VICTORIAN POETS
AND THE
CHANGING BIBLE

Victorian Literature and Culture Series
Jerome J. McGann and Herbert F. Tucker, Editors

VICTORIAN POETS AND THE CHANGING BIBLE

Charles LaPorte

University of Virginia Press   *Charlottesville and London*

University of Virginia Press
© 2011 by the Rector and Visitors of the University of Virginia
All rights reserved
Printed in the United States of America on acid-free paper

First published 2011

1 3 5 7 9 8 6 4 2

Library of Congress Cataloging-in-Publication Data
LaPorte, Charles, 1972-
Victorian poets and the changing Bible / Charles LaPorte.
p. cm. — (Victorian literature and culture series)
Includes bibliographical references and index.
ISBN 978-0-8139-3158-6 (cloth : alk. paper) — ISBN 978-0-8139-3165-4 (e-book)
1. English poetry—19th century—History and criticism. 2. Religion and poetry. 3. Bible
and literature. 4. Bible—Criticism, interpretation, etc.—History—19th century. 5. Bible—
Influence. 6. Bible—In literature. 7. Literature and society—Great Britain—History—19th
century. 8. Great Britain—Intellectual life—19th century. I. Title.
PR595.R4.L37 2011
821'.809—dc22

2011012397

Contents

Acknowledgments

This book has been a long time in the making and accumulated more debts than I can quickly enumerate. It was made possible through funding and research support from the University of Michigan, Vanderbilt University, and the University of Washington. Colleagues and mentors at all of those institutions have been wonderfully supportive. Thanks first and foremost to Yopie Prins, who has inspired and strongly shaped my thinking about Victorian poetics. Particularly warm thanks also go to Martha Vicinus, Ralph Williams, and Julie Ellison for their extensive support and help with this research in its early stages. I also feel a special debt of gratitude to UW colleagues who have read and offered detailed and insightful comments on one or more chapter drafts: Marshall Brown, Gary Handwerk, and Henry Staten. Colleagues at other institutions who have volunteered similarly generous aid include Kirstie Blair, Linda Hughes, and Cynthia Scheinberg. Tricia Lootens helped me to develop key passages in the introduction in particular. Jason Rudy gave me shrewd readings of several chapter drafts and a much-needed source of moral support. Joseph LaPorte offered fraternal advice and a philosopher's perspective on some of the central ideas.

Among many friends, colleagues, and former colleagues whose conversations have helped me think through key issues related to the work, please let me thank Joseph Butwin, Kathleen Blake, Jay Clayton, the late David DeLaura, Carolyn Dever, Richard Dunn, Ella Dzelzainis, James Epstein, Jacqueline George, Erik Gray, Nicholas Halmi, Gillian Harkins, Emily Harrington, Mary-Catherine Harrison, Kali Israel, Marjorie Levinson, Meredith Martin, Christopher Matthews, Elizabeth Miller, Mona Modiano, Ji-Hyae Park, Adela Pinch, Sheshalatha Reddy, Brian Reed, Jessica Roberts, Catherine Robson, David Ruderman, Mark Schoenfield, John Su, and Carolyn

Williams. For help with biblical Greek, in particular, I would like to thank Jay Aultman-Moore and Meilee Bridges. For periodic aid with my German, thanks to Andrea Boboc and Marshall Brown.

I am deeply grateful to the staff of the University of Virginia Press, including Cathie Brettschneider, humanities editor, and Morgan Myers, my project editor. Special thanks go to the Victorian Literature and Culture Series editors, Jerome J. McGann and Herbert F. Tucker, for their support of this monograph, as well as for their insightful readings. My debt to Tucker runs particularly deep, since his virtuosic teaching first inspired me with a passion for nineteenth-century poetics. Last, but not least, I am very grateful to my copyeditor, Colleen Romick Clark.

Some of the material that appears here was first presented at the NASSR conference held at the University of Western Ontario in August of 2002, at the NVSA conference held at American University in April of 2005, at the Victorians Institute conference held at the University of North Carolina at Greensboro in April of 2005, at the VSAWC Conference held at Simon Fraser University in October of 2005, at the Elizabeth Barrett Browning Bicentenary Celebration held at Baylor University in March of 2006, at the Victorian Division session of the MLA conference in Philadelphia in December of 2006, at the "Victorian Genres" symposium at the UC Santa Cruz Dickens Universe in August of 2007, at the Tennyson Society International Bicentenary Conference held at the University of Lincoln, UK, in July of 2009, at the Transatlantic Poetics in the Nineteenth Century Conference held at the University of Pennsylvania in March of 2010, and at the Transatlantic Literature Group of the University of Maryland, also in March of 2010. I remain grateful to the organizers of all of these conferences and events for the opportunity to develop this work.

I have also benefited from assistance at a number of libraries and archives. Thanks to Faye Christenberry and the University of Washington libraries, Judy Avery and the University of Michigan libraries, the Heard Library at Vanderbilt University, the British Library, the Bodleian Library, and the Pierpont Morgan Library. Particular thanks go to Rita Patteson and the Armstrong Browning Library at Baylor University for giving me access to EBB's drafts and correspondence, and to the National Library of Scotland for giving me access to Alexander Main's half of the Eliot/Main correspondence.

The Pickersgill portrait of Elizabeth Barrett Barrett is reproduced by gracious permission of its owner, Captain G. E. Moulton-Barrett. Philip Kelley has very kindly helped me with the reproduction. Susan Casteras, Sandra Donaldson, Barbara Neri, Stephen Prickett, and Melvin Schuetz all helped me to locate my images.

A UW Royalty Research Fund Award in 2007–8 was particularly helpful in developing material that appears in the introduction. I am also grateful to the journals *Victorian Poetry* and *Victorian Literature and Culture* for allowing me to publish revised and extended versions (in chapters 4 and 5) of arguments previously made elsewhere: "George Eliot, the Poetess as Prophet," in *Victorian Literature and Culture* 31, no. 1 (2003): 159–79, copyright 2003 Cambridge University Press, reprinted with permission; and "Sacred and Legendary Artists: Anna Jameson and Barrett Browning in the Hagiography of *Pompilia*," in *Victorian Poetry* 39, no. 4 (2001): 551–72, copyright 2001 West Virginia University Press, reprinted with permission.

Lastly, I would like to thank my parents, my brothers and sisters, my father-in-law, and my two beautiful boys for sustaining my spirits during a long writing process. And I thank Colette Moore, my love, who might not otherwise have spent so many evenings rehearsing tortuous arguments about the evolution of Victorian poetics.

VICTORIAN POETS
AND THE
CHANGING BIBLE

INTRODUCTION

O Poet-Prophets! God hath sent ye forth
With lips made consecrate by altar fire,
To guide the Future, not to tread the Past

—SPERANZA (LADY WILDE)

MID-VICTORIAN POETRY has always gratified historians of British secularization. Religious disputes held a more central place in the intellectual life of nineteenth-century Britain than most of us can easily imagine today, and much of that discord centered upon the Bible's status as the culture's foundational religious text. The eighteenth- and nineteenth-century progress of textual scholarship had recently come to make the scriptures seem more fortuitous, uneven, fragmentary, and literary than had previously been supposed by most of their readers, while major events in the Victorian sciences came independently to militate against many traditional biblical perspectives. To take the most obvious example, Charles Darwin inadvertently followed a century of Western biblical scholarship by implicitly urging his readers to consider the Bible's creation story as a work of literature rather than a strict record of Earth's earliest flora and fauna. Given all this, it comes as no surprise that some of the best-known poetry written in English between the years 1845 and 1875 reflects profound changes in contemporary biblical interpretation, and that it concerns the revolutionary ideas found in such epoch-marking works as Charles Lyell's *Principles of Geology* (1830), Robert Chambers's anonymously published *Vestiges of the Natural History of Creation* (1844), George Eliot's (Marian Evans's) translation of David Friedrich Strauss's *Life of Jesus* (1846), Darwin's *Origin of Species* (1859), the Broad Church collection of *Essays and Reviews* (1860), and Bishop J. W. Colenso's *Pentateuch and the Book of Joshua Critically Examined* (1862–79). In the usual story of Victorian secularization, famous lines like Alfred Tennyson's "Nature, red in tooth and claw" (*In Memoriam* [1850]) or Matthew Arnold's "Wandering between two worlds" ("Stanzas from the Grand Chartreuse" [1855]) stand out not only for their poignancy but also for their handy concision.

For their part, scholars of Victorian poetry have equally relied upon histories of religious decline and the so-called death of God. Poetry lends itself exceptionally well to this version of the secularization narrative because the Victorians found it so well suited to expressing their religious anxieties. Like the Romantics, they associated poetic with religious expression, and to read their poetry for uneasy references to the collapse of Christianity is to inherit a wide-ranging and highly practicable explanation for much Victorian taste, ranging from enthusiasm felt for religious apologetics in Tennyson and Robert Browning to ambivalence felt about the atheistic tendencies of Arnold or Arthur Hugh Clough. A broad criterion of religious comfort or discomfort seems to simplify the unruly diversity of Victorian poetry from the late Romantic era to the fin de siècle, from the devout evangelical Elizabeth Barrett Browning to the devout aestheticist Oscar Wilde. Handy concision again. And this is to say nothing of the scholarly commonplace that the Victorian novel owes its high literary status to the emergence of an unambiguously secular culture.

Such well-trodden literary histories of secularization, nonetheless, tend to lean heavily upon an idea that religion was actually dying in mid-century Britain. It should therefore be of interest to scholars of Victorian poetry and of Victorian literature more broadly that the moribund condition of nineteenth-century British Christianity now seems far less evident than it has seemed to us during most of the intervening period. Recently, historians of religion such as Callum Brown, Jeffrey Cox, Hugh McLeod, and Doreen Rosman have offered to our consideration a Victorian culture where religious beliefs represent much more than the withered remains of a bygone age of faith—where they actually evidence tremendous vitality throughout the century.[1] In like manner, the cultural philosopher Charles Taylor has recently contested the "logic of subtraction" characteristic of most secularization narratives by tracing in modern culture what he sees as a broadening "gamut of [philosophical] positions which descended from Romanticism";

for Taylor, these philosophical positions (both religious and nonreligious) continue to importune modern selfhood.[2] And a new generation of literary scholars, including Emma Mason, Mark Knight, and William R. McKelvy, has begun to outline the consequences of this new historical perspective for Victorian literary studies.[3] Even today's defenders of the old secularization model, such as Steve Bruce, happily acknowledge that to the extent Victorian secularization entails religious decline, it does so for reasons unrelated to the intellectual landmarks by which we have always marked its progress.[4] All parties agree that if Victorian religion declines at all before the twentieth century, it declines from a high tide in the 1850s. By this estimate, "Dover Beach" was written at the high-water mark of post-Enlightenment religion in Britain, the "melancholy, long, withdrawing roar" of its famous "Sea of Faith" perhaps the sound of Arnold's own ear pressed against a seashell.[5]

The Victorian poetry that has for so long served as window dressing for the usual secularization narrative thus deserves another look. As a body, literary scholars have been slow to grapple with the recent scholarly reevaluation of Victorian religious culture in part because the old narratives of disappearance and loss have always served us so well. Secularization of the melancholy Arnoldian model makes not just for beautiful verse, but also for beautiful literary criticism as it appears in such foundational studies as Jerome Buckley's *The Victorian Temper* (1951), John Holloway's *The Victorian Sage* (1953), Walter Houghton's *The Victorian Frame of Mind* (1957), Morse Peckham's *Beyond the Tragic Vision* (1962), and J. Hillis Miller's *The Disappearance of God* (1963). These classic studies remain richly insightful, to be sure, but they attest to the Victorians' impressions of secularization rather than secularization per se.[6]

A fresh appreciation for what Rosman calls "the vigour of Victorian Christianity" (207), by contrast, has begun to reanimate our study of the intersection between poetry and Victorian religion, perhaps especially in those works that reflect the biblical scholarship most frequently associated with secularization. Barrett Browning may provide the most salient example of the kind of poetry ignored for decades by the scholarly heirs of Buckley. And naturally enough; if Victorian literature is really about the disappearance of God, then a work like *Aurora Leigh* (1856) becomes a quaint throwback, whereas if it is about a diversity of religious and secular experience, then *Aurora Leigh* becomes a pragmatic thought experiment in what might be anything but a post-religious world: a means of engaging with the newer paradigms of Strauss and Chambers while affirming a connection to a reconfigured sort of belief. One famous admirer of this text, George Eliot, is herself so often discussed as a standard-bearer of post-religious literary culture that we have a hard time even recognizing how much poetry Eliot wrote in clear and self-conscious imitation of Barrett Browning's vatic mode. A serious look at either poet, though, will give the lie to the idea that biblical scholarship and science simply vitiated contemporary religious culture. As I hope to show, this cliché has things exactly wrong to the extent that such poetry so often gives rise to subsequent religious interpretations.

"Auch Bibel zu sein oder zu werden": Victorian Poetic Ambition and the Higher Criticism

The present study contributes to the ongoing reevaluation of Victorian literary and religious culture by considering how five mutually influential and highly prominent mid-Victorian poets—Tennyson, the Brownings, Clough, and George Eliot—each took a more optimistic and more innovative approach to the changing nineteenth-century Bible than is generally appreciated. These poets all respond to modern biblical criticism and science with extraordinary ambition, asking whether the apparently literary character of the Holy Scriptures meant that modern poetry—even their own modern poetry—might generate the sort of enthusiasm that has historically belonged to the Bible. In this respect, their poetry acts less as a rearguard action to save religion than as a gamble upon its potential future.

The Romantic scholar F. D. E. Schleiermacher frames the crucial scriptural question in this way in his influential work, *On Religion* (1799): "The holy books have become Scripture by their own power, but they prohibit no other book from also being or becoming Scripture [sie verbieten keinem andern Buche, auch Bibel zu sein oder zu werden], and whatever had been written with equal power they would gladly have associated with themselves."[7] Schleiermacher's turn-of-the-century formulation, we see, seems to solicit the reinvention of the sacred canon, and represents a key scholarly counterpart to quasi-biblical poetics of the same period, such as Friedrich Gottlieb Klopstock's claim that he found it "permissible . . . to develop further, in a poetic mode, that which Revelation teaches," or William Blake's representation of his poetry as a "Bible of Hell, which the world shall have whether they will or no."[8] Novalis, another member of the Jena circle, puts this matter still more bluntly: "Who has declared the Bible closed? Shouldn't the Bible be considered as still growing?"[9] For English poetry (as for German), this revelation dovetails with ideas of poetic inspiration that extend back to Milton.[10]

Now, scholars of literary Romanticism ought to find this terrain quite familiar, but Victorianists as likely will not. For both readers, it will be helpful to say a few words about the distinctive scope of the present study. To take up this theme in Victorian poetics is to urge the ongoing interest of this biblical revolution as it develops in mid-century. True, the literary implications of modern scripture scholarship had made themselves felt in British poetry before some of the poets of my study were born: in Blake through acquaintance with the Scottish critic Alexander Geddes, in Coleridge (following Geddes's lead) with the German school of Johann Gottfried Eichhorn, and in Byron still more visibly with a related Continental tradition running from Pierre Bayle to the Count de Volney.[11] An admirable body of scholarship reflects the force of biblical hermeneutics in British poetry of this period.[12] Nonetheless, the breadth of our literary research sharply decreases for the mid-century, in inverse proportion to the increasing social relevance of this issue.[13] Victorian hermeneutics has been taken for a dull interlude between Romantic and twentieth-century theories of interpretation, but such a chronology seems increasingly arbitrary today.[14] Further, it owes largely to an Arnoldian perspective on secularization—partly to Arnold's own deprecation of mid-Victorian thought in works like *The Function of Criticism at the Present Time* and "Obermann Once More."[15]

For the scholar of literary culture, the chronological gap that exists between an idea's origins and its ongoing relevance ought to provide additional interest: the textual groundwork of modern biblical scholarship dates as far back as Thomas Hobbes, Baruch Spinoza, and Richard Simon, yet the institutional machinery of modern biblical criticism as it arose in subsequent centuries increasingly refined these ideas and delivered them to a more extensive audience until they dominated universities and other milieux that could formerly ignore them. The nineteenth century here provides a sort of cultural tipping point. So, for instance, while Simon's seventeenth-century arguments about the composite authorship of the Pentateuch contain an embryo version of Julius Wellhausen's famous "Documentary Hypothesis" of 1878, yet Wellhausen's work has meanwhile come to epitomize the modern critical method. Likewise, while Strauss's *Life of Jesus* openly borrows from Eichhorn's *Einleitung in das Alte Testament* (1780–83) and leans upon David Hume's still earlier essay "Of Miracles" (1752), yet Strauss shook a generation of Victorian scholars who were ignorant of Eichhorn and who had grown accustomed to looking past Hume. Ideas that Volney had delivered to large crowds at the École Normale became newly scandalous—if not altogether new—when they reappeared in the Strauss furor at mid-century.

Biblical scholarship at this cultural moment had a wider circulation than ever before, both within and beyond the universities. *Essays and Reviews* went through twelve editions between 1860 and 1865 and became a best-seller despite being (in the words of one twentieth-century scholar) "almost unreadable."[16] Similar sensations were to be met with in Colenso's *Pentateuch and the Book of Joshua Critically Examined* and Ernest Renan's (eminently readable) *Life of Jesus* (*La Vie de Jésus*) (1863). Mid-century British debates about biblical meaning and translation would culminate in the creation of the New Revised Version (NRV) of 1881 and 1885: the first authorized translation since the time of King James. The progress of this endeavor helps to show the increasing circulation of modern biblical scholarship. In 1780 the Oxford press printed 127,000 copies of the Authorized Version. By 1860 it was up to one million copies, and it remained there over the ensuing two decades. (The missionary work connected to imperialism undoubtedly contributed to this high demand.) In its turn, the NRV generated an unprecedented amount of advance publicity before its appearance in May 1881, exciting, as the *British Quarterly* put it, "greater public interest than any book ever published in England."[17] It sold over a million copies on the first day of publication, and three million copies within the year. This does not count versions that appeared in newspapers—for instance in the United States, where they were simply reprinted out of copyright.

Especially key to the poetics that I treat here is the Victorian experience of what Eichhorn first called the "higher criticism" of the Bible.[18] Its consequences will be unfolded in greater depth in subsequent chapters of this book, but the heart of it is simple: the higher criticism presented the revolutionary practice of studying the Christian scriptures as the collected poetry and mythology of an ancient, primitive people—as a mythical, rather than a strictly factual, record. The significance of higher critical practice is more plainly expressed by Eichhorn's contemporary Johann Gottfried Herder, who reduced this new idea to the maxim that the best manner of reading the Holy Scriptures is *menschlich*: "in the human way."[19] For Herder, crucially, adopting this new "human way" entails abandoning the presupposition that the Bible has been dictated or arranged by God, an idea still prevalent among British Christians in the nineteenth century, but one placed under increasing stress as the independent claims of science supplemented the prior claims of criticism.

Only as the nineteenth century progressed did very large numbers of educated Britons come to ask themselves whether Herder's conclusion was right—whether "the human way" was the most accurate and compelling way to read the scriptures. When Benjamin Jowett of Oxford declares in "On the Interpretation of Scripture" (1860) that Christians ought to read the Bible as "a book like any other book," he places himself squarely in the camp of Herder.[20] Jowett's phrase is by no means original; he plainly echoes Coleridge (himself echoing Herder) in *Confessions of an Inquiring Spirit* (1842), in which Coleridge writes, "I take up this work with the purpose to read it for the first time as I should read any other work."[21] But this expression appeared posthumously in Coleridge's work, and its force was tempered by the context of his earlier and more orthodox *Aids to Reflection* (1825). By contrast, Jowett makes this claim one of the opening flourishes of his contribution to *Essays and Reviews,* a *succès de scandale* whose notoriety eclipsed even that of *The Origin of Species* in Evangelical periodical reviews of the day.[22] Jowett's earlier publication on the Pauline letters had already disturbed his Oxford colleagues enough that his vice-chancellor took the unusual step of having him resubscribe to the Thirty-Nine Articles.[23] "On the Interpretation of Scripture" presents a later and fuller articulation of the idea that religious inspiration lies in a text's literary qualities, rather than its divine origins. In 1860s Oxford, this idea was as revolutionary as it had been in 1780s Jena, and in the 1860s it generated far more widespread discussion.

"The Strongest Part of Our Religion Today": Lowth and the Victorian Meaning of Poetry

Conventional models of secularization today tend to view the Victorian association of poetry and religion as a form of compensation. Hilary Fraser, for instance, attributes to religion's decline that "poetry was invested with so many moral and mystical qualities that it became, in the rhetoric of many Victorians, inseparable from religion."[24] But the distinctive—not to say peculiar—conflation of Victorian poetry and religion ought to be more fully delineated for the study of Victorian poetics. A compensatory model that presumes religion's decline will actually tend to minimize the oddness of Victorian poetic theory's claims for religious significance, including its reliance upon "poetry" in the higher critical sense of the term.[25]

Romantic higher critical discourse, by contrast, adopts "poetry" as part of a general strategy for redeeming the scriptures from Enlightenment deist aspersions. Bishop Robert Lowth's Oxford lecture series *On the Sacred Poetry of the Hebrews* (1753), for instance, presents a seminal articulation of the new idea that the scriptures must be read in the literary or poetic spirit of the culture that created them. Lowth's enthusiasm for biblical aesthetics had important precedents (such as Longinus), but his formulations became central to the literary reevaluation of the Bible in the second half of the eighteenth century.[26] Whereas deists such as Voltaire, Hume, and G. E. Lessing had impugned the biblical authors as primitive dupes or liars, higher critics in the tradition of Lowth would come to argue that the comparatively primitive nature of biblical culture cannot detract from the sublime inspiration of its literature, and that modern culture might be comparatively impoverished. Arnold's lyric "The Future" (1852) reflects just this legacy when it asks,

> Who can see the green Earth any more
> As she was by the sources of Time?
> . . . .
> Who thinks as they thought,
> The tribes who then liv'd on her breast,
> Her vigorous primitive sons?
> (927–33)

Such rhetorical questions explicitly acknowledge the "primitive" nature of biblical culture, but they also bemoan the modern loss of spiritual insight and "vigor" in a way that Voltaire's generation would have found bewildering.

We can easily appreciate how Lowth's unfolding of the Bible's hidden poetry might lend itself to Eichhorn's subsequent consideration of the Bible itself as "a rich collection of true national poesy, which every judge of that kind of composition must hold in high honour."[27] Later, Eichhorn's view of the Bible as a form of "national poesy" lends itself (perhaps inexorably) to Strauss's view of the Gospels themselves as the "poetic" representation of a messianic first-century literary culture: "What we have here is not falsehood, not misrepresentation of the truth. It is a plastic, naïve, and, at the same time, often most profound apprehension of truth, within the area of religious feeling and poetic insight."[28] Whereas Lowth's earlier celebration of the aesthetics of biblical poetry did not forcibly jeopardize traditional interpretations of the Bible's meaning, however, Strauss uses "poetic insight" to argue precisely that it should: that true aesthetic appreciation ought to revise our traditional interpretations of the text. Many Victorians chafed against this link between

Lowth's unobjectionable stance and Strauss's highly objectionable one. But Lowth's aesthetic perspective enjoyed a near-uniform approbation throughout the nineteenth century even while Strauss was widely reviled. Biblical conservatives objected to the higher critical approach only when it implied that the Bible was *merely* poetry: a figurative poetics instead of an inspired one. During the *Essays and Reviews* scandal, Jowett's co-contributor Rowland Williams was brought to trial in the ecclesiastical courts for making claims like the following: "So in the passage of the Red Sea, the description may be interpreted with the latitude of poetry."[29] But few mid-Victorians would question the poetry of the word of God; it was Williams's "latitude" that smacked of heresy.

To appreciate the response of Victorian poets to the higher criticism, then, it helps to keep in mind both the consensus forged by Lowth and also the dissent marking Lowth's implications as pursued by the Germans in particular. Everyone agreed that the Bible epitomized poetic beauty. Victorian readers of the King James translation were especially fervent promoters of what David Norton justly (if awkwardly) terms "Authorized Version-olatry," and conservative devotion to the KJV still runs high in many anglophone parts of the world. But readers from liberal parts of the Victorian political spectrum also objected when a project arose to update the King James with the NRV. Jowett, for instance, is famously said to have lamented that the editors of the NRV seemed "to have forgotten that, in a certain sense, the Authorised Version is more inspired than the original."[30] Whether or not this quip is apocryphal, it certainly brings home how Victorian bibliolatry, with its insistence on the literary perfection of the text, solicits the very higher critical reading against which it ostensibly militates.

Victorian critics of all stripes, moreover, promoted Lowth's ideas even while denouncing their eventual implications. The influential Scottish minister and critic George Gilfillan enjoyed great success with *The Bards of the Bible* (1851), a popular study that treats the scripture authors as full-blooded poets. Whereas Lowth had based his earlier analysis on those parts of the Bible that were explicitly poetic (such as Psalms), Gilfillan finds the Bible's "poetry" in its sentiments rather than its form. Conflating formal and theological arguments in a way that should remind us of Herder much more than of Lowth, Gilfillan argues,

> We have many excellent, elaborate, and learned criticisms upon the Poetry
> of the Bible. . . . Some have laudably devoted themselves to building up anew,

and in a more masterly style, the evidences of the authenticity and truth of Scripture; others are employed in rebutting the startling objections to the Bible which have arrived from across the German Ocean. Many are redarguing the whole questions of supernatural inspiration and the Scripture canon from their foundations; some are disposed to treat Bible poetry as something above literary criticism; and others as something beneath it. *The majority seem, in search of mistakes, or in search of mysteries, to have forgotten that the Bible is a poem at all.*[31] (emphasis mine)

This is an extraordinary reminder, indeed, for Gilfillan's understanding of the Bible as "a poem at all" diverges from what British readers in both prior and subsequent centuries would tend to mean by the term. Gilfillan keeps track of the fact that Lowth had originally associated "poetry" with actual Hebrew verse, but he urges us to see this as an error. Lowth wrongly excludes from the realm of poetry the biblical books that "have no metrical structure or poetic style," argues Gilfillan, for this includes some of the Bible's most significant books, and might produce "a canon which would degrade to dusty prose the 'Be light' of God, and the golden rule of Christ" (62). For Gilfillan, as for many of his contemporaries, the poetic nature of the Bible may be deduced like a syllogism from the two axioms that the Bible is God's eternal word, and that "the language of poetry . . . is the only speech which has in it the power of permanent impression" (ix). "Poetry" is not merely associated with religious truth here; they are effectively synonymous. But the old generic categories remain oddly relevant, as in Gilfillan's caution that Genesis and the Gospels must not be relegated to "dusty prose." When Gilfillan looks for (admittedly pale) analogies to scriptural beauty among secular literatures, he turns overwhelmingly to the poets: to Shakespeare, Milton, Blake, and even Shelley and Byron, but never to the likes of Jane Austen, Honoré de Balzac, or Charles Dickens. In its predisposition to demonstrate correlations between ancient sacred poetics and modern secular poetry, Gilfillan's project becomes strangely arbitrary—something akin to Eichhorn's painstaking study of the book of Revelation by the model of a three-act drama.

There was nothing deliberately tendentious about the mid-century higher critics' continued reliance upon "poetry" as a category term distinct from the new catch-all "literature." But this usage made much better sense in, say, Herder's day than in Gilfillan's, in part because prose genres advanced such strong competing claims for authority during Gilfillan's own lifetime.

It can be helpful to recall, for instance, that Charles Darwin's grandfather, Erasmus Darwin, actually published his biological theories in the form of rhyming epic poetry—*The Botanic Garden* (1789–92) and *The Temple of Nature* (1803). As the elder Darwin explains, he selected heroic couplets as his scientific medium so as "to inlist Imagination under the banner of Science."[32] Darwin's choice was quirky even at the turn of the nineteenth century, but by his grandson Charles's era it would have been unthinkable—not because Victorian scientists were no longer interested in imaginative solutions to their problems, but because heroic couplets could not possibly confer additional status upon their publications. In turn, the emergence of "literature" as a more supple and capacious category term causes "poetry" to appear increasingly rarefied—especially when the terms are used in conjunction with one another. Eliot's Esther Lyon in *Felix Holt* (1866) despairs when she imagines "a life of middling delights . . . where poetry was only literature, and the fine ideas had to be taken down from the shelves of the library when her husband's back was turned."[33]

Hence the perverseness of Victorian enthusiasm for Romantic poetic theory, including Lowthian reverence for the poetry of the scriptures. Romantic poetic theory revolted against the burgeoning world of modern letters: the rising status of the novel, and of scientific studies, and anthropological accounts, and travel narratives, and short fiction, and even penny papers. Gilfillan might happily consign all such writings to the closet of "dusty prose," but this strategy raises questions about what contemporary poets ought to be writing. The poet Alfred Austin offers a typically neo-Romantic view in *The Poetry of the Period* (1868–69), his polemical essay series in the *Temple Bar,* where he affirms that the poet's job is actually to speak the words of God, since "great poets, and great poets only, have . . . channels ready-made for the reception and transmission of [God's] precious messages."[34] Like an arch-conservative reincarnation of Shelley, Austin literalizes *A Defence of Poetry*'s claim that "poets . . . were called in the earlier epochs of the world legislators or prophets: a poet essentially comprises and unites both these characters." If this was a surprising position when Shelley took it, it became ever more so as generations of Victorians repeated it. After all, Shelley clearly hedges on poetry's definition when he calls it "the expression of the imagination"; Austin explicitly specifies that he means verse. And Shelley wrote his *Defence* when the novel remained a low art form; Austin wrote *The Poetry of the Period* as it was beginning to receive universal recognition as a comparable form to poetry. For that matter, Shelley owes his fame to the Victorians: a minor poet in his lifetime, he was made immortal by the mid-Victorian generation that raised Austin.

One need not be Jacques Derrida to see that the mid-Victorian ambiguity between poetry qua inspiration and poetry qua verse partly determines a cultural conception of poetry by strongly associating—and sometimes conflating—these ideas. Arnold, again, puts on display the breadth and scope of higher critical attitudes toward "poetry" in Victorian genre theory when he argues most forcefully that the Bible should be read in a *menschlich* way. The usual joining of the generic and the religious significations of Lowth's "poetry," implicitly qualified in the title *Literature and Dogma,* nonetheless still governs that work once Arnold finally gets around to "the tentative, poetic way in which the Bible-authors used language": "The real germ of religious consciousness, therefore, out of which sprang Israel's name for God, to which the records of his history adapted themselves, and which came to be clothed upon, in time, with a mighty growth of poetry and tradition, was a consciousness of the *not ourselves which makes for righteousness.*"[35] Here in his prose, as in his poetry, Arnold's italics betray his mental strain. The passage is noteworthy for Arnold's "tentative" definition of the poetic, but still more for the fact that it refers to the poetic at all. Usually in *Literature and Dogma,* Arnold avoids the potential ambiguity of "poetry" by sticking to the newer, generically inclusive "literature," as in the following: "The language of the Bible, then, is literary, not scientific language" (189). When he rises to a rhetorical crescendo, though, Arnold reverts to the higher critical tradition, and literature becomes "a mighty growth of poetry and tradition"—not merely literature, but *poetry.*

Like Gilfillan's, Arnold's conflation of poetry and religion is odder than at first appears because he doggedly maintains it when he returns to traditional forms of verse. Consider "The Study of Poetry," Arnold's introduction to Thomas Humphry Ward's anthology *The English Poets* (1880), where he goes so far as to propose poetry as the inevitable heir to traditional religion:

The future of poetry is immense, because in poetry, where it is worthy of its high destinies, our race, as time goes on, will find an ever surer and surer stay. There is not a creed which is not shaken, not an accredited dogma which is not shown to be questionable, not a received tradition which does not threaten to dissolve. . . . But for poetry the idea is everything; the rest is a world of illusion, of divine illusion. Poetry attaches its emotion to the idea; the idea *is* the fact. The strongest part of our religion to-day is its unconscious poetry.[36]

This famous passage might be taken for a routine recapitulation of the ideas of *Literature and Dogma,* but such a reading belies its context as the introduction of Ward's anthology.[37] As its title might suggest, *The English Poets* features poets who actually wrote in verse—not the sort of "poets" who authored the book of Numbers or the Gospel of Mark. Given this context, it is remarkable not that Arnold sought to replace Christianity with poetry, but that he would recommend the English poets from Chaucer to Dryden as sufficient for that particular job.[38] Arnold's literary terminology discourages readers from making distinctions between the poetry found by a Strauss or Gilfillan in the Bible and the poetry anthologized by Ward in the English verse tradition. His resolution to offer the scriptural value of poetry qua verse as a solution to doubts about whether the Bible itself might be arbitrary or culturally determined thus becomes doubly perverse. Still more eagerly than a Gilfillan or an Austin, Arnold demonstrates how tenaciously Victorian poets and critics clung to the promises of Novalis and Schleiermacher. The indubitable fact that the Bible is almost entirely written in prose can be sublimely disregarded. And the unpleasant prospect that the medium of verse was not actually indispensable to the work of religion is explicitly repudiated.

J. Hillis Miller justly urges that "the central assumption of Romanticism is the idea that the isolated individual, through poetry, can accomplish the 'unheard of work,' that is, create through his own efforts a marvelous harmony of words which will integrate man, nature, and God."[39] But the commonplace that the post-Romantic crisis is somehow "poetic" perpetuates an almost schizophrenic understanding of genre during the Victorian era. Critics as different as Gilfillan, Austin, and Arnold clung to formal ideas of poetry tenaciously as their claims for poetic forms became ever more quixotic.

Mid-century Poets and the "Public Mind"

Perhaps the best reason for Victorian literary scholars to follow the mid-century relationship between poetry and contemporaneous biblical scholarship is that Victorian poets were themselves less interested in the genealogical roots of inherited Romantic hermeneutics than in the ways that these hermeneutics resonated in newer contexts, including that provided by science. In the early decades of the century, Oxbridge hegemony and the comparatively small numbers of British universities had made it possible to dismiss this biblical scholarship as "Continental": foreign godlessness with a soupçon of revolutionary menace. But the growing impact of British advances in geology, astronomy, and biology forced many who were not previously interested to take stock of higher critical biblical interpretations, and they variously borrowed from, added to, and reinvented this tradition. If the higher criticism became a mainstay of Victorian intellectual discourse, this seems to have had less to do with the acknowledged efforts of Coleridge or even Thomas Carlyle than with the progress of independent fields of inquiry.[40]

Retrospectives of the higher criticism stress its prominence in Germany, where more than a century of pioneering scholarship culminated in the most detailed source criticism. Yet Victorian poets were demonstrably more concerned with the behindhand and less precise conclusions of their fellow British scholars. The scandalous *Essays and Reviews* collection, Colenso's *The Pentateuch and the Book of Joshua Critically Examined,* and even Arnold's own *Literature and Dogma* all generated tremendous amounts of discussion about the higher criticism, even though none of these works meaningfully advanced the scholarly conclusions of the Germans.[41] Sometimes British scholars failed even to recognize the belated nature of their efforts: Colenso, for instance, had no concept of the state of Continental scholarship, and his readers found high drama in conclusions that Strauss's first audience had taken for granted.[42]

To acknowledge the nineteenth-century superiority of German scriptural scholarship is not, then, the same as suggesting that it affected anglophone literature commensurately. Even mid-century French scholarship exercised an influence that exceeded that of the Germans. Renan's *Life* amounted to little more than a creative adaptation of commonplace German themes, but it enjoyed a far wider British readership than Strauss's *Life* or seminal texts like Schleiermacher's *Über die Schriften des Lukas* (1817, trans. *A Critical Essay on the Gospel of St. Luke,* 1825). Renan's literary panache made his texts much more appealing than the scholarly texts of the Germans—to their extreme pique—and it is clear that British readers were better equipped to handle French authors.[43] Thus, while the British commotion over Renan and anglophone scholarship can seem comically provincial in the light of contemporary German scholarship, still English poets invoke such scholars more frequently than they do German scholarship. Thomas Hardy's satiric "The Respectable Burgher on the Higher Criticism" (1901) culminates in the burgher's resolution to reconsider "that moderate man, Voltaire."[44] The line is a comic one, but still the burgher's reading habits are essential to the literary ambitions that I address here. In his very rejection of the higher critics, he turns to a French deist, rather than to, say, the Wolfenbüttel Fragmentist.

Robert Browning's "Gold Hair" (1864) similarly emphasizes a local (not to say provincial) experience of the higher criticism, although Browning had read Schleiermacher and Strauss for decades:

> The candid incline to surmise of late
>   That the Christian faith proves false, I find;
> For our Essays-and-Reviews' debate
>   Begins to tell on the public mind,
> And Colenso's words have weight[.]
> (141–45)

Here a notoriously difficult poet puts an international revolution in hermeneutics in the most simple and domestic of terms: he affirms the "weight" of Bishop Colenso and the *Essays and Reviews* authors even though he understood perfectly well the belatedness of their conclusions. (The potential ridiculousness of it all may explain the iambs that end lines 141–44 and lend a drinking song air to an otherwise plodding trimeter). That Browning writes a poem about these contemporary clergymen, rather than the German tradition (even as mediated by Coleridge), suggests that Browning took less interest in the theological conclusions per se than the way in which their debate then circulated in Britain—the way that it "began to tell on the public mind." "Our Essays-and-Reviews' debate" and "Colenso's words" caused a stir precisely because their authors held high positions in the established church. Arnold protested that "it is really the strongest possible proof of the low ebb at which, in England, the critical spirit is [that] the book of Bishop Colenso is the critical hit in the religious literature" (736). Nonetheless, here as elsewhere, English poetry evidences an especially acute responsiveness to the vicissitudes of British scholarship, however belated it should be.

English novelists remained similarly preoccupied with British experience. The eponymous hero of Mary Augusta (Mrs. Humphry) Ward's *Robert Elsmere* (1888) finds his youthful faith checkmated by the biblical researches of a fictional English squire, Roger Wendover, and his metaphysical aspirations revived again through a transparent depiction of the (very real) English philosopher T. H. Green. *Middlemarch* (1872) focuses upon Edward Casaubon's obsolescent biblical labors (dismissed by a fellow rector as "Xisuthrus and Fee-fo-fum and the rest"[45]) despite Will Ladislaw's pointed quip that "if Mr. Casaubon read German he would save himself a great deal of trouble. . . . The Germans have taken the lead in historical inquiries, and they laugh at results which are got by groping about in woods with a pocket-compass while they have made good roads" (208). Here Eliot, who had elsewhere upbraided the public for their ignorance of German thought, limits her caricature to the provinciality of English scholarship before work on the NRV finally brought anglophone work into line with that of the Continent. And *Middlemarch* naturally comes from a novelistic tradition that saw young Bertie Stanhope in Trollope's *Barchester Towers* (1857) astonish a group of English clergy-men with his suggestion that "you'll have those universities of yours about your ears soon, if you don't consent to take a lesson from Germany."⁴⁶ Trol-lope's humor depends upon Bertie's apparent disregard for the fact that the intellectual latitude of German institutions was repugnant to conservative Oxford-bred clergymen. But Trollope knew less German than Eliot or Ward; his novel conveys not the results of German scholarship, but the dim sense that traditional English philological and religious scholarship might be quaint and obsolescent.

Cultural anxieties about English provincialism thus both fueled and stymied the translation of higher critical ideas throughout the century. Jowett once reported of the late Tennyson that, "More than thirty years ago I remember his making what appeared at the time a very striking remark, namely, that 'the true origin of Biblical criticism was to be ascribed not to Strauss, but to Niebuhr, who lived a generation earlier.'"⁴⁷ The remark re-flects Tennyson's (and possibly Jowett's) mid-century haziness about the genealogy of Victorian criticism: today scholars generally ascribe "the true origin of Biblical criticism" to neither Strauss nor Niebuhr. But it also affords real insight about the belated and piecemeal way by which this interpreta-tive revolution took root in British culture. Tennyson's poetry engages with the changing Bible because of the way in which his own generation—not Niebuhr's—experienced that change.

Victorian Science and "The Bible Only"

My emphasis is upon a particular and in some ways restricted British experi-ence of the hermeneutic revolution posed by the higher criticism, especially in the wake of Strauss. It also centers upon a diverse Protestant experience that remains distinct from its related forms in the Anglo-Catholic poetry of the Oxford Movement (with its later redactors in figures like Christina Rossetti and Hopkins), Pre-Raphaelitism, or aestheticism.⁴⁸ British Anglo-

Catholics, Roman Catholics, and Jews all felt the force of the higher criticism, yet Protestant believers felt it especially keenly in this context because of their theoretical commitment to the Bible's independence from (or self-sufficient sovereignty over) subsequent traditions of interpretation.[49] As the English minister William Chillingworth (1602–1644) had famously proclaimed in a work widely reprinted throughout the nineteenth century, *The Religion of Protestants* (1637), "The BIBLE, I say, the BIBLE only, is the religion of protestants!"[50] This *sola scriptura* line of theology prospered in the nineteenth century as debates on the Catholic Emancipation laws of 1829 were followed by the Oxford Movement and the rise of Ultramontanism in France. But it is not a theology designed to accommodate itself to the findings of Lyell or Darwin. And while Chillingworth's formula may be helpful for promoting one form of Christianity against another, it is manifestly less helpful when the most vocal opponents of orthodoxy are not Catholics, but skeptics and secularists, and when what is at stake is not the scriptural basis of religion, but the divine basis of scriptures. If Genesis owed its form to Mesopotamian literature, as skeptics such as Volney had suggested before the century's beginning and as scholars such as George Smith had all but proven by its end, then "the religion of Protestants" requires a more nuanced apology than Chillingworth's rubric can easily supply. It is unlikely that Chillingworth would find consolation in the solutions tendered by the evangelical Barrett Browning, let alone Tennyson, Browning, Clough, or George Eliot, but these poets all certainly inherited and wrestled with his religious problem.

For many Victorian readers, the emergence of scientific debate about Genesis helped to bring home the lessons of the higher criticism and to suggest a kinship between contemporary poetry and biblical literature.[51] Our tendency, nonetheless, has actually been to overstate the novelty of Victorian scientific conclusions, instead of seeing how they derive too from earlier periods.[52] For instance, many Tennyson scholars continue to think of geological discovery as a uniquely Victorian problem, more or less coming to light with Lyell's *Principles of Geology* in 1830 and reflected in the famous passage of *In Memoriam* below, in which Tennyson evokes catastrophist evolutionary theory:

> . . . They say,
> The solid earth whereon we tread

In tracts of fluent heat began,
    And grew to seeming-random forms
    The seeming prey of cyclic storms
Till at the last arose the man.
(118)

Indeed, scholars often account for the immense popularity of Tennyson's works—and particularly *In Memoriam*—by claiming that Tennyson there put into words the anxiety felt by his generation toward the scientific revolutions of the nineteenth century.[53] *The Norton Anthology of English Literature* has since its earliest edition reported that "Tennyson is the first major writer to express this awareness of the vast extent of geological time that has haunted human consciousness since Victorian scientists exposed the history of the earth's crust."[54] But, of course, most Victorian "human consciousness" was haunted less by "the vast extent of geological time," per se, than by its evident incompatibility with the cosmogony that appears in scriptures (namely, that God made the Earth in seven days a few thousand years ago, that our first ancestors were created whole from dust, and so on). John Ruskin's complaint of 1851 makes clear that the problem, at least for him, was entirely scriptural: "If only the Geologists would let me alone, I could do very well, but those dreadful Hammers! I hear the clink of them at the end of every cadence of the Bible verses."[55] It is the way the geologists' registers jar with the time or cadence of scripture that makes them "dreadful" to Ruskin.

And it was not Victorian scientists who first exposed the history of the earth's crust at all; rather, it was they who made that history into a powerful new discipline. The vastness of geological time had interested scholars and poets as far back as the reign of George III. If we turn to William Cowper's *The Task* (1785), for instance, published twenty-four years before Tennyson was born, we find that the age of the Earth's crust could already be an important subject for poetry, and that it was treated as such by one whom Tennyson's generation would consider the premier English poet of the second half of the eighteenth century. In a section of his poem devoted to "the vanity of many of their pursuits who are reputed wise," Cowper writes:

. . . Some drill and bore
The solid earth, and from the strata there
Extract a register, by which we learn
That He who made it and reveal'd its date

To Moses, was mistaken in its age.
. . . .
... And thus they spend
The little wick of life's poor shallow lamp,
In playing tricks with nature, giving laws
To distant worlds and trifling with their own.
(134–35)

The key difference between *The Task* and *In Memoriam,* in this respect, is that Cowper can reject the geological register, attacking proto-geologists as benighted souls who need to read their Bibles, whereas Tennyson expresses the need to conform his Bible reading to the findings of a quickly evolving science.[56]

Byron's drama *Cain* (1821) represents a still more sensational example of geological poetry where it relies upon the conclusions of the Baron George Leopold Cuvier. As Byron noted in his preface to that work, "The reader will perceive that the author has partly adopted in this poem the notion of Cuvier, that the world had been destroyed several times before the creation of man. This speculation, derived from the different strata and the bones of enormous and unknown animals found in them, is not contrary to the Mosaic account, but rather confirms it; as no human bones have yet been discovered in those strata."[57] Byron rightly anticipated that his play would be attacked, and he perhaps thought to preempt criticism with such brief explanations as this defense of Cuvier. Indeed, the play caused a tremendous uproar and was condemned in periodicals throughout the 1820s for its blasphemous arguments against the goodness of the Deity. Yet the Cuvier imagery was not especially offensive to *Cain*'s reviewers; many of these conducted extensive analyses of the play's imagery and focused overwhelmingly upon Cain's and Lucifer's extensive arguments against Christian ideas of divine justice.[58] The few people who did focus upon Byron's use of Cuvier's writings, such as his friend Thomas Moore, tended to be poets themselves.[59] Cowper and Byron seem to have been sensitive to what we now call geological research well before their substantial publics were inclined to meditate the problem with them. Tennyson read these poets extensively in early life, and he might have witnessed the *Cain* uproar firsthand as a teenager. Accordingly, he may have been less preternaturally sensitive to the fears of his age and time than simply prepared for them by the English poetic tradition.

The natural sciences rearranged the Victorian intellectual landscape, then, but rarely presented an entirely new one. When Tennyson's speaker in "Parnassus" (1889) recoils at the enormity of "Astronomy and Geology, terrible Muses!" this is not because they are new, but because they are disproportionately sized. His image surely reflects what Robin Gilmour calls the "deep time" of geology and astronomy, but it also hearkens back to Victor Hugo's "Le Satyre" (1859), where Pan, the least prepossessing of the Olympian deities, grows so gigantic as to loom over the mountain home of all the others.[60] In Hugo, as in Tennyson, the moment flags a crisis of theological authority that culminates in the poem's final, riveting line: "Place à Tout! Je suis Pan; Jupiter! à genoux" (Make way for All! I am Pan! To your knees, Jupiter!). One could even debate whether "deep time" is inherently more disconcerting than the proposed afterlife of Christian theology; when Nietzsche writes in *The Gay Science* (1882) that "infinity is the most terrifying idea of all," he points to a constitutive part of the afterlife as the Victorians usually imagined it.[61] What seems beyond debate is that Tennyson's scientific poetry represents a Victorian crisis of authority anticipated by and shared with scripture scholarship and historical study more broadly. Strauss indicates the paramount nature of this problem in his introduction to *Das Leben Jesu:* "What is the precise boundary line between the historical and the unhistorical?—the most difficult question in the whole province of criticism."[62] Or, as E. S. Shaffer puts it, "We are dealing here not with an obscure or isolated phenomenon, but with the rise of the modern conception of history" (32). Science here serves as but one facet of a far broader historical and religious crisis also reflected in the higher criticism.

Science provoked the Victorians to reexamine the higher critics, then, but poetry inspired by the higher criticism almost never comes down to a tactical withdrawal from biblical literalism—or, alternately, from a neo-Wordsworthian natural religion.[63] Post-Darwinian nature could no longer inspire the fond reverence of poets in quite the same way, but post-Darwinian poets decided that neither had it inspired such reverence in Wordsworth. As Wilde dryly put this in *The Decay of Lying* (1891), "Wordsworth went to the lakes, but he was never a lake poet. He found in stones the sermons that he had already hidden there."[64] Nature too must depend upon art, and many Victorian poets saw that inspiration in either milieu might depend upon a poet's ability to generate a religious response from readers. Again, Wilde puts this most economically: "The only effects that she can show us are effects that we have already seen through poetry, or in paintings" (320). But Wilde just as clearly takes his theme from Browning's "Fra Lippo Lippi" (1855):

For, don't you mark? we're made so that we love
First when we see them painted, things we have passed
Perhaps a hundred times nor cared to see;
And so they are better, painted—better to us,
Which is the same thing.[65]

Nothing better suggests Browning's poetic gifts than the clarity with which these few lines presage Wilde's powerful apologia. In Wilde as in Browning (and many of their contemporaries), the demythologizing context of the higher criticism and of science begs for the remythologizing work of a poet. "As for the Church," claims Vivian, the aptly named hero of *The Decay of Lying*, "I cannot conceive of anything better for the culture of a country than the presence in it of a body of men whose duty is to believe in the supernatural, to perform daily miracles, and to keep alive that mythopoeic faculty which is so essential for the imagination" (317). The very fiction of a Fra Lippo or a Vivian is designed in part to throw into relief their artistic life, "that mythopoeic faculty which is so essential for the imagination." What Fra Lippo says about painting, Browning means of poetry: the visible things captured by one art stand in for the invisible perception enabled by another.

Victorian Poets and the Changing Bible

Tzvetan Todorov once summarized M. M. Bakhtin's genre theory with the claim that all genre "forms a modeling system that proposes a simulacrum of the world."[66] But a great deal of Victorian poetic discourse proposes this with a singular zeal—it insists, sometimes against all evidence, that the greatest of poetical forms fashion not just simulacra of the world, but the world itself. If Victorian poets decline to disentangle the scriptures from what Cowper calls "the puzzled skein" of history, this is often so as to reclaim the whole skein as the province of poetry. Among Cowper's boldest self-proclaimed heirs, Barrett Browning insists in *Aurora Leigh* that "The world of books is still the world," and that poetry remains that world's beating heart: "O life, O poetry / —Which means life in life!" (915–16).[67] For this reason, this book devotes its first chapter to Barrett Browning—at that point the most highly regarded female poet ever to have written in English—and traces the extraordinary force with which she reclaims a religious role for poetry, alternately bolstering and challenging her readers' commitments to a changing Victorian Bible. From Barrett Browning, I turn to Tennyson, who as Victoria's poet laureate attained a quasi-religious popular authority unimagined even by Wordsworth and never reproduced since. Chapter 2 focuses upon Tennyson's *Idylls of the King* as an extended intervention into New Testament history as depicted by Strauss in particular. Chapter 3 traces a parallel reconsideration of Strauss in the poetry of Clough, whose skeptical bent causes him to linger upon the hermeneutics implicit in Tennyson: if Tennyson suggests that a believer could finesse the paradoxes of an emerging secular age, Clough takes the same evidence to antithetical conclusions. Browning, the Victorian poet most often connected with the higher criticism, becomes the focus of chapter 4, which concerns his ability to develop a cult following by playing skeptical hermeneutics against the force of religious genre. I here treat *The Ring and the Book* (1868) and *Red-Cotton Night Cap Country* (1873) as poems in dialogue with one another about the import of the changing Bible. And my final chapter is devoted to George Eliot, who takes Barrett Browning's example in a radically different direction from Browning so as to promote her distinctive brand of meliorist humanism. Though often associated with cultural models of religious decline, Eliot risked the favor of an astonished literary world when she interrupted her career as a novelist in the 1860s and 1870s to realize her own vision of a higher critical poetics.

Besides offering dramatically successful and unsuccessful instances of Victorian literary ambition, these five poets show how the higher criticism helped to inspire a great range of Victorian poetic experiments. Since the mid-twentieth century, scholars have often depicted these poets' poetry as a dialogue between "Faith" and "Doubt."[68] This cliché indeed represents how some Victorian readers conceived of their poetry, but it often misses the most interesting parts of the literature. None of my analyses of the following poets' oeuvres can be meaningfully reduced to "faith" and "doubt" unless one principally means an extraordinary new faith in poetry—as Browning put it in *The Ring and the Book*—to "Suffice the eye and save the soul beside" (12.863).

Chapter 1

"MRS. BROWNING'S GOSPEL" AND THE ART OF REVELATION

ELIZABETH BARRETT BROWNING is a paradox in Victorian religious literature. Her fervent devotion to the Romantic cult of poetry made her verses seem quaint even to members of her own literary and social milieu. So did her devotion to the rhetoric of evangelical Christianity. Yet despite such quaintnesses (or possibly owing to them), Barrett Browning came to win greater critical acclaim in her lifetime than any previous woman poet writing in English. She became, in other words, a great voice in Victorian poetry. Even commercial success on the scale that Barrett achieved it was unlikely in the lean years of the 1830s, when poetry seemed to have lost the luster that Byron, in particular, had given it.[1] She struggled to find a literary model that felt neither exhausted nor uncongenial, and she clung to a more overtly religious view of poetry than that afforded by Scott or Byron, a more exalted one than that of Felicia Hemans or John Keble.[2] The first collection of poems to bear Barrett's name, *The Seraphim and Other Poems* (1838), actually suggested to contemporary reviewers an oddly pious, somewhat feminine version of Shelley.[3] (That Shelley himself was never conspicuously masculine seems not to have struck them.) Now, no one would flatter Barrett by pairing her with Shelley, who had yet to outgrow his reputation as a queer and marginal poet, but his own contemporary underappreciation may testify all the better to the distinctiveness of her poetic voice.[4]

The following chapter addresses how Barrett Browning eventually used this distinctive voice to achieve an unlikely prominence in revolutionary Victorian understandings of hermeneutics, inspiration, and poetry. I show at some length how she based her earliest claims to authority upon a literary stance that vacillates between devotional reverence for the traditional scriptures, on the one hand, and a Romantic ambition to craft new religious texts on the other. She intended *The Seraphim,* her first major religious poem, to circumscribe any contradiction between these two goals by means of the philosophy of François-René Auguste de Chateaubriand (1768–1848), a contemporary aesthetic theorist and one of the frankest advocates of the Romantic conflation of poetry and religion. Unhappily for her, *The Seraphim* failed in its design to provoke a passionate religious response from most Victorian readers, and yet its failure to do this helped her to see the promise of a second philosophical muse, Emanuel Swedenborg (1688–1772), who inspired her to new ways of conceiving of the metaphysical as a ubiquitous, hidden presence that only artistic expression could illuminate. (Readers uninspired by her version of Chateaubriand, in other words, could still be potentially inspired by her version of Swedenborg.) The Swedenborgianism of *Aurora Leigh* (1856), her greatest work, is now widely recognized, but this chapter seeks to make explicit how its appeal to Barrett Browning is foremost a literary and strategic one that she uses to grapple with the demythologizing influence of the higher criticism of the Bible. Over time, she comes to see modern poetry as a self-justifying testament to God's divine presence: what we might call the Newest Testament of all. She found the higher criticism incapable of furnishing a true view of divine scriptures—even very new ones. And yet her own conception of poetry clearly derives from the hermeneutic revolution that produced the higher criticism, just as her own reception will be dictated by its paradigms.

Hearing God's Dictation in "Sounds"

To appreciate the full drama of Barrett Browning's religious poetics, it is essential to recall both her lifelong faithfulness to some form of evangelical Christianity, and the ways that this complicates her Romantic commitment to poetry. Uniquely among the poets I consider at length here, Barrett Browning rejected principally literary explanations for the Bible's supernatural histories. Especially in her early years as a Congregationalist, but even later as a vaguely Swedenborgian ecumenist (a "heretic believer," as Marjorie Stone wryly terms her[5]), she resisted the most radical conclusions of the higher critics, affirming a strong commitment to the reliability of biblical history, including even the much-disputed creation account of Genesis. Victorian evangelicals relied overwhelmingly upon literalist hermeneutics and a *sola scriptura* basis for resolving religious disputes, so it is not surprising that they overwhelmingly rejected the early nineteenth-century literary critiques of scripture by the German school of Schleiermacher and Strauss. According to evangelical theory, scripture alone ought to settle doctrinal disputes, and so Barrett also held: "We reason 'out of book' when we reason out of the Book," as she priggishly reminded Hugh Stuart Boyd when she was a twenty-two-year-old aspiring poet and he an accomplished biblical scholar; "for 'only the spirit of God can search the deep things of God.'"[6] Such a taste for dogmatism might be presumed to stymie any sympathy for Schleiermacher's radical notion that the scriptures could be augmented or replaced, and Barrett's letters offer ample evidence that it did so. But Barrett the prig was never safe from Barrett the prophetess, and Schleiermacher's ideas also had their seductive power. Over time, a high Romantic devotion to the poet as *vates* would jar with her Congregationalist impulses and remold them into surprising forms. The tension between the evangelical and the Romantic sides of Barrett, in fact, provides the chief interest of her early religious poetry and much of the interest of her subsequent, more enduring work.

It is tempting to dismiss Barrett's early poetry for its lack of self-awareness, and many critics have done so. The chief advocate for this position is Barrett Browning herself, who correctly guessed that critics would read *Aurora Leigh* autobiographically, and who used this circumstance to disparage her early poetry as an artistic abortion: "I ripped my verses up,/And found no blood upon the rapier's point;/The heart in them was just an embryo's heart/Which never yet had beat, that it should die."[7] These striking images permanently changed a body of early poetry that had been widely praised by contemporary critics, killing them (so to speak) for subsequent generations. Still, these early poems provide a helpful key to the conflict of the later work, especially in regard to its Romantic orientation. Before producing her maturest work, Barrett struggled to emerge from the theological paradox of those who, by legend, burned the ancient library at Alexandria upon reasoning that the library either replicated the ideas of the holy scriptures (making it superfluous) or else advanced alternative views (making it blasphemous). Poetry cannot be meaningfully inspired in a world where the scriptures are sufficient, complete, and uniquely revealed. But Barrett habitually affirmed the revealed scriptures even as she blurred conventional distinctions between forms of inspiration.

Barrett's early poems, indeed, present a wonderfully stark illustration of the conflict between her poetic ambition and her evangelical heritage. For a paradigmatic instance of her loftiest early ambitions, one might take "Sounds," an extraordinary lyric from the *Seraphim* volume that calls for a renewed attention to the voice of God in nature. "Sounds" is a spiritual call-to-arms in the high Romantic mode, composed of five stanzas, of which I print the third below:

> Hearken, hearken!
>   God speaketh to thy soul,
> Using the sùpreme voice which doth confound
> All life with consciousness of Deity,
>   All senses into one,—
> As the seer-saint of Patmos, loving John
>   (For whom did backward roll
> The cloud-gate of the future) turned to *see*
> The Voice which spake. It speaketh now,
> Through the regular breath of the calm creation,
> Through the moan of the creature's desolation
> Striking, and in its stroke resembling
> The memory of a solemn vow
> Which pierceth the din of a festival
> To one in the midst,—and he letteth fall
>   The cup with a sudden trembling.
>   (102–17)[8]

As this passage indicates, the poem's claims are Blakean in their magnitude and Shelleyan in their syntax. Argumentatively, they rely upon the loosely hung metaphor above, comparing the reader's potential perception of God with that of John of Patmos, author of the Christian book of Revelation. Such a comparison flatters us, since that text purports to record the very dictation of God's voice amid dazzling visions of the final days of creation. Our prospect also seems divine: the "As" beginning line 107 does not merely introduce a simile between reader and saint, it functions as an appositive linking adverbial to suggest that John's experience is just one instance of the most intense perception of God. Grammatically, that is, this apposition seems to put the reader in a situation vis-à-vis God's voice that is not merely similar, but identical to John's. Stylistically, meanwhile, the poem's enjambment and repetitions, its syntactic complexity and paratactic interjections, all conspire to reinforce the urgency of this condition. God's voice is everywhere present *just as it was* for the biblical author on the island of Patmos: "It speaketh now, / Through the regular breath of the calm creation." The poem thus elevates the reader to John's level, effectively robbing John of the great distinction of having received God's direct address. Barrett's John is not unique in receiving his revelation (which seems to be ubiquitous), but only unique in attending to it as he did. Others, as Schleiermacher implies, might similarly seize upon such inspiration, and similarly record it.[9]

Barrett's reliance upon the second-person pronoun, further, as in "God speaketh to *thy* soul," belies her attendant interest in the poet's particular role as inspired translator of this divine voice. John Stuart Mill's contemporaneous idea of poetry as "feeling confessing itself to itself, in moments of solitude" never rang truer than here.[10] To appreciate Mill's perspective on poetry as something "*over*heard" is to appreciate "Sounds" as a religious pep talk given by the poet to herself. And the primary advocate of this reading, again, is Barrett Browning, who relates her earliest visions of poetry in book 1 of *Aurora Leigh:*

> Ay, and while your common men
> Lay telegraphs, gauge railroads, reign, reap, dine,
> And dust the flaunty carpets of the world
> For kings to walk on or our president,
> The poet suddenly will catch them up
> With his voice like a thunder,—"This is soul,
> This is life, this word is being said in heaven,
> Here's God down on us! what are you about?"
> (1.869–76)

In such lines, *Aurora Leigh* dilates upon the theme of "Sounds": that God's voice must be hearkened to by poets, who repeat it "like a thunder." John, "the seer-saint of Patmos," himself heard "lightnings and thunderings and voices," as the King James translates him (Revelation 4:5 KJV), as did the prophets before him. Barrett's spiritual mentor Swedenborg would specify (perhaps needlessly) that in a biblical context "voices and lightnings" signify "Truths Divine": "That this signifies a Divine state which was revelation, is evident from the signification of 'voices' which are sounds of thunders, as being truths Divine; and from the signification of 'lightnings,' as being the ruddy glow and brightness of these truths, for truths Divine are bright and glowing from the flame of the light that is from the sun of heaven."[11] Aurora, though, unlike Swedenborg, explicitly gives the voice of God to poets. (More will be said on this below.) "Sounds" also hints that they might claim it, but only hints. Then, too, Aurora's extraordinary claim to know which "word is being said in heaven" confirms the orientation of both poems in Revelation, which unfolds in that distinguished setting. Many versions of the KJV rubricate the words of Christ, and in Revelation this practice produces whole pages of rubrication, since Christ is presumed to be speaking much of the time. In such cases, the entire chapters 2 and 3 serve as bibliographic red flags attesting to the importance of the scripture. So Barrett's instruction that we are all potential Johns of Patmos is indeed bolder than it would be had she given us license to author one of the less prominent scriptures.

The crucial line 107, upon which this argument hangs, gave Barrett a deal of trouble. She first published "As Erst in Patmos, Apolyptic John," until her classicist friends disparaged "Apolyptic" as a monstrosity.[12] The more proper "Apocalyptic" was precluded by her meter, and the present reading seems to have been borne out of compromise. The new "loving John" in the second edition, however, does little to diminish the scope of the poem's implicit hermeneutics. If "Apolyptic" clumsily invokes the Apocalypse, "loving John" suggests the evangelist in his traditional role as Christ's "beloved" apostle, the caretaker of Christ's mother. Barrett's generation was among the earliest to regularly differentiate between these Johns in popular readings; previously, the author of the Johannine gospel had also usually been seen as the author of Revelation and the Johannine letters. Conservative Victorians usually adhered to the tradition of a single John, in fact, and only the broad mid-century circulation of the higher criticism caused the question to become more frequently asked. Barrett's initial wording thus eschews this authorial crux, but her revision exhibits a renewed allegiance to tradition in the face of the higher critics, an allegiance that she would retain as late as *Aurora Leigh*, where John the Divine becomes simply "the apostle" (1.869). Still, exegetical conservatism becomes more daring than higher critical revolution when "Sounds" promotes the reader to evangelist and apocalyptic commentator alike.

Not demonstrably indebted to the higher criticism, then, this arresting lyric nonetheless already suggests a kinship with it, and Barrett's early self-conception as a poet seems to have depended heavily upon it. Barrett Browning scholars have rightly emphasized the extent to which she saw poetry as a masculine tradition, practically if not inherently, requiring that she break into an otherwise male cultural domain.[13] Her extraordinary diligence in acquiring ancient Greek and Hebrew at a time when women were discouraged from such pursuits clearly owes to this ambition. And her pretensions to the loftiest regions of the male literary domain appear earlier still, before she had

H. W. Pickersgill's Portrait of Elizabeth Barrett Barrett (commonly
attributed to Eliza Cliffe). (Courtesy of Gordon E. Moulton-Barrett)

begun Hebrew and before her Greek was very good. A portrait of Barrett
done by H. W. Pickersgill well before the *Seraphim* poems (see figure), for instance, already invites comparison to classical and religious subject painting.
In it, Barrett looks to Heaven as though posing for Poussin's *Inspiration du
poète* (1628), quill poised and parchment ready. Or as though posing for any
of the Evangelists as depicted from Bosch to Rembrandt. Her hair is down
like Saint John à la Alonso Cano and, like a proper evangelist (but nothing
like a late Georgian poetess), she drapes a mantle over one shoulder. She is
missing the angel that by tradition would share the painting, though Barrett
might be said to serve as her own angel. ("Sounds" would encourage such a
substitution.) Contemporary portraits of Hemans and L.E.L. never cultivate
this religious costume-party atmosphere, nor do those of then middle-aged

male poets such as Wordsworth. And though the young Barrett could be scathingly critical of her portrait artists, she seems to have felt quite happy about posing for Pickersgill in the robes of Saint John.[14]

"Earth and Her Praisers": The Evangelical Counterpoint

Not all of Barrett's early poetry so freely invites a higher critical approach to scripture as "Sounds." For a conflicting but equally paradigmatic instance of Barrett's religious mode from the same volume (and nearly the same place in that volume), one might take "Earth and Her Praisers," a lyric designed to distinguish revealed wisdom from that of secular poets and sages. This poem depicts a personified Earth who, depressed at the state of human wickedness, requests that her children raise her spirits with song. Six types respond: a child, a lover, a pedant, a mourner, a poet, and a Christian. These first five pay homage in flawed little odes, until the sixth, the Christian, resolves the matter (conclusively, it seems) by enumerating the beauties of the natural world, which he then calls inferior to the beauties of its future as depicted (again) in Revelation. This thematic scheme is unusually crude for Barrett, but it makes a vivid illustration of her divided goals, for it dramatizes the split focus of her religious and poetic vision: here the true Christian is set apart from, and even against, scholars, poets, children, and the like.

The poem begins by invoking Genesis, surely the most widely debated text of the nineteenth century, and personifying God's creation in a manner that is both pleasingly original and reassuringly familiar:

> The Earth is old;
> Six thousand winters make her heart a-cold;
> The sceptre slanteth from her palsied hold.
> She saith, "'Las me! God's word that I was 'good'
>   Is taken back to heaven . . .
>
> . . . .
>
> Sweet children, I am old! ye, every one,
> Do keep me from a portion of my sun.
>   Give praise in change for brightness!["]
> (1–5, 19–21)

Earth's active personal appeal to her children here clearly corresponds to her passive, readerly appeal for the Victorians. For one thing, Earth doesn't know how to interpret Genesis either. And she is doubtful of her goodness in a nineteenth century full of human industry and corruption. Line 4 ("God's word that I was 'good'") unmistakably points to the famous refrain describing earth in Genesis: "and God saw that *it was* good" (1:10 KJV). But Barrett's Earth inquires whether Genesis still holds true, God's word being "taken back to heaven" (5). This question provides the pretext for the poem.

Such a framework might smack of Schleiermacher inasmuch as the poem's verses (songs of "praise in change for brightness") supplement an original "word" that now seems obscured or withdrawn. But Barrett makes clear that she also cleaves to the literal sense of the Bible. In 1838, to begin a poem with "The Earth is old" is to announce an engagement with Charles Lyell and other contemporary geologists. But Barrett follows with "Six thousand winters" in line 2, signaling instead that her poem has been composed under the auspices of a conservative theology. This is not Charles Lyell's calendar, but Bishop Ussher's, according to which the Earth was created whole by God in the year 4004 BCE. Six thousand years could no longer be "old" to a scientist. The poem requests instead a literary perspective, and an anthropocentric one. When Genesis tells us that Methuselah lived to 969 years of age (5:27), the text implicitly asks us to measure that by our own lifespans, rather than by the age of, say, fossil-bearing geological strata. So, too, the logic of Barrett's poem repudiates recent conclusions that Earth might be older than the Bible tells us: indeed, that it might be so old as to make her plaint totally incommensurate with geological chronology. Mark Twain memorably summed up the incommensurability of geology and human history in the twentieth century when he pointed out that "if the Eiffel Tower were now representing the world's age, the skin of paint on the pinnacle-knob at its summit would represent man's share of that age."[15] Twain's pronouncement, however, only dramatizes the geology of the Victorians, for whom science had sufficient drama already. By 1838, Ussher's position on geological history was already hopelessly embattled, as geology consolidated its conclusions into a recognized science. Yet it was still insisted upon (then as now) by many conservative Bible readers such as Barrett, who would otherwise be pressed into viewing the text's other elements in a more literary light. Even the synecdoche that renders years as "winters" (a common medieval trope) may reflect Barrett's partiality to a premodern, prescientific worldview: for to add the winters of the southern hemisphere to those of London is to have twelve thousand—not "six thousand."[16]

Having begun with a conservative gloss on Genesis, "Earth and Her

Praisers" ends with a conservative Revelation, where the poem's Christian representative invokes Earth's Apocalypse. Here in the poem's concluding lines, Earth receives her highest praise for serving as an old, flawed prototype of a coming heavenly kingdom, where "in God's dear book we read / *No night shall be therein*" (201–2), and for provisionally housing the saintly bodies who will arise from death on Judgment Day, according to John 6:

> Praisèd be thy dwellings cold,
> Hid beneath the churchyard mould,
> Where the bodies of the saints
> Separate from earthly taints
> Lie asleep, in blessing bound,
> Waiting for the trumpet's sound
> To free them into blessing[.]
> (209–15)

Such compliments may seem ungenerous to poor Earth, especially since Barrett's Christian seems unabashedly eager for the Armageddon that he predicts. But though packed with irony, the scriptural glosses are in deadly earnest. Barrett's Christian seems tenaciously literal-minded, and so Revelation's endless day (22:5) and trumpet blasts (8:7, 8:8, 8:10, etc.) are invoked as Earth's literal future. Even the Christian's rhythm and rhyme scheme seem to solicit a rigorously limited hermeneutics: the iambic substitutions of "To free them into blessing" really does feel like liberation after six lines of plodding trochees. But keeping to form seems to be the point. Nothing could be further from the Shelleyean cadences of "Sounds." Additionally, the rigorous limitations governing this poem's theme entirely insulate it from criticism by those who accede to its religious propositions. As I have mentioned, the roles of poets and their critics are always given in this poem. To criticize the meter, by its logic, entails apostasy from the respectable perspective of the Christian.

Indeed, the challenge (or, for some readers, the gratification) of "Earth and Her Praisers" may be found in the fact that it is only this figure of the Christian, and neither the scholar nor the poet, who can find fit praise for the despondent Earth. Barrett was already a fine Grecian when writing this poem, with every ambition to become a great poet. But here she sets aside such minor allegiances in loyalty to Christianity. Her scholar, branded "the pedant," presents a hopeless candidate for songs of praise:

[With] a wrinkle deeply thrid
Through his lowering brow,
Caused by making proofs enow
That Plato in "Parmenides"
Meant the same Spinosa did,—
Or, that an hundred of the groping
Like himself, had made one Homer,
Homeros being a misnomer.
What hath *he* to do with praise
Of Earth or aught?
(77–86)

Worse than a Carlylean "Dryasdust," Barrett's pedant is a benighted soul. His absorption in Greek ought to fit him for songs of praise, since it equips him to appreciate the scriptures. But he wastes time trying to reconcile Plato's lofty "Parmenides" with the materialism of Spinoza, and—worse—apes the offensive theories of F. A. Wolf, whose *Prolegomena ad Homerum* (1795) promoted the sensational idea that "Homer" was the imagined author of a great collection of folk poetry written by unknown hands: "an hundred of the groping," instead of a single genius. Like many Christians of her generation, Barrett regretted the popularity of materialist philosophers, and, lest her libel on Spinoza be thrown away, she added an explanatory footnote to the first edition: "That Plato's high spiritual meanings should ever be confounded with Spinosa's low materialisms, and Homer's individuality be lost . . . are proofs enough . . . that no human errors are too wonderful to be possible" (244). Wolf fares even worse than Spinoza. Barrett badly resented Wolf's thesis on Homer, partly because of her devotion to the Romantic cult of genius, but mostly, one suspects, for the extent to which it reflected badly upon the Bible, an analogous set of ancient legends whose authorship and provenance were also disputed. (Wolf himself readily acknowledged this parallel.) She attacks Wolf throughout her career, here taking her "Homer"/"misnomer" rhyme from Byron's *Don Juan* and applying it to pious ends, but thereby losing Byron's pleasing banter in something nearer to sarcasm.

The poet depicted in "Earth and Her Praisers" cuts a still more hopeless figure than its scholar. In his song, scholarly hubris betrays its petty origins:

Earth, I praise thee! praise thou *me!*
God perfecteth his creation

> With this recipient poet-passion,
> And makes the beautiful to be.
> I praise thee, O belovèd sign,
> From the God-soul unto mine!
> Praise me, that I cast on thee
> The cunning sweet interpretation,
> The help and glory and dilation
>   Of mine immortality!
> (149–58)

Among other things, these lines present an ungracious caricature of the Wordsworthian lyric subject.[17] The poet's boast to complete creation with his own "recipient poet-passion" plainly derives from Kant's epistemology and puts him in a kindred relationship to the speaker of "Tintern Abbey," who famously claims by his senses to "half create" the natural world:

> . . . Therefore am I still
> A lover of the meadows and the woods,
> And mountains; and of all that we behold
> From this green earth; of all the mighty world
> Of eye, and ear,—both what they half create,
> And what perceive; well pleased to recognise
> In nature and the language of the sense
> The anchor of my purest thoughts, the nurse,
> The guide, the guardian of my heart, and soul
> Of all my moral being.[18]

The resuscitated natural theology presented in such lines was highly prized by the Victorians, among whom it ensured Wordsworth's enduring reputation. By contrast, Barrett's Romantic pseudo-Wordsworth demands kudos for his share in Earth's creation and suggests by his vanity that nature might, after all, be an unreliable guardian for the "heart, and soul / Of all [one's] moral being." Note too how even Barrett's ballad meters, though they suffer in proximity to Wordsworth's familiar lines, become positively florid when compared to the plodding simplicity with which her Christian concludes this poem. Barrett has it both ways, granting herself the freedom to play with skipping rhythms and feminine rhymes, and still condemning them as incommensurate with Christian modesty.

We are so accustomed to seeing Wordsworth critiqued from the left (as in Byron or Browning) that it may seem odd to see him parodied from the right, as here. Barrett's condemnation of secular poetics becomes less curious when considered as part of a Protestant religious backlash from secularist triumphs of the late 1820s, such as the foundation of the University of London (the "Godless Institution of Gower Street") and Catholic Emancipation. Barrett's expressed fear that worship of nature is actually the disguised worship of self may seem abrupt: "Earth, I praise thee! praise thou *me!*" Yet it clearly resonated for her contemporaries. It is comparable, for instance, to John Henry Newman's *Tamworth Reading Room* letters of early 1841, where Newman attacks Sir Robert Peel's enthusiasm for public libraries as a tool of godless naturalism: "He considers that greater insight into Nature will lead a man to say, 'How great and wise is the Creator, who has done this!' True: but it is possible that his thoughts may take the form of 'How clever is the creature who has discovered it!' and self-conceit may stand proxy for adoration. This is no idle apprehension."[19] Secularists like Peel are wrong to promote natural theology, argues Newman, because natural theology divorced from revelation leads to mere secular science. The error of Wordsworthian religion, according to the logic of both Newman and Barrett, is that in nature's devotee, "self-conceit" may unwittingly "stand proxy for adoration." Possibly Barrett was especially attentive to the dangers of such misplaced adulation because she herself adored Wordsworth (whom she had not met) with a genuine fervor. As she admitted in an 1842 letter, "I might, if I were tempted, be caught in the overt act of gathering a thistle because Wordsworth had trodden it down . . . [,] of gathering it eagerly like his own ass!" (*Correspondence* 5: 231). And in another: "I w^d have gone on a pilgrimage to see Wordsworth ever since I was eight years old—& if the indispensable condition had been pebbles within side of the pilgrim shoon, I w^d have gone even so" (5: 299). Such promises of pilgrimage making are made partly tongue-in-cheek, but Barrett's Christian enthusiasms frame themselves in similar hyperbole.

My point in discussing these two particular lyrics at such length is that the unresolved conflict between them is paradigmatic of much of Barrett's oeuvre. Neither "Sounds" nor "Earth and Her Praisers" can well be appreciated without the sense of how the logic of each contradicts the other. Similarly, both poems contain the seeds of the other. "Sounds," for all its affinities with what the Victorians might call Spinozian pantheism, culminates in a startling auditory image of the "droppings" of the "victim-blood" of the crucified Jesus, and instructs us to "seek none other sound!" (132–33).

Conversely, the Christian of "Earth and Her Praisers" cannot entirely refrain from enthusiasm for the Earth whose destruction he celebrates. "O Earth," he begins,

> ["]I count the praises thou art worth,
> By thy waves that move aloud
> By thy hills against the cloud
> By thy valleys, warm and green
> By the copses' elms between
> By their birds which, like a sprite
> Scattered by a strong delight
> Into fragments musical
> Stir and sing in every bush.["]
> (168–77)

Such praise is measured, almost reluctantly doled out. But in the context of "Sounds," such Romantic tropes are striking: hills and valleys, elms and birds that "stir and sing in every bush." One suspects that Barrett's Christian regrets the impending Armageddon despite himself. Indeed, it is a proof of this dogma's difficulty for Barrett that she so often rehearsed it in her poems, increasingly often as her individual life became more appealing to her. In these lines, years before meeting Robert Browning, she is already asking the famous question of sonnet 43, "How do I love thee? Let me count the ways"; that is, learning to "count the praises" of mundane things that nonetheless inspire devotion. Note how both "Earth and Her Praisers" and sonnet 43 enumerate her loves precisely so as to distinguish between the limited good of mundane beauty (nature, marriage to Robert) and an ultimate good of divine revelation (Apocalypse, the afterlife).

Poems such as these—and she wrote many of them—even celebrate a death as something to be gladly anticipated in a way that cannot be dismissed for irony. As Barrett Browning closes sonnet 43, "And, if God choose, / I shall but love thee better after death" (14). Indeed, sonnet 43 belongs in a long series of Barrett Browning poems that insist upon death as a joyful condition, especially for jilted lovers ("Bertha in the Lane" [1838]) and unhappy poets ("Insufficiency" [1844]), but also for normally happy folk. In "Isobel's Child" (1838), for instance, a mother's dying infant asks her *not* to pray for its life, because it would prefer Heaven. The mother complies and the child dies. A post-Victorian reader, even accepting the miracle of the child's request, may be hard-pressed to sympathize with its mother's decision or with her satisfaction after its morbid resolution: "A satisfied love meanwhile / Which nothing earthly could despoil / Sang on within her soul" (540–42). Yet Victorian reviewers testified to being strongly moved by the mother's Christian selflessness, which they saw as better fitted to the art of the poetess than were the loftier themes of *The Seraphim*.[20] In turn, an essential part of the drama of the sonnets is that in them the poetess dares to contemplate the pleasures of earthly love ("Let us stay / Rather on earth, Belovèd" [22.9–10]), when she ought in propriety to be contemplating some version of the afterlife.

Poetic Apologetics: Barrett's Seraphim *and* Chateaubriand's Génie

This final irony of "Earth and Her Praisers"—that it is a poem hostile to poetry—succinctly brings home the challenge of measuring poetic ambition against Christian humility as Barrett wished to do. She believed that poets produced the surest representation of God's voice in the world, and, contrariwise, that devotion to the Christ of the scriptures provided a unique guarantee of salvation. Accordingly, she looked for contemporary theorists who wished to reconcile the Romantic cult of poetry with conservative biblical hermeneutics, and during the 1830s, she found the one she needed in François René Auguste de Chateaubriand's famous apology, *Le Génie du Christianisme* (*The Genius of Christianity*) (1802). The *Génie* presents an extensive argument against the Enlightenment skepticism of Voltaire, Diderot, the Count de Volney, and Thomas Paine. It was remarkably influential in the early years of the nineteenth century, and it presents just the hybrid between traditional hermeneutics and a quasi–higher critical poetics that Barrett needed to encourage her: a sort of intellectual platform for the religious poetics that she pursued in her most ambitious poetry of the 1830s and early 1840s, including the long verse dramas of *The Seraphim* and *A Drama of Exile* (1844).

Acknowledging Barrett's debt to Chateaubriand, for instance, helps to clarify her initial resolution of the dilemma found in the conflicting logics of "Sounds" and "Earth and Her Praisers." Given this impasse between the scriptural canon and the art of poetry, Chateaubriand's *Génie* could hardly have been better situated to win Barrett's admiration. A work of remarkable literary panache, it combines a personal and emotional defense of Christian dogma with an aesthetic claim that Christianity lends itself to the creation of beauty in a uniquely powerful way. The *Génie* emerged from the context of a conservative backlash to the French Revolution, but even within this context it demonstrates a singular bravura, as when Chateaubriand advances his foremost proposition, that "of all the religions that have ever existed, Christianity is the most poetic, the most humane, the most favorable to liberty, arts, and letters; the modern world owes it everything from agriculture to the abstract sciences, from hospices for the poor to temples erected by Michelangelo and ornamented by Raphael" (trans. mine).[21] Plainly, this is an ambitious project. For Chateaubriand means to present Christianity as a gift to the secular world, contributing more than anything else to its artistic and intellectual development, to its charity, and even to the progress of individual liberty. Such benefits are reaped by unbelievers, as well as the faithful. But the faithful additionally receive an unparalleled emotional experience from the moment of conversion. In his preface to the first edition, Chateaubriand famously urges that religious sentiment arises from this feeling, rather than from any intellectual proposition: "Ma conviction est sortie du coeur; j'ai pleuré et j'ai cru" (My conviction came from the heart; I wept, and I believed). The manner in which Chateaubriand connects his emotional experience to the broader question of aesthetics over the ensuing six hundred odd pages helped to win over many of his artistic contemporaries. Poetics, after all, comes first in his list of all possible goods: Christianity is "la plus poétique, la plus humaine, la plus favorable à la liberté, aux arts et aux lettres" (the most poetic, the most humane, the most favorable to liberty, art, and literature). Barrett, normally hostile to French royalist Catholic polemic, was apparently swept away.

Neither should this surprise us, for Chateaubriand's articulation of Christianity as a fundamentally poetical religion dovetailed beautifully with Barrett's fundamentally Romantic desire to unite religion and poetry. Like Renan after him, Chateaubriand's genius was not so much to originate ideas (one sees similar formulations in the tradition of Klopstock) as to give them a compelling shape. No doctrinal position could better appeal to Barrett than Chateaubriand's, and in an essay series called *The Greek Christian Poets* (1842), she confesses that her profound investment in his work derives in part from dissatisfaction with the history of Christian poetry. Here, she dilates upon the question of religious poetry—specifically upon why it is often so bad. Chateaubriand instructs that good religion must lead to good poetry, so bad religious poetry presents a theological and artistic conundrum. Barrett solves it by instructing that Christian poets have been insufficiently zealous heretofore:

Of religious poets, strictly so called, the earth is very bare. Religious "parcel-poets" we have, indeed, more than enough; writers of hymns, translators of scripture into prose, or of prose generally into rhymes, of whose heart-devotion a higher faculty were worthy. Also there have been poets, not a few, singing as if earth were still Eden; and poets, many, singing as if in the first hour of exile, when the echo of the curse was louder than the whisper of the promise. But the right "genius of Christianism" has done little up to this moment, even for Chateaubriand. We want the touch of Christ's hand upon our literature, as it touched other dead things—we want the sense of the saturation of Christ's blood upon the souls of our poets, that it may cry *through* them in answer to the ceaseless wail of the Sphinx of our humanity.
(515)

Here we see Barrett take up Chateaubriand as a stick to beat her poetic contemporaries: orthodox "writers of hymns," prosaic translators, Romantic iconoclasts singing either "as if earth were still Eden" or as if the Atonement had not occurred, and finally even Chateaubriand himself, for whom "the right 'genius of Christianism'" had apparently yet "done little." But what is most striking about Barrett's stance here (beyond the gory imagery) is the literalism with which she reproduces certain claims of Chateaubriand, who in writing of Christianity as a poetical religion never meant to suggest that its spirit ought best to be expressed by poets in the craft of verse. He meant, by and large, that the religion lends itself to the kind of inspiration, truth, and beauty that Romantic authors generally associated with poetic beauty.[22] One might say of an individual that he or she has a poetical nature; Chateaubriand says this of a religion. But Barrett's personal investment in the craft of verse drives her to out-Chateaubriand Chateaubriand. She insists not that Christianity might do much more for literature, but that it ought to inspire poets specifically: "We want . . . the saturation of Christ's blood upon the souls of our poets."

Barrett is still more emphatic upon this point in her correspondence of the same period, as in the following to Mary Russell Mitford in January of 1842:

> You are quite right in telling me not to give up poetry for magazine-writing, or for prose of a higher character. You will be satisfied when you hear me say that I could'nt if I tried. Whatever degree of faculty I have, lies in poetry—still more my personal happiness lies in it—still more of my love. [. . .]
>
> Perhaps we may differ a little upon what is called religious poetry . . though

not at all upon the specimens extant. My fixed opinion is [. . .] that the experiment has scarcely been tried . . & that a nobler "Genie du Christianisme" than has been contemplated by Chateaubriand, will yet be developped in poetical glory & light. The failure of religious poets turns less upon their being religious, than on their not being poets. Christ's religion is essentially poetry—poetry glorified. (*Correspondence* 5: 220)

Barrett's claim that "Christ's religion is essentially poetry" makes perfect sense in the context of the *Génie*. (Possibly it *only* makes sense in the context of Chateaubriand's type of Romanticism.) But here as elsewhere, Barrett and Chateaubriand appear to mean something different by poetry and poets, even where she cites him. Beginning this passage, Barrett intends to distinguish the craft of poetry from "magazine-writing," or even "prose of a higher character." She relies upon a generic sense of poetry in a way that Chateaubriand does not, and the consequence of applying this more limited sense of poetry to Chateaubriand's general idea is that verse must then be made to bear the weight of religion. Barrett's formulation demands that the craft of poetry be wedded to "Christ's religion" in a seamless and mutually fitting way.

To understand her impatience for religion to emerge in what she calls "poetical glory & light" is to comprehend the aim of Barrett's most ambitious poetry from the '30s and '40s. *The Seraphim,* her first effort at a major religious poem, conspicuously models itself upon Chateaubriand's proposition that Christianity affords a fuller poetical dispensation than had been enjoyed by the Greek writers of antiquity. Chateaubriand writes in rebuke of deist scoffers: "It is time that we know what they amount to, these accusations of *absurdity, crudeness,* and *pettiness* that are every day made against Christianity. It is time to show that, far from impoverishing thought, Christianity lends itself marvelously to flights of the soul, and can enchant the mind as divinely as the gods of Virgil and Homer" (470, trans. mine).[23] Chateaubriand devotes great effort to expounding this fecund relationship between Christianity and the arts; his "Seconde Partie," the "Poétique du Christianisme," culminates in a parodic tour de force in which, with astonishing chutzpah, he pits the style of Homer against that of the biblical Ruth to maintain the superiority of the biblical style (785–86). Only the rising aesthetic opinion of scripture in the Romantic era makes thinkable Chateaubriand's assertion that Christian art surpasses that of the ancient Greeks. His freethinking opponents could not have imagined such a claim a few years previously, when they dismissed the Bible as a barbarous product of "Oriental" minds. But part of the genius of the *Génie* was its remarkable timeliness. It managed to resituate its skeptical opponents' aesthetic standards as passé even as it bolstered the dramatic reevaluation of the texts that it praises. By the 1820s, even cultured atheists such as Shelley invariably cherished the Bible as literature. They may have come to do so without Chateaubriand, of course, but this in no way reduces his prominence in that aesthetic revolution.

By the 1830s, there was no need for Barrett to defend the Bible from *"absurdity, crudeness,* and *pettiness,"* and yet here she clings to Chateaubriand's idea that Christianity ought "to enchant the mind as divinely as the gods of Virgil and Homer." Her preface to *The Seraphim,* equal in its audacity to Chateaubriand's own, advances the principle that Aeschylus forcibly selected a second-rate subject for his Prometheus plays because he lived too early to consider the superior drama of the crucifixion. As Barrett explains,

> Had Aeschylus lived after the incarnation and crucifixion of our Lord Jesus Christ, he might have turned, if not in moral and intellectual yet in poetic faith, from the solitude of Caucasus to the deeper desertness of that crowded Jerusalem where none had any pity . . . [,] from the taunt stung into being by the torment, to HIS more awful silence, when the agony stood dumb before the love! . . .
>
> . . . The blind eagle missed the sun, but soared toward its sphere. Shall the blind eagle soar—and the seeing eagle peck chaff? Surely it should be the gladness and gratitude of such as are poets among us, that in turning towards the beautiful, they may behold the true face of God.
> (1838 Preface, v–xvi)

Barrett's verse drama, in other words, flies in the face of Shelley and Goethe (who both conceive of Prometheus as an improvement upon Christ) so as to imagine what Aeschylus himself might have written had he only lived in more auspicious times: that is, in Christian ones. This is a bold project under any circumstances, but it is remarkable for a poet who revered the Greek literature of pre-Christian antiquity and who confessed herself to be frustrated with eighteen centuries or so of Christian "parcel-poets."

Crowning this audacity is the fact that Barrett freely borrows from the religious "parcel-poets" whom she belittles. Her mockery in *The Greek Christian Poets* of "poets . . . singing as if earth were still Eden" springs directly from Felicia Hemans's ironic interrogation of Wordsworthian Romanticism in *The Sceptic* (1820): "Is Earth still Eden?—might a Seraph guest, / Still, midst its chosen bowers delighted rest?" (21–22). The bulk of Hemans's religious poem depicts the imagined conversion of another unnamed poet—undoubtedly Byron—whose dubious inspiration, bereft of Christian truth, must pass away like a burning meteor.[24] The opening passage is worth citing, since Barrett's additional metaphor in the *Seraphim* preface of the Christian poet as a "seeing eagle" also comes from here:

> When the young Eagle, with exulting eye,
> Has learn'd to dare the splendor of the sky,
> And leave the Alps beneath him in his course,
> To bathe his crest in morn's empyreal source,
> Will his free wing, from that majestic height,
> Descend to follow some wild meteor's light,
> Which far below, with evanescent fire,
> Shines to delude, and dazzles to expire?
> (5)

Hemans's metaphor is plain enough: why should one soaring on the wings of poetry forsake the steady sunshine of biblical revelation for the evanescent glow of another source? Implicitly, Hemans's rhymes present themselves as a godly alternative to Byron's. Barrett liked this premise enough to recycle it, even while doubting of Hemans's final poetic achievement. Rather than settling for the conversion of a recently dead Byron, Barrett imagines the conversion of Aeschylus, whose distance from Christian revelation was more than a matter of mere inclination. In Barrett's version of Hemans's thought experiment, the payoff is larger, too: Aeschylus comprehends what to do with Christian revelation better than Christian poets themselves. But this is a perverse adaptation of Chateaubriand as well as Hemans, for Barrett endorses the superiority of Christianity for literature without endorsing any actual Christian literature.

Barrett's commitment to Aeschylus in no way diminishes her commitment to Chateaubriand's view of the beauties of Christianity, which she tenaciously maintains throughout the course of *The Seraphim*, in conjunction with her idea that religious beauty is best represented in poetic utterance. For over a thousand lines, these diverse commitments animate a sustained dialogue between two angels, Ador and Zerah, who fly to Earth on the day of the crucifixion. Recognizing the significance of this sacrifice, Barrett's Seraphim prophesy a new poetic dispensation in which Christian literature will prevail over all that has come before it:

> *Ador.* Hereafter shall the blood-bought captives raise
> The passion-song of blood.
> *Zerah.* And *we,* extend
> Our holy vacant hands towards the Throne,
> Crying "We have no music."
> *Ador.* Rather, blend
> Both musics into one.
> The sanctities and sanctified above
> Shall each to each, with lifted looks serene,
> Their shining faces lean,
> And mix the adoring breath
> And breathe the full thanksgiving.
> *Zerah.* But the love—
> The love, mine Ador!
> *Ador.* Do we love not?
> *Zerah.* Yea,
> But not as man shall! not with life for death,
> New-throbbing through the startled being; not
> With strange astonished smiles, that ever may
> Gush passionate like tears and fill their place[.]
> (653–69)

In this dialogue, it is the happy lot of humanity not only to be redeemed by Christ, but also to inherit "the passion-song of blood," a new form of expression so powerful that it threatens to superannuate the very angels' hymns. Under this new dispensation, the Seraphim have only to turn their "holy vacant hands towards the Throne, / Crying, 'We have no music.'" Ador, being a bit slow, initially resists this idea by proposing a harmony in which human and angelic music complement one another: "Rather blend / Both musics into one. / . . . And mix the adoring breath." But the more perceptive Zerah sees that the sacrifice of Christ's atonement produces an utterly inimitable response in its beneficiaries: Zerah admits that the angels love, truly, "But not as man shall! not with life for death, / New-throbbing through the startled being."

Now, one need not be an authority on nineteenth-century religious culture to recognize that the shock, the throb, and the gushing violence of this love response belong to boilerplate evangelical conversion narratives, whereas (as Barrett complains) they are by no means salient in the English poetic tradition. Ador's "passion-song" of Christ's blood anticipates the sort of affect delineated in William Wilberforce's classic *A Practical View of the Prevailing System of Professed Christians* (1797): "When [a sinner] fairly estimates the guilt of sin by the costly satisfaction which was required to atone for it . . . [,] if he be not lost to sensibility, mixed emotions of guilt, and fear, and shame, and remorse, and sorrow, will nearly overwhelm his soul; he will smite upon his breast, and cry out in the language of the publican, 'God be merciful to me, a sinner' . . . Happy, happy souls!"[25] The evangelical believer here comes to appreciate God through an overwhelming, breast-smiting, highly conflicted emotional response to Christ's sacrifice. Like Zerah's "startled being," "he" experiences "guilt, and fear, and shame, and remorse, and sorrow" as the very mark of salvation. And in both works, the paradoxical claims of evangelical awakening amount to a reliable set of tropes, in which the "strange astonished smiles" of "happy, happy souls" will "gush passionate like tears."

Given this evangelical subtext, Zerah's use of the future tense is instructive: the inimitable passion of love does not belong to humanity broadly speaking, or even to the biblical religions; it is specific to what Wilberforce calls "real Christianity" (2). (For Barrett, equally clearly, the evangelical narrative eclipses Chateaubriand's enthusiasm for the Hebrew scriptures.[26]) Seraphim cannot love as humans *shall* love when they come to recognize the sacrifice of Christ. And the model for this new emotional response is identified by Zerah in the woman at the foot of the cross:

> A woman kneels
> The mid cross under,
> With white lips asunder,
> And motion on each.
> They throb, as she feels,
> With a spasm, not a speech[.]
> (476–81)

We find here the jarring rhythms and imagery that would eventually come to cement Barrett's future association with the mid-century Spasmodic poets.[27] In the grief-filled space between spasm and speech, Barrett finds the duty of

the future Christian poet who must convey the heartfelt passion of conversion. Barrett even re-creates a hint of physical confusion (since speech and
sobbing can be mutually exclusive) with metrical substitutions: the apparent collapse of the iambic line in "míd cróss ún-der," and "With white líps
a-súnder," that eventually resolves itself in the strained final iambs of "With
a spá-sm, nót a spéech." This, perhaps, is Chateaubriand's conversion, writ
poetically: "j'ai pleuré et j'ai cru." Barrett, too, emphasizes the poetic potential of weeping one's way to belief: the "passion-song of blood" throbs forth,
and it is the poet's duty to sing it. Whether the woman in question is Christ's
mother or Mary Magdalene, the poem refuses to specify.[28] She is not an individual intercessor, but a general model.

It would be difficult in such cases to overstate the importance of her evangelical emotion to Barrett's poetics, or to overstate the interdependence of
these two. As we will see, she builds her poetic career largely upon the emotional truths of Victorian religion.[29] When her cousin John Kenyon criticized
this emphasis in "The Dead Pan" (1844), she shot back with the following:

> Certainly *I* w^d rather be a Pagan whose religion was actual, earnest, contin-
> ual, . . for weekdays, workdays, & songdays, . . than I would be a Christian who,
> from whatever motive, shrank from hearing or uttering the name of Christ out
> of "Church." I am no fanatic—but I like truth & earnestness in all things,—&
> I cannot choose but believe that such a Christian shows but ill beside such a
> Pagan—What pagan poet ever thought of casting his gods out of his poetry? In
> what Pagan poem, do they not shine & thunder?
> (*Correspondence* 7: 21)

For Barrett, English poets have wrongly shirked religious emotion. "My conviction is that the *poetry of Christianity* will one day be developed greatly &
nobly," she concludes, underlining Chateaubriand's key terms lest Kenyon
miss her point, "& that in the meantime we are as wrong poetically as morally, in desiring to restrain it" (21–22).

This deliberate treatment of pagan themes deserves attention, for it shows
how Barrett's conception merged with other contemporary religious theories, especially the higher criticism. Scholars of the Victorian higher criticism have stressed its reliance upon the development of comparative mythology, and many higher critics invite a conflation of the two. As the American
H. A. Sawtelle aptly observed in the *Christian Review,* "Strauss endeavors to
give plausibility to the theory of myths in the Gospels by seeking to com-

pare those writings with the records of the mythical religions of antiquity."[30] Another American, the Unitarian Theodore Parker, likewise suggests in the *Christian Examiner* that Strauss's conclusions were inevitable as soon as Eichhorn first denied the Hebrew miracles a half century previously on the grounds of comparative mythology: "[Eichhorn] saw that he must deny this [the existence of miracles] of the Bible, or admit it likewise of all ancient religious documents; for they all claimed it."[31] (Unsurprisingly, Parker concedes this ground, whereas Sawtelle disputes it: "But we contend that the Gospel records are entirely different from them" [348].)

Chateaubriand presents an alternative version of comparative mythology, one that held more weight with Barrett. In a breezy prototype of archetypal theory, the *Génie* claims the universality of religious ideas:

> It is impossible to believe that an absurd lie should become a universal tradition. Open the books of the second Zoroaster, the dialogues of Plato and those of Lucien, the moral treatises of Plutarch, the annals of the Chinese, the Bible of the Hebrews, the Eddas of the Scandinavians; take yourself to the lands of the black Africans, or to the sagely priests of India; each of these will recite for you the crimes of the spirit of evil, each will describe to you a brief period of human felicity and the lengthy calamities that followed the human fall from innocence.
>
> (526, trans. mine)

For Chateaubriand, the apparent universality of religious ideas does not diminish the status of Christianity, but rather enhances it. The Bible contains the best of Zoroastrianism and the Eddas, the Analects of Confucius and the Mahabarata, all while having the additional benefit of being historically *true*. (Chateaubriand even defends the scientific basis of the Mosaic cosmogony, which was scarcely more plausible in 1802 than in 1838.) As Barrett's letter to Kenyon indicates, she followed Chateaubriand to this alternative position. In other words, her frustration with Christian poetics grows not from a perceived threat of kinship with pagan religions, but from a recognition that such kinship displays how lamentably short Christian poets have come in taking their due place among the poets of world mythologies. "And then my dear friend, we do not live among dreams," Barrett continues to Kenyon. "The Christian religion is true or it is not—and if it is true it offers the highest and purest objects of contemplation. And the Poetical faculty which expresses the highest moods of the Mind passes naturally to the highest objects" (21). Barrett's many letters on this theme almost justify her later enthusiasm for the outré concept of "automatic writing": they echo her mentor, Chateaubriand, so clearly as to seem to channel him. One might take Barrett herself for a medium if only Chateaubriand had been dead at the time of their composition.

Emanuel Swedenborg's Correspondence School and Barrett Browning's Verse Novel

Barrett's early commitment to Christian poetics, as embodied in *The Seraphim,* nonetheless failed to inaugurate an epoch in "poetical glory & light" or, for that matter, to articulate "a nobler 'Genie du Christianisme'" than Chateaubriand's. Contemporary reviews of the *Seraphim* volume mostly reenact the religious struggle that the poems themselves present, and in much the same language. Reviewers alternately scold Barrett for pursuing such sacred topics (though less severely than she scolds herself) and praise her for the purity of her cause. Overwhelmingly, critics favored her shorter lyrics as comprehensible instances of the tradition of Mary Tighe, Hemans, and Landon, and express only a half-admiring puzzlement at the Shelleyan verse drama.[32] The small number of critics who embraced the *Seraphim* poem without reserve sympathized strongly with its religious bent. The *Sunbeam,* for instance, took Barrett's Romanticism to heart, gushing that "there is something that is preternatural, but not supernatural, in the poems before us. . . . Awake, soul of song, and contemplate the immortal in the infinite. . . . Equally possible this, to the Perfect Poet and the Perfect Christian. Such an one was the Sainted JOHN, but the meagre religionists of this age shrink from this theology, or . . . reduce by accommodation its sublime verities to the standard of modern belief."[33] Clearly, the language of this impassioned review derives largely from Barrett's own "Sounds": the call to awakening, the contemplation of the immortal, the conflation of "Perfect Poet and the Perfect Christian" in "Sainted JOHN." Sadly for Barrett, however, such sympathetic reviewers were scarce. Or, rather, happily—for had the *Athenaeum* printed anything like the above, her poetic ambition might never have increased beyond a long series of celestial dramas charting the various classes of angels: *The Cherubim, The Thrones, The Dominions, The Powers.*

Meanwhile, Barrett felt crushed by the critics' ambivalent response to her most ambitious production, and she downplayed the positive tenor of most reviews. As she complained to Mary Russell Mitford, "But you see, opinion runs almost everywhere . . . *against* the Seraphim, & in favor comparatively, of the shorter poems" (*Correspondence* 4: 74–75). And to R. H. Horne, more despondently, "I wonder to myself sometimes in a climax of dissatisfaction how I came to publish it. It is a failure in my own eyes—& if it were not for the poems of less pretension in its company, would have fallen, both probably & deservedly, a dead weight from the press. . . . Something I shall do hereafter in poetry, I hope" (*Correspondence* 8: 237–38). For their part, Barrett's correspondents agreed with the critics, and urged that she might better utilize her gifts were she to incorporate more narrative and human interest into her longer poems. As Mitford put it in one of many letters on this topic, "I do not believe, my sweetest, that the very highest poetry does not sell at once. Look at Wordsworth! The hour will arrive, and all the sooner if to poetry, unmatched in truth and beauty and feeling, you condescend to add story and a happy ending, that being among the conditions of recurrence to every book with the mass even of cultivated readers—I do not mean the few" (*Correspondence* 4: 123). Critics today invariably side with Mitford on this question. With the privilege of historical retrospect, we can appreciate that over many years, Barrett Browning hearkened to her advice, gradually condescending "to add story and a happy ending" to her most ambitious projects. And that she succeeded wonderfully: *Aurora Leigh* stands out as the consummate example of both. But Barrett's correspondence also attests to the fact that her conversion required years of persuasion by friends such as Mitford and Kenyon.

Barrett also needed an additional theoretical model to Chateaubriand's (or her version of Chateaubriand's) to wean her from the celestial aesthetic of the early poetry. In the mid-1840s, she found a theorist who solicited this literary flexibility, and who seemed equally congenial to her religious spirit. This was the eighteenth-century philosopher, scientist, and mystic Emanuel Swedenborg, and Barrett Browning discovered him about the time of her marriage in 1846. So did everyone else. Swedenborg enjoyed a tremendous mid-century vogue, winning the admiration of figures from the Brownings to Baudelaire, Emerson, Henry James Sr., Schopenhauer, Thoreau, and Walt Whitman. Swedenborgian hermeneutics particularly appealed to metaphysically inclined mid-century intellectuals as a provocative alternative to the higher critical emphasis on probability and evidence. For Swedenborg, biblical interpretation requires fresh revelation, and he routinely attributes his scriptural insights to the private instruction of angels.[34] This approach, it need hardly be said, puts him at odds with ordinary modern exegesis. "He never reasons about the things he learned through spirits and angels," admits James, a devoted proselyte, "or attempts to throw persuasive light upon them."[35] But, for believers, Swedenborg's method circumvents many of the usual stumbling blocks of Victorian hermeneutics, such as textual incongruities or cognate mythologies.

Barrett Browning herself needed little "persuasive light" to embrace Swedenborg's understanding of revelation as a special expression of a spiritual world both within and beyond the natural material world.[36] And Swedenborg's writings freed Barrett Browning to imagine a contemporary author of genuine scriptural authority without the pious misgivings expressed in "Earth and Her Praisers." Consider in this light her depiction of the poet as exegete in *Aurora Leigh*:

> O delight
> And triumph of the poet, who would say
> A man's mere "yes," a woman's common "no,"
> A little human hope of that or this,
> And says the word so that it burns you through
> With a special revelation, shakes the heart
> Of all the men and women in the world,
> As if one came back from the dead and spoke,
> With eyes too happy, a familiar thing
> Become divine i' the utterance! while for him
> The poet, speaker, he expands with joy;
> The palpitating angel in his flesh
> Thrills inly with consenting fellowship
> To those innumerous spirits who sun themselves
> Outside of time.
> O life, O poetry,
> —Which means life in life!
> (1.901–16)

Swedenborg's conception of a correspondent spiritual world fills *Aurora Leigh*, just as it fills this passage. Words do not mean what they say, but they do mean what the poet or angel says. "A man's mere 'yes,'" or "a woman's common 'no,'" will "become divine i' the utterance" thereby. This notion of "consenting fellowship" would be redolent of Swedenborg even without reference to his particular friends: "those innumerous spirits who sun themselves / Outside of time." As formerly with Chateaubriand, however, Barrett

Browning changes the thrust of Swedenborg to her own particular ends in this wedding of "the Perfect Poet and the Perfect Christian." For, in these lines, the "special revelation" belongs not to visionary exegetes, per se, but to poets—in Aurora's case, to a nineteenth-century woman poet. *Aurora Leigh* thus finally genders prophecy and poetry in extraordinary ways that seemed implicit, but were never fully expressed, in the earlier poetry.

Equally important, the Swedenborgian notion of spiritual correspondences affords Barrett Browning a chance to glorify the mundane world of human relations in ways that she had denied herself in early religious work. This revivifies her whole aesthetic by permitting her to borrow from worldly genres in ways that were formerly forbidden. In *Aurora Leigh,* for instance, the novelistic marriage plot and the sexual dynamism of Aurora's prolonged estrangement from Romney drives the narrative and creates the requisite space for her philosophy. The communication problems between Aurora and Romney are wholly typical of the mid-Victorian novel. Like the conflicts animating the novels of, say, Anthony Trollope, they could all have been solved with one timely conversation. Barrett Browning might have called her epic *She Knew She Was Right,* except that this marriage plot was of comparatively little interest to her. Chiefly it functioned to provide an external impetus for her theological position, and thereby to solve the impasse of her earlier work. "There *is* an amount of spiritual truth in the book to which the public is unaccustomed," she acknowledged to her sister Arabella.[37] But she sugared this pill with the secular tropes to which the reading public had become addicted.

The radical nature of Barrett Browning's social investment in *Aurora Leigh* (in society, in sex, or in politics) can hardly be appreciated, then, without a sense of how thoroughly it transforms her former Christian aloofness from the world. Observe how Aurora emphasizes this social world everywhere, even in the very act of deserting Romney, to whom the marriage plot more or less ensures that she will return. She leaves him for the city, "the gathering-place of souls" and the natural setting for what she describes as an experiment in feminist theology:

> ". . . I go hence
> To London, to the gathering-place of souls,
> To live mine straight out, vocally, in books;
> Harmoniously for others, if indeed
> A woman's soul, like man's, be wide enough

To carry the whole octave (that's to prove)
Or, if I fail, still purely for myself.
Pray God be with me, Romney."
(2.1181–88)

The expressed importance of this urban world by no means guarantees that Aurora can depict it faithfully, of course. As Swinburne put it in an otherwise loving appraisal, "The career of Aurora in London is rather too eccentric a vision to impose itself upon the most juvenile credulity: a young lady of family who lodges by herself in Grub Street, preserves her reputation, lives on her pen, and dines out in Mayfair, is hardly a figure for serious fiction."[38] Yet Swinburne's critique, perfectly true, nonetheless misses the point. Barrett Browning did not have to write a realistic novel for her poem to be read as one, and she found herself quite handy with the mechanisms of the genre. David Lodge pinpoints this genre issue when he describes the mode of realism in literature as *"the representation of experience in a manner which approximates closely to description of similar experience in non-literary texts of the same culture."*[39] Mid-Victorian novels, like all texts, adhere to their own generic tropes more consistently than to any external social reality. Since art does so much to create our perception of that reality, of course, there remains a real question about how we can properly judge their relation to one another. Barrett Browning actually takes Lodge's insight one step further: *Aurora Leigh* does not merely replicate the tropes of nonliterary texts of its culture; it visibly replicates their own replication in literary texts with pretensions to realism—that is, novels. And still the result remains as compelling as any "serious fiction." In a well-known critique, Virginia Woolf saluted this where Swinburne had failed to: "We laugh, we protest, we complain—it is absurd, it is impossible, we cannot tolerate this exaggeration a moment longer—but, nevertheless, we read to the end enthralled."[40] But observe how by taking the art of realism to one further remove from the novel, Barrett Browning also ensures that the craft of *Aurora Leigh* can never be far from the mind of her reader. She drives her narrative along while keeping artistic craft in the foreground of the images that she evokes.[41]

This is essential because Barrett Browning was interested in poetic craft immeasurably more than she was in narrative, per se. She returns to this theme repeatedly in *Aurora Leigh*, leading her enthralled readership through recurring episodes of an audacious philosophical *ars poetica*. Lodge meets Swedenborg in any of several passages like the following:

Art's the witness of what Is
Behind this show. If this world's show were all,
Then imitation would be all in Art;
There, Jove's hand grips us!—For we stand here, we,
If genuine artists, witnessing for God's
Complete, consummate, undivided work;
—That every natural flower which grows on earth
Implies a flower upon the spiritual side,
Substantial, archetypal, all a-glow
With blossoming causes,—not so far away,
But we, whose spirit-sense is somewhat cleared,
May catch at something of the bloom and breath[.]
(7.834–45)

Of Swedenborg's contribution to the passage, little need be said. Here we find his distinctive "spiritual side" of the world, a mirror of its material embodiment but more "Substantial, archetypal, all a-glow / With blossoming causes." (To a mid-Victorian audience, indeed, mere mention of "spirit-sense" might call Swedenborg to mind.) But the Romantic conception of the "real" world as an artistic fiction also emerges here. Art does not correspond to "this world's show": on the contrary, art is essential to right experience of the world without being merely imitative of it. Art witnesses for "God's / Complete, consummate, undivided work." It may also stand representative of that alternate reality, witnessing for "what Is" because art "Is," just as the scriptures embody (for believers) God's investment in the world and thereby themselves become (for believers) "Holy Scripture."

Most strikingly for a work that relies so heavily on the conventions of the novel, *Aurora Leigh* consistently professes a literary hierarchy in which poetry "Is" above all other forms of art. As Aurora specifies, poets are "the only truth-tellers now left to God, / The only speakers of essential truth, / Opposed to relative, comparative, / And temporal truths" (1.859–62). Such lines prefigure Bakhtin's famous thesis on "Epic and Novel," except that Bakhtin commends the "relative, comparative, / And temporal truths" of novels over the "essential" truths of poetry, rather than vice versa.[42] Both theorists provide inadvertent evidence of the power of the hierarchies they struggle to maintain or to undo—especially when, as here, their alternative categories seem so empty. Epic affords Bakhtin the inverse of Barrett Browning's straw man, the novel. But what is notable in retrospect is that either should feel pressed to resort to straw men at all.

Let me conclude this discussion of Swedenborgian philosophy in *Aurora Leigh,* then, by recalling how the novelistic marriage plot transpires in the final lines of *Aurora Leigh.* In this final book, Romney shows up blind at Aurora's doorstep in Florence, having had a textbook evangelical conversion to the truth of her gospel: "I came convicted here," he says, "And humbled sorely if not enough. I came / Because this woman from her crystal soul / Had shown me something which a man calls light" (8.1210–13). Chastened, he now agrees that poets are "the only truth-tellers now left to God," and he promises to share her poetic vision. This she graciously accepts:

> My Romney!—Lifting up my hand in his,
> As wheeled by Seeing spirits toward the East,
> He turned instinctively,—where, faint and far,
> Along the tingling desert of the sky,
> Beyond the circle of the conscious hills,
> Were laid in jasper-stone as clear as glass
> The first foundations of that new, near Day
> Which should be builded out of heaven, to God.
> He stood a moment with erected brows,
> In silence, as a creature might, who gazed,—
> Stood calm, and fed his blind, majestic eyes
> Upon the thought of perfect noon: and when
> I saw his soul saw,—"Jasper first," I said,
> "And second, sapphire; third, chalcedony;
> The rest in order,—last, an amethyst."
> (950–65)

There is no need to rehearse here this passage's well-known debt to the biblical book of Revelation, to which the jewels and the newly laid foundation openly allude.[43] What I wish to point out is that Chateaubriand and Swedenborg are still present, orchestrating this culminating religious vision. For that matter, Ador and Zerah, the angelic powers of *The Seraphim,* are still present, pursuing the religious themes of the poetry in an entirely different capacity than formerly. They manifest themselves as the "seeing spirits" of line 951, and they move Romney like a marionette, lifting Aurora's hand and wheeling him toward the East so that his blind, majestic eyes might feed upon her religious vision.

More than anything, it is the erotic charge of this moment in the verse novel that gives us Mitford's "happy ending," a happy ending even—perhaps especially—in the domestic sense that Christina Rossetti used when lamenting Barrett Browning's "happy" marital fortunes.[44] But neither erotic charge nor narrative closure can function here without Romney's and Aurora's shared religious perspective. This is true whether or not the tingling sensation that Aurora attributes to "the desert of the sky" is shared by her readers through their sympathy with her newly revived romantic prospects (as surely it is), and whatever we make of her attention to Romney's "erected" brows. For these are Swedenborgian seers, and they see heaven: "when / I saw his soul saw,—'Jasper first,' I said." What is striking about *Aurora Leigh* is how skillfully Barrett Browning shapes to such visionary ends the generic traits of the mid-Victorian novel. She turns to good use, at last, Chateaubriand's idea that the poetry of Christianity infuses other artistic genres regardless of form. And she turns the momentum of Bildungsroman and marriage plot into something like Swedenborgian mysticism. And all this without compromising her vision: Barrett Browning ends *Aurora Leigh* just as Barrett Barrett had begun *The Seraphim*, with the confidence that Christianity ought still to produce a new poetics, "Which should be builded out of heaven, to God."

Denying Strauss Three Times

Barrett Browning's philosophy in *Aurora Leigh*, especially her emphasis on the inspiration of poetry, ultimately generates curious affinities with the conclusions of the higher critics. Compare her Swedenborgian "Art's the witness of what Is" passage with Ernest Renan's nearly contemporary preface to his famous *Life of Jesus* (*Vie de Jésus* [1864]):

> Religions are false when they attempt to prove the infinite, to define it, to incarnate it, dare I say, but they are true when they affirm it. The greatest errors they blend into that affirmation are nothing compared to the value of the truth they proclaim. The simplest of the simple, provided he practice the religion of the heart, is more enlightened as to the reality of things than the materialist who believes everything to be explained by chance or by finite causes. (trans. mine)[45]

Renan, as I discuss in my introduction, did more to popularize the mytho-logical conclusions of the higher criticism than any of his contemporaries. Not among the most rigorous of higher critics, he was nonetheless their most compelling mid-century expositor and enjoyed an enormous reader-ship. So it is suggestive that Barrett Browning the Swedenborgian proselyte of *Aurora Leigh* and Renan the higher critical populizer of *La Vie de Jésus* end up in much the same place, affirming a metaphysical infinite, disparaging materialism, even defending biblical literalism in a patronizing kind of way. This similarity develops despite the fact that Barrett Browning seems never to have grasped the finer points of the higher criticism. The envious Strauss might point out that neither had Renan, but this is no objection, since Re-nan earnestly sought to portray Strauss's conclusions, however he vulgarized them. Barrett Browning, as we will see, sought only to quash them, and to replace them with her own philosophy.

Barrett Browning's perspective on the myth of Christianity thus evinces some perplexing similarities with the higher criticism. We know that she discussed the higher critics with Browning by the time he wrote "Christmas-Eve" and "Easter Day" in the winter of 1849–50, and so it is easy to imagine her prior engagement with Strauss in something like the following court-ship letter in 1845, in which she invokes Christian mythology in response to Browning's proposition that she rework the myth of Prometheus. (Browning seems to have missed the aim of the *Seraphim* preface, and Barrett restates it here.) "I am inclined to think that we want new *forms* . . as well as thoughts," writes Barrett in her refusal. "The old gods are dethroned. Why should we go back to the antique moulds. . . . Let us all aspire rather to *Life*—& let the dead bury their dead. If we have but courage to face these conventions, to touch this low ground, we shall take strength from it instead of losing it; & of that, I am intimately persuaded. For there is poetry *everywhere*. . . . And then Christianity is a worthy *myth*, & poetically acceptable" (*Correspondence* 10: 135, emphases EBB's). The final sentence here, identifying Christianity as "a worthy *myth*," might suggest a Straussian perspective, especially when quoted out of context. It certainly implies the kinship of Christianity and Greek mythology. But it amounts to a fraught understatement of Chateaubri-and's claim that Christianity offers more to art than its mythological rivals. The "old Gods" being dethroned (as in "The Dead Pan") should make room for a new Christian poetry. Having scolded Kenyon with her insistence that "the Christian religion is true or it is not," Barrett here gently scolds Browning. Further, her claim that "there is poetry *everywhere*" shows precisely how the poetess of "Sounds" develops into the Swedenborgian of *Aurora Leigh*, abandoning Aristotle so as better to capture "this live, throbbing age" (203). As she wrote Thomas Westwood in 1854, "Every *fact* is a word of God, and I call it irreligious to say, 'I will deny this because it displeases me.'"[46] As we have seen, her growing interest in mundane facts corresponds to her increasing power as a poet.

Barrett expresses this investment in Christian "myth" provocatively near George Eliot's monumental translation of Strauss, it is true, after which the very term carried an electric charge. It beggars belief to think that anyone who had eagerly argued the finer points of superannuated anglophone biblical scholarship in the 1830s could by the 1840s overlook what even the least sympathetic reviews acknowledged to be "the most important of those treatises in which the Catholic view of the birth, life, death, and resurrection of Christ has been contested within the last sixty years."[47] Yet Barrett Browning never mentions Strauss in correspondence before 1861. Three explanations appear for this puzzling lacuna, beyond the obvious fact that 1846 (the year of Eliot's translation) was a busy year for the Brownings, between elopement and relocation to Italy. The first is that Barrett Browning was so invested in alternative hermeneutics (Chateaubriand and Swedenborg) that she had no intellectual place for Strauss. Another is that she ignored the Eliot translation because she was already familiar with Strauss, either from the German edition or, more likely, through any of several preexisting and overwhelmingly negative English-language reviews of it. The third and most likely is that she subscribed to a strategy articulated very early in these reviews: that Strauss's attack on more orthodox forms of Christianity ought to be ignored, that it would wither of its own accord if his opponents refrained from giving it gratuitous publicity. All three explanations seem true.

We nonetheless find Strauss in *Aurora Leigh,* despite Barrett Browning's reluctance to name him. She almost certainly conceives of Strauss as a primary model for the conceited German scholar at Lord Howe's party in book 5:

> I heard
> The young man with the German student's look—
> A sharp face, like a knife in a cleft stick,
> Which shot up straight against the parting line
> So equally dividing the long hair.
> (5.627–31)

The portrait, not a flattering one, plays to British stereotypes of the Germans as brilliant but faddish; the mixed compliment was applied to no one oftener than Strauss. Like Browning's "hawk-nosed high-cheek-boned" Göttingen professor in "Christmas-Eve," Aurora's student is sharp in both visage and intellect, and she recognizes in him "the German student's look." She takes note both of his dubious association with Göttingen (where Eichhorn had studied and taught) and of his forward, precocious youth. This youthfulness also strikes his interlocutor in the poem, the Tractarian buffoon, Sir Blaise:

> "You are young,"
> Sir Blaise objected.
> "If I am," he said
> With fire,—"'though somewhat less so than I seem,
> The young run on before, and see the thing
> That's coming. Reverence for the young, I cry.
> In that new church for which the world's near ripe,
> You'll have the younger in the Elder's chair,
> Presiding with his ivory front of hope
> O'er foreheads clawed by cruel carrion-birds
> Of life's experience."
> (5.709–18)

The two characters are coupled here by design, like the pope and professor in Browning's "Christmas-Eve"; they are meant to suggest by contrasting portraits the opposite extremes of Christian faith gone awry. Neither seems quite up to suitable drawing room conversation. Even to the iconoclast Aurora, a cheer like "Reverence for the young" jars as much as Sir Blaise's quaint medievalizing. One thinks of Herr Klesmer's disregard for social mores at Quetcham Hall in *Daniel Deronda,* the "odious German fashion" in which he curtly dismisses Gwendolen's music.[48]

Barrett Browning's Göttingen student differs from both Browning's professor and Eliot's, however, in his unusual youth and iconoclasm, and it is these particularly that call Strauss to mind. Both were strongly associated with him in conservative reviews. Having produced the *Leben Jesu* at the age of twenty-seven, Strauss was regarded by many as a monstrous upstart, the youngest Young Turk of biblical exegesis. A reviewer in the *Christian Examiner and Religious Miscellany* goes so far as to imply that Strauss's personal immaturity alone accounted for his critical audacity:

Not the least remarkable of the phenomena attending this work, is the youth of the author at the period when he gave it to the world. At an age when young men, who by a modern allowance have been permitted to teach their elders, most generally begin to admit modest humility to their true regard, and to realize, by disappointed pride or the vanishing of some delusion, that they know only in part and are just commencing their best education, Strauss published a book which opens with an absolute renunciation of Christianity as a revelation, and closes with instructing those who, like himself, are its ministers, how they may still preach it without believing it.[49]

Implicit in this criticism of parvenu German scholars is surely a criticism of parvenu German universities, which had surged to the vanguard of textual scholarship in a manner bewildering to many in the anglophone world. "Either from contempt of English criticism," continues this unhappy reviewer, "or from a supposition that the German includes it, [Strauss] confines his quotations to the German authorities" (333). The universities of Oxford and Cambridge are half a millennium older than that of Göttingen, which was only founded in 1734; even the American Harvard outdates it by a century. But the young Germans were now "in the Elder's chair" in philology, philosophy, and comparative mythology. Aurora smiles at her student's youth — "He was twenty, certainly" (646) — but she cannot contradict his boast that Göttingen taught him "enough philosophy / To stock your English schools for fifty years" (756–57).

Aurora Leigh's Straussian diverges from Strauss in his antipathy to established Christian traditions, as in proclaiming a gospel of "that new church for which the world's near ripe." In fact, contemporary reviewers puzzled over Strauss's professed allegiance to Christianity, which seems to have been genuine, but which won him few friends during the *Leben Jesu* furor. Opponents variously denounced him as prevaricating, delusional, or (despite the contradiction) both. Much later, in a further instance of life imitating art, the historical Strauss actually did come to reject Christianity, but the materialist tendencies of his *Der alte und der neue Glaube* (1872) apparently shocked even his closest friends and associates as a radical departure. Throughout the 1850s, at least, he was earnestly religious, and as self-interrogating as *Aurora Leigh*'s Straussian is condescending and glib. Strauss could not expect conservatives to appreciate his religious humility, however, when he advocated the apophatic, bare-bones religion mocked in the *Christian Examiner* ("its ministers . . . may still preach it without believing it"). For such reviewers,

the very foundation of Strauss's views was an act of unpardonable intellectual pride; only a minority of critics who strongly disagreed with his prem-
ises deigned to consider the possibility of his personal integrity.

These minority voices are instructive. Peter Bayne of the *Fortnightly*, an
enthusiast of Barrett Browning who identified Strauss (seemingly in earnest)
as an incarnation of the very Antichrist promised in scripture, nonetheless
conceded, "He is no scoffer like Voltaire, measuring the universe with the
plumb-line of a jest, and sneering down all impassioned and self-sacrificing
nobleness, from that of a Mary of Galilee to that of a Joan of Arc."[50] Similarly,
as Parker distinguished Strauss from the English and Continental deists,
"The style is elevated, and manly, and always pretty clear. We do not remember to have met with a sneer in the whole book" (313). Those few critics dis-
passionate enough to consider Strauss's character found it unimpeachable.
From this, we see that Aurora's student is cut not from the mold of Strauss
himself, but rather from conservative perception of him. Her caricature is
a sneering, preening continental European, neither "elevated," nor "manly,"
nor even "pretty clear." Worst of all, he gives little indication of having closely
read his Strauss. Readers expecting a reliable account of the distinguishing
features of mid-century German hermeneutics will have to look elsewhere.

For, beyond embodying conservative misperceptions about Strauss's
character, Aurora's student propagates common misperceptions about higher
critical scholarship. To be sure, Aurora's narrative conveys little of his scholarly acumen, beyond a brief conversation in which he smirks at Lady Wal-
demar (another disingenuous Teuton) as a latter-day Virgin Mary. But the
student makes a point of insisting that the cult of the Blessed Virgin also had
its roots in pagan religion:

["]Be sure that, by some sleight of Christian art,
He has metamorphosed and converted her
To a Blessed Virgin."
"Soft!" Sir Blaise drew breath
As if it hurt him—"Soft! no blasphemy,
I pray you!"
     "The first Christians did the thing:
Why not the last?" asked he of Göttingen,
With just that shade of sneering on the lip,
Compensates for the lagging of the beard[.]
(5.771–74)

To a Victorian, the thrust of this slight sketch might seem obvious: here is German effrontery, "sneering" at the "impassioned and self-sacrificing nobleness" of "Mary of Galilee" (by way of predicting that his own generation of Christians would be "the last").[51] But although the *Leben Jesu* does propose the apotheosis of the Virgin as an instance of early Christian mythology, it repudiates the student's idea that it was "sleight" in any of the common senses of the term, and instead advocates the opposite view that myth should be taken as a natural part of culture. Equally telling is the student's "shade of sneering on the lip"; as even Bayne attests, this is entirely uncharacteristic of Strauss, while it is perfectly characteristic of the French and English deists. *Aurora Leigh*'s scandals come not originally from Göttingen lecture halls, it seems, but from Enlightenment classics such as Edward Gibbon's *Decline and Fall of the Roman Empire* (1776–78), where Gibbon (a British MP) sardonically recounts the ancient controversies around Christ's virgin birth in passages like the following:

> One of the most subtile disputants of the Manichaean school . . . pressed the danger and indecency of supposing, that the God of the Christians, in the state of a human foetus, emerged at the end of nine months from a female womb. The pious horror of his antagonists provoked them to disclaim all sensual circumstances of conception and delivery; to maintain that the divinity passed through Mary like a sunbeam through a plate of glass; and to assert, that the seal of her virginity remained unbroken even at the moment when she became the mother of Christ.[52]

By her own report, Barrett Browning knew Gibbon's work from a relatively young age. Why she would present his conclusions as the latest news from Göttingen is anyone's guess. But most likely she did not clearly differentiate between deist scandal and higher criticism. This is supremely ironic, since the higher criticism emerged largely in order to correct the least generous presuppositions of deism. It is German in its very restraint from Gibbon's signature condescension.[53]

To rehearse the above, *Aurora Leigh* seems unjust to Strauss on three counts: caricaturing his youth, impugning his integrity, and distorting his scholarship. Possibly Barrett Browning can parody Strauss so blithely because she had not read him. We see a final instance of her disinclination to distinguish between deism and higher criticism in one letter that does mention Strauss by way of justifying her spiritualist enthusiasms. As she wrote Fanny

Haworth in January 1861, "But the whole theory of spiritualism, all the phenomena, are strikingly *confirmatory* of revelation; nothing strikes me more
than that. Hume's argument against miracles (a strong argument) disappears
before it, and Strauss's conclusions from a priori assertion of impossibility fall
in pieces at once."[54] The logic of Barrett's argument here is worth explaining.
She claims that the supernatural effects of spiritualism (automatic writing,
table-rapping, and so forth) defy explanation even among reliable witnesses
and thereby defeat Hume's argument that historical accounts of miracles are
most likely the product of liars. Strauss, agreeing to the unlikelihood of miracles but constructing an alternative explanation of their mythical source, is
rendered superfluous. Nonetheless, Barrett Browning's cursory dismissal of
Strauss—juxtaposed with her grudging respect for Hume—reveals undue
irritation with his case against miracles, an irritation that, once again, was
endemic in Victorian conservative treatment of the *Leben Jesu,* and widely
available to those who had not read it. The *British Quarterly Review* complained of Strauss that "to assume [the impossibility of miracles] is to beg the
main question at issue" (211). The *Christian Examiner* cries that "the author
begins with the monstrous assumption of the identity in truth and in destiny
between all religions which depend on documents" (318), and the *Christian
Review* states, "The Gospels tell us of miracles; they cannot, therefore, be
historically true. Is not this a begging of the question?" (411). Thus Barrett
Browning's dismissive aside—her one direct consideration of Strauss's theory—simply parrots a major theme of conservative reviews. What is more,
Barrett Browning did not actually have need of spiritualist miracles in order
to differ from the anti-religious conclusions of Voltaire, Volney, and Hume.
Strauss himself had eviscerated the central arguments of the first two with
regard to the Bible's origins, even going so far as to diverge from Hume in
the question of the scripture writers' integrity (which Hume had doubted).
Further, Barrett Browning's alternative philosophies had rendered irrelevant
to her Strauss's arguments about the limits of historical inquiry. Neither the
Swedenborgian spirit-world nor Chateaubriand's heart-religion depends
upon historical evidence for truth. Truly successful religious movements, as
Wilde points out, will create their own standards for evidence.

The crowning irony of Barrett Browning's response to Strauss, then, is
that she bases her antipathy upon grounds that amounted to little in light of
their shared insight into the literary aspect of religious experience—at least
of most Christian religious experience. Here she attacks Strauss not for the
product of his researches but for their very impetus. Meanwhile, she ignores

the two hermeneutic revolutions that Strauss really does represent: first, the idea that apparent facts in Christian mythological records cannot reliably be distinguished from apparent fictions, and, second, that the gospel representation of Jesus as Christ must be understood in the *literary* context of Hebrew mythology. Both ideas ought to have appealed enormously to Barrett Browning, given their poetic implications. In some ways, she had already internalized the central epiphany of the higher criticism, that the "poetry" of biblical literature served as its own miracle. Strauss was a "heretic believer" much as Barrett Browning herself was, though their beliefs expressed themselves differently. Strauss's position is also close to that later expressed by Arnold in "The Study of Poetry" to the extent that it celebrates the power of the literary as a reality independent of dogmas attached to it. As Strauss and Barrett Browning and Arnold (in that order) agreed, poetry might be better appreciated for its own numinous reality, given the literary character of historical records—that is, the fact that our limited historical understanding relies upon our ability to make sense of historical genres. She thus becomes a secular writer in Charles Taylor's sense of the term, committed to one philosophical stance (in her case, a religious one) but continuously negotiating the claims of alternative stances.

"Mrs. Browning's Gospel"

Aurora Leigh herself conveys the urgency of the higher criticism in a strategic apology for her chef d'oeuvre embedded in the middle of her narrative. We might read the lines as an implied apology for *Aurora Leigh,* since Barrett Browning (once more) rightly counted upon Victorian reviewers to conflate Aurora's views with her own:

> Let us go.
> The end of woman (and of man, I think)
> Is not a book. Alas, the best of books
> Is but a word in Art, which soon grows cramped,
> Stiff, dubious-statured with the weight of years,
> And drops an accent or a digamma down
> Some cranny of unfathomable time,
> Beyond the critic's reaching.
> (7.882–89)

What appears here to be self-effacement is the most extravagant of boasting. "Art," these lines claim, requires constant renewal. Aurora purports to critique her own work ("I'll say with Romney that the book is weak" [7.880]), but her critique instead emphasizes the failure of any critics ever to fully appreciate her highest successes. Even "the best of books" cannot withstand the turn of history, as she instructs in a way that might indict "the Good Book" itself. This is where the hermeneutic context of the higher criticism applies, with its claims that much of biblical meaning has been forever lost—lost like the digamma of the Greek alphabet, which fell out of use in the second century BCE, but which retained a numerological significance in biblical Greek so as to provide the figures of Revelation's infamous "number of the beast" or "666" (Revelation 13:18). These lines of *Aurora Leigh,* indeed, may suggest that Barrett Browning appreciated the vast confusion surrounding this particular *crux interpretum:* what John of Patmos intended now seems lost in "some cranny of unfathomable time." Naturally, such a circumstance did little to quell nineteenth-century speculation upon the topic, but Aurora's point is that the text seems irresolvable. The disappearance of the digamma and its muddled conflation with the final stigma of "χξς" (numerologically, "666") is itself symbolic of the limits of criticism to access the meaning of art. Observe how thoroughly Aurora's notion of "time, / Beyond the critic's reaching" corresponds to Strauss's insistence that "men think they understand the Bible, because they have grown accustomed to misunderstand it."[55] We cannot entirely grasp the Bible because it exceeds our historical understanding. Similarly, Aurora's insistence that Art needed renewal corresponds to the emergence of evolutionary tendencies in Victorian hermeneutics recently traced by Suzy Anger.[56] "I should fear for a revealed religion incapable of expansion according to the needs of man," as Barrett would confess to Fanny Haworth. "What comes from God has life in it, and certainly from all the growth of living things, spiritual growth cannot be excepted."[57] Here, then, is the higher critical promise of the early poetry without any deliberate dogmatic correction.

It is helpful to recognize the distance between *Aurora Leigh* and *The Seraphim, and Other Poems,* or—and this is much the same thing—the distance between *Aurora Leigh* and the poetry of many of Barrett Browning's religiously conservative Romantic predecessors. British Romantic poets between the eras of Christopher Smart and Felicia Hemans regularly appeal to the scriptures in the manner of the early Barrett: that is, they invoke the

Bible as the superlative model for poetry in ways that minimize its foreign character and historical remoteness. Smart's *Jubilate Agno* (ca. 1758) exemplifies the earliest poetic influence of the higher criticism in lines such as "Let Iddo praise the Lord with the Moth—the writings of man perish as the garment, but the Book of God endureth for ever."[58] Writing under the influence of Lowth, Smart here imitates the language of the Authorized Version ("endureth"), but also sets up an antithesis between the evanescent "writings of man" and a fixed "Book of God."[59] Such an antithesis, a key part of early Romantic poetry, remains instrumental as late as Felicia Hemans's final works. Hemans's "The Sacred Harp" (1834) presents a sonnet worthy of Barrett's *Seraphim* volume that mourns the loss of biblical inspiration, "that old victorious tone of prophet-years," so as to promote the idea that God might yet inspire "rekindled chords" and "give the long buried tone back to immortal words!" (13–14). And yet whether Hemans means that the ancient scriptures will themselves be "rekindled" or whether new poets will rekindle their ancient tones does not signify: either way, the couplet insists upon the "immortal" nature of those words in a way that becomes incompatible with *Aurora Leigh*'s frank admission that biblical words are actually quite fragile, and capable of being lost "down / Some cranny of unfathomable time."

Among the intriguing parts of Romantic pronouncements upon the Bible's textual immortality, indeed, is how long they themselves endure. Poets as early as Smart clearly anticipate the complexities of biblical history and textuality that would develop as the higher criticism. The very line here referenced in *Jubilate Agno* names a lost Hebrew scripture, "the visions of Iddo," from a list of what appear to be other lost chronicles in 2 Chronicles 9:29: "Now the rest of the acts of Solomon, first and last, are they not written in the book of Nathan the prophet, and in the prophecy of Ahijah the Shilonite, and in the visions of Iddo the seer against Jeroboam the son of Nebat?" *Jubilate Agno* thus insists upon the Bible's unbroken unity ("the Book of God endureth for ever") by referencing a passage that seems flatly to contradict that idea. Smart's apologetic manner of reading the text had centuries of religious precedent, to be sure. But the higher criticism made increasingly plain the contrariness of such readings. For the higher critics, such moments as 2 Chronicles 9:29 plainly suggest the Bible's kinship with noncanonical scriptures and other contemporary literatures. Smart rejects this hermeneutic in advance; for him, Iddo's name persists as an instance of the perishable "writings of man" in an everlasting "Book of God" from which he has been otherwise excluded (to the evident surprise of the canonical author of Chronicles). By the heyday of the higher criticism in the Victorian mid-century, Smart's resolve would seem less satisfying. For Barrett Browning, as for Strauss, the lost Iddo represents a disappearing digamma. The distinction maintained by Smart between sacred and profane writings is thus dissolved in her later works, and Aurora Leigh offers her own long poem as that of a "prophet-poet" (5.355) not to insist that it must surely achieve that status, but to merely submit that it has a chance. That is, Barrett Browning implicitly concedes *Aurora Leigh* to be an evanescent scripture, but in the knowledge that so, too, were the visions of Iddo. So even, she implies, is the famous thirteenth chapter of Revelation, with its now inscrutable numerological elements. And its power to move and inspire us, for good or ill, clearly outlives our understanding of its design.

In this way, Barrett Browning's ostensible departures from a higher critical perspective of the poetry of the Bible culminate in what looks like a rapprochement. Swedenborg and Chateaubriand, her intellectual heroes, become in her poetry the intellectual siblings of Strauss, and the ideas of Strauss become inspired with a new evangelical enthusiasm. Nothing is more redolent of the mid-century impact of the higher criticism upon poetry than Barrett Browning's full declaration about the "spiritual truth" of *Aurora Leigh* as she first enjoyed its enthusiastic public reception:

> The extravagant things said about that poem, would make you smile (as they make me) -and there's one sort of compliment which would please you particularly—people are fond of calling it "a gospel." That's happy- is'nt it? You suppose perhaps that one unlucky individual calls it so? Not in the least: it's the favorite phrase, in letters from England—in gossip at Florence—And even from America the other day, the publisher writes—"we have received Mrs Browning's *gospel.*" . . . Is it entirely prophane, or simply ridiculous? I leave you to choose. Still, that there *is* an amount of spiritual truth in the book to which the public is unaccustomed, I know very well.[60]

This extraordinary text, written to her sister Arabella, may present Barrett Browning's final resolution of the theological paradox presented by the ancient library at Alexandria, for in *Aurora Leigh* she has found a way not only to reconcile worldly wisdom to her religious creed but also to transform its materials into a new sacred text.[61] Naturally, to credit one's own work with the status of a gospel creates a situation of unusual social awkwardness: Barrett Browning specifies that she records the honor only to gratify her sister, and she duly inquires whether the accolade is "prophane, or simply ridiculous." The sacred poet captured in the Pickersgill portrait, one imagines, might have been unencumbered by such modesty. And yet this mature Barrett Browning remains true to her younger self, in the end, by insisting that her book does have its spiritual truth to bestow upon the public.

It is the way that Barrett Browning's evangelicalism lent itself to the higher criticism that permitted her to play muse to poets such as her husband, Robert Browning, and her admirer George Eliot. As we will see, her own distaste for the higher criticism never diminished her usefulness to them for exploiting its literary consequences. As both recognized, *Aurora Leigh* cuts to the heart of the higher critical debate even in poetry that purports to subvert it. "I shun religious controversy," wrote Barrett Browning in the letter to Fanny Haworth cited above; "it is useless" (421). But both halves of this claim are charmingly disingenuous. Barrett Browning shunned religious controversy in the way that she shunned Continental politics, the American slavery debate, and the Woman Question. The best way to win an argument, after all, is to change the ground of the debate entirely. And it is very easy to argue *sola scriptura* as the author of Mrs. Browning's gospel.

Chapter 2

TENNYSON'S PRECIOUS METHOD
OF INTERPRETATION

I T CAN BE HARD in the twenty-first century to regard *The Idylls of the King* (1859–85) as Alfred Tennyson's supreme poetic achievement. At the middle of the nineteenth century, it was quite easy to do so. When the first edition of *The Idylls* appeared, it was trumpeted by many periodicals as the finest work yet from the era's finest English-language poet.[1] Such praise now seems excessive, but by the late 1850s, Tennyson's generation viewed him as Britain's national bard and looked to him to provide a fitting poetical foundation for its grand industrial and imperial ambitions. As the *Quarterly Review* optimistically put it on *The Idylls*'s first appearance:

> Mr. Tennyson is too intimately and essentially the poet of the nineteenth century to separate himself from its leading characteristics, the progress of physical science and a vast commercial, mechanical, and industrial development. . . . We fondly believe it is his business to do much towards the solution of that problem, so fearful from its magnitude, how to harmonise this new draught of external power and activity with the old and more mellow wine of faith, self-devotion, loyalty, reverence, and discipline.[2]

The stakes of Tennyson's Arthurian poetry, we see, were supremely high for Victorian reviewers like this one, and this one happened to be W. E. Gladstone, chancellor of the exchequer and future prime minister. Even in light of Gladstone's well-known belletristic and scholarly interests, it seems remarkable that any chancellor of the exchequer would single out one "poet of the nineteenth century" for the job of unifying modern culture.[3] Such naiveté almost deserves his enological metaphor, a curious muddling of the gospel injunction to keep new wine away from old wineskins. Yet many readers shared Gladstone's excitement and his heady praise for Arthurian legend as an especially choice subject for this laureate: explicitly "Christian," "national," and (these prior adjectives notwithstanding) "universal" (468). Exhortations like this one were a peculiar feature of Tennyson's extraordinary career.[4]

Only toward the end of that career would it occur to most of Tennyson's mid-century admirers that such demands were exorbitant, or at least that Tennyson could never have fulfilled them entirely. But Tennyson shared his society's expectations about the vital role of poetry in modern culture. If the above quotation risks making Gladstone sound like a latter-day Eurystheus, asking Herculean tasks from his hapless laureate, it helps to remember that Gladstone's convictions about modern poetry derive largely from contemporary poets, who had regularly volunteered to sing the sacredness of British culture much as he recommends.[5] Tennyson's poetry, too, recurs to the Romantic idea of the poet's unacknowledged cultural centrality, from his juvenilia (such as "Timbuctoo" [1829]), to his lyrics ("The Poet's Mind" [1830]), longer narratives (*The Princess* [1847]), and compilations (*In Memoriam* [1850]). By 1859 he could take for granted the application of this general theme to his *Idylls*. And by 1885 the four original poems hailed by the *Quarterly* had grown into a full-blown national epic in a twelve-book format.

This chapter addresses some of the religious implications of Tennyson's Arthurian epic in light of Victorian religious controversy, and considers the extent to which it tried to reconcile Victorian modernity with the "mellow wine of faith, self-devotion, loyalty," and so on. In the twentieth and twenty-first centuries, *The Idylls* has not always been viewed as central in this respect, and yet it presents Tennyson's most arduous intervention into the Victorians' changing understanding of scripture. In particular, it aims at a more profound and comprehensive engagement with the Bible than is to be found in the better-known religious vacillations of *In Memoriam*. *The Idylls* presents a deliberately public expression, rather than an ostensibly personal one: an appeal to religious affect that nonetheless remains impersonally grounded in culture.[6] And though we can trace this impulse back to some of Tennyson's earliest lyrics on biblical topics, still I begin and end this chapter with *The Idylls* because it engages with Victorian religious and hermeneutic controversies in so central and salient a way.

Tennyson's literary remains do not testify clearly to the timing of his acquaintance with the higher criticism, with its arguments about the Bible's mythical nature, compositional heterogeneity, reliance upon diverse manuscript evidence, and overall human character.[7] He never wrote an "Epi-

Strauss-ism" or "Gold Hair." Nonetheless, his poetry affords a significant amount of internal evidence about changing Victorian biblical hermeneutics, and the very manner in which *The Idylls*'s reviewers praised his verse for beating "in harmony with the nation's life" (as the *British Quarterly* put it [481]) might have obliged him to consider the evolution of Christianity if he were not already inclined to do so. Believing in the virtues of a shared national religion, yet seeming also to concede the radical arguments of the higher critics, Tennyson frames Arthurian legend in *The Idylls* in such a way as to construct for the Bible a local, parallel instance of poetic inspiration — one that, like the manuscript of Sir Ralph described in *The Princess,* openly reflects its ambiguous status as "half-legend, half-historic" (30). For today's readers, the religious implications of this gesture tend to be hidden in plain sight. But whereas texts like D. F. Strauss's *Life of Jesus* drew jeers from the conservative Victorian presses for advocating a skeptical Christianity that surrendered historical claims to the events recorded in the scriptures, Tennyson's widely celebrated *Idylls* likewise confesses in advance to the mythological character of his epic — and still asks readers to embrace it as a key part of the national history.

"The Holy Grail" (1869) shows this strategy quite plainly. In Tennyson's retelling, this now-familiar legend interrogates a critical gap between modern skepticism of the sort presented by his own earlier poetry (on the one hand) and medieval devotion of the sort presented by the cult of Joseph of Arimathea, the traditional guardian of the cup used by Christ at the Last Supper (on the other hand). As Victorian believers knew, Joseph of Arimathea appears briefly in all four Gospels in connection to Christ's death, burial, and resurrection (by all accounts furnishing the tomb in which those final two events take place). However, as Victorian medievalists knew, Joseph's greatest interest to the English Church derived instead from apocryphal and pseudepigraphical sources like the Gospel of Nicodemus, auxiliary texts that add to the gospel narrative how Joseph left Palestine shortly after the Resurrection and moved (as Providence would have it) to Glastonbury. Joseph's stature in medieval history owes to his status as Christianity's first missionary to Britain, and this circumstance alone secures his place in Tennyson's national epic. (Many such medieval histories exist, to be sure: Provençal tradition has the biblical sisters Mary and Martha settling down in the Côte d'Azur, and so forth.)

Linda K. Hughes justly describes "The Holy Grail" as among the most successful dramatic monologues of Tennyson's later career: this form permits him to deliver through Sir Percivale the faithful history of the miraculous cup that "the good saint / Arimathaean Joseph, journeying brought to Glastonbury."[8] The device serves so nicely because neither Tennyson nor most of his presumed audience could take this story at face value: as Tennyson put it in an 1859 letter, "The old writers *believed* in the Sangraal."[9] High Church Anglicans could assent to the plausibility of such legends, as in John Henry Newman's Oxford accounts of ecclesiastical miracles. But most Victorian Protestants balked at these apocryphal and pseudepigraphical texts for their Papist affinities (a suspicion Newman's conversion would seem to corroborate) or—still worse—for higher critical suggestions of a kinship between canonized scripture and its various noncanonical antecedents, accretions, and embellishments. Earlier generations of Protestants had declined to make this distinction so sharply even in periods when anti-Catholicism ran high— Elizabeth I, for instance, held that the Glastonbury legend proved the autonomy of the English Church by demonstrating the existence of Christianity on the British Isles before the arrival of Roman missionaries. Tennyson's treatment of the grail legend, by turn, implicitly asks readers to reconsider and even to cherish such local religious tradition. It openly concedes the doubtful foundations of old national mythologies. But it also presumes upon their value to the extent that it proffers itself as an extension of the "Christian," "national," and "universal" tale so much acclaimed in the first *Idylls*.[10]

It is now generally agreed that the political and religious aspects of Tennyson's poetry struck contemporary readers so forcefully in part because of how they reenact a struggle between radical and conservative ways seeing the world, often taking the most radical paths to the most reactionary positions.[11] Eve Kosofsky Sedgwick has famously described the regularity with which Tennyson's poetry can make familiar, respectable bourgeois ideology seem "frothing-at-the-mouth mad."[12] But *The Idylls* has had a diminished place in Tennyson scholarship of the twentieth and twenty-first centuries in part because it so often does the opposite of this: it takes the profoundly alien, potentially alienating religious critique of the higher criticism—including the exacting compromise that Strauss's *Life of Jesus* prescribes to the modern religious believer—and reshapes it into a respectable Victorian idea. Surely it is to Tennyson's credit, then, that so many recent critics have overlooked or shrugged off the poem's audacious adoption—and seeming endorsement— of higher critical hermeneutics. To invert the old formula, Tennyson here takes a conservative path to the most radical religious positions.

For this reason, *The Idylls* may present Tennyson's most significant intervention into the Victorian cultures of religion and secularization, as well as his most deliberate and public one. By 1856 Tennyson had begun to unfold it as the major poetic work of his career, and the following analysis of Tennyson will focus upon its origins. After rehearsing key elements of the mid-Victorian religious landscape vis-à-vis "Gareth and Lynette" (1872), then, I address the ways that higher critical hermeneutics inform "Merlin and Vivien," a poem written between February and March of 1856 and first published as "Nimuë" (1857) and "Vivien" (1859). "Merlin and Vivien" was the least popular book of *The Idylls* in Tennyson's lifetime, singled out by critics from the first as alternately immoral and infelicitous. But Tennyson retained this much-criticized poem with little alteration in every subsequent edition of *The Idylls*, as a sort of grain of sand around which the pearl of his Arthurian project could be formed.[13] With brief excursuses into "The Epic" (1842) and "Timbuctoo" (1829), then, I show how "Merlin and Vivien" puts on display the higher critical ideas about myth at the heart of Tennyson's national epic. And from this, I suggest, we can see how the whole poem seeks to grapple with the crux of the higher criticism.

Tennyson's "Solid Foundation of Facts"

Before turning to "Gareth and Lynette," it will be helpful to address the fraught attitude toward Arthurian legend evidenced in the poem more generally. The faux-chivalric themes that make it an easy target for the critic of bourgeois ideology—truth, honor, loyalty, purity, and Victorian manliness more generally—are earnestly rendered but never merely uplifting in *The Idylls*. As Tennyson's reviewers quickly recognized, his ersatz medieval world owes much to the most advanced medieval Victorian scholarship, and given this real scholarly engagement, it should hardly surprise us that the jarring alterity of the medieval worldview so frequently upends the bourgeois nineteenth-century complacency that Tennyson to a certain extent indulged. Indeed, given *The Idylls*'s thematic ties to sacred history, what should surprise us is that this performance of complacency still overshadows for many readers its jarring interruption throughout the poem. "Nimuë" first appeared with "Enid" in a privately circulated volume called *The True and the False* (1857). But this central theme of truth and falsehood served Tennyson so well in his growing *Idylls* because medieval legend brings home the problems inherent to any premodern history, including the frequent impossibility of retrospectively distinguishing the true from the false at all.

Tellingly, Tennyson was able to dramatize the *False* of that title before he ever got around to *The True*.

This was a scholarly issue, then as now. Tennyson seems to have appreciated very early that the crisis of the higher criticism was a crisis of history *tout court*. At all events, his poetry suggests that the lessons of the higher criticism might be extended to secular history, and the legendary perspective of his *Idylls* has everything in common with the mythical perspective on scripture so forcefully proposed by the higher critics. Arthurian legend presented an ideal subject for an experiment in mythological truth for the very reasons Gladstone gives in his review: its religious and national qualities served to reinforce one another to such an extent that Tennyson could count upon either the nationalism or the religious commitment of his readers to shore up the other. That is, in the hothouse religious atmosphere of mid-century and in the midst of the Victorian Gothic Revival, Tennyson could to some extent count upon a reader's investment in religious ideas to inform his expression of nationalistic ones, and vice versa.

As might be expected, biblically conservative Victorians tended to resist such a framework for thinking about Christian mythology, insisting instead upon the uniqueness of biblical history and scorning the higher criticism as an irresponsible and implicitly atheist scholarly position. Among the most fiercely partisan, the higher criticism was attacked as a foreign threat to British common sense, and this in turn helps make sense of Tennyson's own sustained emphasis on national legend. In 1860 the Oxford dean (and future bishop) John William Burgon of Oriel College, later renowned for defending the King James translation against its updating in the New Revised Version, warned threateningly of the higher criticism that its "precious method of Interpretation" might well be applied to the records of Britain as easily as to those of ancient Palestine. Burgon's writings serve here (and throughout) as a useful foil for Tennyson's, so it is worth recording how in the midst of the scandal surrounding *Essays and Reviews*, he would preach the following to his congregation at St. Mary-the-Virgin Church: "Only let them be sure that they apply this precious method of Interpretation to the History of England, and to everything their friend tells them: and let them not feel surprised if the same kind of ideological handling is bestowed upon everything they tell their friend. Idealize away, and be sure you stick at nothing! *Why* be outdone in logical consistency by such a one as Strauss?" (244, emphasis Burgon's). In Burgon's sermon, we see, Strauss handily serves as the nemesis of true religious interpretation although none of the *Essays and Reviews* essayists mentions him besides H. B. Wilson, who does so negatively as "an example of the critical ideology carried to excess . . . which resolves into an ideal the whole of the historical and doctrinal person of Jesus" (306).[14] Nonetheless, to Burgon's eyes, *Essays and Reviews* presented the apostasy of his fellow countrymen as well as his fellow clergymen, and his rhetoric relies upon the foreignness of this religious threat. Fourteen years had passed since the initial hubbub surrounding George Eliot's translation, but Strauss's name could still serve as a synecdoche for "the German poison" being imported from across the North Sea. By Burgon's logic, to "stick at nothing" was to jeopardize the bedrock of English national culture.

Among conservative Victorians, Strauss's name often invited the kind of reductio ad absurdum that Burgon's argument represents, and this reduction was often tied to national histories in particular. Even before Strauss's translation into English, the Anglo-American religious presses had learned to parody his historiographical method. Twenty years previously, for instance, in a review for the *Christian Examiner,* the American Transcendentalist Theodore Parker offered an extensive comic analogy between the Gospel narratives and the founding of the United States of America, which he declared to be a mythical country:

> The story of the Declaration of Independence is liable to many objections, if we examine it *à la mode* Strauss. The Congress was held at a mythical town, whose very name is suspicious,—Philadelphia—Brotherly Love. The date is suspicious; it was the *fourth* day of the *fourth* month, (reckoning from April, as it is probable that the Heraclidae, and Scandinavians; possible that the aboriginal Americans, and certain that the Hebrews, did). Now *four* was a sacred number with Americans; the president was chosen for *four* years; there were *four* departments of affairs; *four* divisions of the political powers, namely, the people, the congress, the executive, and the judiciary, &c. . . . The *year* is also suspicious; 1776 is but an ingenious combination of the sacred number, *four,* which is repeated *three times,* and then multiplied by itself to produce the date; thus, 444 x 4 = 1776, Q.E.D.[15]

The above is only a small excerpt from Parker's pastiche, which itself forms only a small portion of his review. Even so, the passage makes apparent how such pastiches might lend themselves to recirculation, being easily excerpted and recopied in other publications. (The above passage, for instance, would subsequently be reprinted in the *Congregational Magazine* without Parker's largely sympathetic review of Strauss.) Like any good parodies, they contained a measure of truth. Parker could hardly have been further religiously from Burgon: the one an American Unitarian, the other a conservative Oxford churchman. However, he agrees with Burgon (and, for that matter, with Wilson) that Strauss's genius was "negative, destructive, and unsatisfactory" (314), and he agrees that this is partly because Strauss's method might render half of recorded history suspect if applied with sufficient rigor. "Mr. Strauss, for the sake of consistency, ought to deny that John the Baptist was an historical person," writes Parker, "and doubtless he would have done so, were it not for an unfortunate passage in Josephus, which mentions that prophet" (284). In reality, Strauss's *Life* never disputes that Jesus himself existed, but Bruno Bauer (another of the Young Hegelians) soon outstripped Strauss by arguing against Jesus's having had any historical existence at all.

Characteristically for him, Tennyson's subversively conservative treatment of the national religion pursues a tack antithetical to most conservative mid-century responses to the higher criticism. Tennyson's response, as we will see, offers itself as an alternative to both Burgon's and Parker's. Whereas Burgon implies that true patriotism ought to inoculate citizens from the poison of the higher criticism, Tennyson's poem implicitly endorses the higher critical position by applying it to the history of England in the analogous instance of the Arthurian legends. Whereas Parker facetiously protests that "the whole history of the settlement of New England, for example, we might call a tissue of mythical stories" (311), Tennyson looks far enough back into his national history to find a real tissue of mythical stories. "The shadowy exploits of the British King," as one of Tennyson's earliest reviewers puts it, "are so wholly without any *historical* confirmation, that many antiquarians have been led to doubt whether the traditions which relate to him have any solid foundation of facts to rest on at all" (*Blackwood's*, 608). In this way, more than any other of Tennyson's works, *The Idylls* demonstrates the poet's attempt to wrestle with the implications of contemporary historical biblical criticism by using the national heritage to encourage sympathy for a parallel view of Christianity.

Tennyson's "Wholly Proven King"

Part of the reason a twenty-first-century reader can be hard-pressed to comprehend the scholarly stakes of *The Idylls* is that Tennyson relies so heavily upon mid-Victorian religious controversy to create the poem's drama.

Consider *The Idylls*'s insistent coupling of the figures of the mythical King Arthur and the mythical Christ. It undergirds the whole poem as it does the following exchange from "Gareth and Lynette" (1872), a sunny work written to convey the hopefulness of Arthur's kingdom in its early days. Sequentially positioned as *The Idylls*'s second poem, "Gareth and Lynette" was written in 1869, a dozen years after the first appearance of Gladstone's encomium. In this idyll, Arthur's nephew Gareth resolves to give up his childhood recreations of hunting and gallivanting so as to seek knighthood (and adulthood) in Arthur's court. His mother, Bellicent, agrees to this proposal, but she objects to Gareth's early departure and proposes various arguments for his delay. And Gareth in turn rebukes these arguments as a compromise of his religious and national duties:

> Man am I grown, a man's work must I do.
> Follow the deer? follow the Christ, the King,
> Live pure, speak true, right wrong, follow the King—
> Else, wherefore born?
> (115–18)

The above lines are quite celebrated, historically: the last few merit an entry in *The Oxford Dictionary of Quotations* and are now engraved on the church wall at Somersby for the edification of literary pilgrims to Tennyson's birthplace.[16] In "Gareth and Lynette," however, they do not serve as anything like the matter's final word. Bellicent openly questions the soundness of her son's earnest devotion, and she alerts Gareth to the possible illegitimacy of Arthur's court and kingdom.

Here, and not earlier, is the crescendo to which their argument rises in this early idyll: rumors to the effect that Arthur was not yet proven king, and that perhaps he would never be proven so.

> "Sweet son, for there be many who deem him not,
> Or will not deem him, wholly proven King—
> Albeit in mine own heart I knew him King,
> When I was frequent with him in my youth,
> And heard him Kingly speak, and doubted him
> No more than he, himself; but felt him mine,
> Of closest kin to me: yet—wilt thou leave
> Thine easeful biding here, and risk thine all,

> Life, limbs, for one that is not proven King?
> Stay, till the cloud that settles round his birth
> Hath lifted but a little. Stay, sweet son."
> (119–28)

It is important to note that Bellicent's concerns about legitimacy, a central motif in "Gareth and Lynette," have no precedent in Malory, whose seventh book of *The Morte d'Arthur* (1485) provides the basis for Tennyson's story and who accepts Arthur's legacy with a winning medieval naiveté. By contrast, the skeptical Victorian Tennyson makes authenticity and devotion the prevailing crises of his kingdom even in cases where devotion like Bellicent's is explicitly heartfelt: "Albeit in mine own heart I knew him King." This minor conflict from the lighthearted "Gareth and Lynette" anticipates and serves as a synecdoche for the final crisis of *The Idylls*.

Ultimately, then, the dramatic force of this exchange between Gareth and Bellicent lies more clearly in Victorian religious analogies to her doubts about Arthur than in any career decisions of her son. During the tumultuous religious controversies of the mid-century, the "cloud" that she describes around the circumstances of Arthur's birth bears a distinct resemblance to the similarly opaque cloud surrounding other high-profile historical figures, including Sappho, Homer, Shakespeare, and Jesus "the Christ" of line 116.[17] Bellicent's lines themselves convey something of this uneasiness: graceful yet ambivalent, euphonic yet syntactically tortuous, fueled by Tennyson's distinctive incantatory repetition yet full of equivocation. The long "e" sounds of "Sweet," "be," "many," and "deem" in lines 119 and 120 ("Sweet son, for there be many who deem him not") anticipate the front vowel of "King" so that it rings out more clearly when repeated in lines 121, 123, and 127. Yet this is no ringing endorsement of Arthur's kingship.

Victorian Protestants who insisted upon the sole authority of Chillingworth's "BIBLE [and] the BIBLE only" had particular reason to frown upon such potential analogies. Throughout Tennyson's long poem, nonetheless, Arthur both invites an analogy to Christ and reminds readers that the medieval view (at least the Victorian view of the medieval view) made this analogy an article of faith. Here, for instance, the ending of Gareth's line 116 must at first reading be taken for a possible reference to Christ's divine capacity as King of Kings, Lord of Lords, and so on, reinforcing the parallel between King Arthur and "the Christ, the King." At line 116, the ancillary designator "King" seems to be applied to Christ, whereas by line 117 it seems better suited to Arthur, and any retrenchment and transfer of the term's designation from one figure to the other creates a delicate effect of preterition by which the reader must learn to distinguish Arthur from Christ and to understand when Gareth means one or the other. We do not need the Somersby Church wall inscriptions to appreciate how readily these two figures can be conflated, how the poem on some level solicits their conflation.

Historians rightly point to Strauss's *Life of Jesus* as an epoch-marking event in nineteenth-century higher critical considerations of Jesus, the work that did most to make Christ, like Arthur, the sort of king about whom questions loom larger than certainties; we have seen how in Burgon's writings this certainly holds true. But the gradual composition of *The Idylls* show us how Tennyson responds to the higher criticism less as an event than as a pattern in which the same discoveries about the elusiveness of sacred history are continually remade, to the consternation or thrill of each more or less belated discoverer.[18] Ernest Renan's derivative life of Christ, *La Vie de Jésus* (1863, trans. 1863), once more, generated still more widespread discussion in Britain than Strauss, especially because it appeared in the immediate wake of the religious controversies engendered by *The Origin of Species* (1859), *Essays and Reviews* (1860), and Colenso's studies of the Pentateuch. J. R. Seeley's *Ecce Homo* (1865), also lionized by Gladstone, is more immediately a response to Renan than to Strauss, as is Matthew Arnold's *Literature and Dogma* (1873). And so is Arthur's depiction in "Gareth and Lynette," although Tennyson understood the belatedness of Renan's study and the fact that the religious questions raised by Renan had been anticipated by Strauss, who had (as Tennyson remarked to Jowett) been anticipated by Niebuhr. Tennyson's poetry presents less obviously a response to new events in religious hermeneutics, in sum, than an attempt to break out of a recurring cycle in which various embodiments of a long-standing hermeneutic shift were presented as new events. *The Idylls*'s distinct and repeated conflation of Arthur and Christ presents an interruption (and, Tennyson may have hoped, a sort of fulfillment) of an ongoing hermeneutic revolution. Obviously, Bellicent's preoccupation with authenticity seems apt to trouble the Victorian believer when applied to Jesus: "Wilt thou leave / Thine easeful biding here, and risk thine all, / Life, limbs, for one that is not proven King?" But, similarly, Gareth's unbroken faith in Arthur comes to depend upon something like Schleiermacher's distinction between the Christ of faith and the Jesus of history: Arthur's legitimacy comes to depend upon the practical benefits accrued by believers: "Who should be King," asks Gareth, "save him who makes us free?" (136).

There can be no doubt that Tennyson raises this comparison deliberately. Bellicent's interrogation of Gareth invokes a threatening skepticism widely dispersed in Victorian religious culture but without parallel in Malory's. Malory's contemporaries disputed the real historicity of Arthur, to be sure, just as Bauer would come to dispute the real historicity of Jesus. In the fifteenth century, William Caxton published Malory's *Morte Darthur* expressly to rebuff skeptics who claimed "that there was never suche a kyng callyd Arthur."[19] But Caxton's loyalty to Arthur runs parallel to the religious culture of the nineteenth century, and it has nothing to do with Bellicent's ostensible concerns in "Gareth and Lynette" about Arthur's parentage. In this way, Tennyson's poem pursues an audacious analogy for the mid-Victorian Christian, equating Arthur and Christ as though to invoke the threat that "there was never suche a kyng callyd" *Jesus*—or, rather, that our limited accounts of him provide an insufficient basis for continued belief and devotion. In Tennyson's *Idylls,* these doubts exercise a double and divided influence; they both invite suspicion and suggest its perils. And their narrative trajectory is eschatological: they culminate in the political crisis that will ruin Arthur's kingdom.

For Tennyson, as for many Victorians, nineteenth-century higher critical speculations about Jesus seemed to risk having radical (and, in his view, negative) political ramifications. *The Idylls* also seems to pursue this problem through the analogy of Christ and Arthur. In "The Last Tournament," for instance, Sir Tristram explains that it was only through their quasi-religious devotion to Arthur that his knights secured the kingdom—through such devotion that each knight "Did mightier deeds than elsewise he had done, / And so the realm was made" (675–76). Yet like all civic religions, Tennyson's Arthurian Christianity depends upon the faith of its adherents. When these eventually lose faith in Arthur, the realm loses its stability. As Tristram tells it, "They faild to trace him thro' the flesh and blood / Of our old kings" and came to see him as "a doubtful lord / To bind them by inviolable vows, / Which flesh and blood perforce would violate" (681–84). Such lines can be applied with equal justice to Tennyson's Arthur and to the Jesus of Victorian Christianity, whose austere religious demands seemed for many believers to be suddenly compromised by his "doubtful" status. Here and throughout, *The Idylls* implies that the civic consequences of Victorian doubts about Christ are the modern equivalent of Bellicent's doubts about Arthur. Faith in Arthur brought about political stability, and doubt brings about its collapse. The quid pro quo of this form of religious patriotism is that Tennyson's Arthur cannot ever be the flesh-and-blood king that so many Victorian reviewers also desired.

Later additions to *The Idylls* fortify the analogy between Arthur and Christ, in essence to suggest that the political strength that Christianity had given to the British nation was equally imperiled in the nineteenth century. In 1873 Tennyson added a jingoistic epilogue, "To the Queen," to make his political point more clear. In this lyric, the threatening fragmentation of the British Empire (and, in particular, a proposed partitioning of Canada) mirrors this Arthurian dissolution, because—it is implied—contemporary critics of the imperial government were bereft of the sort of faith that Tennyson champions in *The Idylls*: "Is this the tone of empire?" the lyric pointedly asks, "here the faith / That made us rulers?" (18–19). This epilogue goes so far as to warn us explicitly against the civic dangers posed by "fierce or careless looseners of the faith" that presumably binds the nation together (52). However, while for many conservative Victorians the higher criticism contributed to this "loosen[ing] of the faith," yet Tennyson's poetry also suggests that, on the contrary, a higher critical understanding of scripture ought to be incorporated into modern belief. For Tennyson, the national faith required saving from Strauss's British critics as much as it did from Strauss.

Vivien's "Want of Faith in All"

The disparate nature of medieval Arthurian legends, frequently viewed as an obstacle to the success of Tennyson's final project, may actually provide the best explanation for his attempt. Chief among the formal issues of Tennyson's project is the way that it parallels the fragmentation and dispersal of biblical sources as they were being discussed by Victorian scholars. Tennyson's audience wanted a satisfyingly coherent national epic, whereas his medieval sources present incompatible and conflicting accounts of Arthur and his court that range dramatically in tone and subject matter, from Layamon's *Brut* to the Welsh *Mabinogion*, from Geoffrey of Monmouth's histories to French Cistercian allegories. (And, once more, to Malory.) And while Tennyson attempted to honor the conflicting designs of both his modern readership and his ancient sources, his poem brokers a radical form of compromise: only through the fragmented, halting, broken narrative technique of this poem does Tennyson attempt to depict his nation's religious and cultural history. A minority of Victorian critics took this narrative technique for mere incompetence, as would T. S. Eliot, rather famously, in the 1930s, but Tennyson's painstaking and scrupulous process makes his design seem deliberate.[20] Even after decades of his critics' pleas for a unified epic, Tennyson remained loyal to the idea of a disparate one.

According to Benjamin Jowett, one of the foremost Victorian populizers of the higher criticism and a longtime friend of Tennyson's, *The Idylls* entailed this rigorous higher critical element even in its earliest stages. By Jowett's report, *The Idylls* was always more or less about the historical development of religion, which Jowett understood to be treated in a higher critical manner:

> It is a proof of Tennyson's genius that he should have thus early grasped the great historical aspect of religion.
>
> It may further be doubted whether the work could have been executed, or would have been understood, sixty years ago, at a time when men's minds were so little acquainted with Oriental speculations and were so hide-bound in the controversies of Protestantism and Romanism.[21]

In this context, "Oriental speculations" means comparative mythology, the historical and philological eighteenth- and nineteenth-century scholarship that treated the ancient literatures of mostly non-European peoples. And while such a broad category cannot be reduced to the higher criticism alone, yet there can be little doubt that Jowett had it chiefly in mind. He was a biblical scholar himself, the most prominent of the *Essays and Reviews* essayists, and his reference here to the post-Reformation controversies of "Protestantism and Romanism" confirms a specifically biblical orientation.[22] Before Eichhorn, even German theologians had been reluctant to view the Bible as an "Oriental" work, since Europeans were slow to acknowledge the foreignness of their own sacred text.[23] And, generally, British scholars did remain much less well "acquainted with Oriental speculations," partly because the foremost Orientalists were continental Europeans and regarded with corresponding levels of suspicion. Finally, Jowett rightly notes that British scholars were especially reluctant to leave behind the time-honored ("hide-bound") habits of leveling Protestant and Catholic hermeneutics against one another at a period when interreligious antipathies still ran high.

How Jowett himself conceived of the higher criticism as an antidote to conventional thinking about religion may be gathered from his contribution to *Essays and Reviews,* "On the Interpretation of Scripture" (1860), an essay that he apparently completed while staying at Farringford, Tennyson's residence on the Isle of Wight. In this essay, once more, Jowett characterizes these nineteenth-century biblical "controversies of Protestantism and Romanism" as a hopeless muddle of ideologically driven scholarship and reflexive traditionalism. The higher critic must endeavor to stand free of such dogmatizing, he instructs, and return to the text as it was conceived in its original cultures. Crucial to this endeavor is the Bible reader's ability to suspend any false expectation of narrative or thematic coherence: "The simple words of that book he tries to preserve absolutely pure from the refinements and distinctions of later times. He acknowledges that they are fragmentary, and would suspect himself, if out of fragments he were able to create a well-rounded system, or a continuous history."[24] This controversial stance might be said to present the gist of the higher criticism for Tennyson as well as for Jowett: the textual condition of the Bible itself ought to force our recognition that it cannot be reduced to "a well-rounded system, or a continuous history," because it presents only fragments of a collection of sacred literature from widely different historical periods and circumstances. Indeed, "the refinements and distinctions of later times," properly understood, amount to additional fragments, albeit interpolative ones.

It is supremely unlikely that Jowett could have missed the resemblance of the Arthurian legends to the scriptures. On the contrary, given his scholarly orientation and his closeness to Tennyson, Jowett's observation that *The Idylls* expresses "the historical aspect of religion" might be seen to illuminate that poem's refusal to provide "a well-rounded system, or a continuous history." The very patchwork fabric of the poem reflects an emerging view of the scriptures and a modern concept of history. Again, this is a crucial idea for understanding Tennyson's completed *Idylls*, a deliberately and uncompromisingly fragmented poem. By *The Idylls*'s practical inception in February of 1856, Tennyson had already begun to theorize and even aestheticize textual fragmentation of the sort discussed by Jowett as "the great historical aspect of religion."

"Merlin and Vivien" (then "Nimuë") tells how the enchantress of the title betrays and magically imprisons her mentor, Merlin, with a magical charm that he teaches her. Tennyson's retelling of this story puts to service his renowned gift for lyric and parades literary art as an aspect of the seduction narrative itself. Whereas works like *The Princess* mostly use lyric interludes to break up and vary the course of the narrative, here they lead to its crisis. Vivien chides her lover for his apparent mistrust by singing for him "the tender rhyme / Of 'trust me not at all or all in all'" (381–82):

"In Love, if Love be Love, if Love be ours,
Faith and unfaith can ne'er be equal powers:
Unfaith in aught is want of faith in all.

"It is the little rift within the lute,
That by and by will make the music mute,
And ever widening slowly silence all.

"The little rift within the lover's lute
Or little speck in garner'd fruit,
That rotting inward slowly moulders all.

"It is not worth the keeping: let it go:
But shall it? answer, darling, answer, no.
And trust me not at all or all in all."
(385–96)

The lyric achieves its dreamy faux-medieval air by favoring what Victorian reviewers called "fine old English" words over Latinate synonyms and by a heavy use of alliteration like "little . . . lover's lute."[25] But the faithfulness, of course, remains approximate, and this poem's conspicuous artifice remains charged with irony in its relationship to the literary past. The medieval practice of using alliteration to bridge the caesura, for instance, can hardly be taken for earnest in a melancholy modern lyric alleging that broken halves can never be mended by artifice. "Not" here always contradicts "aught" even where it echoes its sound.

This "tender rhyme" of Vivien, moreover, becomes integral to the higher critical project of the larger poem because of how it performs the contextual problems that the larger poem illustrates: it takes up an ideal of coherence that Jowett dismisses as impossible in a biblical context—and that Burgon insists upon as fundamental. The conundrum of Vivien's song—its paradoxical demand for utter faithfulness—nicely mirrors the conundrum of her listener, Merlin, who wants to believe in her faithfulness but sees (or, rather, hears) that it cannot be absolute. But it also mirrors the conundrum of the religious believer who claims (or even desires) an infallible text or system. The Broad Church theologian A. P. Stanley would come to draw this connection explicitly in his arguments against High Church and Catholic theologies: "It has constantly been argued that we must believe all or nothing. . . . It is the same argument which is used by the false enchantress in the 'Idylls of the King.'"[26] And (as Stanley would recognize) the argument applies equally well to *sola scriptura* interpretation.

Form always informs theme in Tennyson, but this lyric may provide an exceptional case even for him. Consider the masterful line "Unfaith in aught is want of faith in all." Here is a neat parallelism by which the alliterated "t" of "aught" and "want" is embedded within the echo of "unfaith"/"faith." But the chiasmic gap between the two faiths also embodies a tension between the sound and the sense of the whole line, where the vowel sound of "aught" may be only imperfectly mirrored by the vowel sound of "want."[27] Semantically, the line demands a faithful rendering, but the latter sound may or may not be faithful to the former; in the nineteenth century, as now, this pronunciation would vary with the geography of Tennyson's vast readership.[28] Whether the lyric's echoes are true depends upon whether one is from Yorkshire or Kent, from Ireland, New Zealand, or North America. Indeed, the poem makes its reader embody the problem of finding faithfulness in "aught" as a geographical and historical problem. This literally brings home its appeal: "But shall it? answer, darling, answer, no. / And trust me not at all or all in all." This lyric insists upon the wholeness so desired by readers from Tennyson's time to Eliot's ("all in all"), while at the same time demonstrating that it needs a linguistic and historical context to be completed. And this is fitting: the various *Idylls* evoke diverse Welsh, Old English, and French traditions.

Small wonder that "Merlin looked and half believed [Vivien] true" (398), as the poem reports in the subsequent lines. The lyric creates Merlin's hesitation in the poem's very readers, although as "Gareth and Lynette" attests, the greater epic consistently sets unmixed faith in heterogeneous cultural narratives against half-belief in unmixed versions of them. When Vivien finally acknowledges Merlin's hesitation and offers to elucidate her source, she acknowledges that the seeming wholeness of her own poem amounts to an illusion. As she recounts,

> . . . and there is more—this rhyme
> Is like the fair pearl-necklace of the Queen,
> That burst in dancing, and the pearls were spilt;
> Some lost, some stolen, some as relics kept.
> But nevermore the same two sister pearls
> Ran down the silken thread to kiss each other
> On her white neck—so is it with this rhyme:
> It lives dispersedly in many hands,
> And every minstrel sings it differently.
> (448–56)

What Vivien recounts of her own song is manifestly true of the Arthurian legends as a body. These, too, are scattered like "the fair pearl-necklace of the Queen / That burst in dancing" and "live . . . dispersedly in many hands." To represent the fragmented past of such legends in the most scrupulous way entails an admission of their irredeemable fragmentation.

Can it surprise the close reader of "Merlin and Vivien" that as Tennyson gradually expanded his *Idylls* from four poems to twelve, he refused to integrate them into a tightly continuous narrative or to disguise their heterogeneous underpinnings? Tennyson maintained this choice despite great pressure from reviewers, who protested increasingly loudly as subsequent editions of *The Idylls* made clear that no such narrative cohesion would finally be offered. Abraham Hayward protested in the *Quarterly Review* of 1871 that the poems "look like so many pieces of rich tapestry, worked after a pattern for separate panels."[29] Richard Holt Hutton complained in *Macmillan's Magazine* that they are "rich pictoral fancies, taken, certainly not altogether at random, but yet without any really coherent design."[30] Joseph Devey anticipated T. S. Eliot in *A Comparative Estimate of Modern English Poets* (1873) by saying that the "fragmentary treatment" of Arthurian legend in *The Idylls* suggests a "want of power in the artist to handle the story as a whole, and to strike out of heterogeneous materials the unity of a great poem" (qtd. in Andrew 161). It is critical to see that all these reviewers desired from Tennyson precisely what Jowett assures us that a real mythical history cannot provide: "a well-rounded system, or a continuous history." In other words, however justly it reflected the higher criticism, the fragmented design of Tennyson's poem was as frustrating to many Victorians as it would be disagreeable to twentieth-century critics. It does not follow that Tennyson's genius was too feeble or too minute for the task he had set out for himself. Here, at least, far from being the victim of his own lyric impulses, Tennyson indicates in such passages that the fragmentary nature of this epic poetry was its principal condition as a work of art.

Jowett was plainly on to something when he maintained that *The Idylls* needed to be appreciated in the context of nineteenth-century debates about religion. As with Gareth's conflation of Arthur and Jesus, *The Idylls's* textual situation is haunted by mid-century hermeneutics, and the most vivid threat behind this textual contingency lies in the fact that the disparate creation and dispersal of Arthurian materials in the medieval world so plainly reflects the disparate creation and dispersal of the Christian scriptures in the ancient one. Admittedly, Jowett's own enthusiasm for a fragmented idea of the Bible led him to overstate the acceptability of a similar technique from the poet laureate. As we see from other contemporary reviewers, "the great historical aspect of religion" was not at all uniformly embraced in the latter half of the nineteenth century. Still, Tennyson rightly understood his own mid-century prestige to be high enough that he (alone, perhaps) could risk alienating readers when he put it on display.

What is essential to derive from this historical context, once more, is that Tennyson seems to have considered the idea of narrative cohesion and rejected it as a misrepresentation of important cultural truths—both those found in the Arthurian legends and, by analogy, those found in the Christian scriptures. In this respect, *The Idylls* presents a sort of Victorian antecedent to Bernard Cerquiglini's study *In Praise of Variants* (1989). As it happened, reviewers treated *The Idylls*'s earlier editions with greater generosity than the later ones, in part (as Hughes has pointed out) because the earlier ones left open the possibility of being integrated into a coherent whole. But Tennyson spurns such factitious unity—or, rather, demands that such unity be supplied by the reader. Vivien herself dramatizes how the themes and morals of the Arthurian legends tended to be unfinished, to evolve in history, to be radically unresolved. And so "Merlin and Vivien" both anticipates and denies the reviewers' desire that Tennyson resolve the fragmentation and incoherence of his source texts. This desire informs Vivien's seduction of her mentor; it rises with the erotic tension of the narrative and participates in its more unsettling aspects. And maybe what is cleverest about Vivien's refrain is its impossibility when extended to the fragmented Arthurian legends. In such instances, the request to "trust me not at all or all in all," can hardly be fulfilled, for there is really no "all" to be trusted.

Tennyson's Critique of Inspirationism

Interestingly, reviewers who denied the force of *The Idylls*'s religious conflict often objected as strenuously as those who acknowledged it. The High Church critic Anne Mozley, for instance, best known for editing Newman's correspondence, introduces an 1859 discussion of *The Idylls* in *Bentley's Quarterly* by impatiently remarking that "the world in general cares uncommonly little about King Arthur." Her impatience stems not from Tennyson's particular treatment of the myth, but from his decision to honor it in the first place:

> It has, we have assumed, been a mistake, though a very general one, to suggest King Arthur, alive or dead, mythical or actual, as a subject for a poem of

magnitude or seeming aim. A mass of utterly baseless, and often contradictory legend, which nobody ever believed, can afford no foundation for so solid a superstructure; and any attempt to give historic truth to a scene laid in such remote barbarous antiquity, must make matters worse, and reduce it to harsh, dry, probably revolting antiquarianism.[31]

Today, Mozley's hostility toward Arthurian themes seems most conspicuous for its vehemence: medieval legend, however "remote" and "barbarous," no longer seems like anything to get exercised about. But Mozley's rhetoric makes more sense if we see it as an echo of H. A. Sawtelle's indignation toward Strauss as discussed above in chapter 1.[32]

Equally suggestive is the fact that Mozley's mordant tone and demystifying posture ironically mirror mid-century skeptical and freethinking texts that applied the same language to the Bible. The parent and greatest representative of such literature in the Anglo-American tradition is Thomas Paine's *Age of Reason* (1793–1807), which was widely reprinted in the nineteenth century.[33] Consider Mozley's review, for instance, next to Paine's commentary on the biblical books of Kings and Chronicles:

> Like all other ancient histories, they appear to be a jumble of fable and fact, and of probable and of improbable things; but which, distance of time and place, and change of circumstances in the world, have rendered obsolete and uninteresting. (83)

Or of Jeremiah:

> The historical parts, if they can be called by that name, are in the most confused condition; the same events are several times repeated, and that in a manner different, and sometimes in contradiction to each other. (102)

Or of Isaiah:

> . . . one of the most wild and disorderly compositions ever put together; it has neither beginning, middle, nor end . . . except a short historical part, and a few sketches of history in two or three of the first chapters. (98)

One could go on and on with such examples. (*The Age of Reason* does.) Paine has few claims to be considered an avant-garde Romantic biblical scholar, to be sure, but his literary influence and cultural position in nineteenth-century Britain far exceeds his originality as a critic. He served widely as a sort of poor man's Hume: a freewheeling skeptic whose plain-spoken analysis of the Bible appealed to freethinking readers throughout the century. David Norton goes so far as to suggest that *The Age of Reason* actually hindered the progress of the higher criticism in Britain in the first part of the nineteenth century "by producing an inspirationist backlash [that] may have made it more difficult to think about the Bible with freedom" (271).

At the same time, Paine's hostility to the literary character of the Bible, particularly his reluctance or inability to make allowances for the circumstances of its creation, represents exactly what the higher critics hoped to correct. They held the Bible to be anything but "obsolete and uninteresting"; whatever their personal theologies, they argued that the text became increasingly prescient and sublime when seen from a scholarly perspective that conceded up front the fragmented, mythological nature of the scriptures (but that denied its inspiration's contingency upon an imagined authorial or thematic unity). It is in this respect that "Merlin and Vivien" aligns itself clearly with the higher critics against the freethinking tradition of Paine as well as the conservative inspirationist tradition of Burgon. Tennyson's sympathies seem always to have run against both Paine's deism and its inspirationist backlash; certainly by "Merlin and Vivien," Tennyson seems to have believed that the contradictions, omissions, and "baselessness" of neither the Arthurian legends nor the Bible reduced their cultural value as inspirational literature. If "harsh, dry, probably revolting antiquarianism" cannot produce true poetry, then not only is Tennyson's Arthurian project quixotic and misguided, but so might be the rest of Christian literature.

It helps here to appreciate, indeed, how closely Paine mirrors conservative inspirationist views that if the scriptures contradict one another on any historical particulars, "the *disagreement* of the parts of a story proves that *the whole cannot be true*" (118, emphasis Paine's). Michael Nash, an Evangelical contemporary, expressed the sentiments of an increasing number when he described a Bible that was not true *in every particular* as an "amphibious fraud": "Take away the Bible from the Believer (or make him think it an amphibious fraud, which is all one), and you rob him of more than all that earth can give."[34] John Jebb, a student of Lowth's works in the 1820s, who might have been expected to pursue higher critical scholarship, instead pursued the principle that the Holy Scriptures, by definition, must be unified: "Design pervades the whole matter of both Testaments; and unity is the soul of that design."[35] And this brings us to the reactionary mid-Victorians, whose insistence that the sacred canon was either historically true in every particular or it was worthless; as Burgon summarized his own response to *Essays and Reviews* (with a particular dig at Jowett, who was at Balliol): "What I am insisting upon is, that the sacred Writers plainly say,—We stand or we fall together. They reach forth their hands, and they hold one another fast. . . . Verily the Bible is *not* 'like any other Book!'"[36]

Again, what is so pleasing about Burgon's uncompromising response to *Essays and Reviews,* in particular, is that he understood exactly the line of thinking that would inspire Tennyson to apply the higher criticism to British national legends in *The Idylls.* For Burgon, as for Parker, the higher criticism helped make vivid not just the hermeneutic dilemmas inherent to scripture, but the hermeneutic dilemmas of history proper, and the hermeneutic dilemmas of every narrative, from any possible source ("everything their friend tells them," and so on). The widespread incorporation of this intellectual problem into nineteenth-century British thought affords a signal example of why so much of Romantic and Victorian poetry is haunted by basic questions of epistemology. In Burgon, we also see obvious limits to the idea that religious uncertainty helped fuel the ruinous nationalism of the late nineteenth century, if the quasi-sacred national history actually affords no refuge from the problematics of traditional religion.[37] And anticipating Burgon's objection to the higher criticism, Tennyson's *Idylls* already essay to "apply this precious method of Interpretation to the History of England," as Burgon demands in his sermon. Burgon meant this as a rhetorical question, assuming that one must be radical indeed to attempt a debunking of the national history. Yet in a literary maneuver both profoundly conservative and disquietingly radical, his laureate already was attempting to tie the religious and national histories together in the manner that he suggests.

The historical criticism of the Bible caused such shock and furor in Victorian intellectual circles because so many Victorians regarded the question in the terms that Vivien provides, as though the Bible itself said, "Trust me not at all or all in all." This is why Lyell, Chambers, and Darwin met with such contemporary resistance, and why the higher criticism did as well, even though most of the higher critics believed in the Bible's literary—though not literal— inspiration. In "Merlin and Vivien," the literalist response to any scripture is always dubious, and Merlin recounts that the temptation to view things in such stark terms is somehow akin to the curse that destroys him: "But, Vivien, when you sang me that sweet rhyme, / I felt as though you knew this cursèd charm, / Were proving it on me" (432–34). Merlin's tale urges us forward from the stance that we see Barrett Browning adopt in "Earth and Her Praisers" to the one that she adopts in *Aurora Leigh*. As Stanley's analysis would seem to confirm, Tennyson's medievalism provokes Mozley's passion by design.

The Diverse Ambitions of Cultural Narrative: "The Epic"

Unusually for a poet with religious aspirations, Tennyson had often prophesied his own successes with a remarkable prescience. By the 1860s and 1870s, his status had become so high that even antipathetic critics confessed their reservations about him in the language of apostasy. Gerard Manley Hopkins, for instance, came to acknowledge his "doubt" of Tennyson much as he might have acknowledged his "doubt" of the Pauline Epistles: "Do you know, a horrible thing has happened to me. I have begun to *doubt* Tennyson."[38] Darwin, having long resisted his wife Emma's attempts to convert him to Tennyson, makes a special point of his incapacity to appreciate poetry at the close of his autobiography. (Emma did, however, find a companion spirit in Nettie Huxley, with whom she read *The Idylls* aloud. "Only fancy Mr. Darwin does not like poetry," recorded Huxley. "Let us pray for his conversion & glorify ourselves like true believers."[39]) And Alfred Austin, Tennyson's eventual successor to the post of laureate, openly positions himself as a freethinking provocateur in an 1870 attack upon Tennyson's supposed inspiration:

> If one were to enter a modern drawing-room filled with the average polite society of the day, and then and there were to pluck up courage to declare that Mr. Tennyson has no sound pretensions to be called a great poet . . . [,] he would not create more astonishment, or be regarded more unanimously as a heretic, than would another who in a company of *savans* expressed his doubts as to the law of gravitation, or a third who, before a committee of orthodox divines, exposed his utter disbelief in the inspiration of Scriptures.

Even Anthony Trollope, who seemed to be congenitally immune to the excesses of Victorian religious enthusiasm, dryly acknowledged Tennyson's contemporary status as sacred author in the leading article of George Henry Lewes's second *Fortnightly Review:* "It used to be held that a hundred years were wanted to make a poet's reputation, and that no man was a prophet in his own country. We have, I think, changed all that. . . . Alfred Tennyson has received, and is receiving, a homage more devoted than was perhaps ever paid to a living writer."[40] Coming from Trollope—even more strikingly than from Hopkins, Darwin, or Austin—this acknowledgment of the perceived connection between Tennyson's poetic standing and his ostensible prophetic standing provides a clear enough index of the cultural value widely assigned to poetry—to Tennyson in particular—in the mid-century. Trollope's tone manages to combine undisguised admiration for Tennyson's success and doubtful ambivalence about poetry's place in modern culture. After all, "It used to be held that . . . no man was a prophet in his own country," because Christ says so in Matthew's Gospel.[41] Trollope's conclusion, "We have, I think, changed all that," suggests that Tennyson's quasi-biblical status in the mid-century might depend upon a gross devaluation of the original text.

I have mentioned above how Gladstone's appeal to Tennyson to "harmonise" the fragmented and incohesive elements of nineteenth-century culture amounts to a rearticulation of Tennyson's own earlier themes. To convey more thoroughly the centrality of this idea to *The Idylls*, it will help to look at an instance of this perspective. "The Epic [Morte d'Arthur]" published in Tennyson's *Poems* of 1842, but composed around 1837–38, affords an especially good example of such a poem because Tennyson would later incorporate it into "The Passing of Arthur" (1869), which eventually became the epic-crowning twelfth poem and conclusion of *The Idylls*. It is the prologue of the 1842 "The Epic," however, that most clearly invokes the figure of the poet as a redeemer of the religious and social problems of the Victorian age: here the redeeming poet is a fictional university man named Everard Hall, whom most critics see as a thinly disguised self-portrait of young Tennyson. The poem begins with a gloomy discussion among conservative friends about the modern debasement of Christmas. Their host remains upbeat (his social duty), but can only do so by avowing his undiminished faith in poetry, after which the party's shared enthusiasm for literature brings Hall to recite his Arthurian "Morte d'Arthur." All is described by an admiring narrator:

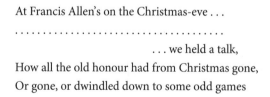

At Francis Allen's on the Christmas-eve . . .
. . . .
　　　　　　　　　. . . we held a talk,
How all the old honour had from Christmas gone,
Or gone, or dwindled down to some odd games

In some odd nooks like this . . .

. . . .

       . . . and half-awake I heard
The parson taking wide and wider sweeps,
Now harping on the church-commissioners,
Now hawking at Geology and schism;
Until I woke, and found him settled down
Upon the general decay of faith
Right through the world, "at home was little left,
And none abroad: there was no anchor, none,
To hold by." Francis, laughing, clapt his hand
On Everard's shoulder, with "I hold by him."
      (1–22)

This prologue's narrator, we see, sympathizes with the religious concerns of the group, but he also dozes during the discussion, signaling some distance from the glum conservatism of Parson Holmes in particular. Scholars of the 1830s and 1840s frequently connect issues of religious tradition to the Oxford Movement—to texts like Keble's *Sermon on National Apostasy*. But for this narrator, religious tradition has greatest interest in its secular incarnations, as in the general lament about "How all the old honour had from Christmas gone / Or gone, or dwindled down to some odd games / In some odd nooks like this." Church commissioners put him to sleep, whereas Hall's "Morte d'Arthur" holds him in rapt attention. "The Epic" might raise the question of poetry's own place among attenuated quasi-religious traditions: the category of "odd nooks like this" potentially includes Tennyson's 1842 *Poems*, as well as the home it depicts. The Victorian tendency to conflate poetic value with Christian value exacerbates, rather than relieves, this possibility.[42]

"The Epic" suggests some accord with the Tractarians about "the general decay of faith / Right through the world," but Tennyson's solution differs radically from theirs, and he remains ironically distant from their type of earnestness.[43] Francis Allen cannot maintain the role of poets in a culture's religious life—cannot assert his faith in Hall as an "anchor . . . To hold by"—without a degree of ironic levity that signals its own distance both from the grave tone marking much of Tennyson's actual Arthurian poetry ("Is this the tone of empire?") and also from the zeal of a previous generation of Romantics, who could entertain the poet's religious duties without smiling at their own ambitions: Novalis and Friedrich Schlegel, for instance, earnestly went about developing new scriptures for a new religion. (It never panned out.) And Thomas Carlyle, who represents the clearest bridge between Novalis's generation of German writers and Tennyson's generation of English ones, seized upon this German idea so enthusiastically as to risk making it vulgar: "Every man that writes is writing a new Bible; or a new Apocrypha; to last for a week or a thousand years; he that convinces a man and sets him working is the doer of a *miracle*" (emphasis Carlyle's).[44] Given these awkward precedents, Tennyson's poem seems rightly cautious of the tastefulness and sense of its position. His alter ego, Everard Hall, has thrown his chef d'oeuvre into the fire as though to relinquish the duty. And yet Hall's friend preserves a relic of it, and it is the favorable reception of this relic (in both "The Epic" and in most of Tennyson's actual reviews) that permits Tennyson to pursue an epic much like the chef d'oeuvre imagined to be lost. That is, *The Idylls* presents both Everard Hall–like ambivalence and a concrete answer to Francis Allen's challenge.

We see from the framing material of "The Epic," then, that when Gladstone, with whom we began, asks Tennyson to redeem the nineteenth century, he essentially delivers lines from a script that Tennyson himself had published years before. Crucially, Gladstone's appeal follows Tennyson's own logic in being implicitly religious, and he identifies medieval Arthurian romance (with its Continental counterpart, Carlovingian romance) as the perfect repository of poetic material for Tennyson to quarry for his lay gospel, his "terrestrial" Christian scriptures:

> The Gospel had given to the whole life of man a real resurrection, and its second birth was followed by its second youth. . . . The life of our Saviour, in its external aspect, was that of a teacher. It was in principle a model for all, but it left space and scope for adaptations to the lay life of Christians in general, such as those by whom the every-day business of the world is to be carried on. It remained for man to make his best endeavor to exhibit the great model on its terrestrial side, in its contact with the world. Here is the true source of that new and noble cycle which the middle ages have handed down to us in duality of form, but with a nearly identical substance, under the royal sceptres of Arthur in England and Charlemagne in France. . . . It is to this rich repository that Mr. Tennyson had resorted for his material.
> (466)

Gladstone fully appreciated the circumstance that medieval Arthurian manuscripts were historically dispersed and aesthetically uneven; he explicitly dismisses true medieval compilations such as Ariosto's and Malory's as hodge-podge and insufficient. (Arnold, in his famous 1860s lectures on Homer, dismisses the German *Nibelungenlied* on the same ground.) And yet Gladstone describes the raw state of Tennyson's material as the mere "childhood" of a text that would come to full maturity in the hands of this great poet (468). He wished to see Tennyson play the roles of both Homer and the so-called Pisistratean compiler, of the evangelist and Saint Jerome, whose Vulgate Bible would help stabilize the canon of received texts for the medieval period. Indeed, Gladstone is explicit about even the biblical analogy that Tennyson implicitly evokes, here praising Arthurian legend as a sort of practical version of the religious truths earlier expressed in scriptures—a sort of "Gospel of the world" that might hide ruptures in the historical record better than the original Gospels had managed to do. It is by no means obvious that Gladstone would have seen the early *Idylls* as a religious project had he not viewed Tennyson's "The Epic" as a blueprint for the work done there.

Put simply, Tennyson's contemporaries were intellectually attuned to Carlyle's stance that potentially anyone could utter prophecy, even as those most often expected to do so—poets—often expressed ambivalence about the endeavor. Critics such as Trollope helpfully remind us of the generic associations that determined the reception of would-be prophets in the mid-century: it is the poet Tennyson, and not the novelist Trollope, who is given this role. (Naturally, there is no reason to believe that Trollope would have wanted it.) Poetry for Tennyson entailed specifically religious burdens "to convince a man," as Carlyle put it, "and set him working," and the higher criticism as he understood it might even be seen as a mandate to shape the nation's sacred literature. This burden also helps account for Tennyson's highly fraught relationship with his reviewers in the critical journals of the day. For decades, critics goaded Tennyson to write a quasi-religious epic of the Victorian age (both before and after *In Memoriam*), and for decades, Tennyson struggled to form one adequately sophisticated for the problem at hand. Edgar Shannon's classic *Tennyson and the Reviewers* (1952) traces this pressure through 1850, but risks leaving the misimpression that *In Memoriam* satisfied Tennyson's critics and ended that concern. This is not the case. The critical public adored *In Memoriam* in part because they saw it as evidence of greater things to come. Gladstone's review, once more, traces Tennyson's career from the 1842 *Poems* to the 1859 *Idylls* as one long crescendo of greatness: "When he published '*In Memoriam*' in 1850," Gladstone writes, "all readers were conscious of the progressive widening and strengthening, but, above all, deepening of his mind. We cannot hesitate to mark the present volume as exhibiting another forward and upward stride" (482). Few today regard *The Idylls* as a unambiguous step "forward and upward" from *In Memoriam*, but it is no surprise that Tennyson followed Gladstone's advice to the letter, eventually reshaping his "Morte d'Arthur" for the growing *Idylls*, and revising and writing new poems in a grander and more antique vein than he had dared to do in the earliest volume of 1859.

Higher Critical Juvenilia: "Armageddon"/"Timbuctoo"

To indicate the truly formative nature of Romantic biblical hermeneutics in Tennyson's poetic career, it is worth pointing out that they may be traced back to his earliest published poetry. "Armageddon" (ca. 1825), written when the poet was fourteen or fifteen and revised as "Timbuctoo" (1829) for his undergraduate Chancellor's Prize poem, demonstrates how very early Tennyson became invested in the poetic possibilities afforded by the higher criticism—a circumstance that itself attests to the belated nature of higher critical hermeneutics as it receives expression in his mid-Victorian poetry. The unlikely story of how "Armageddon" became "Timbuctoo" will be familiar territory to Tennyson scholars: in 1829 Cambridge offered its Chancellor's Prize for verses on the topic of Timbuktu, and the nineteen-year-old Tennyson sent home to Somersby for his childhood "Armageddon," rightly guessing that it might serve him as a strong rough draft.[45] He gutted the poem's biblical elements, relocated its themes in northwest Africa, and added an equal number of lines that were broadly representative of early nineteenth-century European accounts of Timbuktu. His manifest indifference to the assigned theme paid off surprisingly well: not only did Tennyson's revised poem win the Chancellor's Prize, but a review of it brought his poetry (and name) to the world in the pages of the up-and-coming weekly the *Athenaeum* in a review probably written by Richard Monckton Milnes.[46]

Following long critical tradition, I mostly regard these as two versions of the same poem.[47] But it is the transition between "Armageddon" and "Timbuctoo" that shows how Tennyson became invested in the poetic possibilities afforded by the higher criticism, for "Timbuctoo" applies the earlier poem's motif of revelation to an independent (that is, nonbiblical) set of legends in revealing ways. "Armageddon" presents itself as a fairly straightforward guide to the Christian book of Revelation. In it, a visionary narrator receives instructions from an angel about how to understand the celestial warfare associated with what he calls "THE DAY of the Lord God!" To this end, he relates a small series of descriptive vignettes concerning things like gathering armies and supernaturally bad weather. Milton provides the principal stylistic model for the poem:

> Spirit of Prophecy whose mighty grasp
> Enfoldeth all things, whose capacious soul
> Can people the illimitable abyss
> Of vast and fathomless futurity
> With all the Giant Figures that shall pace
> The dimness of its stage,—whose subtle ken
> Can throng the doubly-darkened firmament
> Of Time to come with all its burning stars
> At awful intervals. I thank thy power,
> Whose wondrous emanation hath poured
> Bright light on what was darkest, and removed
> The cloud that from my mortal faculties
> Barred out the knowledge of the Latter Times.
> (1–14)

Tennyson here adopts both Milton's blank verses and his deeply inverted sentence structures.[48] He defers his verb à la *Paradise Lost* until the ninth line—so far, in fact, that he seems to lose his thread, ending lamely with a period. Such an opening gambit risks unintended humor, coming as it does from a boy in his early teens. But it risks humor because it is so generically charged.

Even the awkward punctuation in line 9 might imply a vast ambition, for it brings to mind biblical models such as the incipit of Revelation:

> The Revelation of Jesus Christ, which God gave unto him, to shew unto his servants things which must shortly come to pass; and he sent and signified it by his angel unto his servant John:
> Who bare record of the word of God, and of the testimony of Jesus Christ, and of all things that he saw.
> (Revelation 1:1–2 KJV)

Tennyson's opening sentence apparently follows the King James model, rejecting standard subject-predicate organization in favor of something like a hieratic pause or a more heraldic discourse organization that ignores the syntactic norms of nineteenth-century written language. A subsequent disregard for nineteenth-century grammar in *In Memoriam* brings Isobel Armstrong to reflect that the poem there reaches "the state Nietzsche hoped for but envisaged as a remote possibility: God goes when grammar goes."[49] Nonetheless, it seems plain that God's attendance is required at the battle of "Armageddon."

What do we learn about the end times from Tennyson's poem? Famously little, and much less than the poem initially promises. Part of the problem is that Tennyson's visionary becomes simply too illuminated: he becomes conscious of the "smallest grain that dappled the dark Earth" and the "indistinctest atom in deep air" (30–31), but all this makes him less fit to describe what the end of the world would look like to the rest of us.[50] (Eliot remarks in *Middlemarch* that such supernatural sensitivity would be intolerable, "like hearing the grass grow and the squirrel's heart beat.") Tennyson's visionary himself concedes that "to paint / In dignity of language suitable / The majesty of what I then beheld, / Were past the power of man" (16–20)—rhetorical apophasis here serving as cover for the limitations of the poet.

At the same time, "Armaggedon" presents an earnest attempt to grapple with the problem of sacred history by pinning it down in tangible ways. The narrator places himself precisely in the geography of the poem, claiming in what would become the opening couplet of Timbuctoo: "I stood upon the mountain which o'erlooks / The valley of Megiddo" (24–25). Despite his title, we see, Tennyson chooses not to identify his poetic setting with the King James Bible's translation, "Armageddon"; he rather reproduces the Hebrew *har megiddon,* which early nineteenth-century scholars understood to be a Palestinian valley near the Plain of Esdraelon.[51] In other words, the poem's *title* invokes the biblical event of Armageddon, while the *poem* surprisingly locates its seer in a map of the Middle East. One can contrast Tennyson's practice with that of a long line of eighteenth- and nineteenth-century poets, such as Michael Bruce (1746–1767) or Coleridge's friend, William Lisle Bowles (1762–1850), who treat Armageddon as an event, rather than a geographical location. In Bowles's poem "St. John in Patmos," the very river Euphrates becomes the path by which wicked armies come to Armageddon, but if Bowles were keeping up with biblical geography as closely as the teenage Tennyson was, he would have appreciated that the Euphrates does not lead to Megiddo—one might as soon follow the Thames to Edinburgh. This is not to praise Tennyson at the expense of Bruce and Bowles, but merely to point

out that their interest was eschatological without being rigorously geographical. Tennyson's teenage desire to integrate geography with his eschatology, in
turn, already puts him in conversation with the higher criticism, however rudimentary his grasp of it might have been at this point. Bishop Colenso made
the same sorts of discoveries when the Zulus with whom he worked as a missionary pointed out the apparent geographical irregularities in the Hebrew
Bible. (Colenso labored in ignorance of the higher criticism, once more, but
The Pentateuch and the Book of Joshua Critically Examined includes an epigraph from *In Memoriam;* as Kirstie Blair remarks, Tennyson eventually matters to Victorian biblical criticism as much "because the criticism engages
with the poetry" as "because the poetry engages with the criticism."[52])

To shift the lens of the higher criticism from "Armageddon" to "Timbuctoo" is to see how cleverly Tennyson integrated nascent ideas of the higher
criticism into his early ideas of poetry, for this poem takes up the first draft's
mythological aspirations. As its title might suggest, "Timbuctoo" concerns the
fabled African city, a mythical sort of paradise that Tennyson compares to El
Dorado and the lost city of Atlantis and that his narrator glimpses in a vision
as a marvelous Gothic pile of "rampart upon rampart, dome on dome, / Il-
limitable range of battlement / On battlement, and the Imperial height / Of
Canopy o'ercanopied." As in the former poem, an angel companion explains
his vision to the visionary. To represent African legend, that is, Tennyson
recycles all the machinery of "Armageddon": the angel, the visionary, the
explanation. The difference between these two poems, however, remains instructive. Whereas "Armageddon" attempts to address its mythical subject
with historical and geographical precision, "Timbuctoo" pursues the opposite strategy: it surrenders in advance any geographical truths of its fantastic
subject, and eventually even acknowledges that Western *"Discovery"* shall
find this marvelous city to be a great embellishment upon a dreary reality.

> ["]Oh city! oh latest Throne! where I was raised
> To be a mystery of loveliness
> Unto all eyes, the time is well-nigh come
> When I must render up this glorious home
> To keen *Discovery:* soon yon brilliant towers
> Shall darken with the waving of her wand;
> Darken, and shrink and shiver into huts,
> Black specks amid a waste of dreary sand,

> Low-built, mud-walled, Barbarian settlements.
> How changed from this fair City!"
> (236–45)

As Tennyson realized, the concession contained in these lines throws doubts upon the biblical kingdom of Solomon just as it does upon the legendary kingdom of Timbuktu. If "keen Discovery" were to wave her wand in the direction of Palestine, she might be similarly disappointed. To surrender the Bible to the realm of poetry, as the nineteenth century increasingly learned to do, is to concede that the biblical book of Kings might be no more reliable a history than myths of El Dorado or Timbuktu. This is part of what Jowett calls "the great historical aspect of religion."

Nonetheless, despite throwing over the historical Timbuktu in this startling way, the poem insists upon the spiritual truth of its original vision. The angel holdover from "Armageddon" reassures the visionary that his idea of Timbuctoo remains in some senses truer than the impending version of keen Discovery:

> . . . I am the Spirit,
> The permeating life which courseth through
> All the intricate and labyrinthine veins
> Of the great vine of *Fable,* which, outspread
> With growth of shadowing leaf and clusters rare,
> Reacheth to every corner under Heaven,
> Deep-rooted in the living soil of truth;
> So that men's hopes and fears take refuge in
> The fragrance of its complicated glooms,
> And cool impleachèd twilights.
> (215–24)

These lines instruct us in the value of Timbuktu for Tennyson: while the fantastic riches of this city, previously understood as history, must now be understood as poetry, yet our very real understanding of "Heaven, / Man's first, last home" (212) depends upon such poetry. The Garden of Eden will not be found on a modern map, but this does not make it less true to what the spirit calls "the heart of man." The Christian seraph of "Armageddon" becomes here something like the spirit of comparative mythology but still serves the same basic purpose.

As W. D. Paden first pointed out, the poem's sentiment here very much echoes Wordsworth's long excursus on primitive religions and the imagination in book 4 of *The Excursion,* where a wise old rustic explains to the poem's narrator that primitive religions redeemed humankind from "apathy and destitution, paving the way for Christian revelation." From the context of "Armageddon," however, we see how radically Tennyson's poem alters Wordsworth's argument. For "Timbuctoo" makes no special pleading for Christian revelation within the category of primitive religions, as *The Excursion* does here, and does not set it aside as a special case. "Timbuctoo" makes Tennyson a kind of Strauss to Wordsworth's Herder—he applies to his own Christian religion the logic that Wordsworth had (here) reserved for earlier faiths. Tennyson's poem also reflects dismay at the loss of its fair city, but still promotes myth (or "fable") as essential for human understanding of all religious truth. The seer's guiding genius explicitly states that this truth "courseth through / All the intricate and labyrinthine veins / of the Great vine of *Fable.*" By his report, such fable is rooted in "the living soil of truth," and indeed represents those truths that humankind seems most likely to appreciate. This is less a transcendent metaphor than an organic one: a vine that grows with culture. Like the higher critics, Tennyson maintains that although popular legends might not be true in strict detail, still their literary inspiration redeems both the stories and their readers, and that that alone leads them to "Heaven."[53]

Thus, the lineaments of "Armageddon" within "Timbuctoo" promote an understanding of religious myth very much like the one celebrated by Jowett as peculiar to the mid-century. Tennyson's undergraduate friends agreed that "Armageddon" contains the best elements of either poem: "The bursts of poetry [in "Timbuctoo"] are magnificent," wrote Arthur Hallam, "but they were not written for Timbuctoo; and as a whole, the present poem is surely very imperfect."[54] Similarly, Monckton Milnes's review in the *Athenaeum* concludes with extensive passages from "Armageddon," asking its readers, "How many men have lived for a century who could equal this?" The inquiry about "men" here serves as cover for the fact that a provincial schoolboy wrote the poetry.

Tennyson's poem anticipates Strauss in its allowance that one cannot reliably distinguish between the fabricated and genuine parts of ancient legend, and like Strauss it insists upon the importance of myth itself and myth's organic, human foundation. The angel of "Timbuctoo" never revokes the claims to religious insight made by the angel of "Armageddon," whereas the religious ambition of "Armageddon" fills the later poem, insisting that the very improbability of myth is instrumental to its ultimately redemptive end: "'There is no mightier Spirit than I to sway / The heart of man: and teach him to attain / By shadowing forth the Unattainable[']'" (191–93). Though chastened by probable concessions to historical skeptics, Tennyson thus reinscribes the myth that drives the poem's earlier version, with all of its youthful zeal. He abandons the real Timbuktu, yet he maintains with the higher critics that the meaning behind the fabulous one remains key to "the heart of man."[55]

Tennyson's Lower Criticism: Translation and the NRV

To reapproach *The Idylls* by way of "Timbuctoo" helps, perhaps, to clarify the stakes of the impasse between Tennyson's ambition to rewrite an inspired poetic version of the national past and his corresponding resolve to make visible the hermeneutic problems presented by the sacred texts of Christianity. *The Idylls* really does represent a culminating triumph in Tennyson's career when appreciated for its prolonged struggle between his ambition and his scholarly fastidiousness.[56] Victorian critics' eventual frustration with Tennyson's desire to have it both ways can disguise the extent to which, in some measure, he really did have it both ways. Believers regularly grant the Bible theoretical unity even where it is most palpably fractured, and Tennyson merely aspired to an analogous type of readerly consideration. His decision to invite—or to maintain—a higher critical hermeneutics throughout *The Idylls* suggests that he truly hoped, following Trollope's expression, to "change all that." This struggle resonates not only on the level of the higher criticism but equally on that of the "lower criticism": the criticism of scriptural redaction and translation. *The Idylls* presents the poet as a cultural translator and steward of the nation's heritage even where that heritage remains textually uncertain. Already by 1856, "Merlin and Vivien" featured "translation" as a means of epitomizing both the problem of textual fragmentation and its resolution. Indeed, the very fragmentation and difficulty of access that marked the sacred texts created opportunities for a poet who positioned himself as a translator of otherwise inaccessible texts.

Victorian debates about biblical translation and the lower criticism are the underlying part of this history, although they also derive from Romantic hermeneutics. In mid-century, these debates centered around the King James translation, then over two hundred years old, and which an international community of scholars eventually took it upon itself to update in the New Revised Version that appeared in 1881 and 1885. Mid-Victorian religious conservatives and liberals alike agreed with the principle of having a New Revised Version: virtually everyone agreed that the King James translation contained some obscurities that could be cleared up by a more exact translation, and the problem was felt especially keenly at this time because Britain was exporting enormous numbers of Bibles to its empire, as well as profiting by a religious revival at home. (For the sensational early print runs of the New Revised Version, please see my introduction.)

The purpose of the New Revised Version was to facilitate scriptural understanding by establishing a more definitive text, and, true to this ambition, it adopted an entirely different textual methodology than the one that prevails in the King James. The NRV marked manuscript variants, especially readings that seemed to present interpolations, and included a great number of marginal notes and glosses of ambiguities that had not been present in the Authorized Version. When the first volume finally appeared after ten years of editorial labor, of course, it puzzled and horrified much of its audience, and the scholarly apparatus meant to make it definitive was the most criticized element of its production. Conservative readers of both High Church and Low Church persuasions felt betrayed by the new text. They wanted a reliable, unambiguous text of God's Word, and the NRV editors would only provide one with caveats and variants. To appreciate the significance of these caveats, it will be sufficient to compare a single Revised verse of 1881 with its authorized precedent in the King James translation. Consider Mark 15:39:

> And when the centurion, which stood over against him, saw that he so cried out, and gave up the ghost, he said, Truly this man was the Son of God. (Mark 15:39 AV)

> And when the centurion, which stood by over against him, saw that he so gave up the ghost, he said, Truly this man was the Son of God. (Mark 15:39 NRV)

To most readers, the differences between these two renderings may appear superficial: the translators add one word ("by"), and drop three ("cried out, and"). Certainly in the Victorian period, such variants would attract little attention in most textual situations. That being said, it would be difficult to overstate the importance of these variants in Mark, especially given the literal manner in which the Gospel was presumed to offer God's own utterance. During the *Essays and Reviews* controversy, Burgon preached of the Bible that "every book of it, every chapter of it, every verse of it, every word of it, every syllable of it, (*where* are we to *stop?*) every letter of it, is the direct utterance of the Most High." Burgon's is the strictest of inspirationist perspectives, and for him any variants in ancient source texts, any varying from authorized recensions, present theological problems. One may presume that God does not misspeak, so which of the variants in the ancient Greek texts of Mark 15:39 represents His "direct utterance"? Did Burgon's Most High directly utter that Jesus "cried out, and gave up the ghost" or just that he "gave up the ghost"? Conservative critics wedded to the idea of a text inspired in every word, syllable, letter—*where* are we to *stop?*—were bound to be frustrated by the unfixed nature of the New Revised text, which liberally departed from the previous Authorized Version to accommodate manuscript variations and ambiguities in translation. But this scholarly courtesy put the Victorian editors of the New Revised Version in the midst of an ongoing controversy about the Bible's inspiration; they took a controversial critical position in their decision to acknowledge the unfixed nature of premodern manuscript culture.

Mark 15:39 presents a particularly telling example because the editors of the New Revised also included two footnotes to acknowledge variants in the Greek manuscripts from which this text is derived. The first of these simply acknowledges that the Authorized version has manuscript precedent: "Many ancient authorities read '*so cried out, and gave up the ghost.*'" The second, however, points out that some ancient Greek manuscripts also have "Truly this man was *a* Son of God" instead of the more usual "Truly this man was *the* Son of God." It was the difference embodied in this second instance of manuscript variation that stood out for the Victorians. In most Christian theology, the difference between identifying someone as *a* son of God and identifying him as *the* Son of God is the difference between pious enthusiasm and the dogma of the Incarnation. The NRV records such unsettling alterations with suitable discretion, but much of its Victorian readership could see their revolutionary implications without having them pointed out explicitly.

Biblically conservative Victorian scholars found the inclusion of such manuscript variants deeply unsettling, and they were quick and loud in their protests. Burgon, once more, led the opposition in a series of articles in the same *Quarterly Review* that Gladstone had used to trumpet Tennyson: "Our Revisers stand convicted of having deliberately rejected the words of Inspiration in every page, and of having substituted for them fabricated readings which the church has long since refused to acknowledge, or else has rejected, with abhorrence, readings which survive at this time only in a little handful of documents of the most depraved type." The vehement "abhorrence" animating Burgon's critique sets on display the extent to which the scholarly goals of the NRV were feared to undermine the textual authority of scripture. Burgon acknowledges that the translators of the AV might have known about manuscript variants such as those of Mark 15, but he insists that they rejected them as "depraved." The moral resonances implicit in Burgon's diction—his notion of textual variation as depravity—while not unique to the Victorian period, are nonetheless strategic here. Well into the mid-twentieth century, bibliographers and editors could still speak without irony of textual variation as corruption; in cases like this one, the loaded moral connotations of "depravity" or "corruption" served perfectly to reinforce the conservative critic's disfavor. Even Victorian-era critics, however, occasionally also acknowledge the oddness of viewing textual variation as a sort of moral failing. W. H. Mallock's conservative satire *The New Republic* (1877), for instance, plays wittily on the "corrupt" nature of the Greek Anthology to suggest that Greek love and textual obscurity were not, in his view, morally indistinguishable.[57] Mallock makes Jowett the butt of his jokes, but he could as easily have applied them to the school of Burgon.

This was the state of the lower criticism in English-language biblical studies when Tennyson wrote *The Idylls*. It was a period of immense scholarly discovery in biblical textual studies. The first year of *The Idylls*, 1859, also saw Konstantin von Tischendorf's acquisition of the full text of the Codex Sinaiticus from the Monastery of St. Catherine in the Sinai Peninsula, a fourth-century text that he had discovered there in 1844 and excerpts of which he had published in 1846. (Significantly for our discussion of "The Holy Grail," above, the Codex Sinaiticus includes two apocryphal texts: the Letter of Barnabas and the Shepherd of Hermas.) But this was only the most famous of the biblical manuscripts to come to light at this time, and Tischendorf would never had discovered it without the nineteenth-century revolution in biblical textual studies. The very issue of the *Edinburgh Review* in which Coventry Patmore reviews the 1859 *Idylls,* for instance, also takes up William Cureton's *Remains of a very Antient Recension of the Four Gospels in Syriac, hitherto unknown in Europe* (1858), and the reviewer takes pains to express the foundational nature of such scholarship:

> We can well understand that a reader of the Greek New Testament who has
> paid no attention to textual criticism, looking at the words or phrases which
> this version omits, or which it reads differently from that to which he has been
> accustomed, may feel astonishment almost amounting to indignation at what
> he must regard as daring corruption of the original text. . . . He may turn to
> his Greek New Testament, there to note down the convincing proofs of the
> worthlessness of this newly found Syriac version. But [what happens] if some
> unfeeling critic asks him, "But how do you know that the passages which you
> have noted in Greek are really parts of the New Testament? How are you *sure*
> (in Matt. v. 44. for instance) that the version that you are condemning does not
> contain the true reading?"
> (177)

Victorian religious conservatives saw the creation of the NRV (and, indeed, such preliminary scholarship as Cureton's) as one further threat in the war against liberal criticism that had previously been fought over the grounds of geology and the higher criticism. In the period leading up to the controversies over the New Revised Version, they had increasingly relied not merely upon traditional Greek texts, but also upon the King James translation as a uniform and unvarying text of the Bible, a single and consistent set of scriptures that had ultimately been dictated by God. But during this period other perspectives began to claim much greater authority, as this reviewer also relates: "It was [recently] established, for instance, that the Codex Bezae, which some in the last century, and earlier part of this, contemned altogether because of its interpolations, as though it were wholly a corrupted document, is really one of the very best witnesses of the text of Holy Scripture, as read in the early centuries of the Christian Church" (173). The more liberal scholars behind the New Revised edition, following the methodology of scholars such as Cureton and the famous Tischendorf, felt constrained to include awkward variants in their translations, not least because their very disharmony with modern theology made it all the more likely that they came from earlier forms of the text.

In its treatment of the lower criticism, as of the higher criticism, Tennyson's *Idylls* proceeds by analogy. In "Merlin and Vivien," in exchange for Vivien's rhyme, Merlin recounts the history of his own spell book, a manuscript that descended to him after being recorded centuries previously in foreign lands (and in foreign hands). Vivien, slow to catch the scholarly implications of this complex manuscript history, naively concludes that anyone possessing the book might well reproduce its magic, and she teases Merlin with the possibility that she might steal from him the charm that he refuses to share:

> "Ye have the book: the charm is written in it:
> Good: take my counsel: let me know it at once:
> For keep it like a puzzle chest in chest,
> With each chest locked and padlocked thirty-fold,
> And whelm all this beneath as vast a mound
> As after furious battle turfs the slain
> On some wild down above the windy deep,
> I yet should strike upon a sudden means
> To dig, pick, open, find and read the charm:
> Then, if I tried it, who should blame me then?"
> (650–59)

Plainly, Vivien understands the curse to be more or less legible to her, or rather to any who discover it. Her images of uncovering "vast" mounds and breaking into treasure troves—so different from the gloomy disappointments of Tennyson's "Timbuctoo"—perhaps reflect the glories of mid-century biblical archaeology and European exploration, such as A. H. Layard's exhuming of the biblical city of Nineveh (and subsequent carting of large portions of it back to London's British Museum). At all events, Vivien presents herself as a type of the Victorian explorer.

Yet Merlin's response, no less topical, assures us that his treasure is safe from such explorers as Vivien precisely because of its historical and geographical distance:

> And smiling as a master smiles at one
> That is not of his school, nor any school
> But that where blind and naked Ignorance
> Delivers brawling judgments, unashamed,
> On all things all day long, he answer'd her:

> "Thou read the book, my pretty Vivien!
> O ay, it is but twenty pages long,
> But every page having an ample marge,
> And every marge enclosing in the midst
> A square of text that looks a little blot,

The text no larger than the limbs of fleas;
And every square of text an awful charm,
Writ in a language that has long gone by.
So long, that mountains have arisen since
With cities on their flanks—thou read the book!
And every margin scribbled, crost, and crammed
With comment, densest condensation, hard
To mind and eye; but the long sleepless nights
Of my long life have made it easy to me.
And none can read the text, not even I;
And none can read the comment but myself;
And in the comment did I find the charm.["]
(665–81)

This episode is entirely of Tennyson's invention and not derived from his medieval sources, a fact that seems significant in the religious context of the greater poem. For to the extent that the verses invite a biblical analogy, they seem to suggest that even magical or supernatural books require the learning of "long sleepless nights" and a "long life." Merlin's own example implies that to comprehend a particularly obscure text, one needs context: his long studies suggest a hermeneutic model in which one arrives at comprehension only through context and commentary. Even Merlin confesses not to understand the original text of his special book, and his mode of interpreting this book resembles the practice of nineteenth-century philologists, whose widespread use of one language often (in parallel translations or interlinear glosses) served as a crib for the secrets of another. Thus, for instance, Jean-François Champollion famously decoded the Rosetta Stone through use of its parallel inscriptions. Caedmon's Hymn, quite possibly the earliest piece of recorded English-language poetry, first appears as interlinear marginalia in Bede's eighth-century *Historia Ecclesiastica* (it there appears as the original English transcription of a hymn that Bede records in Latin). And Tennyson's text evokes medieval Talmudic scholarship as well: Merlin comprehends his text only through the marginalia that surrounds it, as one might come to an understanding of Torah through Rashi's commentary more readily than through the text itself. Here the interpretation or gloss becomes part of the import of the inspired text. Merlin's book is incomprehensible outside of the interpretations that have been given to it.

Such an exegetical tradition remained foreign to most of Tennyson's contemporaries even after the mid-century popularizing of the higher criticism. But to compare the power of Merlin's spell book with the traditional power of the Holy Bible, we see the conundrum of the nineteenth-century scripture scholar in the inscrutability of significant portions of the ancient text, in which Barrett Browning's digamma might serve as a telling synechdoche. As mentioned in chapter 1, Strauss would actually come to level this charge of effective inscrutability against the scriptures as a whole; he goes so far as to advocate the adoption of a sacred canon of (German) vernacular literature. To the common man (whom Strauss calls "dem schlichten Mann aus dem Volke") great parts of the Bible remain as incomprehensible as Merlin's book would be to Vivien.[58] Indeed, Strauss submits that not even most scholars can appreciate it: "How many of the theologians understand it? pretend to understand it?" Strauss asks. "Yes, men think they understand the Bible, because they have grown accustomed to misunderstand it."[59] In *The Old Faith and the New,* Strauss essentially smiles at the "schlichten Mann" with a "Thou read the book, my pretty Vivien!"

Just as the problem of textual fragmentation was evident in the theological controversies of the mid-century, then, so was the problem of scriptural translation. As the popular Congregationalist preacher Joseph Parker (1830–1902) observed, even the most conservative of the higher critics posed a threat to belief by emphasizing difficulties within the translation and transmission of the scriptures. Actually *reading* the ancient text according to the best scriptural criticism simply left it outside the ken of the average Christian.[60] Like many evangelicals in particular, Parker held that scholars who maintained the importance of the Bible's translation and transcription were necessarily misguided, for they forcibly surrendered the democratic gains of the Reformation, in which lay Protestants first won the right to read the Bible. "Popery," writes Parker, "says in effect, the Bible is literature; only scholars can understand it; it is written in many languages absolutely locked against the populace, let the priest deal it out discreetly" (75). To Parker, the suggestion that the Bible can be read by only a select few was heresy against Protestantism, whether those few were appointed by the Vatican or by erudition acquired at German universities:

> I am jealous lest the Bible should in any sense be made a priest's book. Even Baur or Colenso may, contrary to his own wishes, be almost unconsciously elevated into a literary deity under whose approving nod alone we can read the Bible with any edification. It is no secret that when Baur rejected the Epistle to

the Philippians as un-Pauline, Christian Europe became partially paralysed, and that when Hilgenfeld pronounced it Pauline Christian Europe resumed its prayers. Have we to await a communication from Tübingen, or a telegram from Oxford, before we can read the Bible? The Bible is not the Bible to me because Herr Baur countersigns it.

(75–76)

Parker does not quite take the rigid position presented by his ideological ancestor Chillingworth, whose famous "BIBLE [and] the BIBLE only" became a litmus test for orthodoxy. Yet he articulates a similar concern that the introduction of any interpretative caste—whether priestly or scholarly—would diminish the religious life of the individual Christian.

In this respect, *The Idylls* plainly comes down on the side of Tübingen. Tennyson dismisses through the mouth of Merlin what Parker reasonably takes to be the gains of the Reformation. The Merlin of Tennyson's poem becomes a medieval "Baur or Colenso," one who smiles at Parker's evangelical hermeneutic "as a master smiles at one / That is not of his school." Indeed, by this analogy, the average English clergyman, untrained in the higher criticism, belongs in Vivien's school, "where blind and naked Ignorance / Delivers brawling judgments, unashamed, / On all things all day long."[61] "Merlin and Vivien" appeals to a sensibility that departs from both religious skepticism à la Paine and inspirationist zeal à la Burgon. Vivien, remarkably, manages to represent both skeptic and zealot at once.

At the same time, Tennyson's poem allows that the power behind such profound study as Merlin's (or, by analogy, Baur's or Hilgenfeld's) had supernatural rewards for the nonspecialist as well as the specialist—a stance that might differentiate Tennyson from Strauss's eventual position. As much as the poem honors a scholarly reading of the book, it also develops the idea that Merlin can relegate his knowledge. For—and here's the catch—the charm actually *works*: Vivien is able to work the magic of the book without being able to read it, once Merlin teaches her how to do it. In other words, to pursue the analogy between Merlin's book and the scriptures, Tennyson insists that the power of the text is indeed translatable and even, in a certain sense, democratic. Even the wicked Vivien can cast Merlin's spell as long as she has a literate mentor like Merlin to teach her. In reformulating the national legends for an adoring nation, then, Tennyson does not entirely revert to the priestcraft model so despised by Joseph Parker. He allows that the cultural past remains partly lost in obscurity, like the language of Merlin's book, and he brings this concept to bear upon the hermeneutic conundrums that caused such a stir in the mid-century. Yet he also celebrates the Arthurian legends as translatable truths—translated by him, and made available to enlighten the nineteenth century although he found it in medieval sources that Parker might well describe as "absolutely locked against the populace." Tennyson maintained throughout his lifetime that *The Idylls* "carefully shadowed forth the spiritual progress and advance of the world" (*Memoir* 2: 128). And he meant there for the lay reader to inherit in the text some measure of that spiritual progress.

According to his son Hallam, Tennyson had little patience for those who demanded a key to the true meaning of *The Idylls,* protesting with Augustine of Hippo that the inspired text contains an infinite number of good readings. "I hate to be tied down to say, '*This* means *that,*' because the thought within the image is much more than any one interpretation," lamented Tennyson. "Poetry is like shot-silk with many glancing colours. Every reader must find his own interpretation according to his sympathy with the poet."[62] Tennyson wished to make the national heritage more alive to his enormous readership; he wished not to eclipse Malory or the *Mabinogion,* but to make them—as he surely did—a more integral part of the national spirit.

"Tennyson as Prophet"

Unlike many of his literary peers, Tennyson left us no record of his encounter with specific works of higher criticism, and it is sometimes difficult to establish precisely how early he was acquainted with it.[63] Yet it will be clear from this discussion that Tennyson evidenced higher critical *modes* of thinking as early as his boyhood verses of 1825, and it may be this early readiness to refigure its central arguments in his poetry that made his religious insights so impressive to many of his contemporaries. As F. W. H. Meyers wrote in his earnest fin de siècle essay, "Tennyson as Prophet" (1889), "Let us briefly consider the successive steps which mark Tennyson's gradual movement to his present position. They show, I think, an inward development coinciding with, or sometimes anticipating, the spiritual movement of the age."[64] Here as elsewhere, Meyers presents Tennyson's poetic progress as an embodiment of the Zeitgeist or of the national faith, his own "development coinciding with, or sometimes anticipating, the spiritual movement of the age." This is not empty praise, for Tennyson clearly beats Burgon to that "precious method of Interpretation" mocked by the latter. The higher critical tendencies of his poetry, though, seem calculated to wean its contemporary readers from the two extremes of skepticism on the one hand and biblical inspirationism on the other. The textual problems detailed in "Merlin and Vivien" certainly urge against these two extremes. And Tennyson displays a higher critical approach to English myth in his very celebration of that myth's value. To the extent that his poem celebrates the national past, it encourages an analogous recuperation of the nation's biblical heritage.

To review the reception history of *The Idylls,* nonetheless, is to appreciate that the critique of inspirationism that Tennyson stages there was only half successful. After its initial excitement, *The Idylls* received the same deflated reaction that the New Revised Bible received, and seemingly for analogous reasons. Its readership was bewildered and deeply disappointed in its conspicuous lack of textual unity. Critics wanted from Tennnyson the kind of seamless legend that he depicts as impossible, and their hunger for textual authority may ultimately have diminished Tennyson's reputation at the close of his career. *The Idylls* remains, nonetheless, a literary achievement of immense proportions. And it remains very much the fruit of the poetic ambitions the fifteen-year-old Tennyson expressed in "Armageddon."

Finally, it is worth pointing out how much Tennyson's yoking of higher critical hermeneutics to a form of British nationalism fosters the idea, so hateful to Joseph Parker, that "the Bible is literature." It clearly offers its own poetic project as a quasi-religious endeavor. In "To the Queen," Tennyson speaks of his completed poem as "sacred" through its dedication to Prince Albert:

> . . . But thou, my Queen,
> Not for itself, but thro' thy living love
> For one to whom I made it o'er his grave
> Sacred, accept this old imperfect tale.
> (33–36)

Reading these lines from a higher critical perspective, it is hard not to suspect Tennyson of a degree of false modesty, in which Prince Albert conveniently appears to justify a sacred ambition that we find in Tennyson's earliest poetry. *The Idylls* may indeed be old and "imperfect," but Tennyson's poetry seems calculated to reconcile his readership to the fact that so is the Holy Bible itself, and that this imperfection cannot diminish its religious value.

Chapter 3

CLOUGH'S DEVIL IN THE DETAILS

T HE RADICAL ENGAGEMENT with Victorian biblical hermeneutics found in the poetry of Barrett Browning and Tennyson also animates the work of less frequently lionized mid-century poets—indeed, poets whose lack of contemporary lionizing caused this engagement to resonate quite differently. Arthur Hugh Clough (1819–1861) stands at the forefront of such poets because of the ways in which his eager engagement with the literary potential of the higher criticism both embraces and rigorously critiques the kinds of poetic gambits we have seen in the above chapters on Barrett Browning and Tennyson. The present chapter attempts to clarify the stakes of some of Clough's best-known work, including the Strauss-inspired lyrics "Epi-Strauss-ism" (ca. 1847, pub. 1862) and "Easter Day: Naples, 1849" (pub. 1865) and the epistolary romance *Amours de Voyage* (1849, pub. 1858). The bulk of my analysis, however, will be reserved for *Dipsychus and the Spirit* (ca. 1850–54, pub. 1865), a closet drama of religious crisis that presents Clough's culminating critique of the literary implications of the higher criticism. Here, I wish to show in particular how *Dipsychus* interrogates the Victorian association of the poetic and the scriptural.

The interest of *Dipsychus*'s relation to the Victorian Bible must accordingly be tied to the degree that nineteenth-century poets entertained the lofty poetic ambitions discussed in previous chapters. Still, Clough himself plainly took such ambition to be characteristic of the age. As his poet-hero puts it in *Dipsychus*, "Lo I am in the Spirit on the Lord's day / With John on Patmos" (2.4.99–100). It would be hard to overstate the implied religious ambition of such an exclamation in the Victorian mid-century. "In the Spirit on the Lord's day," of course, echoes the second verse of Revelation ("I was in the Spirit on the Lord's day, and I heard behind me a great voice, as of a trumpet"), where the verse introduces a very long passage of what has often been taken for God's personal dictation.[1] (Some versions of the King James even rubricate the ensuing pages.) What must not be lost is that Clough's speaker intends to compare himself not only to the biblical author of Revelation but also to Romantic poets like the Elizabeth Barrett of "Sounds" or the Wordsworth of *The Prelude* who writes of sacred and secular literatures alike "as Powers / For ever to be hallowed" (5.218–19).[2] The present chapter will return to the significance of this context; here it suffices to suggest that in such passages, *Dipsychus* flirts with the highest forms of vatic ambition familiar to readers of Romantic poetry, and is in this context evocative of Novalis's and Schleiermacher's proposition that new biblical texts might yet be written.

At the same time, *Dipsychus* gives voice to such sacred ambitions without pretending to achieve anything of the kind. Quite the contrary: the poem's structure as a closet drama facilitates a pointed critique of this type of poetic ambition and secures Clough from the grand posturing that can make a poem like *Aurora Leigh* or *The Idylls of the King* now seem peculiarly Victorian. For the poem presents a contest between the competing characters of its full title: a young Victorian sightseer in Italy and the unnamed, unwelcome, and apparently demonic Spirit who accompanies him. When Dipsychus earnestly preaches the Victorian cult of poetry with his "Lo I am in the Spirit, etc.," he does so only when prompted by his demonic alter ego, who then sneers at his pretensions. Thus, while the dialogue genuinely engages with the potential implications of the higher criticism for the English poetic tradition, yet it does not (and really cannot) presume upon that potential even in the ingenious and artful ways of Barrett Browning and Tennyson. Instead, its staged struggle between sacred ambition and profane mockery creates a very different—but equally important—critique of the repercussions of the higher criticism for Victorian poetry.

All of this makes *Dipsychus* a forbidding work: a tongue-in-cheek philosophical dialogue, a regular crisis-of-faith narrative, a Faustian verse-drama, and perhaps the age's most copious and explicit example of the sort of "dialogue of the mind with itself" that David G. Riede has described, with some justice, as the prevailing condition of nineteenth-century British poetry after Wordsworth.[3] Reide's formulation understates the case, even: *Dipsychus* portrays mental dialogue in much the way that Gustave Flaubert's *Temptation of Saint Anthony* (1857) portrays a desert father with insomnia. And Flaubert's more famous work affords a helpful reference point, since *Dipsychus* gives a similarly extensive treatment to "the conflict between the tender Conscience and the World" (as its epilogue puts it) and to the impact of modern biblical scholarship. Clough's post-Victorian enthusiasts often praise his caginess and uncanny modernity of style, and *Dipsychus* demonstrates these on Clough's largest scale.

The Crux of Clough's Biography: "Epi-Strauss-ism" and "Easter Day"

From the mid-Victorian period to the present day, Clough's biography has served as a case study in what Tennyson famously calls "honest doubt," a perspective that has tended to facilitate certain critical considerations of his poetry at the expense of others. Clough has been chiefly prized for giving a succinct and vivid expression to the shock of German biblical criticism as it came to be felt among the Victorians—a salient example of the belated mid-century reaction to Romantic hermeneutics discussed in my introduction (though, again, not one generally remarked upon for its belatedness). Additionally, Clough's personal religious crisis has always held a special luster for the biographically minded because of his early promise as a sort of literary golden boy for his generation. Clough demonstrated exceptional early promise at Thomas Arnold's Rugby School, and matriculated at Balliol College with high expectations, going on to become a fellow of Oriel. Arnold's influence kept Clough from more than a passing infatuation with John Henry Newman and the Tractarian Movement, but the jarring transition between Rugby and Oxford in the 1840s left him deeply uneasy about the state of contemporary Christianity. He appears to have been shaken by the implications of the higher criticism when he encountered it in George Eliot's translation of Strauss, and he eventually came to feel that he could no longer subscribe conscientiously to the Thirty-Nine Articles. In 1848 he resigned his Oxford fellowship in a symbolically resonant gesture (as Newman had before him, though for quite divergent reasons). He married Blanche Smith in 1854, and he died in 1861. Matthew Arnold's famous elegy, "Thyrsis" (1866), mourns him as a beloved friend and a casualty of his strife-filled age.[4] Nearly all of Clough's significant poetry was written during the period between his acquaintance with Strauss and his marriage.

In some ways, it worked out well for Clough's contemporary literary reputation that his most religiously controversial poetry was posthumously published. As it happened, "Epi-Strauss-ism," "Easter Day," and *Dipsychus* appeared only after the *Essays and Reviews* controversy and Darwin's *Origin of Species,* and this circumstance seems to have helped Clough's readers to appreciate the thrust of his art. After the publication of these Strauss-inspired poems in 1865, the American poet James Russell Lowell could maintain that it was Clough—and not Tennyson—who "will be thought a hundred years hence to have been the truest expression in verse of the moral and intellectual tendencies, the doubt and struggle towards settled convictions, of the period in which he lived."[5] Clough's poetry had always found an especially warm reception in America, but a surprising number of British reviewers would come to agree with Lowell's idea of Clough's symbolic value (if not always of his intrinsic poetic worth).[6] As even an antipathetic *Saturday Review* writer conceded in 1888, "A volume of poems by a dead man . . . does not go through eight editions in eleven years, half a generation after its author's life is closed, without corresponding to some definite, if passing, appetite, taste, disease, or whatever *libentius audit,* of the day and time."[7] Clough's significance as a poet thus increased as the century progressed, growing quickly in New England, and more gradually in Britain.[8] It is no coincidence that this period corresponds to what Charles Taylor calls "the rise of unbelief" in the nineteenth-century North Atlantic world (though Taylor, again, would caution against equating this with a decline in belief).

One unhappy corollary of Clough's posthumous adoption as a personification of Victorian religious conflict, however, is that his poetry has been chiefly read as a symptom of his religious uncertainty rather than as a deliberate exploration of its philosophical principles and possibilities. This remains a significant difficulty within Clough scholarship, exacerbated by the fact that estimates of his poetic worth have varied so widely.[9] Romantic and post-Romantic poetry always solicits autobiographical readings, just as poets have always hedged against it: Browning once prefaced *Pauline,* tautologically, as an attempt to create "so many utterances of so many imaginary persons, not mine."[10] But Clough was dead by the time his poetry required such a public defense as Browning's, and the ensuing half-century of Victorian criticism may be summed up in Charles Whibley's pronouncement that Clough "could make no just separation of the man and poet. He did but attempt to teach in song what he learned in suffering. . . . Instead of a great poet, he became, so to say, the mouthpiece of his own doubting age."[11] According to Whibley, readers are right to conflate Clough and his poetry because it is the record of his interior life.

Strictly autobiographical readings of Clough remain problematic to the extent that they can occlude our sense for how Clough used his poetry as a forum for clarifying his ideas.[12] While Clough's life certainly sheds light on his art, his poetic experiments actually seem to have led him to his eventual stance of religious skepticism, rather than vice versa. My previous chapter shows how Tennyson seized upon poetry as a means of redeeming the Christian scriptures from both Strauss and Strauss's most vocal British critics by presenting analogous sets of sacred histories and potentially inspired texts. Clough entertains similar ideas, but for him the critique of the higher criticism finally seems to encompass all of Victorian bibliolatry, including the kind implicitly recommended by Tennyson. To this extent, Clough's poetry represents less an emotional history of the higher criticism (as it has generally been taken) than a philosophical inquiry into its implications for English poetry. It debates not just the doubtful nature of biblical history but the doubtful nature of secular history as well. And it interrogates not just the composition of the biblical canon but the composition of analogous canons, such as the tradition of English poetry. Here, Clough presciently and powerfully anticipates some of the most egregious excesses of Victorian bibliolatry more generally, such as those of his dear friend Matthew Arnold in "The Study of Poetry" and elsewhere (see Introduction, section 3).

The poems most often cited as expressions of Clough's apostate "suffering" (as Whibley would have it), "Epi-Strauss-ism" and "Easter Day: Naples, 1849," actually provide the clearest evidence that Clough's poetry develops a deliberate intellectual project to realize the implications of the higher criticism. "Epi-Strauss-ism" may present the mid-century's plainest introduction to the impact of Strauss's *Leben Jesu* on its British readers in the 1840s.

"EPI-STRAUSS-ISM"

Matthew and Mark and Luke and holy John
Evanished all and gone!
Yea, He that erst, his dusky Curtains quitting,
Through Eastern pictured panes his level beams transmitting,
With gorgeous portraits blent,
On them his glories intercepted spent,
Southwestering now, through windows plainly glassed
On the inside face his radiance keen hath cast;
And in the lustre lost, invisible and gone,
Are, say you? Matthew, Mark, and Luke and holy John.
Lost, is it? lost, to be recovered never?
However,
The Place of Worship the meantime with light

> Is, if less richly, more sincerely bright,
> And in blue skies the Orb is manifest to sight.[13]

This poem presents a rich starting point for any evaluation of Clough's higher critical poetry because while it plainly rewards Whibley's effusive or "suffering" model of interpretation, yet it also shows how, from the beginning, Clough was searching for ways to reconcile the higher criticism with his culture's religious heritage. The heavily marked conjunctions ("and . . . and . . . and") in the opening couplet, for instance, register everything from aghast befuddlement to wry bemusement. The labored pentameter of the poem's earliest line becomes clipped in the trimeter of "Evanished all and gone"—an embodiment of how abruptly the intellectual habits of Christian poetry are interrupted by this news.[14] But its belabored conjunction also nods to scriptural parataxis ("And in the lustre lost . . .") and bears witness that although the Evangelists may vanish as reliable sources of history, they do not correspondingly vanish as sources of rhetorical example. Likewise the broken meter, signifying the disappearance of the Evangelists, also gives way, intermittently but finally, to a hexameter that both doubles the numbers of these bereaved trimeters and unexpectedly fills them with the promise of a new sun: "And in blue skies the Orb is manifest to sight." Although Clough's poem records the confusion and chagrin of mid-century believers, then, it also seeks to surprise readers with an argument that Christian theology need not be contingent upon the conventional, plodding impulses that the poem endeavors to sustain in the first, middle, and penultimate lines. Newer, unexpected rhythms correspond to the poem's unexpected proposal that "the inside face" of the Christian "Place of Worship" might be more brightly illuminated without recourse to the Gospels. Perhaps, the poem would suggest, Christian theology is important whether the Gospels were historical or not; the poem's final quatrain goes so far as to anticipate a further revelation that will outshine its former sources in scripture.

There is reason to believe that Clough found consolation in this idea. As he wrote to his sister, Anne,

> I cannot feel sure that a man may not have all that is important in Christianity even if he does not so much as know that Jesus of Nazareth existed. And I do not think that doubts respecting the facts related in the Gospels need give us much trouble. Believing that in one way or the other the thing is of God, we shall in the end know, perhaps, in what way and how far it was so.

> Trust in God's justice and love, and belief in His commands as written in our conscience, stand unshaken, though Matthew, Mark, Luke, and John, or even St. Paul, were to fall.[15]

It is unclear whether this letter was written before or after "Epi-Strauss-ism," so here we do not know whether the poem revises the ideas of the letter, or vice versa. What seems sure is that Clough's reference to "doubts respecting the facts related in the Gospels" refers most immediately to Strauss. Strauss's predecessors in the tradition of Eichhorn had largely restricted their historical method to the Hebrew scriptures, partly because historical inquiry into that earlier canon seemed less threatening to Christian belief.[16] Therefore, Clough's appeal to God's "commands as written in our conscience"—rather than, say, the Gospels—reflects his readiness to follow Strauss not just to a different view of scripture, but to a whole new set of scriptures.[17]

"Epi-Strauss-ism" is thus both expressive and argumentative, and built upon a delicate balance between orthodox rhetoric and heterodox religious ideas. It would be a mistake to view this balance as an attempt to redeem the Gospels from Strauss, for it rehearses and celebrates Strauss's own expressed wish that his *Life of Jesus* would be used to promote a new model of Christian dogma. As Strauss wrote in the conclusion of that work:

> In proportion as he is distinguished from the naturalistic theologian, and the free-thinker,—in proportion as his criticism is conceived in the spirit of the nineteenth century,—he is filled with veneration for every religion, and especially for the substance of the sublimest of all religions, the Christian, which he perceives to be identical with the deepest philosophical truth; and hence, after having in the course of his criticism exhibited only the differences between his conviction and the historical belief of the Christian, he will feel urged to place that identity in a just light.[18]

Here, Strauss distinguishes his work from that of natural theologians (who offered what he saw as inadequate defenses of Christian dogma) and free-thinkers (who rejected it altogether). Far from dismissing Christian belief, as the deists had, Strauss's *Life* proposes its radical reformulation.[19] "Epi-Strauss-ism" moreover represents the text more faithfully than do many mid-century British accounts (discussed above in chapter 1). Clough's trope of an afternoon sun progressing westward from the stained glass windows of a church's nave to the "plainly glassed" windows of its body takes up Strauss's expressed hope that Christians would learn to view the beauties of the Christian religion in broader context than that provided by the Gospels, and it couches this transition in Protestant symbolism, as the light passes from an implicitly Gothic or Anglo-Catholic stained glass pane to a plainer, "more sincere," transparent one.[20] Even Clough's sunlight metaphor seems to come from Strauss: the bright rays streaming through the new windows are what will allow the new Christian theologian, as Strauss put it, "to place that identity in a just light."

"Easter Day: Naples, 1849" provides the skeptical side of "Epi-Strauss-ism." Strauss's argument that the Christian scriptures were not materially different from other mythological records may be compatible with a general theism, but it jars with the Bible's own apparent position that Christianity depends upon the historical truth of Christ's Resurrection. "Easter Day" gives voice to this discord:

> Through the great sinful streets of Naples as I past,
>> With fiercer heat than flamed above my head
> My heart was hot within me; till at last
>> My brain was lightened when my tongue had said—
>>> Christ is not risen!
>
> (1–5)

Here the sun of "Epi-Strauss-ism" reappears, stripped of its theological references. Yet these symbolic resonances remain provocatively intact, for now the lines present a risen sun whose former association with Christ has turned ironic. Here both sun and Son are part of the natural world, but unlike the sun (and as the meter beats home), "Chríst is nót rísen!"

Strauss's chief contribution to "Easter Day" lies not in its implicit materialism, but rather in its proposition that the idea of the Resurrection was natural to the culture of first-century Palestine and that it should not be attributed to any willful misrepresentation of the facts of Jesus's natural life. Clough compares the original notion of the Resurrection to a rumor circulating in a vast city:

> As circulates in some great city crowd
> A rumour changeful, vague, importunate, and loud,
> From no determined centre, or of fact
>> Or authorship exact,

> Which no man can deny
>> Nor verify;
> So spread the wondrous fame;
>> He all the same
> Lay senseless, mouldering, low:
> He was not risen, no—
>> Christ was not risen!

(48–58)

This is a Straussian model for the Resurrection: not only does the "rumour" come "from no determined centre," but it grows up spontaneously. As Clough summarizes this point in his posthumously published essay "Notes on the Religious Tradition" (ca. 1853, pub. 1869), "It is conceivable that religious truths of the highest import may grow up naturally, and appear before us involved in uncertain traditions, with every sort of mere accessory legend and story attached to them and entangled with them."[21] Here, as Strauss had argued, religious myth contains "truths of the highest import," but truths that cannot be disentangled from the fantastic mythological cultural climate that originally perpetuated them. Interestingly, the most obvious departure from Strauss in "Easter Day" lies in its very materialism—in its stance that Christ "all the same / Lay senseless, mouldering, low." Strauss was vilified by the Victorian presses for doubting the Resurrection, but *Das Leben Jesu* scrupulously and deliberately eschews any position on what happened "all the same": on the contrary, Strauss's whole point is that from such ancient records as the Gospels no historical facts can be reliably distinguished from mythological "poetry."

Victorian critics, predictably, viewed "Easter Day" as a personal expression of Clough's religious crisis, and many subsequent readers have followed this lead.[22] This can be a perversely reductive approach to the poem, however, as is evidenced by the fact that they applied the same hermeneutic to an untitled fragment that Clough intended as a counterpart to "Easter Day" and that his widow Blanche had entitled "Easter Day II":

> So in the southern city spake the tongue
> Of one that somewhat overwildly sung,
> But in a later hour I sat and heard
> Another voice that spake—another graver word.
> Weep not, it bade, whatever hath been said,

Though He be dead, He is not dead.
>In the true creed
>He is yet risen indeed;
>>Christ is yet risen.

(13–21)

. . . .

In the great Gospel and true Creed,
He is yet risen indeed;
>Christ is yet risen.

(49–51)

This corresponding lyric, as we see, reconsiders the propositions of "Easter Day" to promote something akin to Schleiermacher's idea that religious truth is contingent upon the faith of believers, rather than the occurrences of history. Victorian periodicals like *Macmillan's Magazine* took it for a definitive correction of the first poem, and happily seized upon this "second 'Easter Day,' the burden of which is that Christ *has* risen! As joy and grief intermingle in life, and yet, on the whole, joy conquers grief, so belief and unbelief will mingle, but finally faith is conqueror" (101). Indeed, religiously conservative Victorian reviewers expressed a surprising amount of enthusiasm for Clough as the years wore on. The *Homiletic Review,* the *Free Review,* the *Wesleyan Methodist Magazine,* and the *Primitive Methodist Quarterly Review* all recommend Clough as an earnest seeker of religious truth.[23] The *Contemporary Review,* in a delicious irony, goes so far as to affirm Clough's orthodoxy by appealing to that highest of English religious authorities, William Shakespeare: "Of the essential necessity of faith and of the simple majesty of the Christian hope [Clough] had, as his 'Easter Day' shows, no doubt. Had he lived as long as Shakespeare he would have come to the untroubled outlook on religion of that greatest of poets."[24] Whether Clough's "outlook on religion" runs parallel to Shakespeare's can hardly be answered without undue conjecture about Shakespeare's own outlook. But the *Contemporary Review* commits itself to an extraordinary leap of faith on the issue—faith in the cult of Victorian bardolatry.[25]

Many twentieth-century critics, by contrast, have viewed "Easter Day II" as a feeble apology for the apostasy of the earlier poem; this view, like the Victorian religious view, reflexively and somewhat naively endeavors to extrapolate Clough's "real" views from his poetic ones. "Easter Day" and "Easter Day II" are clearly intended to experiment with different ways of seeing the traditions of Strauss and Schleiermacher, and it is not accidental that they were so often read by the Victorians as mutually exclusive. But if the lyrics are indeed intended to contradict one another, then they must be viewed in tandem. The paired poems, in this way, resemble the two voices of Søren Kierkegaard's *Either/Or* (1843): selecting either of these as the "real" voice of Kierkegaard does violence to the logic of the work. Or, to turn for analogues from Victorian-era texts to recent Victorianist scholarship, we sometimes see studies like those of Isobel Armstrong or Jerome McGann experimenting with opposing voices: this technique (here as in Clough) permits a dialectic to evolve between incompatible positions.[26] What it does not permit is for any of these various positions to be taken, *tout court,* as that of the author.

Just as the championing of Clough as a religious poet by conservative Victorian reviewers relies upon a dubiously effusive model of poetry, then, so does his alternate championing as a Feuerbachian agnostic or closet atheist by unreligious or heterodox admirers. Consider the case of John Addington Symonds, who with Blanche Clough would edit the 1869 *Poems and Prose Remains.*[27] In 1866 Symonds shared with Blanche that his set of university men, dissatisfied with official Oxbridge theology, "look on Mr. Clough's poems as the expression of their deepest convictions and see[k] in him a mirror of themselves."[28] Symonds's published writings cast Clough as the sort of religious reformer that Clough's friend Arnold would really endeavor to become with *Literature and Dogma* and *God and the Bible:*

> The chief value of Clough's religious poetry appears to consist in this—that he sympathised at a very early period with the movement that is unquestionably going on towards the simplification and purification of belief, and that he gave an artistic expression to the thoughts of earnest seekers and questioners in the field of faith. In doing so he did not innovate, or ruthlessly destroy, or sentimentally bewail the past. He simply tried to reduce belief to its original and spiritual purity—to lead men back to the God that is within them, witnessed by their consciences and by the history of the human race.[29]

For Symonds, Clough's poetry purifies religion by returning it to God via the individual believer's conscience. (Symonds skirts the Feuerbachian question of whether God creates the conscience or vice versa.) And yet Clough's writings, by contrast, interrogate the very conceptual basis of Symonds's appeal to "consciences and . . . the history of the human race." Granted, his early letter to Anne Clough does appeal to God's "commands as written in our conscience," but his subsequent poetry and academic writings come to critique this idea of conscience as a reliable basis for judgment or of history as a reliable source of knowledge. Some of these writings Symonds himself first urged Blanche Clough to publish.[30]

The "Notes on the Religious Tradition," for instance, begins by repudiating the sort of history that Symonds takes for granted in the claim that Clough's readers find God "witnessed . . . by the history of the human race":

> It is impossible for any scholar to have read, and studied, and reflected without forming a strong impression of the entire uncertainty of history in general, and of the history of Christianity in particular.
>
> It is equally impossible for any man to live, act, and reflect without feeling the significance and depth of the moral and religious teaching which passes amongst us by the name of Christianity.
>
> The more a man feels the value, the true import of this, the more he will hesitate to base it upon those foundations which as a scholar he feels to be unstable. Manuscripts are doubtful, records may be unauthentic, criticism is feeble, historical facts must be left uncertain.
>
> (415)

The first and third of these paragraphs run toward a more skeptical higher critical position than Symonds himself imagines. Clough confronts the material limits of historical researches—"manuscripts are doubtful, records may be unauthentic, criticism is feeble"—and concludes from these that history, Christian history in particular, is "entirely uncertain." Whether Clough intends "in particular" to mean that the Christian scriptures are exceptionally dubious or merely a particular instance of a general condition, he remains skeptical about the possibility of attaining an "original and spiritual purity" of the religion that they contain.[31] Although the scriptures propagate "the significance and depth of the moral and religious teaching which passes amongst us by the name of Christianity," yet their particular truths resist any kind of appeal to origins. They cannot be returned to an original "purity" because their mythological basis provides no assured original. They come, as "Easter Day" describes, "From no determined centre, or of fact, / Or authorship exact, / Which no man can deny / Nor verify."

Still more important, the "Notes" then goes on to protest that "conscience" could not be relied upon to recognize an "original and spiritual purity" even if one were to exist. Symonds, like Arnold, affirms the value of the conscience as a "witness" (at least the conscience of the cultivated individual). By contrast, Clough proceeds directly from the practical limitations of biblical manuscripts to the fact that his own judgment cannot be held more reliable than the texts themselves: "Even in like manner my own personal experience is most limited, perhaps even most delusive: what have I seen, what do I know? Nor is my personal judgment a thing which I feel any great satisfaction in trusting. My reasoning powers are weak; my memory doubtful and confused; my conscience, it may be, callous or vitiated" (415). For Clough, eventually, religion's presumed relationship with conscience creates more philosophical problems than it solves. As we will see from *Dipsychus,* this, too, is a conclusion that Clough develops in his poetry before he articulates it in the "Notes." Symonds's Arnoldian model for Clough's poetry, like the *Primitive Methodist Quarterly*'s religious model or the *Contemporary Review*'s bardolatrous model, risks obscuring the intellectual work done by the poetry itself.

From a Doubtful History to a Doubtful Conscience: Amours de Voyage

To question the limitations of the effusive model of poetry so widely applied to Clough is not to question the truth that, on some level, poems mean what their contemporaries take them to mean: it is to press the alternative truth that they cannot be reduced to that interpretation, and to wonder whether Clough's warmest admirers did his poetry a disservice when they argued so successfully that Clough's verse gave artistic shape to his radical thinking, instead of generating those radical ideas in the first place. As Clough's American friend Charles Eliot Norton emphatically put this in the *North American Review,* "Verse with him is never the source, but the mere instrument, of inspiration."[32] Norton plainly anticipates Symonds's assumption that Clough's poetry "gave an artistic expression to the thoughts" articulated in his prose. The internal evidence of Clough's oeuvre, however, suggests just the contrary to be the case: rather, the experimentation of Clough's poetry itself seems to bring him to the position he attempts to summarize in the "Notes."

Clough's poetic experiments usually ended up driving his theology, that is, rather than vice versa. Isobel Armstrong, for instance, has shown *The Bothie* (1848) to be a sly political critique of the Oxford Movement, yet Clough's own letters attest that it was born of a metrical experiment.[33] As he wrote to Ralph Waldo Emerson in 1849, "Will you convey to Mr. Longfellow the fact that it was a reading of his Evangeline aloud to my Mother and sister which, coming after a reperusal of the Iliad, occasioned this outbreak of hexameters. Evangeline is very popular here" (*Correspondence* 240). Such protests do not seem to have been arch or disingenuous. We know similarly that early drafts of *Amours de Voyage* (1849, pub. 1858), a comic masterpiece, were born as a metrical experiment and entitled, simply, *Roman Elegiacs and Roman Hexameters April to July 1849.*[34] Like *The Bothie,* this poem seems an immediate product not so much of the Oxford Movement as of what George Saintsbury would later call "the hexameter mania in the middle of the century."[35] Unquestionably, its title suggests Clough's enthusiasm for metrical experiment far more obviously than it does his need for religious expression or—as Norton would have it—his "inspiration." But mechanical experiment itself here becomes an exploration of higher critical principles.

Roman Elegiacs and Roman Hexameters/Amours de Voyage serves as an important transition between "Easter Day" and *Dipsychus.* Unlike the other poems treated here, *Amours de Voyage* does not explicitly address the higher criticism. Nonetheless, the poem's protagonist, Claude, tours Italy at the time of the Roman revolution of 1848, and (in a way that clearly anticipates *Dipsychus*) he engages in a series of epistolary meditations about "the entire uncertainty of history" that will form a central part of Clough's perspective on religion. At one instance, Claude bears personal witness to a scene of mob violence, but upon subsequent reflection about exactly what takes place, he finds he must demur: "History, Rumour of Rumours, I leave it to thee to determine" (2.209). The scene, and its demurral, stand in for broader questions: if Roman history of the mid-nineteenth century is uncertain, surely first-century Roman Palestine must remain shrouded in mystery.

The Victorian hexameter mania itself speaks to a desire for concreteness that the circumstances of mid-century revolution cannot evidently afford. "Classical" English hexameters were alluring to so many of their Victorian practitioners because of their association with the poetic objectivity somehow imagined in Greco-Roman culture and idealized in the tradition of Homer. (Matthew Arnold's *Lectures on Translating Homer* presents the most salient example of this idealization; Arnold repeats Clough's epigraph to *Amours,* "*Solvitur ambulando,*" as an encouragement to those who doubted that true Homeric hexameters could be written in English.[36]) The importance to the Victorians of what Clough calls the "Roman hexameter" can also be reconstructed from the beginning of Ovid's *Amores,* which itself thematizes the difficulty of epic history:

Arma gravi numero violentaque bella parabam
    edere, materia conveniente modis;
par erat inferior versus: risissc Cupido
    dicitur atque unum surripuisse pedem.

(Arms, and the violent deeds of war, I was making ready to sound forth—in
weighty numbers, with matter suited to the measure. The second verse was
equal to the first, but Cupid, they say, with a laugh stole away one foot.)[37]

As Ovid relates, elegiac couplets—hexameters with alternating pentame-
ters—fall a foot short of the weighty numbers required to sing of "violent
deeds of war." Were he not Love's victim, Ovid implies, the *Amores* would
boast the hexameters required to compete with Virgil's *Aeneid,* and would
then be a more serious poem.

    Clough's chief inquiry in *Amours de Voyage* likewise concerns the rela-
tionship between matter and measure presupposed by Ovid. For this reason,
an omniscient third-person narrator frames Claude's love journey in elegant
elegiac couplets. But Clough's hero himself writes most of the poem in an
awkward dactylic hexameter. In a resonant gesture, he turns to the classical
tradition to provide for himself an aesthetic replacement for his uncertainty
in matters of history, culture, and religious devotion. Yet Claude's "weighty
numbers" disappoint him; they do not of themselves provide what Ovid calls
"matter suited to the measure." On the contrary, the very absence of this
objective, epic self, promised by his meter, seems to drive Claude to further reflections on the uncertainty of his views. He describes his founder-
ing conscience as just the unreliable moral authority that Arnold found so
distasteful in Romantic poetry and that Clough himself would later describe
in the "Notes":

What with trusting myself and seeking support from within me,
Almost I could believe I had gained a religious assurance,
Found in my own poor soul a great moral basis to rest on.
Ah, but indeed I see, I feel it factitious entirely;
I refuse, reject, and put it utterly from me;
I will look straight out, see things, not try to evade them:
Fact shall be fact for me; and the Truth the Truth as ever,
Flexible, changeable, vague, and multiform and doubtful[.]
(5.95–102)

Claude grants the existence of "Truth" with a capital "T," but finds it "ever" uncertain, various, and changing. More crucially, he denies that he can intuit "in [his] own poor soul a great moral basis to rest on" (à la Carlyle's *Sartor Resartus,* for instance). His conclusions run all the other way: he continues to mistrust his soul's assurances intellectually ("I see") and emotionally ("I feel it factitious entirely"). The ponderous meter here brings out the halting manner of this thinking. A reader too will "see" and "feel" the comic effect of Claude's excessive conjunctions after the caesura in a dactylic line like "Flexible, changeable, vague, || and multiform and doubtful." Claude's "poor soul," far from obtaining a direct conduit to an unchanging "Truth," instead seems doomed to go on fashioning his own ad hoc self-assurances.

The very *factitiousness* of conscience expressed here will prove important to Clough's artistic and religious thinking. In *Dipsychus*, it comes to occupy a central place. For if conscience and moral sense are factitious, as this passage suggests, then they are surely also constituted (or at least informed) by the varied experience of art and culture. Clough's literary training taught him to find aesthetic excellence chiefly in the classics, while his religious training taught him to find a "great moral basis" chiefly in the Bible. In the wake of the higher criticism, his poetry suggests that such a moral self was not the inevitable result of either, but that it must be cobbled together from whatever cultural material lay to hand. Among other places, Claude finds it by chance in an English psalm tune that he heard played in the streets of Rome:

> Moping along the streets, and cursing my day, as I wandered,
> All of a sudden my ear met the sound of an English psalm tune.
> Comfort me it did, till indeed I was very near crying.
> Ah there is some great truth, partial very likely, but needful,
> Lodged, I am strangely sure, in the tones of the English psalm tune.
> (5.88–92)

Here we have the clearest expression prior to *Dipsychus* of Clough's idea that "religious truths of the highest import" might be found in English artistic traditions. It is explicitly not the sentiment or the syntax of the "English psalm tune" that leads Claude (in Symonds's words) "back to the God that is within" him: it is "the sound" or "the tones" of that psalm tune. In such passages, art literally informs religion because the latter depends upon the affective experience that art is designed to evoke. Claude expressly avoids calling this power universal (on the contrary, it is always "English"), even though the most popular "English psalm tunes" of his day were those celebrating God's universal power.[38] What is most striking about this "great truth," then, is that it is not even located in the words of the psalm, but in the familiar tune to which that psalm has been set. Divine inspiration is not located in a proposition, but in an expression.

Tellingly, Clough's evolving idea of the inspiration of modern European literary traditions also corresponds to Strauss's own evolving ideas: eventually, Strauss too would come to declare his native poetic tradition as inspired as biblical literature. As he writes in *The Old Faith and the New*, "Let it not be deemed that Lessing's *Nathan*, or Goethe's *Hermann and Dorothea*, are more difficult of comprehension, and contain fewer 'saving truths' than an epistle of Paul, or a discourse of Christ, as reported by John."[39] Strauss goes further than Clough's poor Claude. Rather than identifying the "great truths" of German poetry as "partial, very likely, but needful," Strauss proffers them as equal to the Bible's own truths and greatly more accessible. A few pages further, Strauss goes so far as to claim Lessing's *Nathan* as the Bible of post-Christian German humanism: "As every religion has its traditionally sacred books, thus the sacred book of the religion of humanity and morality which we profess, is no other than the *Nathan* of Lessing."[40]

Until *Dipsychus*, Clough seems to have viewed great secular works of literature as lesser companions to the Bible, instead of genuine replacements for it. Yet he anticipates clearly Strauss's idea that secular works are similarly inspired. As early as 1849, Clough was writing his more orthodox friend John Campbell Shairp, "Go to the Bible, thou prude, consider its language, and be wise. Consult also Shakespeare, Milton, Dante also, . . and in fact 'all great poets'" (*Correspondence* 245). At the same time, Claude's expressed enthusiasm for the hymn in *Amours de Voyage* is in some ways more radical than Strauss's Romantic humanism, for Strauss finds "saving truths" in his Romantic heroes Lessing and Goethe, but Claude goes so far as to find them in a popular evangelical (and, by extension, lowbrow) genre. This tension between vernacular classics and popular art will become an important element of *Dipsychus*.

Clough's "Notes on the Religious Tradition" ends with an appeal to the saving lights of literature: "I see not what other alternative any sane and humble-minded man can have but to throw himself upon the great religious tradition" (415), but he there goes on to define that tradition in a startlingly broad way. He looks not only to (by then predictable) non-Western wisdom literature like "the Bhagvad Gita and the laws of Menu; to Persia and Hafiz;

to China and Confucius; to the Vedas and the Shasters; the Koran," and not only to classical literature like "Homer; to Socrates and Plato; to Lucretius, to Virgil, to Tacitus." He extends it as far as to eighteenth-century essayists, analytic philosophers, and theologians: "I will go to Johnson; I will go to Hume, as well as to Bishop Butler" (418). Later in the century, Benjamin Jowett credited Clough with coining the epithet "Broad Church" to describe mid-century figures such as Thomas Arnold, F. D. Maurice, and Jowett himself, whose liberal theological sympathies ran against both High Church and Low. But even "Broad Church" is too narrow a description for Clough's religious thinking, which insisted that each age must create its own set of scriptures. "Every rule of conduct, every maxim, every usage of life and society, must be admitted," Clough instructed in the "Notes," "like Ecclesiastes of old in the Old Testament, so in each new age to each new age's Bible" (418). Through *Dipsychus*, Clough comes to this broadest of positions about the category of redemptive literature.

Dipsychus: The Faust Legend and the Tender Conscience

Victorian critics committed to the religiously effusive model of Clough criticism often celebrate *Dipsychus* as Clough's greatest achievement: a Faustian drama enacted between an idealistic, sensitive young man whose meditations on the higher criticism lead to his temptation (Dipsychus), and the devil who tempts him (the Spirit).[41] To some extent, this structure even prohibits a reader from cleanly distinguishing between the character and author, as when Dipsychus recites Clough's lyrics as poetry that he (Dipsychus) has written. Nonetheless, as with the two voices of "Easter Day" and "Easter Day II," to take Dipsychus as Clough's self-portrait *tout court* is to ignore the fundamentally divided nature of *Dipsychus* and on some level to miss the aim of the dialogue. The title character's name derives from the Epistle of James, a text that condemns a "double-minded man" ("dipsychos" in the Greek original) as "unstable in all his ways" (James 1:8 KJV), and those familiar with this biblical context can appreciate how it sets conventional literary expressions of Victorian Christianity at odds. (For instance, James was the favorite epistle of the Chartists and Victorian Christian Socialists, who often used it to argue that the established Church had lost touch with scriptures of social justice.[42]) Far more insistently than *Amours de Voyage*, *Dipsychus* demands to know what happens when a person's moral grounding is cut off from traditions of textual authority and whether that authority can be supplemented by Shakespeare, Milton, and the "all great poets" recommended in the letter to Shairp.

As is typical of Faustian drama, the poem's opening scene presents an act of diabolical conjuring, the remainder of the work a struggle for the conjuror's soul.[43] Usually, of course, Faustus is seduced with the promise of arcane knowledge and unbridled supernatural power. Clough's hero is less demanding. His hyper-refined moral fastidiousness makes even conventional sin seem enticingly exotic, and his personal demon tempts him with promises of gainful employment, a stable middle-class income, modest personal amusement, and (mostly marital) sex. The effect of this inversion is important: instead of providing the moral lesson of a wicked, terrible Faustus, *Dipsychus* provides that of an excessively good one who loses his soul for things that most of his social peers enjoyed unreservedly. Readers are meant to sympathize partly with the Spirit, especially readers living the sort of lifestyle to which Dipsychus finally succumbs. And lest such readers be "of the Devil's party without knowing it," Clough added a prologue and an epilogue in which the poet explains his symbolic schema to a doubtful uncle:

> "But, sir," said I, "perhaps he wasn't a devil after all. That's the beauty of the poem; nobody can say. You see, dear sir, the thing which it is attempted to represent is the conflict between the tender Conscience and the World—now the over-tender conscience will of course exaggerate the wickedness of the world, and the Spirit in my poem may be merely the hypothesis or subjective imagination, formed—"
>
> "Oh for goodness' sake, my dear boy," interrupted my uncle, "don't go into the theory of it."
>
> (Epilogue, 12–20)

Clough's poem thus presents the unraveling of the type of strenuous moral education that he had received first at Rugby and then at Oxford. But this is not to suggest that Dipsychus's fastidious scruples are ever actually dismissed. On the contrary, the logic of Faustian drama only reinforces them, and as the epilogue accurately reports of itself, "That's the beauty of the poem."

Most versions of this legend also present a Faustus who actually means to conjure a demon in the first place. By contrast, Dipsychus's Spirit is the child of his hypersensitive conscience, and requires no further summons than the doctrinal vacillation so often represented in Clough's poetry. The poem is set in Venice, where Dipsychus has joined the usual ranks of English tourists for the Feast of the Assumption, and the drama begins when he calls to mind the verses that he wrote in Naples on the similar occasion of "Easter Day": "My heart was hot within; the fire burnt; and at last / My brain was lightened when my tongue had said / Christ is not risen" (1.1.24–26). As in the first instance, these lines present a judgment on the poem's setting as much as a theological argument. As Symonds records of their reappearance, "The Resurrection, in any real and modern sense of the word, is just as inconceivable at Venice as at Naples."[44] To Dipsychus's prudish eyes (as to Ruskin's before him), the festival crowd before St. Mark's appears scandalously oblivious to the religious doctrines that comprise their Christian holiday. A true believer should know better than to engage in such revelry, and Dipsychus is forced to conclude that the Venetians lack religious feeling. For them, evidently, "Christ is not risen." The line, though, also gives voice to a skeptical view of the Resurrection and perhaps suggests the shakiness of the very moral foundation from which Dipsychus stands in judgment.

The blasphemy of "Easter Day" produces Dipsychus's Spirit, who assumes—literally—the role of Devil's advocate, and who defends the frolicking Venetians with a wry and unperturbed religious commentary:

> Nay.
> Twas well enough once in a way.
> Having once done it, as we know,
> Some eighteen hundred years ago
> How should he now at Venice here?
> Where people true enough appear
> To appreciate more and understand
> Their ices and their Austrian band
> And dark-eyed girls than what occurred
> So long ago to the Eternal Word;
> Look at them there[.]
> (1.1.36–46)

The two characters' relationship takes off from here. Intertextually, we see, *Dipsychus* begins as a quirky philosophical dialogue in the manner of Nicolas de Malebranche (1638–1715).[45] The difference between *Dipsychus* and Malebranchian dialogue, however, is that Dipsychus's interlocutor concedes in advance all theological arguments (the Venetians seem *not* to appreciate "what occurred / So long ago to the Eternal Word") so as to commend the worldly pleasures condemned by his debate partner: "their ices and their Austrian band / And dark-eyed girls."

It is also significant that Dipsychus summons the Spirit by recalling the "Easter Day" refrain—"Christ is not risen"—because the Spirit's summons is a generically precise element of poetic tradition. The trope derives most prominently from Marlowe's *Tragical History of Doctor Faustus* (1604), in which Mephistopheles appears as soon as Faustus renounces Christ. As Marlowe's demon delineates the generic rules of this tradition,

> *MEPH:* For when we hear one rack the name of God,
> Abjure the Scriptures and his saviour Christ,
> We fly in hope to get his glorious soul,
> Nor will we come, unless he use such means
> Whereby he is in danger to be damned:
> Therefore the shortest cut for conjuring
> Is stoutly to abjure the Trinity[.][46]

In this regard *Dipsychus* strictly follows the generic mold.[47] This attention to genre in *Dipsychus* is worth noting because most modern readers of the poem tend to assume that Dipsychus's personal struggle with the Spirit derives from sheer sexual anxiety—that his sexual repression creates his religious frustration, rather than vice versa. John Maynard represents this position when he posits that the Spirit is a direct expression of the poet's "unfulfilled sexual nature": "The ideas so dramatically present in the poem range over philosophy, religion, views of society and of the individual. They center, however, in Dipsychus' unresolved sexual dilemma, which provides the situation for much of the dialogue (looking over the Venetian girls) and the motivation for bringing in related issues."[48] In such readings as Maynard's, the poet's sex drive operates as a sort of hydraulic system to force out his metaphysical commentary. This amounts to a twist on the effusive model, except that now the pressure is sexual instead of religious. Plainly, though, the poem cleaves to literary tradition: the Spirit requires a blasphemous summons before he can turn Dipsychus's attention to the sexual issues that will feature in their later discussions. And sex is by no means the only moral question to preoccupy Dipsychus, who also worries a good deal about violence, sloth, social justice, and the difficulty of choosing an honorable profession. (By contrast with

Maynard, for instance, Symonds locates the struggle between "the spiritual and natural" parts of Dipsychus first in religious doubt and later in his deliberations about whether to fight with an Austrian military officer [607–9].)

From sexual continence to personal honor, such scruples as Dipsychus expresses throughout the drama are so often lampooned as quintessentially Victorian that it is worth remembering how much Clough's verse anticipates sharp twentieth-century parodies of Victorian mores. In the Epilogue, for instance, when the poet's uncle complains about Dipsychus's excessive virtue, the poet rejoins with a wry account of Victorian religious sentiment, especially as expressed in the preaching of Oxford's Newman (though the text refrains from actually naming him directly): "The real cause of the evil you complain of, which to a certain extent I admit, was, I take it, the religious movement of the last century, beginning with Wesleyanism, and culminating at last in Puseyism—This overexcitation of the religious sense, resulting in this irrational almost animal irritability of conscience was in many ways as foreign to Arnold as it is proper to . . ." (83–89). What is most surprising and insightful about this broad characterization of the Victorian religious experience is not its vivid description of the "irrational almost animal irritability of conscience"; rather, it is its depiction of the Oxford Movement (here "Puseyism") as a natural growth of the Evangelical revival. To its contemporaries, Tractarianism usually seemed to militate against Evangelical enthusiasm: one might think of the animosity between Dr. Arabin and Mr. Slope in Trollope's *Barchester Towers*. Nonetheless, by depicting the Oxford Movement as the end result of "Wesleyanism," Clough can encompass the whole nineteenth-century religious conscience as the product of a single, Evangelical hermeneutic. And, in Clough's view, the higher criticism made that Evangelical hermeneutic (in all its forms) extremely vulnerable. "The thing which men must work at will not be critical questions about the Scriptures," he wrote his sister in the previously cited letter, "but philosophical problems of Grace, and Free Will, and of Redemption as an idea, not as a historical event. What is the meaning of 'Atonement by a crucified Saviour?' *How* many of the Evangelicals can answer that?" (*Correspondence* 182, emphasis Clough's).

Dipsychus attempts to "work at" the philosophical problems "of Grace, and Free Will, and of Redemption," in a manner antithetical to evangelical principles, but it also betrays how hard Clough finds this without what Claude calls a "great moral basis to rest on." Even Dipsychus's reactions to temptation are measured by the pieties of his culture and of its inspired literature, whether that literature means the Bible or the "all great poets" that he recommended to Shairp. The Venetian pleasures that form the basis for Dipsychus's temptation remain a cliché of the British literary tradition, from Shakespeare's *Othello* (ca. 1603) to Byron's tragedies, from Eliza Haywood's *Idalia* (1723) to Charlotte Dacre's *Zofloya* (1806). Venice is always, in the British literary imagination, heavy with vice. Thus, even if the Spirit actually does represent "the subjective imagination" of Dipsychus, as proposes the Epilogue, this imagination springs from the English national literature, and runs exclusively in the channels that this literature has already dug for it. In this respect it makes no difference whether the Spirit is a true devil or not, for his temptation never exceeds the boundaries of this literary tradition. Clough's hero often conceives of himself as a Byron manqué, conscious that Byron had forged a new mythology, and yet—at the same time—conscious that Byron's approach would be factitious in him, trapped as he was between the clichés of Byronism and his own mid-century "overexcitation of the religious sense."[49] *Dipsychus* dramatizes what Vivian will describe half a century later in Oscar Wilde's *The Decay of Lying*: "Paradox though it may seem— and paradoxes are always dangerous things—it is none the less true that life imitates Art far more than Art imitates life."[50]

Fascinated by the manner in which art can dictate the terms of conscience, Clough cultivated a taste for its relentless ironies. During his stay in Massachusetts in 1853, he wrote his fiancée to share the comical ironies of New England Puritan theology: "Did I tell you of the aged Calvinist woman, who being asked about the Universalists said, Yes, they expect that everybody will be saved, but 'we look for better things'" (407). The phrase here—"we look for better things"—comes from the pen of the Puritan Mary Winslow (1630–1663), who wrote a well-known series of meditations called *Walking with Jesus.* Clough may have doubted that it would be a "better thing" for most of humanity to be damned in the afterlife, but he delighted in the idea that Winslow's phrase should be held up in this manner against humane sentiment, or even coherence. His letter shows less interest in the experience of conscience, per se, than in its mechanical deployment of literary expressions. He enjoys the aged Calvinist's expression because her religious literary heritage so perversely dictates her reasoning.

English Poetry as Biblical Substitute: "A great moral basis to rest on"

Just like "the aged Calvinist" woman's reliance upon Mary Winslow, Dipsychus's reaction to the Spirit's temptation seems to provide a commentary upon his own reading habits in the great English tradition. When Dipsychus comes to see that his "Easter Day" blasphemies have conjured an evil spirit, for instance, his reaction comes from Milton's biblical poetry more immediately than from the Bible itself: "Off, off—Oh heaven, depart, depart, depart / Oh heaven. [The] toad that whispered in Eve's ear / Whispered no dream more poisonous than this" (1.2.30–32). "The toad," of course, is the Satan of Milton's *Paradise Lost,* book 4, who assumes this shape to disguise himself in Eden. The allusion—not to be found in Genesis—speaks to a number of the poem's motifs. Among other things, it demonstrates how even Dipsychus's spontaneous exclamations are informed by his reading habits and his unobjectionable tastes. In *Dipsychus*'s Prologue, the poet has explained to his uncle that "there is an instructed ear and an uninstructed. A rude taste for identical recurrences would exact sing-song from 'Paradise Lost,' and grumble because 'Il Penseroso' doesn't run like a nursery rhyme" (10–13). Far from evidencing "a rude taste for identical recurrences," Dipsychus remains a prisoner of his own "instructed ear"—so much that when he starts with fright, it is in blank verse with spondaic substitutions: "Óff, óff! Oh héav'n, depárt, depárt, depárt!" Clough was so very invested in the natural boundaries of this "instructed ear" that some contemporaries wondered whether he could escape from it if he tried. Walter Bagehot, for instance, accused Clough of having "an over-cultivated taste," claiming, "He was so good a disciple of Wordsworth, he hated so thoroughly the common sing-song metres of Moore and Byron, that he was apt to try to write what will seem to many persons to have scarcely a meter at all" (324). Yet the relation between *Dipsychus*'s Prologue and its many poetic meters puts beyond doubt the deliberate way that Clough used poetic rhythm. The rhetorical question of whether Clough might escape from it misses his point that Dipsychus cannot do so.

Dipsychus thus exploits the metrical differences between the chosen language of its two characters. Dipsychus gravitates toward richer, more pretentious meters than the Spirit; his blank verse, as Kathleen Chorley points out, links his expressions to poets of the highest moral and intellectual standing in Victorian culture: Shakespeare, Milton, Wordsworth.[51] Nonetheless, English poems of high moral and intellectual purpose apparently do little to exorcise his Spirit, and this may present the primary importance of the Milton allusion near the drama's opening. It establishes that Dipsychus will not find it easy to substitute English poetry for the Bible (the book that usually serves for exorcism). Dipsychus's invocation of Milton cannot have the desired effect, that is, if Milton too fails to provide "a great moral basis to rest on." Even Dipsychus's decision to identify himself with Eve seems unfortunate, since in that particular narrative (the Bible's as well as Milton's) the human will eventually succumb to the serpent's temptation.

Milton having failed him, Dipsychus finds himself forced to look for solace elsewhere in the English poetic tradition. When the Spirit next teases him with vulgar raillery, Dipsychus tries presenting himself as a new Romantic poet, and he requests succor from the Nature that surrounds the city:

> Ah me, me
> Clear stars above, thou roseate westward sky
> Take up my being into yours: assume
> My sense to know you only: fill my brain
> In your essential purity: or Great Alps,
> That wrapping round your heads in solemn clouds
> Seem sternly to sweep past our vanities
> Lead me with you—take me away, preserve me[.]
> (1.2.50–57)

Metrically, of course, these lines are also the product of what the Prologue calls "an instructed ear," and it is in light of this instruction that they appear so ridiculous. As J. P. Phelan notes, Dipsychus's "attempt to transform the Alps into the guardians of [his] moral being obviously owes a good deal to Wordsworth's treatment of the mountains of his native Lake District" (164). Similar claims might be made for John Keats's "Ode to a Nightingale" with its hankerings after a sort of natural oblivion: "O for a beaker full of the warm South! . . . That I might drink, and leave the world unseen / And with thee fade away into the forest dim" (15, 19–20). In truth, it is the cliché built into Dipsychus's appeal that creates the ironic bathos of the lines. Modern English poets are no more effective than Milton had been in saving Dipsychus from temptation. Even a truly stirring imitation of the great Romantics—of which Dipsychus seems incapable—seems unlikely to deter this Spirit, who points out his unresponsiveness to such prophets:

> By Jove we've had enough of you,
> Quote us a little Wordsworth, do;
> Those lines which are so true, they say:
> "A something far more deeply" eh

"Interfused" what is it, they tell us?
Which and the sunset are bedfellows?
(1.5.256–61)

Here, then, we see an important difference between Clough's literary experiments and Strauss's sanguine theory that the great works of Romantic
secular literature might function like the Bible in Western culture, might
contain "saving truths" as priceless as "an epistle of Paul, or a discourse of
Christ, as reported by John." *Dipsychus* suggests that even if such truths
should be found in the English poetic tradition, newer scriptures would still
lack the talismanic properties widely granted to the traditional text. As far
as British literature goes, Milton in particular represents an inspired choice,
for *Paradise Lost* did more than any other work to recreate mid-Victorian
myths of Genesis. Its contents were often confused with the Bible itself: William Neil suggests that the mid-century controversy over Darwin's *Origin of
Species* "was not so much a controversy between Darwinism and the Book
of Genesis as between Darwinism and Milton's interpretation of Genesis."[52]
This widespread adoption of Milton for Genesis obviously contributes to
Clough's interest, as *Dipsychus* expressly invokes the potential replacement
of the scriptures by literature.

Eventually, Dipsychus appeals to Shakespeare himself, the apogee of
modern literature in both German and British Romantic canons. *Dipsychus*
everywhere alludes to Shakespeare, both directly and indirectly. And while
direct allusions to *Hamlet* in particular are regular and conspicuous, far more
striking is Clough's habit of using what Phelan glosses as "Shakespearian-
sounding phrase[s] of no specific provenance" (208). Thus Dipsychus regularly warns himself against "the empty garnished tenement of the soul"
(1.3.72) and struggles against the demands of "base compliance, e'en that
same / Which buys bold hearts free course" (2.3.86–87). In part 1, scene 3,
when the Spirit recommends prostitutes, Dipsychus reinvents himself as a
nouveau Hamlet, fulminating on "the rank sweat of an enseaméd bed":

Ask not! for oh, the sweet bloom of desire
In hot fruition's pawey fingers turns
To dullness and the deadly spreading spot
Of rottenness inevitably soon
That while we hold, we hate—Sweet Peace! no more!
(1.3.109–12)

It is difficult to isolate such examples of faux-Elizabethan excess without giving the impression that *Dipsychus* goes overboard in its literary pastiche. For some Victorians, it plainly did. And yet it evokes the English poetic tradition to wonderful effect—jarringly, vividly, but never dully. As Wendell V. Harris rightly claims of the above passage, "It is subtly done, the accent and phrasing near enough to suggest Shakespeare's, but far enough away to avoid wholly humorous parody" (90). Clough's elusiveness is further attested by the fact that late Victorian critics so regularly conflated Clough and Dipsychus as to come to regard Clough as a sort of Hamlet figure in his own right: "Thus moving, like a Hamlet, through the strifes of theology and religion, [Clough] resembles Hamlet in another way," wrote Stopford Augustus Brooke. "When the Prince is suddenly flung into the storm of action, he takes momentarily a fierce part in it, and enjoys it, till overthinking again seizes on him. Clough repeats this in his life."[53] Life surely imitates art for Clough, but art imitates art first and foremost.

In order to convey how ubiquitously Clough weaves into his poem what he called the English tradition, in fact, it is easiest to appeal to the testimony of the Victorian critics who received his works. Upon the whole, his contemporaries were nonplussed by the frequency with which *Dipsychus* echoes other literary works. Many expressed unhappiness at the allusive quality of his poetry. Henry Sidgwick, for instance, felt impressed by Clough's metrical virtuosity, but tempered his praise in the *Westminster Review* with the observation that Clough's blank verse was palpably derivative: "The blank verse too in parts, though only in parts, seems to have been carefully studied, and, though a little too suggestive of Elizabethan models, to attain a really high pitch of excellence" (181). The *Saturday Review* article on Clough's *Poems and Prose Remains* is considerably blunter and less forgiving: "Clough is always an echo. Longfellow, Tennyson, Browning, Matthew Arnold, Emerson, ring by turns on the ear trained to detect such ringing; and his letters contain the very best bit of imitated Carlylese we know. . . . But this last, of course, is intentional parody; the poetical echoes clearly are not" (26). Martha Hale Shackford repeats this accusation, complaining that "there are too many influences operative in *Dipsychus*"; among these she finds obtrusive Goethe, Alfred De Musset, and—*pace* Bagehot—Byron (quoted in Thorpe 393). R. H. Hutton agrees to Goethe's obtrusive influence, calling it "very powerfully marked" (253), but also concludes surprisingly that "there is something of the . . . vascular Saxon breadth of Chaucer's poetry in Clough" (260). (This last observation might have pleased Clough.) Even Clough's most devoted champions, such as Norton, concede that "his intimate study of the great poets" certainly shapes his versification and diction (445). Clough's prose essays occasionally earn similar censure, as when John Mackinnon Robertson complains, "They never write themselves: they are composed; and smack of Carlyle and I know not how many other intellectual fashions of his young days" (312).

Such critics of Clough's supposed unoriginality rightly note that he cultivated in his verse a refined, ironic, almost constant echo of the British poetic tradition as conceived in the mid-century. But they are wrong to consider such echoes haphazard. In *Dipsychus,* at least, these remain crucial to the critique of Victorian bibliolatry and the crisis of the higher criticism. The poem performs a pointed critique of the bibliolatrous Romantic culture invoked by Strauss by suggesting that our readiness to make sacred the literature of the English canon is premature at best. Strauss, of course, reserved his bibliolatry for the German Romantics, yet in *Der Alte Und Der Neue Glaube,* he will compare their achievement with Shakespeare's, citing the latter as the consummate example of a modern sacred literature (127). And though Strauss arrives at his bibliolatrous position decades after the *Leben Jesu,* Clough more swiftly extrapolates from that early work to Strauss's final stance. When Dipsychus denies the significance of Clough's experimental verses, pleading, "I but wrote it" (2.1.42), the Spirit smirks back at him, "Perhaps; but no sane man can doubt it / There is a strong Strauss-smell about it" (43–44). *Dipsychus* illustrates the difficulty of taking a secular tradition for scripture, as Strauss will eventually advocate; its first lesson is that such literature may always lack the cachet that has given the biblical scriptures their extraordinary influence. Its second lesson, described below, is that the English poetic tradition affords no better moral influence than the superannuated scriptures.

"The Devil oft the Holy Scriptures uses": Dipsychus, *Victorian Morality, and the Collapse of "Modern Bibliolatry"*

As we have seen, Victorian reviewers were quick to suggest that Clough would profit by Shakespeare's "untroubled outlook on religion." One of the consequences of the mid-Victorian association of poetry and religion is that it so often took for granted the moral and religious righteousness of great poets, particularly great poets of whose lives almost nothing is known. As an 1863 review in the *Christian Remembrancer* explained, "The three who are considered in the present age to occupy the highest thrones in the realms of poesy, Homer, Dante, and Shakespeare, are all (according to their light) earnest believers" (400). The peculiarity of this critical stance may be felt in the fact that Homer and Shakespeare remain (famously) lost to biographers, and Dante, an Italian Catholic, seems an imperfect model for the Anglican *Christian Remembrancer.* Undaunted by such apparently contrary details, the reviewer calmly concludes that Clough, too, would have been a stronger poet, had he only been more religious.

The irony of such criticism is that *Dipsychus* seems written in part to interrogate this line of thinking. The moral value of Shakespeare, after all, is not always plain (and neither does our limited evidence suggest that he lived an especially devout life). When the Sturm und Drang Germans began heralding Shakespeare as a worldwide genius, for instance, they also felt compelled to expurgate from his plays passages of excessive vulgarity; "coarse" characters such as Mercutio and Juliet's nurse were left off the German stage for decades.[54] Even Herder, among the Bard's most zealous enthusiasts, conceded that such expurgation was demanded by our remoteness from Shakespeare's time. And Clough himself, in "The Development of English Literature" (1869), maintains that only received opinion makes Shakespeare a moral authority:

> It is impossible I should suppose for any reader who does not come to the plays of Shakespeare with a judgment overborne by the weight of authority or the force of general sentiment—it is impossible I should imagine for any ingenuous dispassionate reader not to find himself surprised, checked, disappointed, shocked[,] even revolted by what in any other author—in an author of modern times, he would call gross defects—in points of plot, flagrant inconsistencies of character. . . . Whom does the marriage of Angelo and Mariana leave quite easy in his mind? Whose moral sensibilities are not a little ruffled by a strange phantasmagoria of good people becoming bad of a sudden, and all of a sudden good again, good and happy too: after every sort of misconduct, after the wickedest and foulest actions . . . ?
> (336–37)

Dipsychus, we see, is haunted not just by the Spirit but by the villains of Shakespeare's comedies: figures like Angelo from *Measure for Measure* or Oliver from *As You Like It.* In turn, *Dipsychus* pries back what Clough here calls "the weight of authority [and] the force of general sentiment." It asks, what makes the English poetic tradition particularly moral at all? The Spirit

submits that, indeed, one could develop from the English poetic tradition—
and Shakespeare in particular—a worldview thoroughly antithetical to even
the most liberal mid-Victorian religious mores.

Whenever Dipsychus turns to the poetic tradition, then, the Spirit always
trumps him, citing the same authors to better effect. He responds to Dipsychus's chaste Hamlet impression, for instance, with a suggestive pastoral
lyric from *As You Like It*:

> It was a lover and his lass
>> With a hey and a ho, and a hey nonino
> Betwixt the acres of the rye
>> With a hey and a ho, and a hey nonino
> These pretty country folks would lie—
>> In the spring time, the pretty spring time.
>
> (1.3.126–31)

In Shakespeare, naturally, these lines comprise two stanzas, rather than one:
the Spirit accelerates the lovers' progress through the rye field, as though
adopting the play's own dictum that such carpe diem lyrics must not delay
listeners from applying their lessons. He shows himself to be as careful a literary judge as Dipsychus, yet one liberated from the critical pieties common
to Victorian literary theory. The Bard, he reminds us, champions ribaldry
and experience as often as the mid-century prudery and innocence valued
by Dipsychus.

The lesson here is not that the great literary and artistic tradition of Western Europe provides Dipsychus with insufficient ammunition to fight his
moral battles; it is that the Spirit can clearly draw from the same literary
stockpile. It is important that both adversaries draw from the poetic tradition, rather than Western traditions of romance or novel, which were not yet
granted anything like the same moral weight. In mid-century, novel-reading
was still largely an indulgence; poetry-reading a means of self-improvement,
particularly if the poet was Shakespeare. But Western poetry provides many
more vivid examples of the Spirit's permissiveness than of Dipsychus's prudery, which is why the former can defend the Venetian festival merely by
singing lines from Béranger's suggestive "Ma Grand'Mère": "Ah comme je
regrette / Mon bras si dodu, / Ma jambe bien faite, / Et le temps perdu" (Ah,
how I miss my plump arms, my shapely legs, and the days that have gone
by [1.2.40–44]); or Rossini's *Barber of Seville:* "Figaro sù Figaro giù / Figaro

quà Figaro là" (Figaro up Figaro down / Figaro here Figaro there [1.1.72–73]). Clever double rhymes serve to "put in a just light" pious readings of Goethe: "Trust me, I've read your German sage / To far more purpose e'er than you did / You'll find it in his wisest page / Whom God deludes is well deluded" (1.5.88–91). And, moreover, the grand English poetic tradition provides the centerpiece of the Spirit's point of view, as well. He finally wins his poetic argument with Dipsychus (and begins to win the corresponding theological one) when he convinces the latter that the style of the high English tradition cannot function as a warrant of a work's inspiration:

> . . . but let me say
> I too have my *grandes manières* in my way.
> Could out-blank-verse you without much ado
> Have my religion also in my kind
> For dreaming—unfit, because not designed.
> What! you know not that I too can be serious
> Can speak big words, and use the tone imperious;
> Can speak—not honeyedly of love and beauty,
> But sternly of a something much like Duty?
> Oh, do you look surprised? were never told
> Perhaps that all that glitters is not gold[?]
> The Devil oft the Holy Scriptures uses
> But God can act the Devil when he chooses.
> (2.5.51–64)

The Spirit here inverts the paradigm that begins the poem: as Chorley observes, Dipsychus tries to dismiss the Spirit's lighter airs with the gravity of a fuller poetic idiom. But the Spirit trumps his efforts by demonstrating the unruliness of poetic language.

The Spirit's literary tastes range from the Gospel of John to "Little Bo Peep" (a nickname for his absent rival, Christ, who "is not risen" [2.7.56, 85]). Sometimes he cleverly combines these in parodies of scripture, claiming Dipsychus as "My lost sheep in the wilderness" (2.3.185), and consoling him with: "Fear not, my lamb, whate'er men say / I am the Shepherd; and the Way" (2.5.214–15). Indeed, *Dipsychus*'s blend of secular and scriptural sources contributes most to its modern flavor, particularly his repeated, ironic use of distinctly Shakespearean phrases that had become proverbial in nineteenth-century English. The most unlikely of these reappear in

Dipsychus, out of context and usually misapplied, as when Dipsychus repeats to himself the blundering Polonius's advice to his son, Laertes: "To thine own self be true, the wise man says." To look for wisdom in Shakespeare is reasonable enough, but to attribute to Shakespeare the sentiments of his characters leads to absurdities. Despite this, such attributions became increasingly common in the Victorian period. Seventy years after *Dipsychus,* James Joyce could reinvent this joke (or, conceivably, borrow it) in *Ulysses* (1922) when Mr. Deasy advises Stephen Dedalus on finance and attributes to Shakespeare expressions taken from Iago in *Othello:* "What did Shakespeare say? *Put but money in thy purse.*"[55] In *Dipsychus,* as in *Ulysses,* such misquotation is the rule, and is used to a variety of effects.

In the long passage quoted above, for instance, as Phelan indicates, the Spirit's suggestion that "all that glitters is not gold" derives from *The Merchant of Venice,* where it is delivered by Portia's initial suitor. It comes from secular literature, then, rather than sacred; however, its rhetorical power is reflected in Dipsychus's response, when he willingly accepts the Spirit's rebuke as indicative of an established truth: "Ill spirits can quote holy books I knew, / What will they not say? what not dare to do?" (2.5.68–69). In his response Dipsychus not only accepts the Shakespearean idiom, but he instinctively propagates it as well. For he, too, misquotes a now proverbial part of *The Merchant of Venice:* "Mark you this, Bassanio, / The devil can cite Scripture for his purpose" (1.3.98–99). And lest a good joke be lost, Clough repeats this play upon literary authority in the poem's Epilogue, when the young poet defends his work:

> "I don't very well understand what it's all about," said my uncle, "I won't say I didn't drop into a doze while the young man was drivelling through his later soliloquies. But there was a great deal that was unmeaning, vague, and involved; and what was most plain was least decent and least moral."
>
> "Dear sir," said I, "Says the Proverb, Needs must when the devil drives, and if the devil is to speak—"
>
> "Well," said my uncle, "why should he? Nobody asked him."
> (231)

This dialogue takes the terms of the poem and extends them into the ostensible theories behind it. "Needs must when the devil drives" comes not from Proverbs, as the poet's citation might imply, but from *All's Well That Ends Well;* it is not a biblical citation but a Shakespearean one.

Here we see the religious project of higher critical Victorian poetry in crisis. On one hand, the surest proof that English literature might attain biblical status is found in the fact that its aphorisms could attain the status of received truths, to become such sacred texts as Shakespeare became for many in the nineteenth century. Yet such texts often remain perversely at odds with their sacred hermeneutics: "Whom does the marriage of Angelo and Mariana leave quite easy in his mind?" asks Clough to suggest that an unbiased modern mind will revolt at the Shakespearean resolution, in which a despot and would-be rapist is compelled to marry his foremost victim. Such a rhetorical line of questioning will sound very familiar to readers of, for instance, *The Nemesis of Faith* (1848), by J. A. Froude, a friend of Clough's who would voice similar moral objections to biblical episodes like the slaughter of the Amalekites from the first book of Samuel. (Before quitting Oxford, Clough suggested to his provost that *The Nemesis of Faith* would give him a better sense of the doubts besetting Clough's own generation. The provost, Edward Hawkins, replied that he had heard too much about Froude to be tempted.) The most revered English poetry jars on too many levels with Victorian mores: are Touchstone's carpe diem lyrics or Mercutio's lewd puns integral to the Bard's sacredness? If so, can we draw distinctions between nursery rhymes and Genesis? The Spirit suggests not when he pooh-poohs the distance between John's "Good Shepherd" (2.5.215) and "Little Bo Peep."

Clough and the Function of Poetry

In an often-cited chapter called "The Rise of English," Terry Eagleton's *Literary Theory: An Introduction* (1996) posits that the academic study of English emerges in modernity chiefly as substitute for the nineteenth-century "failure of religion."[56] As I have discussed in my introduction, more recent scholarship has given us much reason to doubt that nineteenth-century Christianity collapsed in quite the manner implied here (and lately Eagleton himself has taken to defending religion's legitimacy).[57] Still, Victorian apprehensions about religion's demise can nonetheless help us to appreciate *Dipsychus*'s probing engagement with what McKelvy calls "the English cult of literature." As we have seen, Dipsychus at times flirts with Arnold's view of poetry as an "ever surer and surer stay" from the vicissitudes of Victorian religion. Yet *Dipsychus* gradually devolves into a satire of the very notion that poetry should result in the spiritual betterment of its readers. Doubts expressed by Eagleton about the moral and ethical value of literature in "The Rise of

English" are here anticipated by Clough, who depicts a poetry that aspires to an inspired, vatic role but invariably must settle for a comic one instead. Dipsychus's seduction by the Spirit traces his retreat from an inspired theory of literature to a merely whimsical one, to an expression of the mere pleasure of language. And mere pleasure is what the Spirit has advocated all along.

It is central to this idea that Dipsychus's vatic understanding of poetry entails actual moral and social good, such as a believer might seek from the Bible. This makes sense of both Dipsychus's professional uncertainties and his concern for social justice. An example may be found in the well-known Gondola episode:

> Afloat; we move. Delicious! Ah,
> What else is like the gondola?
> This level floor of liquid glass
> Begins beneath it swift to pass.
> It goes as though it went alone
> By some impulsion of its own.
> (1.5.3–8)[58]

As the *Macmillan's Magazine* reviewer put it, "Dipsychus breaks forth in these lines. . . . Yet the next minute he cannot but bethink him of the boatman at work out there in the hot sun to procure him this delicious movement of the gondola" (100). Recent scholars have rightly linked this lyric to Samuel Rogers's *Italy* (1830) and to the early ("Didst ever see a Gondola?") stanzas of Bryon's *Beppo* (1818). But Dipsychus's lyric is at once less crafted than Byron's ottava rima (the Victorians rarely associated 4 × 4 measures with the height of metrical virtuosity) and yet more sensuous than Rogers's labored blank verse. It reproduces a struggle between the pleasure of its art and the material conditions that make such art possible: the Venetian gondola goes "as though" it went alone—but not without the labor of the gondoliers. And while *Beppo* describes this labor, Byron does not overtly worry about its justice; Dipsychus does not describe it, but worries.[59]

This is because Dipsychus so actively strives to apply his bibliolatrous theory of literature to the actual moral, ethical, and social problems of the external world. Even the famous rhymes of *Beppo*, to which the poem gestures, suggest a tacit indifference to social inequality. As Dipsychus puts it, "So live, nor need to call to mind / Our slaving brother set behind!" (Oxford 4.35–36). The worldly Spirit, of course, intervenes when Dipsychus's lyric becomes a serious meditation on unjust conditions of labor. To the qualms of Dipsychus's awakening post-Christian conscience, the Spirit offers the laissez-faire counterargument, claiming that it is Dipsychus's very exploitation of the gondolier's labor in the market system that most systematically leads to future gondoliers' happiness. When Dipsychus muses,

> To make one's fellow-man an instrument—

the Spirit replies,

> Is just the thing that makes him most content.
> (Oxford 4.41–42)

Dipsychus finds such laissez-faire arguments disingenuous, but still he listens to the Spirit's bluster:

> Oh come, come, come! By Him that set us here,
> Who's to enjoy at all, pray let us hear?
> You won't; he can't! Oh, no more fuss!
> What's it to him, or he to us?
> Sing, sing away, be glad and gay,
> And don't forget that we shall pay.
> (Oxford 5.55–60)

Here in questions of social justice, as in earlier questions of sex or violence, Dipsychus becomes seduced by the Spirit's literary argument, rather than by his analysis of the situation. As in the earlier scenes, the Spirit resorts to a clipped version of a Shakespearean byword. Line 58 of his reply evokes Hamlet's famous "What's Hecuba to him, or he to Hecuba, / That he should weep for her?" (2.2.569–70). The Spirit frames the argument in terms of sheer histrionics: here, as in *Amours de Voyage*, the hero's "great moral basis to rest on" is merely performative and "factitious entirely." The Spirit acknowledges social injustices but mediates them through Shakespearean tragedy and comedy. That is, his goal seems to be to turn Dipsychus from a real social problem to a more satisfying literary one. Far from presenting a moral solution on par with the Bible, Shakespeare here presents a moral problem. Nonetheless, Dipsychus's reliably "instructed" ear and tongue respond with lines that recall *Hamlet* again: "All as I go on my way I behold them consorting and coupling; / Faithful, it seemeth, and fond; very fond, very possibly faithful" (Oxford 5.72–73). True to the *Saturday Review*'s depiction, Dipsychus "is always an echo": here with his self-conscious literary affectations (note the archaic "-th" suffixes), he evokes Polonius's "pity 'tis 'tis true" stammering before Shakespeare's Claudius and Gertrude (2.2.98).[60] Dipsychus experiences life most readily when it corresponds to his poetic sensibilities.

When Dipsychus returns to social questions later in the scene, the Spirit continues his literary assault by different measures, interrupting Dipsychus's qualms with a crass Epicurean impromptu first composed by Clough for a different context (and there entitled "Spectator ab Extra"):

> As I sat at the cafe, I said to myself,
> They may talk as they please about what they call pelf,
> They may jeer if they like about eating and drinking
> But help it I cannot, I cannot help thinking
>> How pleasant it is to have money, high-ho
>> How pleasant it is to have money.
>
> (1.5.125–31)

As is true for the previous lyrics, these verses evoke many possible sources. Isobel Armstrong, for instance, cites the radical Spasmodic poetry of R. H. Horne as a model for this particular lyric. Yet the song's chorus ("How pleasant it is to have money, high-ho / How pleasant it is to have money") more plainly connects it to such brutal social satire as Thomas Love Peacock's "Levi Moses" (1806). Peacock's poem, with its similar refrain, "Oh, a very goot ting ish de monish!" takes much the same tone and meter to relate the financial successes of a parvenu Jewish stockbroker whose father sold rags for a living.[61] The point of Peacock's anti-Semitic verse, of course, is to stymie social revolution of the sort ardently hoped for by Horne and dimly hoped for by Dipsychus. It vilifies social climbers and perpetuates ugly stereotypes about their lack of culture. And the Spirit's endorsement of "Levi Moses" cuts both ways: while it implies that only an anti-Semitic demon could embrace Peacock's song wholeheartedly, it also may reinscribe the idea that such social climbing is, by extension, demonic.

At all events, the Christian Socialism of the gondola episode is drowned out in an implied threat to the social order by nineteenth-century cosmopolitanism:

It was but last winter I came up to town,
But I'm getting already a little renown
I enter good homes without much ado,
Am beginning to see the nobility too
   So pleasant it is to have money, high ho
   So pleasant it is to have money.

Oh dear what a pity they ever should lose it,
For they are the gentry that know how to use it,
[So] grand and so graceful, such manners, such dinners,
But yet in the end it is we shall be winners
   So pleasant it is to have money, high ho
   So pleasant it is to have money.
(1.5.168–79)

The Spirit's song entails a threat of social upheaval—the gentry "lose it" to an implicitly demonic parvenu—that pushes aside thoughts of the gondolier. It distracts Dipsychus from wishing to improve the lot of his social inferiors by making him anxious about his social betters. It also captures Dipsychus's conflicted ideals; the Spirit here both mocks his suspicion of commercial and legal professions and reminds him of the unsettled nature of his social position: so unpleasant it is to lack money.

Clough had a complex relationship to such satire, being in some ways the very arriviste whose vulgarity *Dipsychus* parodies as satanic. In *Amours de Voyage,* Claude shrinks from his love-interest's family as "Middle-class people these, bankers very likely, not wholly / Pure of the taint of the shop" (1.125–26). But neither was Clough "pure of the taint of the shop": his father was a Liverpool cotton merchant who removed the family for many years to Charleston, South Carolina, a city remote enough from London that Clough's obituary in the *Cornhill Magazine* carelessly places his childhood "in South America."[62] *Amours de Voyage* may even suggest the readiness with which a parvenu adopts the suspicions of elite culture. But *Dipsychus* also portrays the perils of their literary and social education. As Samuel Butler (schooled at Shrewsbury) bluntly puts it, "A public school education cuts off a boy's retreat; he can no longer become a labourer or a mechanic, and these are the only people whose tenure of independence is not precarious—with the exception of course of those who are born inheritors of money."[63] When beginning *Dipsychus,* Clough was circumstanced in precisely this manner. He was not a "born inheritor of money," but his education had given him the acquired prejudices of those who were. Clough became a scholar of the Latin and Greek disparaged in "Levi Moses" ("'tish all nonshenshe, I shay, / Vhich occasion to shtudy dere none ish" [13–14]), but after his resignation from Oriel, this education seemed unlikely to earn him a comfortable living. A political radical possessed of "manners" to meet the Spirit's (mock) admiration, he felt mixed loyalties to the genteel classes whose eclipse is predicted in the Spirit's boorish song.

Although the Spirit's seduction of Dipsychus returns us to the poet's biography, moreover, it need not bring us to an effusive critical model that minimizes the poem's intellectual work. These passages do not merely show Clough "attempt[ing] to teach in song what he learned in suffering," as Whibley has it: they show how his impecunious circumstances might present intellectual, as well as social, problems:

> O, you have paths of your own before you, have you?
> What shall it take to? literature no doubt?
> Novels, reviews? or poems! if you please!
> The strong fresh gale of life will feel no doubt
> The influx of your mouthful of soft air.
> . . . .
> Breathe out your dreamy scepticism, relieved
> By snatches of old songs; People will like that, doubtless.
> (2.5.138–42, 150–51)

The Spirit's sarcastic professional advice, of course, describes just the sort of poem that *Dipsychus* actually represents: a "breathing out" of "dreamy scepticism." As we know, Clough was himself too doubtful of this poem's reception to risk sending it to the public, and he was probably right to refrain. Not even its "snatches of old songs" would have made it palatable to a large audience in the early 1850s. Had it made an impression at all, it would have caused the sort of commotion exemplified by Froude. Markham Sutherland, the (anti) hero of *The Nemesis of Faith,* laments that "modern Bibliolatry" limits itself to a single set of scriptures and insists that "he should make another version of the Bible for [his parishioners] in what is for ever before their eyes, in the cornfield, in the meadow, in the workshop, at the weaver's loom, in the market-places and the warehouses."[64] And yet Sutherland finds only spiritual ruin when he accepts an ecclesiastical post for heterodox reasons.

The above passage takes on a particular pathos in light of Clough's own letters from the 1850–53 period, when he was enormously worried about his future. As late as 1853, Clough even considered opening a school in Massachusetts, using such friends as Emerson and Lowell to get himself started, but he worried that rumors of his religious heterodoxy would lead to the school's failure. Such worries, too, are taunted by the Spirit:

> Or perhaps you'll teach youth . . .
> Will parents like that, think you? he writes poems,
> He's odd opinions—hm—and's not in orders
> For that you won't be. Well, old college fame,
> The charity of some freethinking merchant,
> Or friendly intercession brings a first pupil;
> And not a second.
> (2.5.164, 171–76)

Here, finally, is the practical financial side of "Easter Day," the consequence of Dipsychus's not taking religious orders like Froude's Sutherland, and the consequence of Clough's resignation of his Oriel fellowship. When Dipsychus submits to be guided by the Spirit, it is because such practical considerations have filled the void left by the Evangelists. The void looms so large because Dipsychus loses faith not only in the ancient scriptures but in the inspired English tradition as well.

Dipsychus attempts to take seriously the possibility of making "another version of the Bible," but he cannot, on a practical level, see how it is to be done. The poem puts on display this intellectual problem as much as any emotional response, and it is for its solution that Dipsychus is fighting by the poem's end. The couplet with which this chapter began pronounces the beginning of the literary argument that culminates in the Spirit's *"grandes manières."* Only in his culminating poetic ecstasy, when Dipsychus goes so far as to align himself with the biblical author of Revelation, does he begin to realize the limits of his vision:

> Lo I am in the Spirit on the Lord's day
> With John on Patmos. Is it not enough[?]

> [One day in seven?] and if this should go
> If this pure solace should desert my mind
> What were all else?
> (2.4.99–104)

As mentioned above, this passage explicitly invites comparison to the biblical author, John. As we have now seen, however, Dipsychus relies perhaps less upon the authority of that celebrated allonym than upon the newer authority of the English poetic tradition. Literature can remain a "pure solace" if literary inspiration can provide a substitute for the supernatural inspiration of scriptures, implicit in the belief that "Christ is risen indeed." The problem is that English literature might not work as well. John of Revelation claims to reproduce God's own dictation. But Dipsychus cannot finally "hear behind him a great voice," as the biblical author claims to do. Worse, the voice that he does hear smirks at the pretensions of modern literature as well as ancient, and Dipsychus finds himself hard-pressed to argue that any English poetry, least of all his own, can be expected to fill the religious void indicated by his "Easter Day." Dipsychus's Spirit avers that English poets need no divine afflatus to fill the void of scripture. Quite the contrary: inspiration is so plentiful already that one need not contribute to it. As the Spirit laughs, "The strong fresh gale of life will feel no doubt / The influx of your mouthful of soft air."

Clough's Poetic Agnosticism

As committed to the sacred English canon as many of Clough's contemporaries were, they regularly misunderstood his reasons for abandoning poetry and propagated his story as that of a "failed poet" (as in Arnold's "Thyrsis"). Coventry Patmore might be said to represent the opposite side of the religious spectrum from Arnold (Patmore's quest for form led him to Roman Catholicism), but he, like Arnold, mistook Clough's literary lassitude for a lack of proper perspective. In the *St. James's Gazette,* Patmore belittles Clough as a hapless follower of Emersonian transcendentalism, and he laments,

> Now Emerson, at his very best, never approached greatness. He was at highest only a brilliant metaphysical epigrammist. But a religion without a dogma, and with only one commandment, "Thou shalt neither think nor do anything that is customary," had great attractions for Clough; to whom it never seems to have

occurred that the vast mass of mankind, for whose moral and religious welfare he felt so keenly, has not and never can have a religion of speechless aspirations and incommunicable feelings, and that to teach men to despise custom is to cut the immense majority of them adrift.

(qtd. in Thorpe, *Clough: Critical Heritage*, 337–38)

Patmore plainly finds in Clough a thirdhand expression, via Emerson, of *Sartor Resartus*'s famous description of philosophy: "Nay, what is Philosophy throughout but a continual battle against Custom; an ever-renewed effort to *transcend* the sphere of blind Custom, and so become Transcendental?"[65] Yet, in retrospect, Patmore's analysis could hardly be more wrongheaded. Clough's theological position seems quite antithetical to the maxim "Thou shalt neither think nor do anything that is customary." Far from being inattentive to social custom—or from imagining it to be beneath him—Clough dramatized his culture's inability to escape from it.

As we have already seen, Clough's own religious position after the religious stalemate of *Dipsychus* was to become to many Victorians unrecognizable as a position at all. His "Notes on the Religious Tradition" calls for a canon that simply knows no bounds: "Every rule of conduct, every maxim, every usage of life and society, must be admitted." Since the higher critical method had demonstrated the factitiousness of the biblical canon, so Clough insists that nothing ought now to be ruled out from potential new sets of scriptures, "so in each new age to each new age's Bible." But accepting everything into a sacred canon effectively means surrendering the idea of a canon at all—including a canon of English poetry. No longer believing in the cult of English poetry, Clough quit attempting to contribute to it: he never bothered to put *Dipsychus* into a definitive form, and his brief attempt to imagine a worldly, successful middle-aged Faustus—provisionally entitled *Dipsychus Continued*—was abandoned almost as soon as begun.

In some ways, *Dipsychus* presents an anticlimactic conclusion to the flurry of verse that Clough wrote while inspired by Strauss at the Victorian mid-century, from "Epi-Strauss-ism" to *Amours de Voyage*. But in part owing to its unfinished nature, *Dipsychus* remains among the mid-century's most powerful demonstrations of the role of literature in the formation of religion. It explores the literary implications of Strauss's *Leben Jesu* much as Strauss himself would later learn to do, and brings them home more vividly. And it never amounts to just the record of conscience that so many Victorians took it to be. Far from suggesting that individual consciences could serve as independent arbiters of religious dogma, *Dipsychus* demonstrates how these consciences might themselves be products of literary history in first place— not merely literary history as found in the Bible, but in nursery rhymes, and not just in Milton, but in Peacock, and not just in Shakespeare, but in what Clough calls "every usage of life and society." If this is "a great moral basis to rest on," it is not "great" in an aesthetic, bibliolatrous, or even an evaluative sense. It is great only in a vast, inclusive sense. And when "every usage of life" can be canonized, one need not strive to join the canon.

Chapter 4

ROBERT BROWNING'S SACRED
AND LEGENDARY ART

R OBERT BROWNING's relationship to the Bible generates a good deal of commentary. It has always done so. Browning's late Victorian disciples were rather given to religious speculation, and their response to his work provides one of literature's more intriguing cases of modern bibliolatry. The London Browning Society of 1881–92, for instance, routinely alienated nonreligious members in its zeal to demonstrate the spiritual value of Browning's poetry. Even the society's freethinking co-founder, F. J. Furnivall, sometimes expressed irritation with the group's religious tendencies. (The other, the poet Emily Hickey, later became a Catholic.) And fin de siècle readers throughout the Anglophone world subscribed to what some contemporaries called a "Browning cult," and what William S. Peterson delineates as an apparent "answer to . . . spiritual ills, an embodiment of Christian values, and a link with the unseen world."[1] Furnivall's remonstration that "the Browning Society is not made up of idolaters" now smacks of wish fulfillment, even though Browning's poetry won enthusiasm from the skeptical as well as the devout. At all events, readers from a variety of theological and scholarly perspectives have always found Browning to be an invaluable compass point for evolving mid-Victorian ideas of scriptural authority.

Browning scholars who take an interest in the poet's complex relationship to the changing Victorian Bible thus follow in the footsteps of Victorian readers. A devotional view of Browning emerges in particular after the critical triumph of *The Ring and the Book* (1868), a work that cemented Browning's nineteenth-century reputation and that demonstrates his engagement with hermeneutics on its largest scale.[2] Among other things, this poem generated a tremendous amount of deference to Browning as an interpreter of sacred texts. As the poet Robert W. Buchanan puts it at the opening of his prominent 1869 *Athenaeum* review,

> At last, the *opus magnum* of our generation lies before the world. . . . The fascination of the work is still so strong upon us, our eyes are still so spell-bound by the immortal features of Pompilia (which shine through the troubled mists of the story with almost insufferable beauty), that we feel it difficult to write calmly and without exaggeration; yet we must record at once our conviction, not merely that *"The Ring and the Book"* is beyond all parallel the supremest poetical achievement of our time, but that it is the most precious and profound spiritual treasure that England has produced since the days of Shakespeare. Its intellectual greatness is as nothing compared with its transcendent spiritual teaching. (399)

This passage testifies equally well to Browning's sudden arrival at the pinnacle of the Victorian poetic pantheon (where Tennyson had previously reigned alone), and to the newness of his place there in 1869. Buchanan labors to reassure readers—and possibly himself—of his earnestness: he struggles "to write calmly and without exaggeration," being "spell-bound" in particular by the "immortal features" of the poem's heroine. Yet Buchanan's enthusiasm can be ascribed neither to any personal religiosity nor to rhetorical bombast. Contemporaries of every stripe agreed. The stridently freethinking Furnivall took for granted that *The Ring and the Book* was Browning's greatest and most inspired work.[3] Likewise, James Thomson ("B.V."), best known for his atheist manifesto, *The City of Dreadful Night* (1880), called *The Ring and the Book* a "stupendous Poem," claiming that he knew no other work "more impressive and authentic of rapt prophetical possession and inspiration," and adding that it would "rank among the world's masterpieces."[4] And even today, although critical estimations of the poem have cooled a bit, it remains perfectly fair to call *The Ring and the Book* "the *opus magnum* of [its] generation" and "the supremest poetical achievement of [its] time." At least, one would be hard-pressed to identify patently "supremer" Victorian poetical achievements.

The following pages promote the idea that Buchanan's experience of the "almost insufferable beauty" of this poem not only testifies to Browning's radical engagement with the Victorian changing Bible, but itself helps to substantiate that engagement. It is widely recognized that the poem solicits from readers a leap of faith in the integrity of its chief characters, particularly in the heroine whose "immortal features," at least for Buchanan, "shine through the troubled mists of the story." But it should be better appreciated how the poem's excitement of the nineteenth-century religious imagination itself contributes to—or in some cases constitutes—the meaning of the work. Put simply, *The Ring and the Book*'s religious truths are pragmatic ones. It represents a higher critical analogy akin to the one that Tennyson pursues in his *Idylls of the King* (as we saw in chapter 2), but one that is more spectacularly successful. Whereas Tennyson solicits a reader's emotional assent to the kinship between national and religious narratives, leaving both in jeopardy, Browning secures a reader's personal investment in the resolved truth of his fantastic and doubtful story.

It is hard to overstate the importance of this literary gambit in Browning's career. Jerome McGann's remark that in poetry, "knowledge will appear as a form of activity rather than as a content, possession, or an idea" can hardly be truer than in this part of Browning.[5] Buchanan, Furnivall, Thomson, and the fin de siècle Browningites did not receive Browning's "transcendent spiritual teaching" as a bequest. Rather, *The Ring and the Book* provided the material from which they crafted that teaching, and their zeal in doing so conditioned the reception of Browning's oeuvre in ways that the poet himself could not fully control. This chapter concludes, therefore, with a discussion of *Red Cotton Night-Cap Country, or, Turf and Towers* (1873), a profoundly skeptical later poem that presents a qualification or retraction of a number of the religious implications of *The Ring and the Book*. Significantly, no generation of Browning readers has counted *Red Cotton Night-Cap Country* among "the supremest poetical achievement[s]" of his oeuvre, and its very neglect testifies to the genius with which Browning's earlier poetry fashions itself. The universally disliked *Red Cotton Night-Cap Country,* that is, shows just how effectively the universally admired *The Ring and the Book* uses the model of the higher criticism to anticipate and eviscerate critiques of its religious claims (including Browning's own subsequent critiques). His readership's devotion to *The Ring and the Book* not only supersedes Browning's, but also shows the irrelevance of his own reservations about its true inspiration.

The Art of Browning's History

Browning, as I have mentioned in this book's introduction, took an abiding interest in the manner in which art dictates the terms of knowledge, history, and even ordinary perception. Earlier poems like "Fra Lippo Lippi" had given him occasion to present this idea as something not merely plausible but self-evident and demonstrable. (No Browning reader, for instance, can now view a Lippi without something of Browning's Lippi in mind.) But the very vastness of *The Ring and the Book* brings home this lesson about the mutual dependency of art and history in a way that Browning's much-anthologized dramatic monologues cannot. Like the triple-decker novel, it creates a whole world for its readers. But unlike that novel, it insists upon the historical truth of its world even as it delivers that world in conspicuously "poetic" language, refusing the devices of realism in pursuit of something very unlike most Victorian fiction. The craft of poetry here asks to what extent historical representation always depends upon art and—despite this term's negative connotations—artfulness.[6]

As appreciated by contemporary reviewers, *The Ring and the Book*'s true story resembles a cliché Gothic romance in the century-long tradition of Horace Walpole's *Castle of Otranto* (1764). It tells of a pregnant seventeen-year-old named Pompilia who flees Arezzo with the help of a dashing young priest, Giuseppi Caponsacchi, in order to escape her evil old husband, Count Guido Franceschini. Guido tracks down the fugitives near Rome and, after a period of legally enforced separation, contrives to murder Pompilia (who nonetheless lingers long enough to tell her tale). Meanwhile, Guido is himself taken, judged by Pope Innocent XII, and executed. Those familiar with *Otranto* and its innumerable literary offspring will recognize here the formative elements of the English Gothic: the pre-Enlightenment Italian Catholic setting, the wicked nobleman, the good and beautiful young woman, the virtuous and attractive hero of noble family but impoverished circumstances, the inevitable bloodletting when these elements come finally together. (Thus Guido might be given the role of Walpole's Manfred, Caponsacchi Theodore, Pompilia Matilda, Pope Innocent Alfonso, and so forth.) Browning's familiarity with this Gothic tradition would presumably have alerted him to the promise of the story when he found it (as 1.33–83 recounts) in a bona fide Roman court document sold in a Florence bookstall.

But for the Victorians, as for subsequent readers, much of the power of *The Ring and the Book* lay in Browning's method of presenting this story as a sort of forensic experiment—and a sort of workshop in the higher critical perspective that even true histories must always be mediated by a literary imagination.[7] To achieve this, Browning sacrifices the particular dramatic elements that make his plot resemble Walpole's. He spills his plot outright, for instance, in the first book of the poem, and in subsequent books only repeats the established facts of the case from the vantage of its various participants: the gossips of half of Rome followed by the other half of Rome, cynical social aspirants, Guido under trial, Caponsacchi, Pompilia on her deathbed, the two opposing lawyers, Pope Innocent, Guido awaiting execution, the poet *in propria persona*. This experimental mode refuses ordinary narrative effects, including any attempt to engross a reader with the machinery of an unfolding story (what John Stuart Mill calls the interest of "incident"). As Thomson points out, Browning aims to "deliberately sacrifice all that he might have gained by a slowly evolved narrative, the interest of expectancy, surprise, suspense, doubt, fear, terror" (690), yet while still managing to secure his reader's profound investment in the truth of the story. And the catch? Browning still insists that the varied colors of these diverse monologues, when spun together in the color wheel of poetry, "whirl into a white" and produce "the eventual unity / Which make[s] the miracle" of perception (1.1362–65). This experience he leaves to his readers: "See it," he dares them, "for yourselves . . . !" (1365–66).

Naturally, many readers have rejected the prospect of this "eventual unity" and denied its "miracle." Every religion has doubters as well as devotees.[8] But the poem offers a dazzling history lesson even to those disinclined to credit it with a religious interpretation because of how it puts on display a reader's inclination to fill in the gaps of an incomplete narrative—and to what devotional effect. Because Browning's technique relies upon the disharmony between conflicting narrators, it has sometimes been compared to Wilkie Collins's *The Moonstone* (1868), which similarly unfolds the individual voices of its depicted characters. This comparison, however, minimizes several crucial differences of genre, including the circumstance that poetry was in the 1860s granted a higher seriousness than prose fiction, and the equally obvious circumstance that Browning never resolves the innocence or villainy of his principal characters. Whereas Collins's detective story holds readers in high suspense before gratifying them with a straightforward explanation for a fictional diamond heist, Browning holds no one in suspense and never gratifies readers with a straightforward explanation for his ostensibly true history.[9] Browning's poem, not being a novel, does not finally illuminate readers with *les nouvelles*. Its revelations are everywhere or else they are nowhere at all.

Marveling at this technique, James Thomson describes Browning as a magician who scrupulously exposes the mechanics of his legerdemain beforehand so as to increase the wonder of his performance. As is generally true of stage magic, such tricks require a degree of complicity in their audience. A reader's prior commitment to the historical truth lurking behind this story grants Browning much of the leverage that he needs to inspire such devotion to his heroine Pompilia without conclusively demonstrating her innocence, or such admiration for the Pope's wisdom without confirming his chief assumptions, or such resistance to Guido's logic while allowing that he may have been rightly suspicious of his young wife's virtue. In some respect, Browning's characters more closely resemble those of Thomas Babington Macaulay's *History of England* than those of the Victorian novelist. At the same time, Browning's artistic design provides leverage to vindicate his protagonists in ways that Macaulay could never, say, vindicate King William III of the Glencoe Massacre. Macaulay's readers already believe something of Hanoverian history, whereas Browning unearths an obscure Italian history and asks his readers to take its relevance on faith. Just as Browning's earlier Fra Lippi had promised the lover of art and beauty that "you'll find the soul you have missed, / Within yourself" (219–20), so *The Ring and the Book* promises readers their own souls. And for significant numbers of Victorian readers, it delivered.

Today, *The Ring and the Book*'s perverse truth claims and its bewildering scope can make its experimental fragmentation of perspective more disquieting than conventional Gothic à la Walpole or sensation fiction à la Collins. Suzanne Bailey speaks to the "nightmarish quality to interpretative issues in *The Ring and the Book*" as though the real Gothic horror of the poem were to be found in its hermeneutics.[10] Many post-Victorian readers will agree. Nonetheless, and critically, the poem was not nightmarish to readers like Buchanan or to Thomson (who might be trusted to know a nightmare when he saw one). They appreciated its quasi-Gothic as an active engagement with the higher criticism and with religious history more broadly.[11] Surprising numbers of Victorian readers were willing to meet Browning halfway, to create meaning out of his material in a ritual performance of higher criticism pulled inside out. The religious implications of his practice may be clearly felt in comparison with Annie Besant's *Autobiographical Sketches* (1885), in the episode where she describes her youthful frustration at being unable to "harmonise" the passion accounts of the four canonical Gospels. In retrospect, what stands out about young Besant's dabbling in higher critical modes of exegesis is her initial confidence that the four accounts ought to dovetail seamlessly, once put together.[12] The curious part, perhaps, is not that generations of Victorians should record their shock at being disabused

of a naive view of the scriptures' seamless unity; it is that they should conceive of seamless unity as being central to their religion in the first place. By
contrast, early readers of *The Ring and the Book* (preemptively disabused
from assuming clear harmonies between its constituent parts) worked dili-
gently to create just the kind of coherence that Besant and others had taken
for granted in scripture. Browning's poem, we see, pulls Besant's experience
inside out.

Strauss, again, had appreciated the vitality of contemporary biblical
hermeneutic traditions, but he insisted upon the practical impossibility of
distinguishing between the Bible's factual and fanciful parts. Browning found
in his Roman murder story an apparently dead history that could serve as a
useful analogy for the potential vitality—the factuality, even—of the scriptures. Can these dry bones live? Can they talk? And can their meaning be
translated in a self-consciously modern era? "'Tis a credible feat," instructs
the poem, "with the right man and way" (1.771–72). The poem dramatizes
Browning's implicitly religious view that interpretation melds itself to historical fact so thoroughly that one cannot be said to adulterate the other. The
centrality of this interpretative process accounts for the *"Ring"* of Browning's title, for he compares the historical imagination to gold metallurgy and
avers that the alloy of representation does nothing to adulterate the final
purity of this history. "Fancy with fact is just one fact the more" (1.464), he
pronounces—a believer's half-concession to a Straussian view of history.

Tellingly, then, the poem almost immediately foregrounds the biblical
application of Browning's central metaphor. In an early flourish of higher
critical apologetics, the narrator/poet proposes an analogy between his "resuscitation" of the Franceschini characters and the history of the Bible. I cite
the passage at length because it provides not just Browning's *ars poetica* but
also his biblical orientation:

Well, now; there's nothing in nor out o' the world
Good except truth: yet this, the something else,
What's this then, which proves good yet seems untrue?
This that I mixed with truth, motions of mine
That quickened, made the inertness malleolable
O' the gold was not mine,—what's your name for this?
Are means to the end, themselves in part the end?
Is fiction which makes fact alive, fact too?
The somehow may be thishow.

                    I find first
Writ down for very A.B.C. of fact,
"In the beginning God made heaven and earth;"
From which, no matter with what lisp, I spell
And speak you out a consequence—that man,
Man,—as befits the made, inferior thing,—
Purposed, since made, to grow, not make in turn,
Yet forced to try and make, else fail to grow,—
Formed to rise, reach at, if not grasp and gain
The good beyond him,—which attempt is growth,—
Repeats God's process in man's due degree,
Attaining man's proportionate result,—
Creates, no, but resuscitates, perhaps.
Inalienable, the arch-prerogative
Which turns thought, act—conceives, expresses too!
No less, man, bounded, yearning to be free,
May so project his surplusage of soul
In search of body, so add self to self
By owning what lay ownerless before,—
So find, so fill full, so appropriate forms—
That, although nothing which had never life
Shall get life from him, be, not having been,
Yet, something dead may get to live again[.]
        (1.698–729)

This extrapolation from Genesis 1:1 ("In the beginning, God made heaven and earth") plainly takes its impetus from higher critical hermeneutics. It suggests that Genesis, a sublime work of literature, is neither God's dictation nor pure history (whatever that might entail), but a divine reflection of creation repeated "in man's due degree." By 1868, in the wake of related astronomical, geological, and Darwinian revolutions, any endorsement of the Genesis creation account as an "A.B.C. of fact" required either bluster or an ingenious poetic caveat. Browning offers the latter in an apologia derived from Schleiermacher: he appeals to the hermeneutics of believers with a believer's willingness to meet the holy book halfway. God alone creates from nothing, but the literary text and act of literary creation resuscitate the world in a secondary act also requiring a "surplusage of soul," which revivifies the dead parts of God's first creation. Browning interestingly anticipates Jacques Derrida's twentieth-century hermeneutics of the "supplement" insofar as what is supposed to be surplus and superfluous here proves constitutive of the original case. We see here how Browning's literary position quickly exceeds the confines of Schleiermacher's theological one: he asserts that if the literary text cannot resuscitate that which was never created, then the living Bible cannot misrepresent religious history, either. This is reader-response criticism with a vengeance: only what lives for readers is alive. Like the biblical prophet Elisha, whom he here invokes as a religious antecedent (1.760–71), Browning resurrects dead bodies without fear of misinterpretation because, he affirms, his literary method can only animate that which had life already. According to this principle, the sacred Moses of the biblical literature cannot misrepresent the historical Moses, for the literary mechanism itself would not admit such resuscitation, nor can the divine Christ of scriptures misrepresent the historical Jesus. Nor, by extension, can the characters of *The Ring and the Book* misrepresent their historical antecedents to the extent that Browning's remains an inspired retelling of their story. Browning trusted that his poem's reception history would create its validity as history. His work solicits a believer's response so as to provoke, by analogy, a justification of the Bible's own truths for believers.

Without Browning's plain religious provocations in the frame of this poem or the context of 1860s Victorian religious controversy from Darwin and *Essays and Reviews* to Renan and Colenso, the mid- to late Victorians' strongly devotional response to it might be less intriguing. Today, extravagant praise like Buchanan's stands out for its gushy devotional tone: expressions such as "precious and profound spiritual treasure" and "transcendent spiritual teaching." Such expressions suggest a pious sensibility now absent from twenty-first-century Browning studies, but also—and more significantly—absent from Browning's early career. Buchanan goes on to boast that Browning's "perfection of spiritual insight" actually exceeds that of "the Biblical poets" (399–400): an ardent profession of faith even if Buchanan only means the Bible's formal verse and not, let us say, the four Gospels. Thirty years of prior reviews in the *Athenaeum* had rarely flattered Browning, and no one had previously taken him for an oracle.[13] After 1868, by contrast, Browning's quasi-prophetic status rivaled that of Tennyson, and neglected or badly reviewed early works like *Christmas-Eve and Easter-Day* (1850) and *Men and Women* (1855) quickly became "precious and profound spiritual treasure[s]" in turn. Browning's openness about borrowing higher critical models of religious truth in *The Ring and the Book* similarly helps to account for the emphasis paid by the most zealous Victorian Browning-ites to other biblically themed works such as *Christmas-Eve and Easter-Day;* "Bishop Blougram's Apology," "Saul," "An Epistle Containing the Strange Medical Experience of Karshish the Arab Physician," and "Cleon" from *Men and Women* (1855); "Gold Hair," "Rabbi Ben Ezra," "A Death in the Desert," and the epilogue of *Dramatis Personae* (1864). (Plus, eventually, *Ferishtah's Fancies* [1884] and *Parleyings with Certain People of Importance in Their Day* [1887].) A poem like "Rabbi Ben Ezra," rarely taken for a crucial intervention into nineteenth-century hermeneutics, resonates differently in light of Abra-ham Ibn Ezra's twelfth-century appreciation of the multiple authorship of the book of Isaiah—six centuries before Eichhorn rediscovered it and seven centuries before many Victorian readers reluctantly conceded the point. And while *The Ring and the Book* eschews direct reference to Colenso à la "Gold Hair," or to Renan à la *Dramatis Personae,* still its oblique invocation of such Victorian biblical criticism left little doubt about the religious stakes of the poetry that, as Thomson puts it, "must surely be as clear as noonday to even the most purblind vision" (250).

In short, Browning's bold use of the genres of religious discourse in *The Ring and the Book,* more than compensating for the freedom with which he reproduced them, made that freedom seem wonderful to behold—a sort of miracle in and of itself. Scholars have long appreciated Browning's nods to the hagiography of St. George (which in turn has been irresistibly applied to the poet's own biography and marriage). But this famous hagiographical narrative in *The Ring and the Book* competes for space with other, equally persuasive and irreconcilable religious narratives: if on one page Caponsac-chi appeals to the role of St. George rescuing his princess, on another he poses as the celibate St. Francis famously exorcising the demons of Arezzo. While Pope Innocent's deliberations clearly solicit comparison with earlier hagiographical models, still Guido, too, is supposed by his supporters at the close of the story to have miraculously healed a lame beggar (12.159–62). And most Victorian reviewers found the poem's weightiest hagiography in what Buchanan calls "the immortal features" of "Pompilia"—an extraordi-nary study in the mold of a virgin martyrdom. It is this version of the story that I delineate below as illustrative of Browning's method in *The Ring and the Book:* never fully compatible with the poem's competing hagiographies, this virgin martyr narrative deserves special consideration for the neatness with which it serves as a synecdoche for higher critical issues in *The Ring and the Book.* Its prominence, its blatant artifice, its Continental character (especially vis-à-vis the true-blue English story of Caponsacchi/St. George), its perverse resilience (especially in light of Pompilia's motherhood), and its power with the Victorian faithful all speak to Browning's active engagement with the changing Victorian Bible and the terms of the higher criticism.

Browning's Borrowed Catholicism and the Cult of Saint Pompilia

Like many Victorians, Browning associated hagiography with Catholicism, with its distinctive cult of saints and its modern-day Virgin apparitions.[14] But he also associated it with the problems of the higher criticism and religious hermeneutics. Indeed, many mid-century Protestants viewed Catholicism as the mirror reflection of the higher criticism, a religious failing of the opposite extreme. This is plain from *Christmas-Eve,* in which an ungainly and somewhat absurd British chapel meeting reveals its true grace only through comparison with jarring and antithetical alternatives: the high Roman mass at St. Peter's, on the one hand, and the demythologizing German lecture hall at Göttingen on the other. (Conveniently for its Victorian readership, the poem offers British Protestantism as a sort of sensible middle-ground.) In an analogous manner, Arthur Hugh Clough's "Notes on the Religious Tradition" (discussed above in chapter 3) disparages the modern demystification of the Gospels as a sort of religious indiscretion directly antithetical to—and grotesquely mirrored by—"Romish" mystification:

> I do not see that it is a great and noble thing, a very needful or very worthy service, to go about proclaiming that Mark is inconsistent with Luke, that the first Gospel is not really Matthew's, nor the last with any certainty John's, that Paul is not Jesus, &c. &c. &c. It is at the utmost a commendable piece of honesty; but it is no new gospel to tell us that the old one is of dubious authenticity.
>
> I do not see either, on the other hand, that it can be lawful for me, for the sake of the moral guidance and the spiritual comfort, to ignore all scientific or historic doubts, or if pressed with them to the utmost, to take refuge in Romish infallibility, and, to avoid sacrificing the four Gospels, consent to accept the legends of the saints and the tales of modern miracles.[15]
>
> (416)

To a mind like Clough's, Catholicism too plainly represented the flip side of the higher criticism: whereas the higher critics abdicate any claim to the traditional value of the scriptures, Catholics retain this only by abdicating their right to question history sanctioned by the Church, including "the legends of the saints and the tales of modern miracles." "Romish infallibility" affords a sort of solution to problems raised by the higher criticism, but Clough finds this solution more offensive than the original problem.

For his part, Browning was possessed of no more native sympathy than Clough for "Romish" religion, but he found in this antithesis between the "modern miracles" of Catholicism and the ancient ones of biblical narrative a means of testing the relationship between poetry and religion. Nineteenth-century Catholic legend, so problematic for Clough, brought to life Browning's poetic ambition, and the "tales of modern miracles" disparaged by Clough provide Browning with the machinery of a modern mythical poetry. The earliest higher critics had consistently implied that the myths of scripture originally emerged because they could circulate freely in premodern "Oriental" cultures. In theory, at least, the modern West had become less fertile ground for religious movements. But religious legend continued to emerge in modern cultures. The new Mormon scriptures were clearly important in this respect, as was the hubbub recently created in 1839 (and, before that, 1751) by an apocryphal English-language book of Jasher passed off as the lost text mentioned in the Hebrew Bible. As F. Max Müller recounted of the story that Froude's *Nemesis of Faith* was publicly burnt at Oxford, "The story is interesting as showing how quickly a myth can spring up even in our own life-time."[16] And even as Clough composed his "Notes," the Virgin Mary was appearing before the faithful at Paris, Périgord, La Salette, Valence, and most recently at Rimini in Italy.[17] During the next five years, she would appear more famously at Lourdes, and by the 1870s she would regularly perform miracles throughout Germany and Italy, in Ireland and America.[18] Browning's *Red Cotton Night-Cap Country,* to which I will return, will depict these Virgin apparitions as a hazardous illusion on the part of the Catholic world, but, by contrast, *The Ring and the Book* seems to embrace the possibility of modern miracles, and the truth of virgin hagiography in particular.

What Browning so stunningly dramatizes in *The Ring and the Book* is that, in practice, the legends of the nineteenth-century Catholic Revival afford striking religious parallels to the ancient religious traditions that Clough invokes when he concedes that a biblical literature could "grow up naturally" among an illiterate people to express "religious truths of the highest import" ("Notes" 417). If biblical miracles might articulate "truths," then contemporary miracles might do so as well. *The Ring and the Book* carefully re-creates the religious enthusiasm that Clough decries, and its central figure, Pompilia, carefully negotiates the religious conundrum of those contemporary legends scorned by Clough. Browning makes with Pompilia a hagiography for a post–higher critical Protestant world; rather than wondering at the persistence of "modern miracles," as Clough does, he endeavors to harness their power. "Pompilia," in sum, solicits the very religious response that Clough associates with Catholic excess.[19]

Given the Roman setting of the drama and Browning's historical rigor, it makes sense that Pompilia's supporters would use their familiarity with martyr hagiography to articulate her story: thus the sympathetic half of Rome reveres her martyrdom in book 3 (111–12), Caponsacchi insists upon her sainthood in book 6 (1880–81), and Pope Innocent pronounces upon her holiness in book 10 (111–12), even requesting her postmortem intercession: "stoop thou down, my child, / Give one good moment to the poor old Pope / Heart-sick at having all his world to blame" (1005–7).[20] But we should not take for granted the frequency with which nineteenth-century enthusiasts of Browning's poem echo these ideas of Pompilia as "a saint, / Martyr and miracle!" (1.207–8). This hagiographical lens raises genuine questions about the nature of the higher critical history lesson provided in the first book of the poem. Anticipating by a few years John Dalberg-Acton's dry observation that "Kritik grew up on the lives of Saints," Browning asks his readers to grow up on them again.[21]

The Ring and the Book insists repeatedly upon the "facts" of its history: "Here it is all i' the book at last, as first / There it was all i' the heads and hearts of Rome" (1.414–17). Neither did the poet waver from his poem's most forceful historical claims. To Julia Wedgwood, his proofreader, he wrote steadfastly, "I think this is the world as it is," and of Pompilia, in particular, he insisted, "I assure you I found her in the book just as she speaks and acts in the poem."[22] Clear evidence from Charles Hodell's *Old Yellow Book* (1908) and Beatrice Corrigan's *Curious Annals* (1956) has long confirmed Browning's finding of Pompilia to be selective in its emphases, but such evidence falls beside the point of Browning's generic experiment.[23] The strongest Victorian responses to the poem clearly advance the generically constructed ideals of sanctity that the poem itself provides. "For Pompilia," bids Caponsacchi, "build churches, go pray!" (6.1880–81). And reviewers who subscribed to the English cult of poetry did not need to be told twice. What Browning's biographer Alexandra Sutherland Orr calls "the saintly glory of Pompilia" animates many Victorian reviews, and literary scholars discuss "Pompilia" as a hagiographic text *tout court* well into the twentieth century.[24] Still, it is one thing for the *Christian Examiner* of 1868 to describe "Pompilia" as "the most touching passage in the literature of our time" because Pompilia is a "perfect . . . saint" (306). It is quite another for Harriet Gaylord in 1931 to write of Pompilia's ability to "hallow lives," or for Kay Austen in 1979 to argue for Pompilia's real significance as "a Christian saint" (290). The *Christian Examiner* betrays the religious enthusiasm that animated nineteenth-century Browning societies, but Gaylord and Austen demonstrate something more important: the extraordinary effectiveness of Browning's poetic devices and the peculiar longevity of his religious effects.

Browning both asks readers to believe in the truth of this story and rewards their commitment to his hagiography. If his explicit claims to historical truthfulness seem difficult to reconcile to the fact that Pompilia's representation in the poem is a generically mediated event, still the genre anticipates this difficulty. The conflation of the generic and historical terms of saintly biography is the response that all hagiography solicits, because hagiography generates most enthusiasm and authority from readers willing to elide the space between textual representation and historical manifestation. The sympathetic and deliberately naive reading of Pompilia that began with Browning and prevailed for over a century is less a historical accident or misreading of this text than it is the calculated effect of the poem's construction as a virgin martyr hagiography.[25] Sacred literature animates religious experience by dint of its aesthetic and generic properties: the poem both insists and demonstrates that "the world as it is" requires the lens of genre.

Admittedly, the central features of Pompilia's history must generally coincide with the tropes of virgin martyrdom for this all to work. Female martyr hagiography seldom departs from its stock history of a pious young Christian beauty coveted, captured, and finally executed by an evil pagan nobleman. But not only does Pompilia resemble a textbook virgin martyr, we may even feel confident which textbook Browning liked best: his friend Anna Jameson's *Sacred and Legendary Art: Containing the Patron Saints, the Martyrs, the Early Bishops, the Hermits, and the Warrior Saints of Christendom, as Represented in the Fine Arts* (1848).[26] This popular study generated widespread interest in Continental hagiography from the 1840s through the 1860s, and indeed made Jameson into what Adèle Holcomb calls "the first professional art historian."[27] Jameson made a career of *Sacred and Legendary Art,* with supplementary volumes entitled *Legends of the Monastic Orders* (1850), *Legends of the Madonna* (1852), and the unfinished *The History of Our Lord* (1864).[28] Throughout, Jameson organizes her thoughts by genre, and virgin martyrs receive particular attention as instances of quintessentially Catholic aesthetics: noteworthy for their primitive, Gothic, poetical nature.[29] And although Jameson's interests remain ostensibly historical and artistic, she also takes note of contemporary hagiography such as the recently canonized St. Filomela, whose martyrdom by the pagan emperor Diocletian was discovered through the visions of a nineteenth-century mystic in one of the Catholic "modern miracles" so troubling to Protestants and skeptics such as Clough (672). Browning might well have participated in Jameson's composition process for this work: she accompanied the Brownings to Italy on their famous journey of 1846 so that she could finish research for the manuscript.

Attention to the hagiographical basis for Pompilia's character, as represented by Jameson, explains several crucial and otherwise unaccountable additions to the story as Browning had it from his sources in the "Old Yellow Book." In virgin martyr hagiography, the nobleman is invariably a pagan, and the maiden invariably consecrated to Jesus. Invariably, too, he avenges his abortive love by putting her to death, just as she performs miracles or receives visits by angelic beings. The poem's descriptions of Pompilia's home life in Arezzo, then, suggest not the usual forms of Victorian domestic violence, but rather a sort of costume-drama pagan sacrifice: "all was sure / Fire laid and cauldron set, the obscene ring traced, / The victim stripped and prostrate: what of God?" (1.580–83).[30] While Browning's source material attests to domestic brutality of a "My Last Duchess" variety, yet *The Ring and the Book* freely switches genres, borrowing from Jameson's hagiography its depiction of Guido's Arezzo as "the woman's trap and cage and torture-place" (1.502) and the locale of "foul rite[s]."[31] According to *Sacred and Legendary Art,* St. Justina of Antioch and St. Celia were immersed into just such a cauldron as Browning describes (*SLA* 576, 586) and (having been miraculously preserved from scalding) subsequently put to death by knife and sword like Pompilia. (Celia, like Pompilia, also lives for three days that she might perform good works before being taken up to God.) St. Agnes is stripped and burned before decapitation (*SLA* 603), St. Agatha scourged and mutilated before being incinerated, and St. Euphemia smashed with a wooden mallet. Grotesque torture being strictly de rigueur for virgin martyrs, two saints depicted on the frontispiece of Jameson's volume 2—Lucia and Agatha—are identifiable only because they hold aloft body parts that were torn off by their persecutors.

Similar elements from the virgin martyr legends animate book 3, Browning's explanation of "how, to the other half of Rome, / Pompilia seemed a saint and martyr both!" (1.908–9). Here the genre is indicated by Monna Baldi's announcement of Pompilia's healing powers ("Her palsied limb 'gan prick and promise life / At touch o' the bedclothes merely,—how much more / Had she but brushed the body as she tried!" [3.55–58]), coupled by Maratta the painter's claim that "a lovelier face is not in Rome" (3.63).[32] "The Other Half Rome," skeptical of such popular credulity, remarks that Pompilia was never before considered a beauty, but still acknowledges that Pompilia endured at the hands of Guido the sort of trials that have traditionally qualified women for a place in the canon: "Thus Saintship is effected probably; / No sparing saints the process!" (3.111–12), and by the middle of the monologue, even uses the genre to defend her innocence: "If it were this? / How do you say? It were improbable; / So is the legend of my patron-saint" (3.1049–51). A contemporary Italian audience would be aware of the means by which "saintship is effected" and would know to what extent Pompilia's story fulfills them. They could not have been surprised when, by its end, he confidently claims of Pompilia that "The couple were laid 'i the church two days ago, / And the wife lives yet by miracle" (3.1640–41).

Sympathetic voices in *The Ring and the Book* insist upon Pompilia's peerless beauty and affirm their faith in her miraculous powers. But unsympathetic voices contribute equally to this hagiography. Take Guido's extraordinary death row confession that he has always secretly subscribed to the paganism of his distant Roman ancestors:

> I think I never was at any time
> A Christian, as you nickname all the world,
> Me among others: truce to nonsense now!
> Name me, a primitive religionist—
> As should the aboriginary be
> I boast myself, Etruscan, Aretine.
> (11.1914–19)

This rhetorical gesture presents a radical departure from Browning's source documents. And though Browning must be allowed a degree of poetic license in Guido's character, here such license operates in generically precise ways, according to the conventions of *Sacred and Legendary Art*. Only a genuine "primitive religionist" can be expected to lay fire and set cauldron, to trace "the obscene ring" in the approved fashion. Guido's startling decision to emerge from the closet of paganism thus presents an independent—and

otherwise extraneous—confirmation of Pompilia's claims to virgin martyrdom. The same might be demonstrated of Caponsacchi's role as the sort
of comforting angel sent to the virgin martyr saints Catherine (*SLA* 473),
Theclea (560), Dorothea (569), and Cecilia (584).

Finally, and triumphantly, Pompilia's own monologue in the poem's seventh book embraces the virgin martyr hagiography as its own most fitting
antecedent. Pompilia prefaces her history with the exact details of her execution, the foremost credential for her canonization: "The surgeon cared
for me, / To count my wounds,—twenty-two dagger-wounds, / Five deadly,
but I do not suffer much" (7.37–39). Most female martyrs receive their death
before submitting to marriage with pagan noblemen, it is true, but Pompilia
maintains that utter innocence kept her from comprehending what St. Augustine calls "intercourse of the flesh": "—Well, I no more saw sense in what
[Violante] said / Than a lamb does in people clipping wool" (7.386–87). Here
and throughout, Pompilia presents herself as a holy innocent. She emphasizes that her marriage had always admitted questions of authenticity—
"People indeed would fain have somehow proved / He was no husband: but
he did not hear, / Or would not wait, and so has killed us all" (7.156–58)—and
repeatedly yokes the circumstances of her marriage and murder so as to un-
derscore the truth of the martyrdom in contradistinction to the dubiousness
of the marriage.

Pompilia insists that her narrative requires a Continental religious perspective that departs from the everyday and the natural: "Thus, all my life,— / As
well what was, as what, like this, was not,— / Looks old, fantastic and impossible" (7.198–200). As Herbert F. Tucker puts it, only a rhetoric of religious virginity permits the socially suspect flight from Arezzo with a handsome young
priest.[33] Thus Pompilia doggedly associates herself with the virgin heroines
of her religious culture, insisting that she was innocent, virtuous, beautiful,
committed to God and to her virginity, and put to death for being just those
things. Even for the sake of her newborn son, Gaetano, she specifies,

> . . . I hope he will regard
> The history of me as what someone dreamed,
> And get to disbelieve it at the last:
> Since to myself it dwindles fast to that,
> Sheer dreaming and impossibility.
> (7.108–12)

This appeal to the "fantastic and impossible" nature of her history is, of course, central to the hagiographical strategy of her monologue, and while it serves Pompilia to redeem her name from accusations of adultery, it also serves Browning to redeem his heroine for the British public. In either context, the strategy depends upon her tale's fantastic nature, for it is only the fantastic nature of hagiography that allows Pompilia to acknowledge circumstances that might solicit a less forgiving interpretation, and that allows Browning to present her as dazzlingly pure to a British readership accustomed to conceiving of female sexual virtue in more straightforward ways.

As her story nears its most socially questionable moment, then, her flight with Caponsacchi and their stay together in an inn at Castelnuovo, Pompilia appeals directly to the cultural power of virgin martyr hagiography:

> An old rhyme came into my head and rang
> Of how a virgin, for the faith of God,
> Hid herself, from the Paynims that pursued,
> In a cave's heart; until a thunderstone
> Wrapped in a flame, revealed the couch and prey:
> And they laughed—"Thanks to lightning, ours at last!"
> And she cried, "Wrath of God, assert His love!
> Servant of God, thou fire, befriend His child!"
> And lo, the fire she grasped at, fixed its flash,
> Lay in her hand a calm cold dreadful sword
> She brandished till pursuers strewed the ground,
> So did the souls within them die away,
> As o'er the prostrate bodies, sworded, safe,
> She walked forth to the solitudes and Christ:
> So I should grasp the lightning and be saved!
> (7.1389–1403)

Now, the deathbed audience to whom Pompilia recounts this tale may be presumed to know that when Guido overtakes the fugitive pair at Castelnuovo, Pompilia will indeed "grasp the lightning" of his sword in a failed attempt to kill her husband. And, given *The Ring and the Book*'s peculiar narrative structure, so do Browning's readers. Pompilia prefaces her attempt on Guido's life with this holy virgin story not to inform her listeners of the circumstances of her forthcoming encounter, but rather to provide the genre in which she wishes her Castelnuovo encounter understood: hagiographical narrative.[34] She who "grasp[s] the lightning" to strike "Paynims" must be a "virgin" with true "faith of God." Pompilia's acknowledged role model emerges "sworded [and] safe" from the episode, as Pompilia cannot, but many virgin martyrs initially resist subjugation to no ultimate avail. Guido serves nicely as the demon that haunted St. Justina and the dragon that devoured St. Margaret: he is Pompilia's "master, by hell's right" (1586), "the serpent towering and triumphant" (1589), "the old adversary," and, perhaps redundantly, "the fiend" (1623).

In a moment of self-fulfilling prophecy toward the end of her monologue, Pompilia remarks of Guido, "I am saved through him / So as by fire; to him— thanks and farewell!" (1738–39). By this point, even her early mention of her "own five [patron] saints" (107) may retrospectively be considered to include herself. There exists no "St. Pompilia" in the Catholic canon, as Browning surely knew when in a final draft he revised the poem's manuscript from "my own four saints" to "my own five"; either the revised line contains an anachronism (listing two Saint Angelas, although just one was canonized by 1698) or it includes Pompilia herself in the company of Saints Francesca, Camilla, Vittoria, and Angela.[35] In either case, the manuscript alteration points to the profusion of the Catholic cult of saints and to its handiness as a paradigm for one situated in Pompilia's circumstances. It both organizes diverse elements of her story and brings that story to life. And the final words of Pompilia's monologue—"And I rise"—helps bind us to such "old rhyme[s]" as the best generic model for her story.[36]

Despite the wonderful effectiveness with which Pompilia's history lends itself to virgin martyr hagiography, however, the visible factitiousness of her hagiography puts on display the limits, as well as the reaches, of a generic self-defense. Browning refuses to conceal the hand of the artist in this hagiographical creation, and he throws into jeopardy the saint hailed in Victorian reviews (and honored even in much subsequent criticism) by crafting her hagiography out of materials that prohibit its generic logic from operating cleanly. Thus, Pompilia's most ambitious attempts to free herself from culpability sometimes violate the rules of the very genre that establishes her innocence. Here the example of Pompilia's pregnancy and childbearing of Gaetano looms rather large.[37] It is both a consequence of the Victorian cult of motherhood and a tribute to the immense power of *The Ring and the Book*'s hagiographical themes that critics and reviewers have so much understated the audacity of Pompilia's apparent claims to virgin motherhood, her means of reconciling sexual innocence to the fact that she was carrying someone's child when Guido overtook her at Castelnuovo. Almost none of the poem's contemporary reviewers expresses confusion about how Browning leaves this point ambiguous as does J. R. Mozley in *Macmillan's Magazine:*

> We accept for the present, and are content to accept, that view of the subject of the plot—the story of Pompilia—which Mr. Browning evidently means us to believe. . . . And thus we assume, as we are clearly intended to assume, that Guido was a desperate rascal . . . Pompilia a model of pure trustful innocence. *But yet it cannot but be observed that the story lends itself to another interpretation, which Mr. Browning has hardly done his utmost to ward off.*[38] (emphasis mine)

On one level, Mozley is plainly right. But Browning does not "ward off" the possibility of this other interpretation—that Gaetano is the child of Caponsacchi, and Pompilia is not "innocent" in the Victorian sense of the term—because that would destroy the generic experiment that he wishes to effect. Browning was interested in the operation of hagiography as a form that disambiguates such circumstances on its own terms and through its own literary power.

By way of analogy, here, one might think of the story of Strauss's groomsman, who famously quipped of the higher critic's celebrity marriage to the opera singer Agnes Schebest, "It is certainly a strong proof in favour of Strauss' theory, that so many untruths are circulated about his wedding—nay, that it is turned into a myth only a few days after the event."[39] While Strauss's *Leben Jesu* does not itself question the profusion of myth in the modern world, it raises this question nonetheless. In turn, Browning's *Ring and the Book* performs its own latter-day "proof in favour of Strauss' theory" whenever it elides meaningful distinctions between historical fact and poetic fancy. Possibly it does so especially when it elides these distinctions against unequal odds, as in the case of Pompilia's baby, whose appearance drives Pompilia to reach for the most extraordinary claims about her own purity. Pompilia initially suggests the notion of virgin motherhood only tentatively, suggesting that her son will have "No father that he ever knew at all, / Nor ever had—no, never had, I say! / That is the truth,—nor any mother left" (91–93). This early claim she hedges by parallel reflections upon their similar orphanhood: "I never had a father,—no, nor yet / A mother: my own boy can say at least / 'I had a mother whom I kept two weeks!'" (131–33). Yet 1,500 lines later, when her audience is moved by her rhetoric of saintliness and its hagiographical weight, she returns to this theme without any qualifications at all: "My babe nor was, nor is, nor yet shall be / Count Guido Franceschini's child at all—/ Only his mother's, born of love not hate!" (1762–65). It is an extraordinary moment in the poem. She cannot identify the baby as that of Guido (the fiend) or of Caponsacchi (the angel) and so her rhetoric lays claim to a sort of religious parthenogenesis. But this claim is not, as some modern critics have supposed, the consummate example of hagiographical pretensions in a culture where the fantastic is taken for truth. It continues a hagiographical theme of innocence, certainly, but it also indicates where such hagiography must break down. Anyone can become a Catholic saint (at least in theory), but no one else can become the Virgin. However many virgin martyrs proliferate in the Christian tradition, there remains only one Virgin Mother, as Browning knew and as Anna Jameson reminds us by publishing as a separate volume her third work in the *Sacred and Legendary Art* series: *Legends of the Madonna.* The virgin birth entails what Hilary Mantel calls a "one-off by the deity," and the cultic diversity of the religion, sprawling elsewhere, remains bounded here.[40]

This disjunction between Pompilia's vindication in the virgin martyr tradition and the audacity of her pretensions to virgin birth thus exposes a philosophically richer character than either her admirers or her more recent detractors have acknowledged. When today's scholars (such as Walker) first began to question the cult of Pompilia, they called her disingenuous, pragmatic, and evasive, but her rhetoric does not add up to this. It amounts to the cultural power of a particular combination of tropes regardless of Pompilia's sincerity (which might be perfect), and without necessitating any deliberation on her character's part to deploy a generic strategy (beyond taking "an old rhyme" as a model for her demeanor at Castelnuovo). Anna Jameson once recounted having encountered on the streets of Paris a gaily dressed child in beads, flowers, and veils. "Rather surprised at her appearance, I asked her name; she replied blushing, *'Madame, je suis la sainte Vierge'* [Madam, I am the Holy Virgin]."[41] Even if Browning's Pompilia makes the same innocent mistake as Jameson's Parisian girl, she also reveals the problematics of self-canonization. Jameson's story is comical because it shows off the difference between the sacred and the mundane. "Pompilia" is sublime because it shows how religious texts can simultaneously admit and efface that distinction.

In this manner, the generic construction of religious and historical truths becomes essential to Browning's poetic vocation and to his reception as a poet. Browning agreed with Strauss that the Bible's sacred truths were literary, and he understood that Anna Jameson's hagiographies were, like the Gospels, literary sites where fact and embellishment become indistinguishable and still demand to be read as truth. He took seriously the possibility of finding truth in the "legends of the saints" of which Clough complained, and for the same reason. So "Pompilia" presents a clear and important extension of the logic of "A Death in the Desert" (1864), an earlier dramatic monologue that purports to represent the death speech of St. John the Evangelist. In a twist upon the Gospel of John, which records the author's presence at Christ's crucifixion ("And he that saw *it* bare record, and his record is true" [19:35 AV]), Browning's St. John concedes that he was not present at the crucifixion, while insisting upon the fundamental truth of that biblical account in which he claimed to be there.[42] The analogy between Pompilia's hagiography and St. John's Gospel ought to be plain: both are fantastic religious tales by authors who insist upon their truthfulness even as they reveal their own historical dubiousness. Browning, like his own St. John, elides the difference between the generic and historical elements of his religious text when he insists that Pompilia "is just as I found her in the book." And Browning's St. John performs exactly the ideal of poetic creation offered by *The Ring and the Book:* that to "write a book shall mean, beyond the facts, / Suffice the eye and save the soul beside" (12.862–63). For Browning, no literature could be more eye-sufficing and soul-saving than the Gospel of John, so it is all the more compelling that he takes a Johannine approach in his construction of "Pompilia." Like St. John with his gospel, Browning composes "beyond the facts."

The Protestant Truths of Catholic Poetry

There is no reason to take the religious meaning of Browning's poetry to be always in keeping with, or reducible to, his personal religious commitments. On the contrary, to appreciate Browning's genius with religious symbols, it actually helps to distinguish the religious operation of his poetry from his presumed beliefs. Any analysis of Browning's response to the higher criticism in *The Ring and the Book* must accommodate the difference between Browning's ability to marshal the religious vision of seventeenth-century Rome and his ongoing commitment to nineteenth-century evangelical nonconformism. While we cannot speak with certitude about Browning's private beliefs, yet we can confidently maintain with William O. Raymond that "so far as Browning can be claimed by a religious party, his affiliations lie with the Evangelicals" (595), and we can certainly affirm that such denominational difference remained an issue of some moment in Victorian Britain. We can even agree that Browning regularly demonstrates what one twentieth-century biographer calls an "anti-Catholic prejudice," a prejudice noted with resentment by nineteenth-century reviewers in Catholic periodicals such as the *Dublin Review.*[43] Therefore, Browning's reliance upon a Catholic aesthetics in his most ambitious poetry ought to be better appreciated as a means of engaging with higher critical models of religious sacralization. "Pompilia" operates through a disjunction between what Browning insists to be "truth" and what he shows to be a generically achieved canonization. Although Browning clearly celebrates Pompilia's virtue, he also deliberately acknowledges the problematic nature of such auto-hagiography; and although he establishes the cult of her sainthood, he provides as well suggestions (or reminders) that her generic pretensions are just that: generic pretensions. This paradox (as I hope to show) does not contradict Browning's religious engagement; on the contrary, its exploration is essential to his kind of Protestantism in the 1860s.

Jameson's *Sacred and Legendary Art,* in addition to providing a handbook to the hagiographical themes of *The Ring and the Book,* also suggests religious motivations for Browning's artistic choices. First among these is Jameson's view that Catholic hagiographical legend represents an artistic foundation of Western culture, a genre without which European civilization might never have survived. "It is a mistake to suppose that these legends had their sole origin in the brains of dreaming monks," says Jameson in the preface to her work. "The wildest of them had some basis of truth to rest on, and the forms which they gradually assumed were but the necessary result of the age which produced them. . . . In these universally diffused legends, we may recognize the means, at least one of the means, by which a merciful Providence, working through its own immutable laws, had provided against the utter depravation, almost extinction, of society" (2–4). Jameson forestalls anti-Catholic criticism on the part of her readers by openly sharing their distaste for "dreaming monks." But instead of depicting medieval hagiography as a tool of a malevolent Catholic hierarchy (and enduring threat to British souls), she reenvisions it as folk art and a sort of primitive antecedent to a more enlightened Protestantism. This rhetorical maneuver allows her Protestant readers to appreciate Catholic art for its poetic insightfulness while feeling gratified about their own presumably more sophisticated religious identity. Victorian ideas of evolution and progress facilitate this handy religious transvaluation, and indeed much Victorian anthropology rests upon its self-congratulating teleology. As an art critic, Jameson views Catholics much as the anthropologist Edward Tylor will view the benighted subjects of his *Primitive Culture* (1871), in which religion itself becomes a symptom of the primitive mind. But comparison with Tylor brings home the tenuousness of Jameson's position: the benighted religion (or irreligion) of the Victorian other can always be pitied as a halfway house to the enlightened religion (or irreligion) of the Victorian self.

In actuality, Jameson's usefulness to Browning springs from her aesthetic resistance to her own denominational complacency: when her engagement with the art of foreign legend requires her to suspend her assumptions about the superiority of Protestant Christianity, and when the dialectic inadvertently set in motion between Protestant religion and Catholic art drives her in the direction of the higher criticism. For instance, while she dismisses many of her fantastic virgin martyr legends as mere fictions (as those of Saints Ursula and Filomena), she insists on the essential factuality of others (Saints Agnes and Perpetua), and her inability consistently or systematically to separate "historic truth" from the "poetic fiction" of hagiography serves at first to emphasize, and then to elide the importance of distinguishing between them at all. Ultimately in *Sacred and Legendary Art,* such legends come to represent a site at which religion, art, and history can become intertwined and indistinguishable from one another. In the tale of St. Cecilia, for example, she writes, "There can be little doubt that the main incidents of her life and martyrdom are founded in fact, though mixed up with the usual amount of marvels, parables, and precepts, poetry and allegory. . . . In this, as in other instances, I shall make no attempt to separate historic truth from poetic fiction, but give the legend according to the ancient version, on which the painters founded their representations" (583–84). The very profusion of material in *Sacred and Legendary Art* tears Jameson between her twin goals of redeeming "genuine" historical antecedents to the truths of Protestant Christianity and celebrating the legends' Catholic fusion of "fact" and "fancy." Ultimately, like Strauss before her, Jameson concludes that "historic truth" and "poetic fiction" are not worth distinguishing even if they can be distinguished. In her incidental and admittedly clumsy manner, she becomes a Straussian *avant la lettre*—or, rather, *après la lettre,* but without the benefit of knowing Strauss. Still, even as an unthreatening middlebrow art historian, Jameson bespeaks the revolution of the higher criticism when she celebrates the "poetical" nature of these legends as genuinely sacred. Despite her text's anti-Catholic orientation, she insists that even the most bizarre and obscure of these legends "may be said to hallow . . . daily life when considered in a right spirit" (621).[44]

While Jameson unfolds saintly history for its redemptive capacities as art, Browning adds art to history in the creation of his own saint. His virgin martyr, too, comes to instantiate Browning's claim that "fancy with fact is just one fact the more" to precisely the extent that it succeeded with Victorian readers. No religious facts can be made for a skeptical reader such as Mozley, who doubts the cult of Pompilia, but religious facts are made for born skeptics such as Furnivall and Thomson—to say nothing of Buchanan, the idolaters of the Browning Society, and twentieth-century critics such as Gaylord and Austen. "Pompilia" reworks the terms of Jameson's "poetic fiction[s]" to explore not their history but their genesis as a literary construct. Jameson determines not to distinguish between history and art, and Browning creates a legend geared to drive his readers to the same resolve. The poem's reviews unwittingly celebrate Browning's gifts as a hagiographical embellisher of the type mistrusted by Jameson's Protestant readership, yet if "art remains the one way possible / Of speaking truth" (12.839–840), as Browning maintains, then the rhetorical feats of "Pompilia" express an essential element of faith while providing a clinic in the mechanisms of history. According to his own famous analogy, when finally the pure "gold" of Pompilia's history is shaped into a ring by her generic construction here, his own fancy is washed out of the mixture, leaving unalloyed fact. He took this idea of truth very seriously, once more, if his letters to Julia Wedgwood are any indication. Flying in the face of what we know to be hagiography, Browning insists of the poem that "the business has been, as I specify, to explain fact—and the fact is what you see. . . . Before I die, I hope to purely invent something,—here my pride was concerned to invent nothing: the minutest circumstance that denotes character is true" (emphasis Browning's).[45] The hagiographical elements of Pompilia considered in this chapter thus, if Browning's letters are to be trusted, serve for him a historical function in addition to a sacred function. Genre conditions sight—"and the fact is what you see."

Browning's deployment of the generic authority of hagiography bears particular interest with reference to this history of the changing Bible of Victorian poets because he learned much of his technique from Barrett Browning. Indeed, his "business" of explaining *"fact"* concerns her own subsequent reception as much as his. As Browning's friend Alexandra Orr recorded, "The ingenuously unbounded maternal pride, the almost luscious maternal sentiment, of Pompilia's dying moments can only associate themselves in our mind with Mrs. Browning's personal utterances, and some notable passages in *Casa Guidi Windows* and *Aurora Leigh*."[46] Nina Auerbach rather understates the case when she claims that with Pompilia, Browning "added his wife to the chorus of his creations" (106). *The Ring and the Book* remains a major event in Barrett Browning's reception history, so it can be helpful to recognize the extent to which Browning's motivation in writing Pompilia dovetailed with his religious commitments and his bold gambit into the construction of history. Once more, however, his enshrinement of Barrett Browning only magnified a process begun many years before by the poet herself. Pompilia's cunningly rendered self-createdness celebrates Barrett Browning not as sacred muse and holy virgin, per se, but as Protestant artist and Victorian mother who appropriates and wields the power of muse and virgin. Victorian pronouncements on "Mrs. Browning's spiritual presence" in "Pompilia" are entirely in keeping with the religious encomia that Barrett Browning herself so often solicited and received when alive: for instance, Dinah Mulock Craik's "So, go thou in, saint—sister—comforter! / Of this, thy house of joy, heaven keep the doors!" which she confessed touched her "to the quick."[47]

Likewise, Tricia Lootens has shown how mid-century religious and poetic canonization had very powerfully converged and blended to "sanctify" the life and afterlife of Barrett Browning, and at no time more so than the years in which her husband outlived her. One must take further Lootens's shrewd argument that "if we are to understand what canonicity has created and cost, we must address the power of legend—and must acknowledge, too, how significantly such power has been shaped by cultural traditions linked to the lives of the saints."[48] And this is especially true of Browning's canonicity, because Browning was so aware of the mechanisms of such canonization; he witnessed how his wife's death had contributed to her already-weighty status in Victorian poetic and religious legend, and he, more than any other person, helped shape his wife's legacy in the years after her death, accomplishing this largely through such works as *The Ring and the Book*.[49]

Barrett Browning's work, and *Aurora Leigh* in particular, had taught Browning the value of the generic tropes of hagiography. "Pompilia" represents an earnest development of religious issues addressed in *Aurora Leigh*: single motherhood, saintliness, and a Protestant adoption of Mariology. In Aurora's promises to Marian Earle, for instance, we see an early picture of the poetical devotional paradigm that would later serve Browning: "And in my Tuscan home I'll find a niche / And set thee there, my saint, the child and thee, / And burn the lights of love before thy face" (7.126–28). If "Pompilia" mirrors Barrett Browning's appropriation in *Aurora Leigh* of the hagiographical culture of Italian Catholicism (the niche, the Madonna, the devotional candles), it mirrors, too, the zeal of a believer in the availability of religious truth to poets. *The Ring and the Book* as much as demonstrates this availability, reproducing these tropes so skillfully as to contrive a religious reading of itself. Like the story of Marian Erle (who also had a "poor unfathered child" [7.327]), Pompilia's story might well cause revulsion in its readers, but it does so in service of a religious impulse that many nineteenth-century readers endorsed. The factitious nature of the religious experience provided by *The Ring and the Book* solicits a higher critical critique of the poem's religious logic; like *Aurora Leigh,* this poem openly wagers that its cumulative emotional effect will trump the reader's reservations on that head.

Later in life, Browning maintained that his ideas "were made beautiful and blessed by my perfect knowledge of one woman's pure soul. Had I never known Elizabeth, I never could have written *The Ring and the Book*" (qtd. in Gaylord, 20). The praise is purely generic: its sense relies upon the popular success of "Pompilia" as a devotional text. Then, too, the popular Victorian conflation of Barrett Browning and Pompilia provides its own evidence of the success of Browning's generic experiment. As a rule, established Victorian poets did not gratuitously associate their private names with adulterous teenage fugitives. Had Pompilia's virtue remained a doubtful proposition, as it appears in Mozley's review, any direct parallel between Pompilia's "pure soul" and Barrett Browning's might have reflected badly upon both Brownings. But with the overwhelming success of *The Ring and the Book,* Browning's subsequent literary persona could rely upon the integrity of his artistic creation.

For this reason, Pompilia's openly self-generated hagiography may be seen as a devotional work for all its apparent disclosure and demystification of religious narrative. It uses traditionally Catholic generic structures in a specifically Protestant celebration of woman and a specifically Victorian hermeneutic. It perpetuates his wife's canonization in a way that celebrates religious truth as the effect of genre. And Browning's faith in Christianity rests upon the redeeming qualities of just such a poetically generated canonicity as "Pompilia" realizes. We cannot upon internal evidence doubt the integrity of the poet's devotion to his late wife in this instance without at the same time doubting his religiosity, because they operate by the same principle. Pompilia's sainthood, like Barrett Browning's, is effected by the saint herself through a combination of history and literature, fact and fancy. Browning's conviction in the sanctity of both rests upon his conviction in the redemptive power of literary texts. *The Ring and the Book* was written to redeem and inspire, operating in part as an exposé of Barrett Browning's secular sainthood, but much more as a devotional text. Browning's version of the Barrett Browning legend, like his version of St. John, stands or falls upon his religious conviction that "fiction which makes fact alive" might prove, in the end, "fact too."

To all appearances, the poetical and historical conflict that shapes the genre of "Pompilia" remained as pertinent to Browning as the Bible itself and as personal as his relationship with Barrett Browning. That Browning capitalizes upon these does not forcibly diminish his devotion either to the Bible or to *Aurora Leigh*. It raises questions about how much such poetry depends upon the Victorian cult of poetry, but in considering these questions, we would do well to remember how deist biblical critics reflexively questioned the integrity of the scriptural authors before the higher critics offered a more satisfying—as well as a more generous—model of authorship. More successfully than any other poet in this study, Browning both gathers the fruits of historical biblical criticism and shows how more fruit can be grown.

Browning's Futile Retraction: Red Cotton Night-Cap Country

The Ring and the Book established Browning as a sage and poet of the first order, and to read it as a tribute to Barrett Browning's "pure soul" is to grasp anew the depth of his engagement with the higher criticism and the shrewdness of his faithfulness to *Aurora Leigh*. And the strongest evidence of the power of genre in *The Ring and the Book* may reside in its power to trump the logic of Browning's own subsequent poetry wherever apparent conflicts arise. In other words, the poem's religious power persisted even in the face of Browning's later attempts to undo it. The clearest instance of this may be found in *Red Cotton Night-Cap Country, or, Turf and Towers,* a long poem that seems intended to chasten the very religious response to Browning that *The Ring and the Book* encourages. In the years immediately following 1868, Browning turned away from "the legends of the saints and the tales of modern miracles" in order to write *Balaustion's Adventure* (1871), *Prince Hohenstiel-Schwangau* (1871), and *Fifine at the Fair* (1872): of these, the first provides a radically different image of Barrett Browning, and the latter two were subjects of which she strongly disapproved. (The notion of Balaustion in particular as a corrective of sorts to the figure of Pompilia may be found in Charles Hodell's caution that "it takes, however, both the throbbing humanity of Balaustion and the saintly glory of Pompilia to express fully the nature of Elizabeth Barrett Browning as she appeared to her husband" [281].) But with *Red Cotton Night-Cap Country,* Browning returns anew to the themes of virgin martyr hagiography and Marian devotion. And far from provoking a religious response in the manner of "Pompilia," *Red Cotton Night-Cap Country* seems to mirror it grotesquely, like a parody of the religious mechanisms of that earlier poem.

Like *The Ring and the Book, Red Cotton Night-Cap Country* uses poetic hermeneutics as a tool to pry open a homicidal legal case. The subject excited Browning, and John Pettigrew and Thomas J. Collins reasonably maintain that "part of the reason for his excitement is unquestionably the parallels between the materials and the treatment of them in *The Ring and the Book* and *Red Cotton Night-Cap Country*" (2. 986). *Red Cotton Night-Cap Country* concerns the estate of one Monsieur Léonce Miranda, a Norman gentleman whose weakness for his lover drives him to a series of desperate acts of Catholic piety—including that of burning off his hands. These acts culminate in a suicidal leap from the tower of his château, a leap that Browning's poem imagines as precipitated by his vision of the Holy Virgin of La Ravissante (one of a great number of nineteenth-century Virgin apparitions in France), whom he trusts to hold him aloft in the sky as a reward for his unmixed faith. But the Virgin, apparently unmoved by Miranda's zeal, declines to have angels suspend him in midair. Falling from the towers of his religious imagination, Miranda dies on the turf of the physical world.

Far from soliciting the religious response of Browning's earlier poem, we see, *Red Cotton Night-Cap Country* seems designed to steel readers against it. The poet dryly defends his protagonist by insisting that a vision of the Virgin based upon the evidence of the senses makes such suicide sane and reasonable. This is a bit like Nietzsche's mock relief that Christians do not generally pluck out their own eyes in accordance with the dictates of the Gospels.[50] In any case, Miranda's excuse only extends to believers who have been favored with personal apparitions, and his ultimate fate would normally seem to militate against the nineteenth-century cult of the Virgin—or at least suggest the foolhardiness of presuming upon it as he does. The text thus presents a dramatic correction of any dangerous Mariolatrous tendencies in *The Ring and the Book, Aurora Leigh,* or even Anna Jameson's *Legends of the Madonna,* the last volume in the *Sacred and Legendary Art* series completed by her before her death.[51] In that work, Jameson urges her Protestant readership to acknowledge the historical significance of Marian devotion: "Worship of the Madonna did prevail through all the Christian and civilized world for nearly a thousand years [and] in spite of errors, exaggerations, abuses, this worship did comprehend certain great elemental truths interwoven with our human nature."[52] Barrett Browning's use of the Marian image in *Aurora Leigh* reifies the "great elemental truths" found by Jameson, and "Pompilia" probes deeply into the radical literary implications of doing so. By contrast, *Red Cotton Night-Cap Country* makes these truths seem hazardous as well as doubtful. "Pompilia" proffers itself as a mixture of history and "errors, exaggerations, [and] abuses," but resolves these abuses in "the miracle" of religious perception. *Red Cotton Night-Cap Country* divorces perception from any miracle.

Browning remained as emphatic about the historical accuracy of *Red Cotton Night-Cap Country* as he had been about *The Ring and the Book*. Whenever discussing the poem, he pointed out, "Indeed the facts are so exactly put down, that, in order to avoid the possibility of prosecution for Libel—that is, telling the exact truth—I changed all the names of persons and places."[53] Here, "the exact truth" of history seems called upon to debunk religious enthusiasm much as it was called upon to engender enthusiasm in the earlier poem. This poem, like *The Ring and the Book*, meditates upon the contributions of emotion and perception to truth: "Truth I say, truth I mean: this love was true, / And the rest happened by due consequence, / By which we are to learn that there exists / A falsish false, for truth's inside the same, / And truth that's only half true, falsish truth" (1487–91). Attending to such passages, Donald Hair convincingly analyzes *Red Cotton Night-Cap Country* as a dialogue between two divergent views of religious epistemology: Lockeian empiricist and "Germano-Coleridgian" idealist.[54] More important to Browning's legacy, however, is that it also seems designed to qualify the generic experiment of *The Ring and the Book*, with its demonstrations that religious truth is composed of generic form. *Red Cotton Night-Cap Country* puts on display how the generic forms of religious discourse may be used to deceive the hapless and credulous. Miranda's apparent delusions and suicide embody the price of that deceit.

Consider the iconographic depiction of Miranda's lover, Clara de Mille-fleurs, as she acknowledges her dubious past as a stage actor and kept mistress of one Lord N.:

As the meek martyr takes her statued stand
Above our pity, claims our worship just
Because of what she puts in evidence,
Signal of suffering, badge of torture borne
In days gone by, shame then but glory now,
Barb, in the breast, turned aureole for the front!
So, half timidity, composure half,
Clara de Millefleurs told her martyrdom.
(1543–50)

Here, as in *The Ring and the Book,* Browning seizes upon the iconography of virgin martyrs outlined in *Sacred and Legendary Art* and elsewhere. But unlike "Pompilia," *Red Cotton Night-Cap Country* does not readily permit its readers to approve for themselves the auto-hagiography of the heroine, still less to adopt it. A hundred lines on, Clara de Millefleurs confesses herself to be really Lucie Steiner, sometime milliner and estranged wife of Ulysse Muhlhausen—by no means the flower (*"fleur"*) that she initially seems to Miranda. Clara presents a Duessa to Pompilia's Una, or a sort of Arabella Donn to Pompilia's Sue Bridehead (Hardy's *Jude the Obscure,* to be sure, appears only in 1895). The poem's narrator admires Lucie/Clara's pragmatism and spirit, but takes no pains to hide her mendaciousness and opportunism.

Miranda, at all events, remains unhappy about his moral compromises, and in the episode upon the tower with the Virgin of La Ravissante, he fantasizes about redeeming a whole host of social and moral ills through his miraculous show of faith:

Regenerated France makes all things new!
My house no longer stands on Quai Rousseau
But Quai rechristened Alacoque: a quai
Where Renan burns his book, and Veuillot burns
Renan beside, since Veuillot rules the roast,
Re-edits now indeed "The Universe."
O blessing, O superlatively big
With blessedness beyond all blessing dreamed
By man! for just that promise has effect,
"Old things shall pass away and all be new!"
Then, for a culminating mercy-feat,

Wherefore should I dare dream impossible
That I too have my portion in the change?
My past with all its sorrow, sin and shame,
Becomes a blank, a nothing! There she stands,
Clara de Millefleurs, all deodorized,
Twenty years' stain wiped off her innocence!
There never was a Muhlhausen, nor at all
Duke Hertford: naught that was, remains, except
The beauty,—yes, the beauty is unchanged!
Well, and the soul too, that must keep the same!
And so the trembling little virgin hand
Melts into mine, that's back again, of course!
(3553–75)

From a historical perspective, Miranda's catalog of events here falls into anticlimax, if not bathos: his view narrows from a restored monarchy and a "Regenerated France" to the chastisement of infamous skeptics (Sister Margaret Mary Alacoque displaces Rousseau and the orthodox Louis Veuillot burns the higher critic Renan) and from there to Miranda's own life. From Miranda's personal perspective, however, this same catalog of social healing presents a glorious crescendo; his love's redemption becomes the "culminating mercy-feat" of this miraculous encounter with the Virgin: "Clara de Millefleurs, all deodorized, / Twenty years' stain wiped off her innocence!"

It is needless to add that the restitution of Clara's virginity (and accompanying restitution of Miranda's hands) recalls Pompilia's own reconstituted virginity in truly unflattering ways. Miranda demonstrates little subtlety in metaphysics. He has his lover's hand already (as that synecdoche goes), but wants to see it restored to him as a "trembling little virgin hand." He trips upon the awkward question of how to divorce "soul" from experience, but insists that Clara's soul "must keep the same," beautifully embodied in its assumed name but without past lovers (Hertford) or husbands (Muhlhausen), whom his fantasy obliterates with a thoroughness more shocking than the imagined burning of Renan at the hands of Veuillot. At the same time, Miranda's desire to have de Millefleurs ("a thousand flowers") "all deodorized" provides the most unnatural image in the passage: even the most ardent Victorian champion of female virginity ought to recoil from the prospect of a thousand deodorized flowers.

Strikingly, however, *Red Cotton Night-Cap Country* did little to discourage religiously minded fin de siècle Browningites, or even to alter the tone of their criticism. Victorian Browning enthusiasts did not care for this skeptical view of the generic experiment that had done most to secure Browning's literary immortality. Many voiced their displeasure that their hero had so dramatically departed from the sacred tenor of his early work. Sir Henry Jones, a typical example, protested in his book-length study that Browning himself "had Pompilia's faith" (89) and that "his faith, like Pompilia's, is held fast 'despite the plucking fiend'" (17). So it is unsurprising that Jones rejects *Red Cotton Night-Cap Country* and champions instead the earlier work, in which, as Jones puts it, "his inspiration was more direct and full" (322). Jones's understanding of Browning's earlier "inspiration" holds particular interest because he appreciated Browning's engagement with sacred text without setting apart the biblical scriptures as uniquely inspired: "It is because I thus regard Browning as not merely a poet but a prophet, that I think that I am entitled to seek in him, as in Isaiah or Aeschylus, a solution, or a help to the solution, of the problems that press upon us when we reflect upon man, his place in the world and his destiny" (15). Such statements plainly echo the Reverend J. Kirkman's inaugural address to the London Browning Society, which also compares Browning to the prophet Isaiah; Jones pairs ancient Hebrew and Greek poets as a jointly sacred heritage.[55] But his philosophy becomes what we might term fin de siècle "art for wisdom's sake." Browning must help solve "the problems that press upon us when we reflect upon man, his place in the world and his destiny," and wherever Browning's instruction leans toward skepticism, it may be rejected on pragmatic grounds. Jones treats late Browning poems like *Red Cotton Night-Cap Country* as a sort of Browning apocrypha: interesting and worthy of study, but wanting in the "full" inspiration of the earlier canonical poetry.[56]

The mechanical operation of religious belief in *The Ring and the Book* thus contains a degree of proof against even Browning's own critique in *Red Cotton Night-Cap Country*. Ironically, the more Browning attacked it, the more pure and disinterested *The Ring and the Book*'s validation of religious difference came to seem. That poem relies upon a wary sympathy with various elements of Continental Catholicism, as Browning himself saw in the poem's opening book, where he defends his story to a Catholic critic:

> ["]And it tells
> Against the Church, no doubt,—another gird
> At the Temporality, your Trial, of course?"

"—Quite otherwise this time," submitted I;
"Clean for the Church and dead against the world[."]
(1.433–37)

The Ring and the Book here solicits sympathy with "Catholic" material even as the poet hastens to add that he himself runs no risk of Romish conversion (or, as the Victorians had it, "perversion"), assuring readers that he is not to be "manned by [Henry Edward] Manning and new-manned / By [John Henry] Newman and, mayhap, wise-manned to boot / By [Nicholas] Wiseman" (444–46). Naturally, Browning often used alternative religious positions to explore the implications of the higher criticism for his Christianity. Thus we find a supposed insider's view of first-century Arab monotheism (possibly the cult of El) in "Karshish," of Judaism in "Jochanan Hakkadosh" (1883) and (more lightly rendered) in "Rabbi Ben Ezra," of Islam in *Ferishtah's Fancies,* and of Catholicism in poems like *Sordello* (1840), "Soliloquy of the Spanish Cloister" (1842), "The Bishop Orders His Tomb at Saint Praxed's Church" (1845), and "Bishop Blougram's Apology" (1855). Throughout the period of these poems, Browning ran no more risk of being taken for a closet Catholic than he did of being taken for a closet Muslim. But his perceived distance from Catholicism sometimes lent more credence to his "Catholic" poems where they became most sympathetic or ecumenical.

Even where Browning's poetry places alternative religious traditions in an unflattering light, his dramatic representation of religious alterity provides him with a crucial degree of philosophical distance. His Protestant readership found such "insider" depictions entirely compelling, as in John Ruskin's famous praise of "The Bishop Orders His Tomb" in the fourth volume of *Modern Painters:* "I know of no other piece of modern English . . . in which there is so much told, as in these lines, of the Renaissance spirit,—its worldliness, inconsistency, pride, hypocrisy, ignorance of itself, love of art, of luxury, and of good Latin." In reality, Ruskin's catalog of Italian vices might derive from any number of texts in the English Gothic tradition or—alternately—from nineteenth-century evangelical anti-Papist religious pamphlets. What impresses Ruskin is Browning's vivid expression of historical detail, at once economical and copious. While such remarks upon Browning's endeavors with Catholic religious genres tell us little directly about Browning's religious investments, they help to clarify aspects of its perceived truthfulness. *The Ring and the Book*'s religious tropes resonate so powerfully in part because of their borrowed Catholicism, and not despite it. Harnessed into the service of a reliably Protestant spiritual transcendence, such borrowing testifies to its own integrity in a way that the attacks of *Red Cotton Night-Cap Country* cannot subsequently efface.

Browning's Pragmatism

To view *The Ring and the Book* in conjunction with *Red Cotton Night-Cap Country* is to see how the force of genre trumps Browning's own religious allegiances even where it relies upon the idea that he had them. In all such cases, it remains worth differentiating between questions of Browning's religion and the more germane question of how Browning's poetry contrived to generate his extraordinary religious following. Even many Victorian critics of Browning's poetry realized that they needed to distinguish the sacredness of the poetry from questions about the poet's personal beliefs—a realization that became increasingly urgent as Browning's friends increasingly relied upon hearsay to interpret his poetry. Alexandra Sutherland Orr's "The Religious Opinions of Browning" (1892), for instance, uses private conversation to ground her position that the epilogue of *Dramatis Personae* refers to the person of Christ.[57] Business at the London Browning Society, similarly, was sometimes postponed so that Furnivall could consult the poet on thorny problems of interpretation. Orr's statement now seems facile, and Furnivall's practice ridiculous, but this is because in hindsight Browning seems more like one of his own unreliable narrators and less like what Roland Barthes calls the Author/God. While no Browning scholar today will dismiss the interest of Orr's account or fail to admire the aplomb with which Furnivall pronounces on Browning's brand of Christianity, still one need not be deeply versed in Barthes's or Michel Foucault's ideas of the "death of the author" to be struck by such uncritical acquiescence in Browning's behindhand ideas about the meaning of his own poetry. Browning himself anticipated Barthes's general idea clearly enough that when cornered by the inquiries of eager Browningites, he eventually took to recommending the conclusions of the Browning Society—as though to seal that hermeneutic loop.

More recent Browning scholarship, too, has struggled to divorce itself from questions about Browning's personal beliefs. When E. S. Shaffer describes "A Death in the Desert" as "a masterpiece of convincing casuistry" (210), she seems to solicit a critique of Browning's underlying aims ("casuistry" meaning "rationalization" in addition to applied religious doctrine). Subsequent critics have pursued Browning's higher critical understanding of history and science as heuristic fictions (Suzanne Bailey), his attention to the fraught problem of manuscript authentication and transmission (Adam Roberts), and his higher critical understanding of language theory (Michael Johnstone).[58] And although such scholarship nowhere surrenders to a naive Victorian understanding of Browning's authorship, still it generally takes Browning's poetic representation of the higher criticism to be in keeping with his personal views. Linda H. Peterson rightly urges us to consider how often Browning forces us "to interpret for ourselves and to decide, if we can, what Browning means."[59] But for most readers, the poetry's unreliable narrators and marked emphasis upon language and mediation seem to bespeak the poet's epistemological skepticism as the chief grounds for his affirmation of religion.

Browning's bold experimentation with the higher critical hermeneutics in *The Ring and the Book,* by contrast, could short-circuit such skepticism and also escape the purview of Browning's own religious commitments. The public's rejection of *Red Cotton Night-Cap Country* might show this if its enthusiastic embrace of *The Ring and the Book* did not. In the end, *The Ring and the Book* demonstrates the fundamental unruliness of the inspired text, especially when viewed in relation to *Red Cotton Night-Cap Country,* and shows how Browning's involvement with the higher criticism in some ways trumped his own ultimate intentions or beliefs. *The Ring and the Book* may feel like a game in higher critical hermeneutics, but its inspiration was felt by Victorian readers even where Browning tried to curb the feeling.

What remains of Browning's contributions to higher critical hermeneutics may be an object lesson in a view of religion and history that hinges upon its usefulness, an intriguing antecedent to the philosophical pragmatism that William James would later articulate in *The Will to Believe* (1897) and *Varieties of Religious Experience* (1902). Here Orr's report of Browning's personal statements on religion becomes freshly relevant. "I grant even that it may be a fiction," said Orr's Browning, "but I am none the less convinced that the life and death of Christ, as Christians apprehend them, supply something which their humanity requires, and that it is true for them" (367). Given the contradictions inherent in Browning's poetry, such a wedding of apprehension and religious truth may seem comical, or even ironically poignant. But if Victorian Browningites found in *The Ring and the Book* "something which their humanity require[d]," at least Browning himself ought to have understood why they should so zealously hold by its truths.

Chapter 5

GEORGE ELIOT'S FITS OF POETRY

G EORGE ELIOT COULD hardly have picked a worse time to publish her first volume of poetry, *The Spanish Gypsy,* than the fall of 1868. A few weeks previously, her friend Robert Browning's *The Ring and the Book* had created a great critical hubbub, partly by orchestrating its own quasi-religious reception in ways that I describe in the previous chapter. To the extent that Browning's poem capitalizes upon the changing hermeneutics of the Victorian Bible, as I argue, Eliot found herself taken to school in a subject to which she had made real contributions as the translator of David Friedrich Strauss and Ludwig von Feuerbach. Browning himself had recently deferred to Eliot's judgment about "Gold Hair" (1864, a poem I address in my introduction).[1] Nonetheless, Eliot's view of the Victorian Bible brought her to a very different poetic ideal than Browning, whose most stunning poetic achievement in *The Ring and the Book* took up what she clearly saw as the wrong parts of their shared religious heritage.

To put all of this into practical terms, Eliot's inordinate hopes for *The Spanish Gypsy* rather quashed the sympathetic pleasure that one might normally take in a friend's successes—even the extravagant sort of sanctification enjoyed by Browning. When Eliot's publisher, John Blackwood, suggested that sales of *The Spanish Gypsy* had faltered because critics had "got it into their heads . . . to praise Browning," she responded with distaste that she, too, had been reading *The Ring and the Book* to her husband, George Henry Lewes:

> At present it verifies the fear we have always had when we have heard Browning talk of the poem, namely that the subject is too void of fine elements to bear the elaborate treatment he has given to it. It is not really anything more

than a criminal trial. . . . I deeply regret that he has spent his powers on a
subject which seems to me unworthy of them. . . . The review in the Athenaeum especially was a laughable mixture of impertinence and attempted
compliment.[2]

It is hard to resist reading the above lines as a case of professional jealousy,
given Eliot's preoccupation with her literary legacy by the late 1860s and the
disappointment openly expressed in the correspondence with Blackwood.
Could Eliot truly have missed the force of Browning's religious analogies
and seen his poem as "not really anything more than a criminal trial"? Alternately, did her familiarity with its mechanisms add pique to the comparative failure of her own poem? Either case presents a great novelist who had
famously lavished her genius upon a humanist cult of sympathy failing to
extend that sympathy to a more successful poet.

Still, to make sense of Eliot's disappointment requires both a more serious
view of her poetry than most scholars have heretofore granted it and (by way
of this) a keener sense of the ongoing link between poetry and inspiration in
the nineteenth century, particularly as reconfigured by the higher criticism.
It should surprise no one familiar with Eliot's journals and correspondence
that she responds so strongly to Browning, for she basically agrees with him
that religious belief derives from the poetic imagination, and that the best
poetic practice should inspire the human spirit to reverence. Nonetheless,
she rejects as unfitting Browning's design of soliciting the religious response
traced by the higher critics. Her poetry instructs readers in the impulses
behind such sacred writing, but she does this to evoke a deeper appreciation
of the Bible's historical moral role in the culture, a role that she imagined
would increasingly be reshaped—even replaced—by modern literature. She
thus takes Elizabeth Barrett Browning's example in a rather different direction from Browning's, and (like that precursor) she puts her immense gifts
and intellectual might in the service of a discernibly feminine poetics and a
commitment to social good. We can recall in this context her gushing *Westminster Review* account of *Aurora Leigh* (1856), with its claims that "Mrs.
Browning has shown herself all the greater poet because she is intensely a
poetess" (306). This review provides a salutary corrective to the antifeminist
bent of more often-cited reviews like "Silly Novels by Lady Novelists" (from
the *Westminster* a few months previously) and helps to make sense of Eliot's
own eventual contributions to the Victorian poetess tradition. Eliot more or
less admits that the plot of *Aurora Leigh* resembles her "silly novels," but she

argues that its sublime poetry so far overshadows any deficiencies in plot as to raise the bar for what modern poetry might achieve.

In like manner, Eliot's *Spanish Gypsy* and *The Legend of Jubal* (1874, expanded 1878) explore in conspicuously artistic forms the idealistic themes familiar to readers of her prose fiction, themes such as sympathy, altruism, and duty in the face of adversity. The heroine of *The Spanish Gypsy* devotes herself to a newly discovered Zíncalo heritage even when it means abandoning her prospects of domestic happiness; the title character of *The Legend of Jubal* finds himself tragically slain by those whom he has endeavored to enlighten and to serve; the lesser poems take up similarly weighty themes. Eliot made no secret of her belief that verse presented a more natural medium than prose for such flights of sympathetic imagination. And so in Eliot, as in the poets previously discussed in this work, we see the Romantic reformulation of genre norms give rise to a curious paradox, whereby poetic praxis struggles to maintain its association with a poetical ideal—or, to put this differently, whereby poetry struggles to merit the status of "poetry" as the self-evident site of revelation.

The widespread Victorian dissemination of the higher criticism, as we have seen, raised the stakes of this struggle in many places where it might as easily have put it to rest. Browning magnificently capitalized upon the transcendent claims of poetry and the changing norms of Victorian hermeneutics, as did Barrett Browning and Tennyson. Eliot's poetry never achieved this measure of success, but still her scrupulous negotiation of its paradox merits critical consideration. For her as for Clough, apparent failure might itself increase the interest of engagement with this major literary question. It helps here to keep in mind the Russian genre theorist Yuri Tynyanov's dictum that literary works only resonate within genre systems and that to take a work out of its generic context is to change its literary function. Henry James, who was partial to novels, asks in an American review of *The Legend of Jubal* why anyone should attempt poetry at all "if one has at one's command the magnificent vehicle of the style of *Middlemarch*."[3] But Eliot poured her heart into poetry both before and after *Middlemarch* (1872). Her sense of the poetic nature of the changing Victorian Bible helps explain why she devoted herself to the genre as she did.

"That Condition" of Poetry

Eliot's novels themselves regularly invoke or gesture to the Victorian cult of poetry. When Dorothea Casaubon, the heroine of *Middlemarch*, asks her future love Will Ladislaw whether he might become a poet, he responds with some zeal:

> "That depends. To be a poet is to have a soul so quick to discern, that no shade of quality escapes it, and so quick to feel, that discernment is but a hand playing with finely ordered variety on the chords of emotion—a soul in which knowledge passes instantaneously into feeling, and feeling flashes back as a new organ of knowledge. One may have that condition by fits only."
>
> "But you leave out the poems," said Dorothea. "I think they are wanted to complete the poet. I understand what you mean about knowledge passing into feeling, for that seems to be just what I experience. But I am sure I could never produce a poem."
>
> "You ARE a poem—and that is to be the best part of a poet—what makes up the poet's consciousness in his best moods," said Will, showing such originality as we all share with the morning and the spring-time and other endless renewals.[4]

To a seasoned reader of nineteenth-century novels, such passages crackle with erotic passion as Dorothea tempers and deflects Will's flirtatious (though, by the narrator's admission, unoriginal) repartee. But they also crackle with the heat of Romantic genre theory, and literary scholars unaccustomed to thinking of poetry might be forgiven for catching the passion and missing the theory, or for presuming that when Eliot writes of "knowledge pass[ing] instantaneously into feeling, and feeling flash[ing] back as a new organ of knowledge," she has in mind creative works such as *Middlemarch*. Eliot's correspondence strongly suggests that what Will calls "that condition" really does refer to "fits" of poetry in some exclusive generic sense. So may even this passage of *Middlemarch* do so, albeit in a milder way: whereas Will takes the Romantic discourse about poetry in a generically sloppy fashion ("You ARE a poem"), Dorothea protests that Will's theories ought not to "leave out the poems," since "they are wanted to complete the poet." This theme—that inspiration must find its completion in real praxis or craft—receives a parallel dramatization in Eliot's lyric "Stradivarius" (1874), written at the time she was writing *Middlemarch,* in which the famous violin maker chastises a painter friend for shrinking from the duty of labor: "'Tis God gives skill, / But not without men's hands: He could not make / Antonio Stradivari's violins / Without Antonio" (140–43). Dorothea here acts the part of Eliot's Stradivarius for Will (significantly, another painter and dilettante), strongly pressing him to devote himself to a cause. One condition of having poetry is that discernment serve as "a hand playing with finely ordered variety on the chords of emotion," but an equally imperative condition is that one must, after all, write poems.

Throughout her correspondence, Eliot remained deeply invested in poetry as a key to understanding religious expression and experience, if only as a cultural legacy. In 1844 she argues with Caroline Hennell Bray the thesis of Chateaubriand's *Génie du Christianisme* (1802) as though it were a new idea, original to her:

> By the way, I never said that the canons of the Council of Nice, or the Confession of Augsburg, or even the 39 articles are suggestive of poetry. I imagine no *dogmas* can be. But surely Christianity with its Hebrew retrospect and millennial hopes, the heroism and Divine sorrow of its founder and all its glorious army of martyrs might supply and has supplied a strong impulse not only to poetry but to all the fine arts.
> (June 18; *Letters* 2: 177)

In an 1862 letter to Bray's sister, Sarah Hennell, she writes in the vein of Strauss,

> What pitiable people those are who feel no poetry in Christianity! Surely the acme of poetry hitherto is the conception of the suffering Messiah, and the final triumph, "He shall reign for ever and for ever." The Prometheus is a very imperfect foreshadowing of that symbol wrought out in the long history of the Jewish and Christian ages.
> (December 26; *Letters* 4: 71)

And to Lady [Mrs. Henry Frederick] Ponsonby in 1875, she urges,

> Consider what the human mind *en masse* would have been if there had been no such combination of elements in it as has produced poets. All the philosophers and *savants* would not have sufficed to supply that deficiency. And how can the life of nations be understood without the inward life of poetry—that is, of emotion blending with thought?
> (February 11; *Letters* 6: 124)

One could produce many other such instances of Eliot's reverent attitude toward poetry as the heart of religion and the ground of culture. These few,

though, suffice to indicate the manner in which Eliot recurrently and reflexively invokes verse as well as "poetry" in the broad Romantic sense. Again, as
I discussed in my introduction, one need not be Jacques Derrida to appreciate
how the nineteenth-century ambiguity between poetry qua inspiration and
poetry qua verse invariably serves to strengthen the association of verse with
inspiration by partially conflating the terms. A critic like Anna Jameson, as we
saw, addresses painting as "the poetry of sacred and legendary art" to claim
for it the numinous quality reflexively granted to poetry in the nineteenth
century. But Eliot makes plain that she views the art of poetry as preeminent
among the beaux arts: Christianity "has supplied a strong impulse not only
to poetry but to all the fine arts," she explains, with the latter too evidently an
afterthought. Twenty-first-century readers invariably extend to the novel Eliot's ideal of poetry as she puts it to Lady Ponsonby: "that is, of emotion blending with thought." But this gesture risks anachronism: we cannot easily substitute "the novel" (or even "literature") for "poetry" in the first two quotations
above. For instance, one cannot imagine Eliot writing to Sarah Hennell, "What
pitiable people those are who feel *nothing of the novel* in Christianity!"

Just as in Matthew Arnold's *Literature and Dogma* (1873), then, Eliot's
conception of "poetry" betrays a tendency to blur the distinction between
verse and inspiration in a manner that perversely literalizes the ideas of earlier Romantic theorists. Neither need we turn to Arnold for a comparison:
Eliot's own partner George Henry Lewes wrote *The Principles of Success in
Literature* (1865) with the expressed aim of reconsidering Victorian truisms
about literary art and its production. Lewes's marriage to one of the great
novelists of the age presumably motivated this reconsideration, at least in
part; accordingly, Lewes restricts himself to genre terms such as "books,"
"authors," "works," and "writers," and he even specifies at the outset that "literature" must evoke all of its myriad mid-century forms if it is to trace the
unstable and shifting ground of modern aesthetics.[5] Nonetheless, Lewes soon
finds his own restrictions cumbersome, and five of his six essays revert to
using "poetry" in a loose Romantic way. After the first installment, *Principles*
regularly combines "poet" and "artist" in such semi-tautological expressions
as "Vigorous and effective minds habitually deal with concrete images. This
is notably the case with poets and great literates" (46). In Lewes, poetry evidently doubles as an artistic standard and an art form; if run-of-the-mill "poets" serve as interchangeable (if only syntactically) with other "great literates,"
presumably "great poets" hold a higher place altogether. Lewes's ambiguity
on this point thus brings home the enduring cachet of poetry better than

Arnold's (Arnold was, after all, a poet) or than his theoretical sources such as Hegel's *Aesthetics,* which assigns poetry an exalted and even prophetic role without bothering to fix the mundane details of genre theory.

Given the nineteenth century's reflexive association between or conflation of poetry and high literary art, it should surprise no one that Eliot's success as a serious novelist eventually drives her to take up verse in an earnest and thoroughgoing way. For some Victorian admirers, as for nearly all readers today, verse was irrelevant to the type of poetry that Eliot seemed best equipped to write. In 1863, when Browning himself wished to praise *Romola,* he wrote of it as "the noblest and most heroic prose poem" that he had ever read (*Letters* 4: 96). But other Victorians remained stuck on verse. Even the term "prose poem" was newfangled and jarring when Browning used it—Charles Baudelaire's *Petits poèmes en prose,* for instance, would only appear in 1869—and would remain controversial through the fin de siècle. And Eliot's critics eschewed it. Her friend Frederic Harrison praised *Felix Holt* (1866) in more representative terms when he urged her to devote herself to the creation of a great nineteenth-century positivist epic:

> I find myself taking it up as I take up Tennyson or Shelley or Browning and thinking out the sequences of thought suggested by the undertones of the thought and the harmony of the lines. Can it be right to put the subtle finish of a poem into the language of a prose narrative? Is it not a waste of toil? And yet whilst so many readers must miss all that, most of them even not consciously observing the fact, that they have a really new species of literature before them (a romance constructed in the artistic spirit and aim of a poem) yet it is not all lost. I know whole families where the three volumes have been read chapter by chapter and line by line and reread and recited as are the stanzas of In Memoriam. . . . Are you sure that your destiny is not to produce a poem—not a poem in prose but in measure—a drama? Is it possible that there is not one yet existing or does it lie like the statue in the marble block? I am no fortune-teller but I believe it is in the Stars.
> (*Letters* 4: 284–85)

In these letters, as in so much other nineteenth-century writing, we see "poetry" invoked in praise of prose as a level of achievement rather than as an alternative art form. Such comparisons also occasionally crop up in early Romantic criticism of novels like Samuel Richardson's *Clarissa* (1748) and not infrequently thereafter, but there is a difference between Harrison's usage and theirs.[6] In both cases, the best of prose writing becomes poetry much as Harrison instructs, and it may well be recited "chapter by chapter and line by line." However, what is interesting about Harrison's argument is not its belated genre-bending Romanticism, but the perverseness with which it subsequently avers that Eliot's poetic prose qualifies her to write "a poem— not a poem in prose but in measure—a drama." When early Romantic critics praised the poetry of *Clarissa*, they certainly did not mean that Richardson ought to have taken himself for Homer or Shakespeare. But this is just what Harrison means in praise of *Felix Holt*.

Harrison's letter merits especial mention as well because it made a well-documented impression on Eliot, who apparently thought long and hard about what it would take to become a new Homer. Eliot's response to Harrison assures him that she read his letter "many times," and even two years afterward, she claimed to have "always kept it at hand" (*Letters* 4: 300, 448). As it happens, Eliot had already been seriously pursuing verse for a year or so when Harrison wrote, and she was acutely sensitive to the Victorian hierarchy of genre. She agreed with Harrison's sense of the "subtle finish" of poetry, for she complains to him of "the miseries one's obstinate egoism endures from the fact of being a writer of novels—books which the dullest and silliest reader thinks himself competent to deliver an opinion on" (300).[7] Likewise, she responds warmly to Harrison's request that she consider writing a "great comprehensive poem" representing the spirit of Comtean positivism. She does not commit to finishing such a work, but she promises to pursue his dream according to her abilities: "My whole soul goes with your desire that it should be done," she writes, "and I shall at least keep the great possibility (or impossibility) perpetually in my mind, as something towards which I must strive, though it may be that I can do so only in a fragmentary way" (301). Eliot finally entrusts to Harrison that she has begun writing what would become *The Spanish Gypsy*: "It is—but please, let this be a secret between ourselves—an attempt at a drama . . . I find it impossible to abandon it: the conceptions move me deeply, and they have never been wrought out before. There is not a thought or symbol that I do not long to use" (301, emphasis Eliot's). *The Spanish Gypsy*, of course, would never become the positivist epic that Harrison had in mind (it is not really an epic, and Harrison would later deplore its implications for positivism), but the fact that she brings it up in partial answer to his plea for one suggests Eliot's desire to use poetry to build an artistic foundation for post-Christian morality, to use poetry as a tool to "urge the human sanctities" (301), as she put it, in a nation that seemed destined to outlive its Christian past.

Still more clearly, Eliot's private "Notes on the Spanish Gypsy and Tragedy in General" (hereafter "Notes") make clear that she conceived of this poem à la Chateaubriand as an undervalued part of Christian literature and mythology:

> The subject of "The Spanish Gypsy" was originally suggested to me by a picture which hangs in the Scuola di San Rocco at Venice. . . . It is an Annunciation, said to be by Titian. . . . It occurred to me that here was a great dramatic motive of the same class as those used by the Greek dramatists, yet specifically differing from them. A young maiden, believing herself to be on the eve of the chief event of her life—marriage—about to share in the ordinary lot of womanhood, full of young hope, has suddenly announced to her that she is chosen to fulfil a great destiny, entailing a terribly different experience from that of ordinary womanhood. . . . Here, I thought, is a subject grander than that of Iphigenia, and it has never been used.
> (Cross, *George Eliot's Life*, 3: 42)

In Eliot's statement that her prospective heroine ought to be "grander" than Euripides's heroine Iphigenia, we find again the associations of her correspondence, where Prometheus serves as "a very imperfect foreshadowing" of the sublime Christian sacrifice. (One thinks of Barrett Browning's claim in *The Seraphim* that Aeschylus would have taken up the tragedy of the crucifixion had he only known of it.) Eliot's princess Fedalma is explicitly modeled upon the Christian Virgin, and Eliot preserved her "Notes" to confirm this connection. (They were accordingly published by her future husband, John Cross.) To all appearances, Eliot fully agreed with Harrison that her novels had proven her fit to take up work that so many Victorians understood as the province of poetry. And she apparently conceived of *The Spanish Gypsy* as the sort of grand subject that could only be fully realized in verse. In this manner Eliot reflects Dorothea Casaubon's literalism to a startling degree: she agrees with Will Ladislaw's Romantic view of poetry but protests that one must not "leave out the poems," since these "are wanted to complete the poet."

The Spanish Gypsy *and Eliot's Cult of Duty*

The ensuing pages treat *The Spanish Gypsy* and *The Legend of Jubal* as Eliot's attempts to advance the wedding of poetry and religious feeling through an affective, implicitly feminine poetics compatible with secularization and materialism but plainly growing out of English Christian tradition. To return, by way of this, to Eliot's severe judgment upon *The Ring and the Book* from the perspective of her 1860s correspondence is to see it as much more than sour grapes. Browning's poem does indeed lack "fine elements," if by "fine elements" one means something like a dramatization of Victorian notions of Christian (or, as it were, post-Christian) duty. Might not Eliot's chagrin in 1868 derive partly from the fact that her *Spanish Gypsy* presents the sort of luminous moral parable that Browning never develops? Eliot scholars will be familiar with F. W. H. Meyers's famous description of Eliot as a modern-day sibyl: walking in the crepuscular light of Trinity College, ruminating upon the prospects of *"God," "Immortality,"* and *"Duty"* (italics Meyers's), and pronouncing upon the peremptory nature of the third. Seen in this light, Browning's epic might appear a craven falling off from the intrepid humanism of his wife's *Aurora Leigh*. Pompilia's virtue lies mostly in being stabbed to death, rather than in Fedalma's selfless action or Aurora's bold decision making. Browning, that is, sets into motion the machinery of Christian canonization and apotheosis, but without a corresponding moral program; his hagiographies are neither specifically moral nor applicable to ordinary life in any obvious way.[8] Susan B. Anthony famously dedicated her copy of *Aurora Leigh* to the United States Library of Congress with the wish that "women may be more & more like Aurora Leigh," but it is hard to imagine anyone wishing all women to be "more & more like" Pompilia. *The Ring and the Book* does not even try to inspire the sort of good that Eliot believed to be the real heart of the Christian legacy, and so from Eliot's perspective, it assumes the glory of a religious authority while shirking its highest duties.

The moral attitude that Eliot sought in post-Christian poetry becomes quite explicit in her correspondence with an enthusiastic Scottish admirer, Alexander Main, to whom she explains how she meant *The Spanish Gypsy* to be read. Her correspondence here even entails a sort of close reading of a few key lines from the poem (unusually for Victorian poetry criticism) and repeatedly considers the prospect of a secular literature to supplement or replace the Bible. Ironically, Eliot's epistolary friendship with Main began— eagerly on his part, guardedly on hers—with a conversation about whether the novel served religious inspiration just as well as poetry. For his part, Main glorified Eliot's fiction as a source of spiritual insight comparable to Shakespeare's:

August 7th 1871

Dear Madam,

. . . Notwithstanding my professed admiration of your genius you will probably think me deficient in reverence, thus to venture to write you once more. But "perfect love casteth out fear." And one who has delightedly kept you company from the time you took the field with Dinah Morris and Parson Irwine till you parted with Romola and Savanarola: one who has just finished "Adam Bede" & "The Mill on the Floss" for the seventh time, and found them as fresh and feeling as at first and vastly richer to thought: one who, though a devotee of Shakespeare, Scott, Wordsworth, Shelley, Thackeray, & Tennyson, yet holds firm faith, that in fullness, richness, massiveness and majesty, of heart and intellect, the first alone has surpassed George Eliot, and *no other* comes near . . . one who believes that you have for ever *sanctified* the novel as a vehicle of grand moral truth, because, while others have been, & are, content to amuse and to please, you have boldly dared to preach and to instruct; one who conceives that George Eliot is the *first complete MAN* who has uttered him-(her) self since the "Secretary of the Ages" laid down his pen; one who, in short, might go on thus *ad infinitum* & still have to leave something unsaid:—such an one knows his own sincerity, and is not fearful lest his enthusiasm should be misinterpreted by her who has called it forth.[9]

Main, we see, argues that Eliot has "*sanctified* the novel as a vehicle of [that] grand moral truth" for which she herself habitually turned to poetry. Even Thackeray receives a place in the company of Shakespeare, Scott, Wordsworth, Shelley, and Tennyson, and Main avers that among these nineteenth-century English writers, Eliot alone is the "*MAN*," the complete man who lives in the company of Shakespeare and Goethe, the "Secretary of the Ages" (whose own novels nonetheless fail to "*sanctif[y]*" the genre). Given that most of the above quotation is composed of a single sentence, we have little reason to doubt Main's assurances that he "might go on thus *ad infinitum*" in praise of Eliot. But her ongoing doubts about the spiritual reaches of the novel as a genre drive her to respond to Main by asking him whether he has read her poetry. Main spares her any painful admissions on this head before repairing his deficiency.

Significantly, Main's ensuing letters on *The Spanish Gypsy* receive from Eliot a much warmer response than does his effusive praise of *Romola, Adam Bede,* and *The Mill on the Floss.* These letters vie to exceed the superlative praise that he had previously lavished upon her novels:

> Aug 31ˢᵗ . . . This inspiration is as real as was ever that of the Hebrew
> prophet or apostle. . . . What are all the sermons preached in all the pulpits
> of our land from year's end to year's end compared with the 165 pages I have
> now read! . . . No living writer (and scarcely any one dead) has grappled with
> thoughts so powerful, fathomed such depths of the soul of man, and with such
> majestic calm fronted the Destinies of Life.
> (Main, "Letters")

But the second, following quickly upon the first, adds explicit commentary
upon the text by way of announcing that "I have now finished your noble
poem; and the impression on my mind at this moment is, that it is the fullest
& grandest expression of yourself yet before the world." Tellingly, but predictably in light of the Harrison correspondence, Main's effusions over her poetry
win Eliot's heart as his praise for her novels could never succeed in doing.
Eliot's next letter explains to Main that he has won her confidence at last:

> September 11. 71.
>
> My dear Sir
> Mr. Lewes, who generously sifts my morning letters for me, read me your
> last when I went down to luncheon, and I confess it made me cry.
> You have thoroughly understood me—you have entered with perfect in-
> sight into the significance of the poem—and without that, no amount of praise
> could have had much value for me. In the passages which you quote from the
> Fifth Book, you have put your finger on the true key. . . .
> Always yours with high regard
> M. E. Lewes
>
> (*Letters* 4: 184–85)

Now, it is a very sad commentary on the disrepute into which George Eliot's
poetry had fallen by the late twentieth century that Gordon Haight's multi-
volume set of her correspondence includes this letter ("You have thoroughly
understood me") without bothering to include Main's letter on *The Spanish
Gypsy,* which explains precisely how she is to be thoroughly understood, and
what exactly made her cry when Lewes read it aloud.

In part for this reason, I reproduce from Main's letter the largest of the
excerpts of *The Spanish Gypsy* as cited by him and with all of his emphases. The following are, by Eliot's own lachrymose account (above), "the true
key" to "the significance of the poem." Both passages present Eliot's heroine

Fedalma's explanation to her lover the Duke de Silva that she must break off their engagement out of duty to her newly rediscovered people and to her slain father, Zarca. She could not love Silva so much, as the line goes, loved she not honor more:

> Nay, Silva, think of me as one who sees
> A light serene and strong on the sole path
> Which she will tread till death . . .
> *He trusted me, and I will keep his trust:*
> *My life shall be its temple.* I will plant
> His sacred hope within the sanctuary
> And die its priestess—*though I die alone.*
> *A hoary woman on the altar step*
> *Cold 'mid cold ashes. That is my chief good*
> *The deepest hunger of a faithful heart*
> *Is faithfulness.* Wish me nought else.

And again:

> Our marriage rite
> Is our resolve that *we will each be true*
> *To high allegiance, higher than our love.*
> Our dear young love—its truth was happiness!
> But it had grown upon a larger life
> Which tore its roots asunder. We rebelled—
> *The larger life subdued us.*
> (NLS MS 942; emphases all Main's)

Here in Main's citation of *The Spanish Gypsy,* we see explicitly the theme that the "Notes" compares to the Annunciation and, not incidentally, the moral thrust that Eliot found so lamentably absent in Browning. Fedalma has a moral duty to her people and to her late father, and she puts this duty before her prospective love life with the Duke de Silva. She binds herself "*To high allegiance, higher than* [her] *love*" and sanctifies this role in explicitly religious terms: "*My life shall be its temple.*" Main's letter compares Fedalma's fortitude to that of the biblical Job in a way that must have pleased Eliot still more than his general assurances that the poem's inspiration equaled "that of the Hebrew prophet or apostle":

And . . . Fedalma leaves the Spanish shore and her first love, unhappy, it may be, but certainly not *unblessed*. I have never been able to perceive, in the holy raptures of the most famous Saints anything so impressive and grand as the noble old Job's attitude of mind and heart when he cried—"Though He slay me yet will I trust in Him;" and in the midmost heart of a nature like Fedalma's there must have been a joy in conscious well-doing surpassing far any *pleasures* however sweet. (emphases Main's)

Eliot's Fedalma acts a self-sacrificing moral agent in the way that Browning's characters do not and so to readers like Main she can therefore be tragic in a way that Browning's characters cannot. Main's assurances that he finds nothing so lofty in "the holy raptures of the most famous Saints" amounts to a dig at the sort of hermeneutic explored by Browning to such great effect: it is no wonder that Eliot found satisfaction there.

What will by this point have become clear about Eliot's poetic ambition, I hope, is that from about 1865 until the second *Legend of Jubal* collection, she hoped by verse to achieve something distinct from (and loftier than) what she had achieved with novels. Correspondence in 1867 in which she complains of the prevalence and popularity of "trashy literature" finds her adding, "The book I am writing is not a novel, and is likely to be dead against the taste of that large public which a publisher is for the most part obliged (rather unhappily) to take into account" (4: 377). As though responding to Harrison's suggestion that *Felix Holt* was a romance, Eliot writes to Blackwood in March 1867, "The work connected with Spain is not a Romance. It is—prepare your fortitude—it is—a poem" (354). She means by this to register a difference between the sacred art of "poetry" and pretender genres (here "Romance") that do not carry the cachet to which she aspires. Yet such remarks also show how the limits of poetry remain flexible and how this becomes a source of anxiety in itself; these clearly contribute to what Adam Roberts calls the "orgy of generic markers" by which the post-Romantics attempted to evaluate their own chefs d'oeuvres.[10] In 1870 Alfred Austin belittled Tennyson, Browning, and others by insisting that no poetry could be called "great" except epics or dramatic romances combining "love, patriotism and religion"; this description certainly fits *The Spanish Gypsy*, and Eliot shares Austin's generic anxiety, yet she draws lines between romance, epic, and verse drama that he plainly does not see.[11]

The lack of uniform values for generic nomenclature in 1868, conversely, helps to account for the great weight that the prose/poetry distinction it-

self is made to bear in Eliot's writing, as when she tells Blackwood to prepare his fortitude because *The Spanish Gypsy* "is—a poem." Despite such
shows of modesty, Eliot yearned for a broad circulation: "I care for the sale,
not in a monetary light (for one does not write poems as the most mar-
ketable commodity) [but] because sale means large distribution" (466). She
returns repeatedly to the difference of this work from her novels: "I seem
to have gained a new organ, a new medium that my nature had languished
for" (465). And to Caroline Bray, "Don't you imagine how the people who
consider writing simply as a money-getting profession will despise me for
choosing a work by which I could only get hundreds, where for a novel I
could get thousands? I cannot help asking you to admire what my husband
is, compared with many possible husbands—I mean, in urging me to produce a poem rather than anything in a worldly sense more profitable."[12] Eliot,
we see, dismisses the novel in evangelical terms as more profitable than verse
only in a "worldly" sense. (Mr. Bulstrode of *Middlemarch* would have picked
just these terms if he were a post-Christian poet, too.) Lewes, meanwhile,
shared with Blackwood his private doubts about the success of the project,
though he seems to have put on a good face for Eliot. "My poem has been a
great source of added happiness to me," she writes, "all the more, or rather
principally because it has been a deeper joy to Mr. Lewes than any work I
have done before" (*Letters* 4: 465).

Extravagant praise of her poetry always gave Eliot particular joy. Robert
Hogarth Patterson, editor of the *Press,* wrote Blackwood (and, by extension,
Eliot) that *The Spanish Gypsy* "*dwarfs* all the poems that were ever written,
it is so grand and high in its theme and scope, and so beautiful in its detail,
so marvellously perfect in plan and working out" (*Letters* 4: 455). Eliot's well-
documented satisfaction in Patterson's praise (via Blackwood) gives the lie
to some of her hedging with Main: she longed for superlative praise for her
poetry, and not merely judicious praise. (What could be less judicious than
to say that a contemporary poem "dwarfs all the poems that were ever written"?) Still, such thirst for praise does not amount to mere egotism here. Harrison's projected epic, for which Eliot's "whole soul" also yearned, needed
to merit Patterson's extravagant praise if it was to complement and build
upon sacred literature like the Bible. And the Victorians tended generally to
believe that someone of the age would produce so important a text as Patterson was pleased to find in *The Spanish Gypsy:* "so beautiful in its detail, so
marvellously perfect in plan and working out." A great deal of literary theory
at that time seemed to speak of its imminent arrival.

Finally, then, between the correspondences with Harrison and Main and in the wake of *The Spanish Gypsy*'s mediocre reception, Eliot began plans for a greater poem than *The Spanish Gypsy*, and one which would better satisfy the world. She had for some weeks been planning *Middlemarch* when she decided to pursue this more lofty venture. In her journal she records, "But I am not yet engaged in any work that makes a higher life for me—a life that is young and grows, though in my other life I am getting old and decaying. It is a day for resolves, and determination. I am meditating the subject of Timoleon" (November 1868; *Letters* 4: 490). She repeats this on January 1, 1869: "I have set myself many tasks for the year—I wonder how many will be accomplished—A Novel called *Middlemarch*, a long poem on Timoleon, and several minor poems" (5: 3). Again, plainly, her planned novel *Middlemarch* appears separate from and subordinate to the more ambitious poetic project, which was to "make a higher life" for her. The long poem on Timoleon was never written, but it helps to answer Henry James's question with which we began.[13] The legend of Timoleon provides just the moral thrust that Eliot found so central to poetry: this ancient general's personal integrity demanded that he put his brother to death for attempted tyranny—a sacrifice if possible more austere than that of Fedalma, and certainly more so than those of Dorothea Brooke or Daniel Deronda. Eliot's reasons for writing an epic thus appear in her proposed subject. Here as elsewhere, Eliot wished to achieve in her poetry stark moral dilemmas and heroic resolutions.

The Resilience of Jubal

For their part, most reviewers of *The Spanish Gypsy* gave Eliot little enough reason for devoting herself to more poetry: they alternately question her poetic gifts and mourn for the prose ones that she had evidently set aside. "Up to this moment," sniffs the *Atlantic Monthly*, "she has scarcely proved herself a poet."[14] The *London Quarterly Review*, which praised the drama, still concludes "the abandonment by George Eliot of her own walk of art for the continued production of works in the manner of *The Spanish Gypsy* would be a national calamity."[15] And Henry James's *North American Review*, cited above, complains that "it is not a genuine poem," adding, "I shall indicate most of its merits and defects, great and small, if I say it is a romance,—a romance written by one who is emphatically a thinker" (635). (This last line may have caused Eliot chagrin, if her letter claiming that "the work connected with Spain is not a Romance" may be trusted.) Even the *Edinburgh Review*, the

most encouraging among these reviews, still concludes, "If in the future contributions of George Eliot to our literature there is to be a choice between the
poet and the novelist, we earnestly plead for the latter, . . . In as far as George
Eliot can be a poet 'Romola' is, undoubtedly, a finer poem than the 'Spanish
Gypsy.'"[16] This last comment, an echo of Browning's letter, seems especially
worth noting. Not only was the Victorian poetic hierarchy in disarray at this
time, but poetry itself, so powerful in abstract theory such as Lewes's *Principles,* was distinctly losing its hegemonic influence in practical theory.

Can novels be more poetic than poetry? The question sounds facile to us,
just as it would have sounded facile to Shelley or to the philosophers of the
Jena circle.[17] But it presented an epistemological crisis for many mid-century
anglophone critics who found something crucial in the terms. The *London
Quarterly Review* devotes ten pages of its *Spanish Gypsy* review to this generic conundrum before addressing the specifics of Eliot's work, where it
responds emphatically that prose must sometimes be more poetic:

> If "the good, the beautiful, and the true" can be embodied in a prose work of
> art with wider effect than in verse, as is unquestionably the case in the pres-
> ent crisis, then the artist who elects to address that wider circle, and attains
> supremacy, can hardly be called upon to take rank second to any artist, be he
> who he may, on the mere ground that prose is not verse.
>
> (163)

"The present crisis," once more, remained one of audience as much as of craft.
Poetry was in many contexts being called upon to replace a quasi-ubiquitous
sacred text, and a literature not read ubiquitously, chapter and verse, cannot
replace it. Perhaps inspired by such reasoning, the *London Quarterly* reviewer
even advances the paradoxical claim that the best prose (here represented by
Eliot) is really more difficult than poetry because poetry corresponds more
naturally to the spirit of literary genius:

> In writing high-toned and intensely-poetic prose, a besetting difficulty is to
> avoid breaking into rhythm. To one with a thorough command of language,
> the mere transit from prose to blank verse would present no difficulty what-
> ever, and would often be a great relief; but the great feat, when under the
> excitement of working prose artistically, is to keep it thoroughly true to prose
> principles.
>
> (169)

This reviewer goes so far as to suggest, in other words, that since blank verse is the natural language of genius, Eliot wrote prose at a special disadvantage: she *denied herself* the relief of meter, and restrained herself in particular from the temptation of blank verse. This bold metrical hypothesis might not hold up under an extended application to Eliot's prose oeuvre; among other things, it raises the question of why her blank verse should not outshine her prose. But such inconsistencies reveal the Victorian critic's strain to realign the grinding gears of generic ideology.

In reality, Eliot's plans for the unwritten Timoleon epic change the aspect and appearance of the 1874 and 1878 *Legend of Jubal* collections, which treat similar issues in various ways. Eliot scholars have tended to give these poems still less attention than *The Spanish Gypsy;* they have seemed to many a sort of recreation from Eliot's real vocation. But Eliot's letters give ample reason to think that, on the contrary, they represent forays into potential matter for a "work that makes a higher life for me," promised in the November 1868 journal. We might even view them as fragments of the great unfinished "something towards which I must strive" promised to Harrison, "though it may be that I can do so only in a fragmentary way." During the few years following Harrison's letter, at all events, Eliot published a verse retelling of a story from *The Decameron,* "How Lisa Loved the King" (1869), a miniature sonnet cycle called "Brother and Sister" (1869), and the weighty title poem of her collections, "The Legend of Jubal" (1870), a work designed to interrogate the extent to which a modern poetess tradition might craft new moral truths from scripture. This body of poetry grows out of the ambition of the Timoleon period, and its diversity shows Eliot trying out new poetic roles just as Barrett Browning had done from *The Seraphim* (1838) to the *Sonnets from the Portuguese* (1850) to *Aurora Leigh.* The older Eliot remains more cautious and tentative than the young Barrett Browning (writing eleven sonnets instead of forty-six, translating Boccaccio instead of Aeschylus), yet she too looks for a way to formulate a great modern epic.

"The Legend of Jubal," for example, shows Eliot an enthusiastic heir to Barrett Browning, boldly embellishing a difficult passage from Genesis in a way that both admits the obscurities of revelation and lays implicit claim to the revelatory power of modern poetics. It retells the lives of the seventh generation of Cain and of the earliest creation of "the Arts" in human history. Whether by design or by happenstance, Eliot's source passage in Genesis seems to connect such innovation to violence in the antediluvian world, and herein Eliot finds her subject:

And Lamech took upon him two wives: the name of the one was Adah, and the name of the other was Zillah.

And Adah bare Jabal: he was the father of such as dwell in tents, and of such as have cattle.

And his brother's name was Jubal: he was the father of all such as handle the harp and organ.

And Zillah, she also bare Tubal-Cain, an instructor of every artificer in brass and iron: and the sister of Tubal-Cain was Naamah.

And Lamech said unto his wives, Adah and Zillah, Hear my voice; ye wives of Lamech, hearken unto my speech: for I have slain a man to my wounding, and a young man to my hurt.

If Cain shall be avenged sevenfold, truly Lamech seventy and sevenfold.

(Genesis 4:18–24 KJV)

Now, Genesis itself devotes no more than the above cited passage either to Lamech or to his gifted sons, so to a modern reader, the obscurities of this text might overshadow its religious significance.[18] The etiologies are comprehensible enough as a primitive history: the world's first cattle herder, first musician, and first metalworker here are presented as a remarkable set of brothers. However, the text never makes clear what connection exists between the legacies of these inventors and the man or men whom their father Lamech boasts about slaying in lines 23–24. Eliot's poem invents a connection.

In its utter contrast with the cryptic brevity of Genesis at this point, Eliot's couplet scheme resembles a great deal of other Romantic Orientalist poetry, from Thomas Moore's *Lalla Rookh* (1817) to Jean Ingelow's *Story of Doom* (1867), and at first glance it might seem to have little bearing upon the changing Victorian Bible:

When Cain was driven from Jehova's land
He wandered eastward, seeking some far strand
Ruled by kind gods who asked no offerings
Save pure field-fruits, as aromatic things
To feed the subtler sense of frames divine
That lived on fragrance for their food and wine:
Wild joyous gods, who winked at faults and folly,
And could be pitiful and melancholy.
He never had a doubt that such gods were;

> He looked within, and saw them mirrored there.
> Some think he came at last to Tartary,
> And some to Ind; but, howso'er it be,
> His staff he planted where sweet waters ran.
> And in that home of Cain the Arts began.
> (91)

Some Eliot scholars have even described this poem as light verse that Eliot "accordingly distances . . . by setting it in the remote, mythic past."[19] But the evidence stacks up against this reading. Not only did Eliot associate poetry with serious religious art, but this poem's paradise manqué clearly corresponds to her instruction to Harrison that "great epics" tend to possess "a frankly Utopian construction, freeing the poet from all local embarrassments" (448). By turn, Cain's search for other gods than Jehova suggests the hermeneutic reconfiguration brought about by F. Max Müller's argument that the Pentateuch features a religion of henotheism but not monotheism. (This useful term, coined by Müller in 1860, denotes the exclusive worship of one god while acknowledging the existence of other peoples' gods. Since Müller, scholars have broadly agreed that it fits the Lord in most of the Hebrew Bible.) And Cain's intuition that his own emotions might be trusted to find a more congenial deity ("He never had a doubt that such gods were; / He looked within, and saw them mirrored there") equally applies to his situation Feuerbach's idea of religion as an idealized projection of the human spirit. (Eliot, once more, had translated Feuerbach's *Das Wesen des Christentums* [1841] in 1854 as *The Essence of Christianity.*) Herbert Tucker has recently suggested the significance of Fedalma's allegiance to the godless Zíncali in light of Feuerbach's higher criticism.[20] The same critique applies to Eliot's godless Cain, who lingers in the space between henotheism and a coming monotheism from which he is already exiled.

The emotional work of this poem, moreover, plainly counts for still more than the intellectual work. Like Byron before her, Eliot takes for granted Cain's innocence in the face of the Bible's impenetrable "Jehova." Neither is Eliot's Lamech at all to blame for the violent tendencies of his forefather. Far from Genesis's violent boasts or threats ("I have slain a man to my wounding, and a young man to my hurt"), Eliot crafts a pious domestic circle, and an accidental rediscovery of death in the world. Her Lamech neither intends the young man's death nor even comprehends it when it happens:

Till, hurling stones in mere athletic joy,
Strong Lamech stuck and killed his fairest boy,
And tried to wake him with the tenderest cries,
And fetched and held before the glazèd eyes
The things they best had loved to look upon;
But never glance or smile or sigh he won.
The generations stood around those twain
Helplessly gazing, till their father Cain
Parted the press, and said, "He will not wake."
(92–93)

By framing events in this way, Eliot clears away the obscure violence of Genesis and provides a tender sentimental vignette. In the nineteenth century, Eliot's narrative becomes not merely comprehensible (as the original may not be) but predictable. Lamech's outpouring of parental grief at the loss of his child is a leitmotif of the nineteenth-century poetess tradition, and sentimental overtones here unmistakably alert the reader to this mode of literary grief: "the fairest boy," "the tenderest cries," "the glazèd eyes," the "glance," the "sigh," the "smile." By turn, Eliot's account effaces the puzzling ambiguities of Genesis: there is one boy killed; it is Lamech's fairest child and Jubal's brother. These are further effaced, perhaps, by the meter that she chooses, the regular lines supposed to characterize the poetess tradition.[21] Even in the few instances where Eliot retains the poetic devices of Genesis—for instance, the parataxis of "And tried to wake him with the tenderest cries / And fetched and held before the glazèd eyes"—these devices are turned to the end of this inevitable meter that reigns until Cain himself arrives to announce the death of the child in monosyllables that interrupt the poem's regular iambics (the point is that the boy will NOT wake).

The poetess tradition makes itself equally felt in the connection between heartfelt grief over the young man and the dirge that arises from such feeling. Making explicit a connection that Genesis admits (but does not pursue), Eliot proclaims this event as the catalyst for Jubal's future as the inventor of music, "father of all such as handle the harp and organ" (Genesis 4:21):

And a new spirit from that hour came o'er
The race of Cain: soft idleness was no more
But even the sunshine had a heart of care,

Smiling with hidden dread—a mother fair
Who folding to her breast a dying child
Beams with feigned joy that but makes sadness mild.
Death was now lord of Life, and at his word
Time, vague as air before, new terrors stirred,
With measured wing now audibly arose
Throbbing through all things to some unknown close.
(93)

This is the atmosphere, Eliot instructs, in which song, music, and poetry would be invented by Jubal, an atmosphere in which "even the sunshine had a heart of care," and in which a vast portion of women's nineteenth-century sentimental poetry was composed. Cheryl Walker, Germaine Greer, Paula Bennett, and others have called the dead child the signature trope of the women's sentimental tradition (though women were not the only poets writing such verse).[22] Eliot defends the tradition by embracing these conventions, by associating them with existing sacred texts and the possibility of future ones. She identifies the mysterious victim of Genesis as Lamech's son and commemorates the scene with the image of a mother clutching her dying child. Indeed, Eliot composed the first 100 lines of *The Legend of Jubal* at the sickbed of her stepson, and composed the rest shortly after his death. At that time, she explained her preoccupation with his death to Eugène Bodichon: "He is gone and I can never make him feel my love anymore. Just now all else seems trivial compared with the powers of delighting and soothing a heart that is in need" (*Letters* 5: 61). The generic importance of this is striking. Eliot's relations to her husband's sons were normally strained, awkward, and distant (as Rosemarie Bodenheimer has demonstrated), and yet Eliot, in search of an epic theme, feels moved to adopt this powerful nineteenth-century trope of bereaved motherhood as soon as it presents itself.[23] The truth of her feeling permits the trope of her feeling, just as the trope facilitates the truth. "What a passage is that about Death!" wrote Lewes to Main. "It was written under the shadow of a great grief, when our second boy in his 25th year passed away from us after six months of frightful agony" (*Letters* 5: 205). Here, as in the poem, the power of this signature trope of the poetess tradition trumps even Eliot's own peculiar personal circumstances in reference to her state of adoptive parenthood.

The translation of grief into music for which this tradition was known also governs the form of Eliot's lines in a way that helps to justify her turn from prose fiction. Human finitude in this poem is not simply apprehended in the death of Lamech's son, it is metrically realized in the passage of the poem and figured in "Time" itself. The couplet quoted above announces its own prosody: "With measured wing now audibly arose / Throbbing through all things to some unknown close" (93). If the "measured wing" of the first line doesn't alert the reader to its metrical self-referentiality and poetic importance, the trochaic "thrȯbb-ing" and spondaic "un-knȯwn clȯse" of the second may. This is Eliot's version of the "broad Homeric lines" commemorated in book 5 of *Aurora Leigh,* which "with their spondaic prodigious mouths . . . lap the lucent margins" of the page (1251–52). Here a throbbing departure from iambic regularity instructs Eliot's readers to consider that song is originally born of parent's grief.[24] She proceeds: "Now glad Content by clutching Haste was torn, / And Work grew eager, and Device was born" (93). If the first couplet suggests the birth of poetry in a mother's loss, this one explains the mechanisms by which a poetical commemoration of the event operates. Poetical "Device" is literally born of eagerness to "work out" grief, suggesting Eliot's endorsement of the improvisatrice model of poetry so important to women's poetry after the appearance of De Staël's *Corinne* (and whose recent study can be credited in large part to Ellen Moers).[25] If the stereotypical poetess leans heavily upon device to facilitate hasty verses (as in the improvisatrice tradition), yet Eliot relocates this impulse in the genesis of song itself. The slippage between a poetic symbol and its referent is created when "Content"—either contentedness or semantic import—is torn by Haste, which in turn is necessitated by Time and Death. This wedding of music with grief rings throughout *Jubal:* "Thus to Cain's race death was tear-watered seed / Of various life and action-shaping need" (93). Here the poetess tradition represents not an artificial refinement of earlier poetry, but a return to the roots of what made it sacred at all.

Eliot never pits poetry's emotional basis against its mechanics, that is, but tries to reconfigure their relationship. The untimely death of the nameless young man drives Jubal's brother, Tubal-Cain, to craft the world's first forge, and its prominence in the poem makes plain that Jubal's art requires not merely nature but also the mechanical example of that brother craftsman's industry:

Jubal, too, watched the hammer, till his eyes,
No longer following its fall or rise,
Seemed glad with something that they could not see,

But only listened to—some melody,
Wherein dumb longings inward speech had found[.]

Such lines articulate a sort of genealogy for stress-based meter in English poetry: here the hammer blows of a regular stress compete with the logic of syntax, and music (as poetry scholars generally recognize) emerges from the interplay of stress and import. "Dumb longings" corresponds not to Lamech's "hidden dread," but to a correlative melody that Jubal must learn to recreate. Tubal-Cain's hammer serves both as origin and as foundation of Jubal's music. And once he finds it, he finds it everywhere:

The mother's call, the children's answering cry,
The laugh's light cataract tumbling from on high;
The suasive repetitions Jabal taught,
That timid browsing cattle homeward brought
The clear-winged fugue of echoes vanishing
And through them all the hammer's rhythmic ring.
(94)

In this miniature *ars poetica*, then, we see something akin to Browning's insistence that art creates nature—or perceptible nature, which is the same thing. At least, Jubal can invent musical art only once his brother has inadvertently provided him with a mechanical basis: "And thróugh [it] áll the hám-mer's rhýth-mic ríng."

For Eliot, too, this invention of the lyre—and, by extension, the lyric—remains crucial to the place of memory in culture. Jabal, Jubal, and Tubal-Cain all invent their arts in deliberate response to the demise of their brother:

["]Come, let us fashion acts that are to be,
When we shall lie in darkness silently,
As our young brother doth, whom yet we see
Fallen and slain, but reigning in our will
By that one image of him pale and still."
(94)

Device (or "act") openly serves to counter the oblivion of death. Genesis may be said to provide its own precedent for this ambition, since, as some Victorians were always shocked to rediscover, it provides none of the New

Testament's assurances of an afterlife. And memory, by turn, serves like the divinity of Christian mythology:

> And the last parting now began to send
> Diffusive dread through love and wedded bliss,
> Thrilling them into finer tenderness.
> ·Then Memory disclosed her face divine,
> That like the calm nocturnal lights doth shine
> Within the soul, and shows the sacred graves,
> And shows the presence that no sunlight craves,
> No space, no warmth, but moves among them all;
> Gone and yet here, and coming at each call,
> With ready voice and eyes that understand.
> And lips that ask a kiss, and dear responsive hand.
> (94)

Eliot felt particular pride in this passage: the 1874 manuscript of *The Legend of Jubal and Other Poems* reinscribes the initial three lines above ("And the last parting, etc.") "To my beloved Husband, G— H— L—, Whose cherishing tenderness for twenty years has alone made my work possible to me."[26] In a biographical context, surely, the deep feeling behind this mingling of marriage to Lewes and death's "diffusive dread" must be linked to Eliot's doubts regarding an afterlife. But, equally clearly, memory here acts like the evangelical Jesus, attending each disciple personally ("coming at each call, / With ready voice and eyes that understand / And lips that ask a kiss, and dear responsive hand") and not merely standing against death, but soothing it away.

English poetesses often turned to biblical subjects because the Bible afforded them examples of female prophetic authority, an authority made particularly compelling by the quasi-divine moral perspective credited to many women in nineteenth-century culture. Cynthia Scheinberg traces this phenomenon in the work of Felicia Hemans, Elizabeth Barrett Browning, Christina Rossetti, and Grace Aguilar, and F. Elizabeth Gray's more recent and wider-ranging study reminds us of the tremendous denominational diversity presented by this poetic movement.[27] Any biblical retelling must be understood in the broader context of Western nineteenth-century Orientalism, yet it also represents an especially important refiguring of the terms of English moral and religious thought, as Scheinberg and Gray make clear. Eliot believed, as she put it to Harriet Beecher Stowe, "that religion too has to be modified—'developed,' according to the dominant phrase" (*Letters* 5: 31).[28] But scholars generally fail to recognize her poetry as an attempt to cultivate religious "development."

Eliot's rewriting of biblical narrative, in sum, demonstrates faith in the evolution of biblical hermeneutics away from inspirationism and toward a tradition of sentiment and humanism, as well as Barrett Browning's desire to help sculpt that evolution. Lewes must have bolstered Eliot's sense of the moment's opportunity, for he exclaimed of Arnold's *Literature and Dogma* (1874), "What a singular spectacle is presented by the contrast of the general tone of men's minds on this subject of Religion at the present day and that of some twenty years ago!" (6: 87). Still, as the much-maligned translator of Strauss, Eliot also appreciated the resiliency of a literalist hermeneutics to an assault upon its historical bases. Poems like "The Legend of Jubal" attempt to inspire readers with an unobjectionable and yet flexible view of sacred literature. And the higher criticism could only serve to emphasize the kinship between her appropriation of the biblical events and the sacred reconstructions of the original scripture authors.[29]

"The Death of Moses" and the Death of Eliot

A clear parallel to "The Legend of Jubal" may be found in "The Death of Moses" (1878), a lyric that revisits Jubal's idea of how art, music, and poetry redeem us from death and do (as Arnold hoped) the cultural work of the Bible without requiring our endorsement of its doubtful historical propositions. Eliot's theme derives from the Devarim Rabbah, a midrashic account of how the Lord God descended from the heavens to gather up Moses's soul at the end of that prophet's life, after the angels themselves had balked at so great a task. The poem explicitly takes up the ancient Jewish and Christian tradition that Moses authored all of the Pentateuch (a tradition repeatedly invoked in the Christian scriptures where Christ asks about Moses's view on one point or another), and it unguardedly affirms that Moses's name remains interchangeable with Law (Torah). By the late nineteenth century, commitment to Mosaic authorship had become a distinctly conservative position, but as a literary achievement, the figure of Moses still presents what may be the ultimate instance of Jubal's immortal "Memory" with "her face divine." By Eliot's view, it is Jubal's tragedy and his glory that he becomes a name: "The immortal name of Jubal filled the sky / While Jubal lonely laid him down to die" (705–6). And so it is with Moses.

At the same time, no reader familiar with the nineteenth-century historical crisis in scripture studies would need reminding that the authorized biblical account of Moses's death poses famous problems for traditional exegesis. To modern eyes, indeed, this text seems plainly to contradict the traditional premise of Mosaic authorship:

> So Moses the servant of the LORD died there in the land of Moab, according to the word of the LORD.
> And he buried him in a valley in the land of Moab, over against Bethpeor: but no man knoweth of his sepulchre unto this day.
> (Deuteronomy 34:5 AV)

Centuries of exegetes, it is true, have found this text perfectly compatible with the idea of Moses's authorship, and very conservative Jews and Christians continue to do so. But it provided an obvious site for inquiry once modern biblical criticism began to probe the structures of traditional exegesis. After all, the idea of Mosaic authorship here requires not just that Moses compose an account of his own death and burial in the land of Moab, but also that he include a jarring deictic reference ("unto this day") to an otherwise unspecified present.³⁰ It remains possible that God dictated these words, jarring deixis and all, to Moses while he was yet living. But readers from Hobbes and Spinoza onward have been better satisfied to conclude that some other hand authored the lines. For the higher critics, this became a foregone conclusion as early as the eighteenth century, and it remains one for mainstream scholars.

Beth-Zion Lask Abrahams describes the Devarim Rabbah as a "well-known *medrash*," but the story would not have been known to the bulk of Eliot's Victorian readership.³¹ Her text clearly represents the period of her studies under the great Hebraist Emanuel Oscar Menachem Deutsch, and, in fact, Eliot seems to present its first significant English translation as a useful alternative to the hide-bound controversies over Deuteronomy 34. The midrash, that is, provides space for Eliot to engage with the most conservative elements of Judaism and Christianity (Mosaic authorship) while still articulating the higher critical notion of prophecy as a generic and poetical construction. En route, she celebrates Moses as literature's most salient precedent for the humanist celebration of memory and literature that animates "Jubal." It was apparently Eliot's last completed lyric, written in December 1875 when her great epic projects had fallen by the wayside and when she was in the midst of writing *Daniel Deronda* (1876). And like *Deronda* itself, the poem celebrates Jewish scriptural tradition as a living heritage conveniently alien to Evangelical Christianity, with its emphasis on the Atonement and the afterlife.

A comparison with the more recent English translations of Louis Ginzberg and J. Rabbinowitz shows how far Eliot imbues her text with the sort of sentimental flavor that she also gives to the story of Lamech in Genesis.[32] Eliot remains upon the whole faithful to the Devarim Rabbah, including God's conversations about Moses with the angels Gabriel, Michael, and Zamaël. But where other translations focus on the events, as in "At that hour God said to Gabriel: 'Gabriel, go forth and bring Moses' soul'" (Ginzberg 466; Rabbinowitz 184), Eliot dilates upon the instruction in highly sentimental terms:

> God spake to Gabriel, the messenger
> Of mildest death that draws the parting life
> Gently, as when a little rosy child
> Lifts up its lips from off the bowl of milk
> And so draws forth a curl that dipped its gold
> In the soft white—thus Gabriel draws the soul.
> "Go bring the soul of Moses unto me!"
> (196)

By Eliot's simile, we see, the archangel Gabriel gathers souls as a celestial Miss Muffet might draw stray curls from her curds and whey. Eliot focuses on the affective and poignant elements of the ancient text, omitting passages that might prove distasteful to an audience of nineteenth-century humanists. She ignores, for instance, that Moses ought to abuse the death angel Zamaël with his angry words and beat him with his staff (Rabbinowitz 185–86; Ginzberg 467–71). In more traditional translations also, Moses speaks of his own greatness in a way that the nineteenth-century poetess decorously avoided (Rabbinowitz 185–86; Ginzberg 468–69). Eliot simply excludes such passages from her poem, the better to dilate upon the striking parental love with which the Lord in this midrash finally addresses Moses's soul: "O child, come forth! for thou shalt dwell with me." She thus lingers upon those textual moments of the midrash that might appear most fitting in the poetess tradition. The key moment, when the Lord takes Moses's soul with a kiss— "Thereupon God kissed Moses and took away his soul with a kiss of the mouth" (Rabbinowitz 187; Ginzberg 473)—Eliot expands into a metaphysical flight of fancy: "But behold! upon the death-dewed lips / A kiss descended, pure, unspeakable— / The bodiless Love without embracing Love / That lingered in the body" (198–99). All this is not to imply that Eliot takes wild liberties in her rendering of the poem. Lask Abrahams fairly defends Eliot's as "a great Jewish poem which no born Jew could have bettered" (57). Still, Eliot certainly betrays modern and—more important—generically defined sensibilities. Her sentimental expansion of the affective moments of this extraordinary text demonstrates a profound reverence, but a different kind of reverence than the midrashic author had formerly envisioned.

The Devarim Rabbah translated à la poetess thus makes luminous the reconciliation that the poetess tradition effects between the religious spirit of the scriptures and secular humanism. Eliot takes up midrashic tradition as Tennyson takes up the apocryphal legends of Joseph of Arimathea in "The Holy Grail" (1869) and for analogous reasons. The importance of extra-canonical scriptures, including midrash, had struck anew nineteenth-century scholars of canon formation.[33] L'Abbé Migne's monumental two-volume *Dictionnaire des apocryphes, ou collection de tous les livres apocryphes relatifs à l'ancien et au nouveau testament* (1856, 1858) was, as J. H. Charlesworth notes, "followed by a cascade of publications . . . in Austria, Italy, Russia, France, Britain, and especially in Germany" (9). "The Death of Moses," although its story does not appear in Migne's volume, may be seen from the perspective of nineteenth-century Protestantism as work in the same tradition.

Further, Eliot's disinclination to acknowledge a religious difference between apocryphal scriptures and canonical ones represents a tendency in nineteenth-century women poets generally, who showed a keen interest in apocryphal texts.[34] The peculiar liminal status of such texts afforded women poets a certain power, for the texts were not sacred in the Protestant churches, yet they were manifestly cousin to much that is, and they showed how sacredness in texts is culturally selected.[35] Southey's American friend Maria Gowen Brooks made a poetical career of apocryphal texts, moving from an 1820 retelling of the book of Judith in her *Judith, Esther, and Other Poems* to a 1833 revision of the book of Tobit in her *Zóphiël, or The Bride of Seven*, reprinted in both 1849 and 1879. Adah Isaacs Menken evokes them in her 1868 "Judith," which ends with the startling triplet: "I am starving for this feast. / Oh forget not that I am Judith! / And I know where sleeps Holofernes."[36] And Christina Rossetti reifies a Johannine or Danielic apocalypse in her beguiling 1862 "My Dream," which begins with a vision "beside Euphrates while it swelled" but which comes around to deconstruct the biblical historical approach that its opening solicits: "What can it mean? you ask. I answer not / For meaning, but myself must echo, What? / And tell it as I saw it on the spot."[37]

Eliot's use of the Devarim Rabbah is more radical than these examples to the extent that it suggests a poetess's claims to share even the unique place of Moses in traditions that associate him with the text of Torah. The final quatrain of Eliot's poem makes explicit this association by which Moses lives in the minds and hearts of the practicing religious, who initially feel dismay at the loss of their great leader:

> Then through the gloom without them and within
> The spirit's shaping light, mysterious speech,
> Invisible Will wrought clear in sculptured sound,
> The thought-begotten daughter of the voice,
> Thrilled on their listening sense: "He has no tomb.
> He dwells not with you dead, but lives as Law."
> (199)

Here "Invisible Will" thrills on the listening senses of all the faithful, like the revelation of Barrett Browning in "Sounds." But Eliot's vision of Moses is foremost a textual one, generic and poetical. Moses "lives as Law" because his text, the beauty of Torah, continues to speak to us. Moses has become a name more fully than Jubal, for he personifies the wisdom of the texts that bear his name. In a certain sense, this idea appealed to Eliot the post-Christian humanist as deeply as it had to Marianne Evans the young Evangelical.

To turn from "The Death of Moses" to "O May I Join the Choir Invisible" is to find the same theme applied to Eliot's own oeuvre. This lyric became Eliot's most popular and most acclaimed poem, briefly enshrined in Francis Turner Palgrave's canon-forming Golden Treasury.[38] It professes (and attempts to realize) the goal of literary immortality that Eliot nursed in the years before her death. As she wrote in confidence, "'Non omnis moriar' ["I shall not wholly die"] is a keen hope with me" (*Letters* 9: 226). This is the poem's matter:

> O may I join the choir invisible
> Of those immortal dead who live again
> In minds made better by their presence: live
> In pulses stirred to generosity[.]
> . . . .

So to live is heaven:
To make undying music in the world.
(49)

Though skeptical of the Christian afterlife, Eliot sees promise in the pagan tradition of poetry's afterlife, and she turns to poetry to achieve that salvation. Eliot's 1867 hymn to literary influence might be said to offer the most direct expression of her wish to fulfill the role that she elsewhere assigns to Jubal and to Moses.

Non omnis moriar comes from Horace's *Ode* 3.30. But whereas the Horatian ode presents the boast of an imperial poet at the apex of his career, Eliot strikes a humbler pose, appearing neither as hero nor even necessarily as a distinct voice, but as a member of a celestial choir or a canon of secular saints. Eliot selects not heroic terms, but domestic and sentimental ones, terms that the Victorians associated with femininity. Her poem concludes,

This is life to come[.]
. . . .
May I reach
That purest heaven, be to other souls
The cup of strength in some great agony,
Enkindle generous ardour, feed pure love,
Beget the smiles that have no cruelty—
Be the sweet presence of a good diffused,
And in diffusion ever more intense.
So shall I join the choir invisible
Whose music is the gladness of the world.
(50)

Eliot desires not to be remembered for a Horatian *"Exegi monumentum,"* but to be felt as a nurse to the sick in spirit, to enkindle generosity, to engender love. Eliot's cliché invocations of "purest heaven," "great agony," and "pure love"—impossible in Horace's *Ode* 3.30—here are perfectly in line with Eliot's ambition to share the "sweet presence of a good diffused." And this is particularly so if, as Virginia Jackson and Yopie Prins persuasively argue, the poetess tradition understands itself to be one of recycled tropes and echoed voices.[39] What Eliot proposes is less a pagan alternative to Christian immortality than a sentimental alternative: "O May I Join" puts its faith in the recycled poetics of the poetess tradition, a tradition of piety that lives through its repetition and circulation, in "pulses stirred," in "other souls." This sentimental alternative to Heaven is presented as the likelier afterlife of the two.

Christianity operates as a foil for the poetic salvation that Eliot wishes to achieve. Even at its most heterodox, that is, the poetess tradition owes much to Christian moral culture but refines that culture in important ways. Eliot takes Christian bywords—purity and harmony—and translates them into the language of the poetess tradition: "sweet purity" and "meeting harmonies" that eschew the fundamentals of Christian doctrine.

> So we inherit that sweet purity
> For which we struggled, failed, and agonised
> With widening retrospect that bred despair.
> Rebellious flesh that would not be subdued,
> A vicious parent shaming still its child
> Poor anxious penitence, is quick dissolved;
> Its discords, quenched by meeting harmonies,
> Die in the large and charitable air.
> (49)

Christian imagery here serves a humanist manifesto: goodness derives from a struggle with nature ("Rebellious flesh") that ends in Heaven ("in the large and charitable air"). But Eliot employs this formula to suggest a terrestrial paradise that dwells in the realm of living memory, so her poem announces the borrowed nature of its symbols just as it celebrates their import. This is the "double poem" that Isobel Armstrong has taught us to look for in Victorian poetry—on the one hand, a straightforward celebration of important cultural symbols; on the other, a reification or investigation of their limited scope or validity. "This is the [only] life to come," Eliot suggests, this life in others, this heaven made possible by literacy and memory.

"O May I Join" is as much a Straussian meditation as a Horatian one; like much nineteenth-century poetry, it remains fixed to Christian symbols without laying claim to historical or even religious bases for that sacredness. Eliot would have known a similar wedding of Horatian ambition and biblical sentiment in "Le Tombeau de David à Jérusalem" ("The Tomb of David at Jerusalem," 1839) by Alphonse de Lamartine, a poem that explicitly applies classical tropes to Christian texts.[40]

Is that dying, O prophet?
What? For an eternity
to feel the breath lent one
to breathe in humanity?
. . . .
To have one's cry in every mouth,
one's accent in every accent?

Is that death? No! It is life,
made more alive in the written word!
By each eye which turns to the sacred book,
it is to multiply one's spirit!
(trans. mine)[41]

Like Eliot's poem, Lamartine's "Tombeau de David" skirts metaphysical speculation not by contesting the idea of life after death, but by suggesting that a postmortem poetic life amounts to the same thing. Rather than imagining David in the Christian heaven, Lamartine depicts the circulation of the Psalms as the immortality experienced by David. David's poetry becomes the most divine part of him even if most of the poems attributed to David were surely written by others.[42] This reflection, that the sacredness of a text resides in its genre (as a Psalm) rather than its authorship (as a work of David), reframes and refigures the province of sacred verse. The Psalms, sacred by definition, are not sacred because they were written by the historical David: the prophetic book creates the prophet, rather than vice versa. The anonymous authors who composed the Psalms live in David, and have their "cry in every mouth," their "accent in every accent." That one need not be Israel's king to write sacred verses suggests why Lamartine was so engaged with the genre. Eliot, taking this up, presents the poetess tradition as a similarly inspired instance of communal wisdom, of "a good diffused." A reader who admired the Psalms as David's voice (or God's) could not regard Eliot's work in the same light before coming to see the Psalmic wisdom as shared, or communal. Eliot could anticipate such readers, could hope to join "the choir" of which David was himself a member.

   If Eliot wishes to play the harp of David, she shows a significant measure of confidence that sentimental lyric can share the Psalms' longevity. "O May I Join" risks appearing comically ambitious after having lain mostly unread for a century, yet at her death, Eliot's place was perceived by many in Britain and America as commensurate with her aspirations. The American poetess Rose Elizabeth Cleveland (sister of U.S. President Grover Cleveland), launched a critical career with her 1885 book *George Eliot's Poetry and Other Studies,* arguing that Eliot's achievement falls only short of Barrett Browning's, the poetess par excellence.[43] Other American poetesses promised her in eulogies that "thou hast joined 'the choir invisible,' / Thy fancy leads us forth."[44] "O May I Join" was widely hailed as a masterful hymn, set to music by five or six composers, and actually sung in Positivist congregations (Vogeler, "Choir Invisible," 77–79). Not only were nineteenth-century poetesses quick to "measure to [themselves] a prophet's place," as Romney Leigh puts it, but they frequently discussed the Bible's female prophets specifically as poetesses.[45] Grace Aguilar notes in *The Women of Israel,* "The Hebrew word . . . translated prophetess, means also, a *poetess,* and the wife of a prophet, and is applied sometimes to a singer of hymns,"[46] and Eliot's friend Harriet Beecher Stowe observes in *Women in Sacred History,* "The prophetess was always a poetess" and "That pure ideal of a sacred woman springing from the bosom of the family, at once wife, mother, poetess, leader, inspirer, prophetess, is peculiar to sacred history."[47] Eliot capitalizes upon this association in her volume of lyrics. "O May I Join" shows her turning the biblical hermeneutic of "Le Tombeau de David" to the advantage of her own work. Its placement as the volume's envoi demonstrates her faith in its success.

The Turn to Music in "A Minor Prophet"

From our vantage, the unflagging earnestness of Eliot's poetry might have been profitably counterbalanced by the humor characterizing her prose fiction. But Eliot seems to have both entertained and rejected this possibility, to judge by "A Minor Prophet," of January 1865, which represents the start of her serious attempts at poetry.[48] The first portion of this poem satirizes the views of an American Quaker ("a friend, a vegetarian seer, / By name Elias Baptist Butterworth") who harbors millennial hopes of a coming ecological Utopia (31–35). Henry James, sensitive to the ridicule of loquacious Americans, considers this satire the heart of the poem and identifies the title character as "a gentleman, presumably, who under another name, as an evening caller, has not a little retarded the flight of time for the author."[49] American politics of the 1860s presented an obvious target for mid-century English satire, of course; Eliot's Butterworth anticipates by a few years Trollope's Jonas Spald-

ing and Wallachia Petrie, caricatures similarly meant to suggest the superior
common sense of British thinking. But James's sensitivity to the American
satire diverts him from the point of this poem. In reality, the Butterworth
pastiche serves as window dressing for the reflections of the narrator, whose
discourse about domestic life composes the bulk of the poem. Ultimately, it
is she who best merits the poem's title.[50]

The very dreariness of Butterworth's millennial vision brings Eliot's narrator to muse—at considerably greater length than he does—about her familiar, distinctly antemillennial English world, which includes childhood
Christmases, "patched and plodding citizens," and tasty baked goods. Her images of mundane community life replace the fantastic imagery of the American prophet, and she defends in particular "nature's blunders, evanescent
types / Which sages banish from Utopia" (36). She moreover suggests that the
comparative ugliness of her friend's Utopia should prohibit it from attaining
the status of true prophecy:

The earth yields nothing more Divine,
Than high prophetic vision—than the Seer
Who fasting from man's meaner joy beholds
The paths of beauteous order, and constructs
A fairer type, to shame our low content.
But prophecy is like potential sound
Which turned to music seems a voice sublime
From out the soul of light; but turns to noise
In scrannel pipes, and makes all ears averse.
(39)

"Scrannel pipes" here derive from Milton's "Lycidas"—an image of disharmony and clerical hypocrisy of which Ruskin assures us, "No English words
are more familiar to us."[51] Not only is religion poetical for Eliot, but the
unpoetical can hardly be religious. Here the nostalgic female domestic ideo-
logue overtakes the male vegetarian radical in her claims to modern day
prophecy. She too risks "speaking in parable" (as she puts it) to defend her
humble domestic realities, the "ungainly forms / inherited from toiling generations." Her poem instructs that such cultural forms, like the poetic forms
that call them to mind, are by nature imperfect but can be redeemed by
"high prophetic vision." Her very interruption of Butterworth presents this
on the smallest scale; excusing herself from his company, she suggests that

they revisit the topic at some future date: "No, not to-morrow—I shall have a cold—/ At least I feel some soreness—this endemic—/ Good-bye." The comic evasion of this moment is not meant to degrade prophecy so much as to render it local. The humor of this poem, far from tempering the earnest prophetic voice, hereafter becomes overwhelmed by it.

Eliot took humor to be the province of prose. She had initially conceived of *Silas Marner* (1861) as a poem, but reworked it as a novella when she realized its comic potential. Conversely, "A Minor Prophet" began as a prose piece called "My Vegetarian Friend" (*Letters* 4: 175), but became a poem when the poem's second voice took a commanding role. This reversal, whereby the prophetic status promised by the poem's title is transferred from one character to another, reflects equally Eliot's view of comedy and her understanding of high art. "In the later development of the poetic fable," she observes in her 1870 *Notes on Art*, "the αναγνωρισις [anagnorisis, "recognition"] tends to consist in the discernment of a previously unrecognized *character*, and this may also form the περιπετεια [peripeteia, "reversal"] according to Aristotle's notion that in the highest form the two coincide" (*Writings*, 359). The previously unrecognized character of "A Minor Prophet" is plainly the narrator, who begins with wry deference to her friend but who by the poem's conclusion has progressed to her own hierophantic claims: "Even our failures are a prophecy / Even our yearnings and our bitter tears" (40).

Eliot did not believe in the supernatural power of prophetic vision, but she felt it lost none of its importance when seen from a positivist perspective. She offers for a metaphor a pair of facing mirrors, looking backwards at the past and projecting it onto the future:

> Full souls are double mirrors, making still
> An endless vista of fair things before
> Repeating things behind: so faith is strong
> Only when we are strong, shrinks when we shrink.
> It comes when music stirs us, and the chords
> Moving on some great climax shake our souls
> With influx new that makes new energies.
> (39)

"Full souls," we see, are the essential element of the proleptic hermeneutic by which prophetic texts make themselves received: a claim with clear higher critical as well as sentimental antecedents. One of the most resounding

scholarly insights of modern biblical criticism is that many salient examples
of biblical prophecy seem to present the past as a prediction of the future in
order to explain the present, like a figure set between facing, parallel mirrors that reflect one another into "an endless vista." For instance, in Daniel's
vision of Alexander the Great, or in Jesus's vision of the destruction of the
Jerusalem temple, scripture writers with positive knowledge of historical
events record their historical anticipation.[52] In such cases, even a natural,
generically conceived prophecy can dictate the future, just as Daniel's imagery may have influenced the outcome of the Maccabean War and the Gospels
brought about the rise of Christianity in the Roman Empire.

As had the higher critics before her, then, Eliot locates prophecy in sympathy—the sympathetic soul reflects its earnest desires in its future, as well
as its past. We see here too Feuerbach's idea that the idea of God comes from
within: in art, too, we are stirred "At labours of the master-artist's hand/
Which, trembling, touches to a finer end,/Trembling before an image seen
within" (39–40). In fact, Eliot's choice to introduce a higher critical understanding of prophecy illustrates her desire to render the proleptic operation of
prophecy in familiar, even cliché terms. Her narrator embraces and embodies the contention of Jackson and Prins that the nineteenth-century poetess
tradition always understands itself to be one of recycled tropes and echoed
voices: "One reason for the perpetual disappearance and reappearance of the
Poetess is that she is not the content of her own generic representation: not
a speaker, not an 'I,' not a consciousness, not a subjectivity, not a voice, not a
persona, not a self."[53] Eliot was almost uniquely positioned to see that the poetess tradition of recycled tropes operates like the prolepsis of prophecy as the
higher critics understood it, for both traditions make "an endless vista of fair
things" before themselves, the "double mirrors" of future and past prophets
or poetesses framing poetic image within image. That Eliot should intuitively
retrace the analogous relation of these models should not surprise us.

For all its tongue-in-cheek attitude toward political radicalism, then, "A
Minor Prophet" participates in a discourse outlined by mid-century "feminine" publications like the American *Ladies' Repository* (1841–76), which advocated women's poetry with arguments like the following: "Why and how
is it that woman is now wielding the mightiest power in literature? The solution, we think, is found in the fact that she is nearer the heart of humanity,
her whole nature responsive to its throb of sympathy, and her whole soul
kindling with the revealings of its faith" (170). "A Minor Prophet" gives us
every reason to believe that Eliot took seriously the generic cachet of such

claims about women's poetry as the revealed faith of "the heart of human-ity." Her poem is essentially a celebration of national domesticity, but one that attempts to imbue this "mighty power" of feminine sympathy with the emerging power of a literary perspective on scripture. The poetess as under-stood by a higher critical model demonstrates the power of the vatic figure as Eliot saw her—a power that derived from sympathy, from a sentiment that in Eliot's culture had become the province of women.

Assuming the mantle of the prophetess, Eliot's narrator encourages an alternative future much as the scriptural authors did, by asking her readers to share her meliorist vision of domestic sentiment even as she concedes the human, individual basis for that vision. She embraces faith of the sort celebrated in the *Ladies' Repository*—a secular, internal faith, but one that is not less real for that:

> The faith that life on earth is being shaped
> To glorious ends, that order, justice, love
> Mean man's completeness . . .
> > . . . that great faith
> Is but the rushing and expanding stream
> Of feeling, fed by all the past.
> (39)

This internal faith remained for Eliot truth of the most exalted kind; indeed, Eliot believed that many of history's most important religious works derived from this source of feeling. The domestic terms of "A Minor Prophet" vener-ate prophecy even as they demystify and qualify themselves as expressions of human knowledge and feeling from the past. Without recourse to the supernatural, Eliot deifies individual, sentimental history as a positive truth and its own self-fulfilling prophecy.

This scriptural and prophetic element of Eliot's poetry helps to clarify just why the changing Victorian religious landscape might draw Eliot away from the realist prose tradition and into the field of sentimental verse-making. Eliot's scholarly understanding of prophecy derives from her read-ing in German biblical criticism, but her poetic use of it makes most sense in the light of a tradition that maintains the sacredness of recycled visions. Eliot uses the image of prophecy to elevate the figure of the poetess, and she does so even as she admits to the paradoxes that she presents, even when her poetry shows readers its own devices. As we better understand the nuances of classifying women's poetry of the nineteenth century, we can better account for its frequent characteristics and aims: not just sentimentality, piety, inter-referentiality, and strict attention to form, but increasingly also a prophetic investment in crafting a meaningful post-Christian culture. To read such a poetess as Eliot, one must observe her allegiances to nineteenth-century categories and then explain the kind of place she claims for herself. It was a gender-coded place, although Eliot knew as well as we do that Victorian gender essentialism is a box into which no nineteenth-century poetess actually fits.

The Poetry of Prophecy, the Prophecy of Fiction

Eliot's poetry remains an important and puzzlingly neglected aspect of her literary oeuvre. And even a rudimentary appreciation for her engagement with the women's sentimental poetic tradition can make better sense of Eliot's literary career than can a study of her fiction alone. It is no coincidence that *Daniel Deronda* (which I have no space to treat here) is both the only novel written after Eliot had finally given up on verse and the least novelistic of her major prose works. Having failed to write a poem that "dwarfs all the poems that were ever written," Eliot put her last great literary efforts into a novel that resembles in some manner the poetry of *Jubal* and (as has often been remarked of its plot) *The Spanish Gypsy.*

Here it is telling that Henry James's query about why one should write poetry "if one has at one's command the magnificent vehicle of the style of *Middlemarch*" might as easily have been posed about *Daniel Deronda,* a lopsided novel interlaced with what we might call religious prose poetry. James himself all but poses this question a few years later in a dialogue entitled *Daniel Deronda: A Conversation* (1876) imagined between a theological reader (Theodora), a superficial beauty (Pulcheria), and a persevering reader (Constantius), whose views mediate between those of the women and seem closest to those of James himself. Theodora adores the religious "burden" of the story whereas Pulcheria deprecates it, and Constantius himself confesses a "temptation to skip" it so as to get on to the domestic plot of Gwendolen and Grandcourt.[54] Theodora aside, James's readers want a novel and are dissatisfied when "Deronda clutches his coat-collar, Mirah crosses her feet, and

Mordecai talks like the Bible," protesting that "that doesn't make real figures of them. They have no existence outside of the author's study" (686). (Being a scholar of Victorian poetry and religion, I confess to generally skipping the Gwendolen plot in favor of the Mirah / Mordecai one. But James is perfectly right to call this a genre issue.) Emma Lazarus selected equally significant genre terms when describing the Zionism inspired by *Daniel Deronda:* "Could the noble prophetess . . . have lived but till today to see the ever increasing necessity of adopting her inspired counsel . . . she would have been herself astonished at the flame enkindled by her seed of fire, and the practical shape which the movement projected by her in poetic vision is beginning to assume."[55] Seeing Lazarus's association of "poetic vision" and "the noble prophetess" is instrumental to understanding much women's literature of the mid-nineteenth century. Almost despite themselves, James and Lazarus drive at Eliot's feeling that the novel as a genre could not suffice to engage the religious elements of our secular modernity.

Alexander Main, perhaps the most charmingly naive of Eliot's admirers, may here also provide the clearest example of how Eliot cultivated a religious and a poetic hermeneutic of her own oeuvre. Main's own greatest literary work was an edited volume of his favorite Eliot passages, republished with the author's blessing and entitled *Wise, Witty, and Tender Sayings in Prose and Verse, Selected from the Works of George Eliot* (1873). This compilation went through no fewer than eleven editions and was reprinted into at least 1904. Main's idea derives from the tradition of devotional and commonplace books, and might be classed with that distinctively Victorian sub-genre that collates Bible truths alongside those of the bard: works like J. B. Selkirk's *Bible Truths, with Shakspearean Parallels* (1862). Indeed, Main's preface reverts to the themes of his earliest correspondence with Eliot: "I only express the ripest fruit of sound critical inquiry when I affirm, that what Shakespeare did for the Drama, George Eliot has been, and still is, doing for the Novel" (ix). At the same time, Main's volume clearly works against the narrative logic of the novel: in one section, he excerpts all the snatches of wisdom and bons mots that come from Maggie Tulliver; in another, those from Philip Wakem. Even where he reprints whole sections of a work (like the whole preface to *Middlemarch*), Main's volume, like Selkirk's, solicits a hermeneutics that has much more in common with biblical reading practices than with the normal practices of novel readers.[56] Finally, both Eliot and Lewes hoped the *Wise and Witty* collection would have a religious function, as appears in Eliot's reply to Main's compilation proposal:

Bertel Thorvaldsen (1768–1844). Marble statue of Christ in the Church
of Our Lady, Copenhagen, 1839. Copenhagen, Denmark. (Photo credit:
Bildarchiv Preussischer Kulturbesitz/Art Resource, NY)

26 September 1871.

My dear Sir

Mrs. Lewes you will be sorry to hear is too weak to answer your letter—she
is only now recovering from a sharp attack which for two or three days kept
me very anxious. However she is now fairly on the way to recover again and it
was a real gratification to her—as to me—to receive your letter with its "happy
thought." Some years ago a lady suggested that "texts" should be selected from
the works to hang up in schoolrooms and railway waiting rooms in view of the

> banal and often preposterous bible texts, thus hung up and neglected. Your idea
> is a far more practical one. . . .
>
> Very truly yours, G. H. Lewes
>
> (*Letters* 5: 192–93)

Rather than "banal and often preposterous bible texts" hung up in schoolrooms and railway stations, Lewes looks forward to Eliot's original and judicious wisdom disseminated in a more convenient manner. Eliot herself
eventually responded to Main's initial compilation by urging him to include
more of her poetry.[57]

It is interesting that Eliot saw poetry—potentially including her own poetry—as the most obvious site for the promotion of a philosophical melior-
ism that we now associate with her fiction. But for her, the deliberateness of
poetic art and its nineteenth-century conflation with religion made this pref-
erence seem unexceptional. Then, too, many readers today will balk at the
sentimentality of much of Eliot's poetic oeuvre. But this amounts to a failure
of our scholarly hermeneutics if we cannot imagine why one of the great
literary minds of the nineteenth century would use this mode when engaging with biblical issues and the higher criticism (to say nothing of the other
dangers attendant to cursorily dismissing the bulk of nineteenth-century literary expression by women). Our failure here seems only the more striking
because Eliot's personal experience with the higher criticism literally made
her feel the appeal of sentimental religious meditation such as her poetry
offers us. Caroline Bray wrote of her during the *Leben Jesu* translation that
she was "Strauss-sick—it made her ill dissecting the beautiful story of the
crucifixion, and only the sight of her Christ-image and picture [a cast and
engraving of Thorvaldsen's figure of the risen Christ] made her endure it."[58]
What stands out about Bray's letter is not that Eliot would rely upon religious
art to help her through the revolution that Strauss represented. It is that she
would lean upon Thorvaldsen's Jesus (see figure), a somewhat kitschy speci-
men of nineteenth-century religious art. It is to Thorvaldsen's sentimental
Jesus, and not, say, to Michelangelo's Moses, that Eliot turns for the "cup of
strength in some great agony," as her best-known poem will later put it. So
Emma Lazarus seems mistaken only when she imagines that Eliot would
feel astonishment at moving readers to the religious response that *Daniel
Deronda* came to provoke. Eliot kept faith in poetry even when seized by the
apprehension that her own verse might not live forever.

CONCLUSION

Ist das Thema nicht erledigt,
Schelte Keiner mich darum:
Wer erschöpft in einer Predigt
Je das Evangelium?

(If the topic has not been exhausted,
No one should scold me.
Whoever exhausted the Gospels
With a single sermon?)

—D. F. STRAUSS, *"Vortrag über Lessings
Nathan" ("Lecture on Lessing's Nathan")*

CHOLARS HAVE LONG acknowledged the cultural importance of Victorian developments in modern biblical criticism and—less often—the equal importance of its widespread dissemination during this same period. It has been my attempt here to show how changing nineteenth-century perceptions about the Bible both stimulated the ambitions of the most prominent Victorian poets and conditioned their contemporary reception. Victorian biblical criticism often invoked the "poetic" nature of scripture, and Victorian poets often took this language literally as in some sense paradigmatic of their craft. Where the critic might take up "poetry" to indicate the fragmented, historically uncertain composition of the sacred canon, the poet might take up criticism as a challenge to reconfigure the very contours of contemporary religion. Poetry could assume this extraordinary role because of the cultural place of the poetic register: its function to move and to inspire. Still, it remains an extraordinary charge.

The above chapters center upon the poetry of Barrett Browning, Tennyson, Clough, Browning, and George Eliot, but this analysis should speak to the work of other poets as well, from both sides of the Atlantic. The crucial point here is that the changing nineteenth-century Bible put the meaning of textual inspiration up for grabs, and thrilled many poets with the prospect of contributing to what Carlyle called "a new Bible; or a new Apocrypha."[1] We see its American repercussions, for instance, in Emerson's famous divinity school lecture (1838) and his essay "The Poet" (1844), which positively solicit new inspired texts.[2] Inspired in part by Carlyle, Emerson calls Christ a "poet," but he also expresses dissatisfaction with holy scriptures that "have no epical integrity; are fragmentary; are not shown in their order to the intellect."[3] (The Gospels, that is, fail to achieve the highest levels of poetry, and Emerson looks for a work with "epical integrity" to take their place.) This point of view lost little traction as Carlyle's and Emerson's immense literary influences gave way to that of Arnold, who (as we have discussed) would go so far as to advocate poetry itself as "the future of religion." By the fin de siècle, even a popular journalist such as W. T. Stead could advocate incorporating the poetry of Tennyson and the Brownings into a new national "Bible" composed of English poetry and philosophy.[4] Apparently writing in earnest, Stead in 1893 recommends that Chaucer might serve for a new book of Ruth, *Paradise Lost* for Job, Shakespeare's sonnets for the Song of Solomon, Anglophone folk sayings for Proverbs, and so forth. (Tellingly, Stead's vision excludes prose fiction, though it admits sermons, scientific papers, and philosophical prose.) Stead's proposal might almost seem to parody Arnold's mature views on poetry—then, to us, Arnold's views seem sometimes to parody themselves.

At all events, this Victorian aspiration to re-craft the scriptures was tied to evolving nineteenth-century conceptions of poetic genre more radically—and in some ways more incidentally—than was clearly appreciated by Carlyle, Emerson, Arnold, or (certainly) Stead. The higher criticism presented an unprecedented crisis not just of literary authority but also of literary language. It is not that the Victorians failed to grasp the difference between "poetry" and poetry; it is that their shifting literary taxonomies facilitated a blurring of that important distinction just where this religious crisis occurred. Scholars rarely emphasize the sheer unlikelihood and persistence of mid-Victorian poetry's tendency to measure itself against the Bible, the resilience of the Victorian expectation that English verse forms might prove crucial to supplementing the Bible in the secular age of modernity. But we need this context to account for, among other things, the increasingly rarified role that poetry was expected to play, the longevity of key precedents in Romantic poetry, and the ongoing discussions of the poet as *vates* even at a moment that other literary forms (most notably the novel) made sweeping incursions into the cultural prestige of verse.[5] What is more, the vigor of Victorian Christianity created a sort of serial repetition of the specifically biblical elements of this crisis of modern hermeneutics, which played out again and again in varying configurations among the religiously minded throughout the course of the century. We should strive to understand better both the habits and the vicissitudes of Victorian hermeneutics, including the perennial recurrence of key themes and tensions between different ways of constructing the religious world.

In this way, and for these reasons, religious aspiration contributes a great deal to the shape, focus, and meaning of Victorian poetry. Happily, such aspiration becomes easier to comprehend when we move away from still-dominant models of secularization predicated upon the demise of Western religion or the "death of God" and toward a more capacious (albeit messier) model of secularization such as that suggested by the recent work of Charles Taylor, who discusses secularization as a condition of modern life that helps to constitute modern selfhood and that—at least historically—brings about both the deterioration and rejuvenation of religious forms.[6] The opposing or antithetical forces apparent in the poetry treated here, for instance, remain a function of a broader modern condition: one best conceived of not as a retreat from religion but as an unresolved tension between variously appealing ways of imagining the world. In *Sources of the Self* (1989), Taylor pursues "the cultural mutation by which alternative sources to the theistic became available" (316), and in his more recent *A Secular Age* (2007), he critiques prevalent "subtraction" models that presume urbanization, industrialization, science, and technology to produce religious decline in and of themselves:

> My aim is to suggest, in place of the supposed uniform and unilinear effect of modernity on religious belief and practice, another model, in which these changes do, indeed, frequently destablilize older forms, but where what follows depends heavily on what alternatives are available or can be invented out of the repertory of the populations concerned. In some cases, this turns out to be new religious forms. The pattern of modern religious life under "secularization" is one of destabilization and recomposition, a process which can be repeated many times.
> (461)

Taylor's point is that once we stop taking for granted the disappearance of religion, we can begin to take stock of the various ways that religion continues to function in modern secular climates. Among other things, this will help us to understand better the reasons for the dissolution of religion's former intellectual hegemony. Taylor refers to the Victorians as "our Victorian contemporaries" so as to indicate both the newly widespread viability of diverse atheist and materialist models during this period and also the relevance of ongoing and newly emergent theistic models. As I have striven to show, Victorian poetry does significant religious work in this context. To us, its literary power might seem incidental to its religious value, but mid-century poets took it as axiomatic that these should constitute one another.

For Barrett Browning, Tennyson, Browning, Clough, and Eliot, the religious possibilities of what Taylor calls "a secular age" clearly proved a marvelous stimulant. The very theoretical machinery of secularization provided a scaffolding for their poetry: Tennyson went to Shakespeare for scriptural solace, and Eliot went to Tennyson.[7] The mid-Victorians called *Aurora Leigh* "Mrs. Browning's Gospel" and its author a "saint"; the late Victorians compared Browning to Isaiah and one (sadly anonymous) Browningite believed his very voice to be God's own.[8] These days, such fervor will appear excessive, but the striking and apparently sincere reverence inspired in many readers of Victorian poetry produces what we ought to consider real modern religious expressions, regardless of our attitude toward sacred literature more generally. This poetry emerges from a lively religious context that serves as an enabling condition for its creation, and it engages with religion in hugely ambitious ways. Barrett Browning's poetry attests to the force of the higher criticism although she leaves little independent evidence of having read it. The same might be said of Tennyson. Browning and George Eliot then build in antithetical (indeed, mutually exclusive) ways upon the foundational poetics of Barrett Browning, and Clough revises the hermeneutic implicit in Tennyson to show both its attraction and the attraction of its antithesis. All five figures evidence a marvelous sensitivity to mid-century intellectual and religious change. And, in very different ways, all five took these winds of change for a divine afflatus. If they came to hold a more exalted view of the power—or, at least, the stature—of modern poetry than circumstances warranted, still that attitude gives life to much of their most important poetry.

Novalis and Schleiermacher, moreover, were perfectly right to suggest that enduring modern Bibles could always be written—though verse was never a sine qua non for their creation. It is the American Joseph Smith whose writings provide the most conspicuously successful example of a modern Bible, and the cadences and diction of *The Book of Mormon* (1830) clearly hearken back to the King James prose, rather than to Milton or Cowper.

Smith's better angel wisely kept him from translating his divine inspiration into iambic pentameter.[9] One finds nothing like the poetry of Smart, Blake, or Wordsworth in *The Book of Mormon,* nothing like Barrett Browning, Tennyson, or Clough, nothing even like Psalms, the Song of Songs, or Isaiah. And Smith's exclusive devotion to prose surely augmented, rather than diminished, his scripture's claims to religious authority. Scholars of literature will likely continue to find greater interest in the more conspicuously literary works of a Browning or a George Eliot, for these remain in conversation with the overall development of modern Anglophone poetry, fiction, and literature.[10] It is precisely their participation within the English poetic tradition that lends such interest to their extraordinary sacred ambitions. Yet Smith's alternative model reminds us of the persistence, even peculiarity, of Victorian devotion to a biblical conception of poetry such as these chapters describe—the mild but tenacious sort of category error that allowed poets to flatter themselves about an inherent connection between their craft and potential new scriptures.

In the end, the literary fruitfulness of Victorian higher critical poetry often seems to depend upon a poet's willingness and ability to negotiate a dual allegiance to English poetic form and to poetical religion. Our most eager proponent of an open religious canon, Barrett Browning, found her greatest successes when working with well-established secular poetic forms (blank verse, sonnets) and modes (bildungsroman, novel of ideas). Tennyson's more subtle accommodation or transformation of the terms of the higher criticism depends upon the epic, national character of *The Idylls:* his work has great implications for the stakes of the higher criticism, but it arrives there only by analogy and indirection. And if Browning's hermeneutic experiments boldly claim a kinship with biblical modes of instruction, yet they too can only emerge as a religious intervention through the prodigious poetic craft on display in *The Ring and the Book.* Clough here stands out for what we might consider his more judicious appreciation of the distance between the English poetic tradition and the received scriptural canon, but this apprehension seems also to have robbed his art of its appeal for him: we can see clearly how his earliest sacred ambitions enable his greatest works, *Amours de Voyage* and *Dipsychus,* to probe the boundaries of a vatic poetics in intriguing and exquisite ways. When Clough lost his faith in poetry, the world lost his poetry. George Eliot, by turn, offers to Clough a useful foil in her enduring devotion to this quest between the periods of *The Spanish Gypsy* and *Daniel Deronda:* Eliot's poetry has been rather neglected, but it shows us the limits of Victorian prose fiction as she saw them, and it delivers intricate religious ideas that required, as she saw it, the more deliberate craft of verse.

Looking back, we can appreciate the usefulness to Victorian poetry studies of an idea of secularization in which "new [religious] forms . . . can flourish."[11] The Browning Societies did not have the staying power of other contemporary religious movements (like Mormonism or the Catholic Marian devotions critiqued in *Red Cotton Night-Cap Country*), but they present an important reification of Victorian poetry that we miss entirely where we presume a narrative of religious decline and disappearance, as we so often have tended to do. Consider in this light Thomas Hardy's late lyric "An Ancient to Ancients" (1922), which strives to recapture the wrecked aftermath of the Victorian cult of Tennyson:

> The bower we shrined to Tennyson,
> > Gentlemen,
> Is roof-wrecked; damps there drip upon
> Sagged seats, the creeper-nails are rust,
> The spider is sole denizen;
> Even she who voiced those rhymes is dust,
> > Gentlemen![12]

Hardy's poem here traces (and in some measure mourns) the diminishment of a certain religious model of Victorian poetry, not as something risible but as a treasure somehow mislaid. The tone feels wistful, closer to that of "The Darkling Thrush" than to the mordant satire of "The Ruined Maid." The Tennysonian prophecies heard by Victorian readers from Anthony Trollope to F. W. H. Meyers had become awkwardly hollow by the second decade of the twentieth century. But part of Hardy's wonder is that Tennyson once had a shrine in the first place. And despite Hardy's own assumptions about the modern death of God, Tennyson haunts the imagery and meter of this poem, from the rusted nails of Mariana's grange to the nostalgic half-rhymed dactyls in "Tennyson" and "Gentlemen." Angela Leighton has recently suggested of the high modernist poets that "the sound of Tennyson rings on their ears and in their writings": this observation applies still more unmistakably to the twentieth-century secular poetry of Hardy.[13]

Mid-Victorian poetic interventions into the hermeneutics of the changing Victorian Bible remained artful and oblique. They never simply claim an acquaintance with angels or biblical figures in the manner of Swedenborg or

Blake, of Joseph Smith or the mid-century peasant children visited by the Virgin. They sometimes seem chastened by the example of the English Romantic poets. But the most ambitious mid-Victorian poetic projects plainly continue to draw inspiration from the great Romantic promise of an open canon. This promise animates their poetry in powerful ways and drives it into unexpected, extravagant, and often beautiful forms.

Notes

INTRODUCTION

1. Brown, *Death of Christian Britain;* Cox, *English Churches;* Mcleod, *Secularization in Western Europe* and *Religion and Society;* Rosman, *Evolution of the English Churches.*

2. Taylor, *Sources of the Self,* 408, and *Secular Age.*

3. I single out Mason and Knight (*Nineteenth-Century Religion*) and McKelvy (*English Cult of Literature*) because they expressly acknowledge a debt to the historians cited above and to their reconceptualization of the secularization hypothesis. Many other literary scholars have acknowledged religion's vitality in this period, of course, which includes important work by Gauri Viswanathan (*Outside the Fold*), Cynthia Scheinberg (*Women's Poetry and Religion*), and (for many years now) Stephen Prickett (*Origins of Narrative, Words and the Word,* and *Narrative, Religion and Science*). But our habits of viewing secularization à la Buckley have made it much harder to incorporate the fruits of such scholarship.

4. Bruce, *God Is Dead.*

5. This is the difference between the newer models of secularization and older models like that of Owen Chadwick's classic *Secularization of the European Mind.* Chadwick traces the intellectual history of educated elites and assumes that their beliefs inevitably trickle down to the masses. But many recent scholars, even those as divergent as Brown and Bruce, agree to discount the "European mind" as of minimal sociological relevance; their interest lies in the broad trends in religious belief.

6. As McKelvy puts it, "Yesterday's truisms appear, at the least, one-sided. Take J. Hillis Miller's elegant study *The Disappearance of God. . . .* The religious professionalism lurking in the background and emerging in the conclusion of Miller's study has the virtue of quietly compromising his major assumption" (13). Nowadays, Hillis Miller seems to agree with McKelvy: "These days I find [my] hypothesis of such a universal spooky Zeitgeist extremely dubious. How would you prove such a thing? . . . God, wherever he is, does not I think consider it worth his time to appear and disappear like that" (xi).

7. "Die heiligen Schriften sind Bibel geworden aus eigener Kraft, aber sie verbieten keinem andern Buche, auch Bibel zu sein oder zu werden, und was mit gleicher Kraft geschrieben wäre, würden sie sich gern beigesellen lassen" (Schleiermacher, *Über Die Religion,* 203, trans. Crouter, *On Religion*).

8. Balfour provides a fuller context for Klopstock's claim in *Rhetoric of Romantic Prophecy,* 42. Blake, *Complete Writings,* 158.

9. Qtd. in Balfour, *Rhetoric of Romantic Prophecy,* 43.

10. Edward Young, James Thomson, and Christopher Smart, for instance, all see poetry as what Thomson calls "the peculiar Language of Heaven" (*Poetical Works,* 165).

11. Shaffer, *"Kubla Khan";* McGann, "Indeterminate Text"; Prickett, *Words and the Word;* Thorslev, "Byron and Bayle"; Balfour, *Rhetoric of Romantic Prophecy.* See also the preface to Looper, *Byron and the Bible.*

12. In addition to Balfour, McGann, Prickett, Shaffer, and Thorslev (above), examples of such work may be found in M. H. Abrams's classic *Natural Supernaturalism* (1971), Shaun Irlam's *Elations: The Poetics of Enthusiasm in Eighteenth-Century Britain* (1999), and David Jasper's *The Sacred and Secular Canon in Romanticism* (1999).

13. Shaffer, for instance, overstates Coleridge's impact upon Victorian hermeneutics when she claims that "the mythological school of German higher criticism enabled him to move . . . towards a new apologetics that ultimately he would use to transform Anglicanism and make it viable for another century" (*"Kubla Khan,"* 25).

14. As is powerfully demonstrated in Suzy Anger's *Victorian Interpretation.*

15. For more on the connection between the higher criticism and Arnold's poetry, especially "Empedocles on Etna" and the Obermann poems, see Culler, *Imaginative Reason.*

16. Shea and Whitla, *Essays and Reviews,* 4, 20.

17. *British Quarterly Review* 71 (July 1881): 128.

18. The phase *Höhere Kritik* comes from Eichhorn's *Einleitung in das Alte Testament,* 3 vols. (1780–83). It apparently took hold quickly, for in Eichhorn's 1787 preface to the second edition of this text, he could write, "It was necessary to apply my chief pains to a field hitherto unbroken, namely, to an inquiry into the internal structure of the separate books of the Old Testament by means of the higher criticism, a term strange to no scholar" (Eichhorn, *Introduction,* xi).

19. "Es bleibt dabei, mein Lieber, das beste Studium der Gottesgelehrsamkeit ist Studium der Bibel, und das beste Lesen dieses göttlichen Buchs ist *menschlich.* Ich nehme dies Wort im weitesten Umfange und in der andringendsten Bedeutung.

Menschlich muß man die Bibel lesen: denn sie ist ein Buch durch Menschen für Menschen geschrieben: menschlich ist die Sprache, menschlich die äußern Hülfsmittel, mit denen sie geschrieben und aufbehalten ist; menschlich endlich ist ja der Sinn, mit dem sie gefaßt werden kann, jedes Hülfsmittel, das sie erläutert, so wie der ganze Zweck und Nutzen, zu dem sie angewandt werden soll" (Herder, *Theologische Schriften,* 145, emphasis his).

(It remains a fact, my dear, that the best divinity study is the study of the Bible, and the best manner of reading this godly book is a human reading. I take this word in the widest possible way [compass, scope] and by its most urgent meaning.

We must read the Bible in a human way, since it is a book written by humans, for humans: the language is human, [and] human are the external resources [auxiliary means] by which it was written and preserved; finally, human is the sense with which it can be grasped, every resource that explains it, as well as the entire purpose and use to which it is to be applied [trans. mine].)

20. Shea and Whitla, *Essays and Reviews,* 482.

21. Coleridge, *Confessions,* 8.

22. Nixon, "Kill[ing] Our Souls"; Mason and Knight, *Nineteenth-Century Religion,* 156.

23. Shea and Whitla, *Essays and Reviews,* 107.

24. Fraser, *Beauty and Belief,* 5.

25. Fraser does offer a significant discussion of the role of genre here, as does, more recently, F. Elizabeth Gray's *Christian and Lyric Tradition.*

26. Stephen Prickett and Robert Barnes offer a succinct account of Lowth's influence in their Landmarks of World Literature volume, somewhat confusingly entitled *The Bible* (91–98). Another good account is Norton, *History of the English Bible,* chapter 10.

27. Eichhorn, *Introduction,* 11.

28. Qtd. in Moore, *History of Christian Thought,* 114–15.

29. This passage was among those cited as evidence of heresy in Williams's trial at the Court of Arches in 1862 (*Essays and Reviews,* 185).

30. Jowett, *Life and Letters,* 1: 406.

31. The clearest exception to this majority, he adds, is Herder (Gilfillan, *Bards of the Bible,* xix–xx).

32. Qtd. in Roberts, *Romantic and Victorian Long Poems,* 38.

33. Eliot, *Felix Holt,* 426.

34. Austin, "Poetry of the Period," 320.

35. Arnold, *Dissent and Dogma,* 196.

36. T. H. Ward, *English Poets,* 1: xvii.

37. In these famous introductory lines, Arnold reprints most of the final paragraph of his own recent introduction to the "Poetry" section of Wallace Wood's *The Hundred Greatest Men: Portraits of the One Hundred Greatest Men of History* (1879). Interestingly, Wood lists under "Poetry" a few authors mostly known for prose (Rabelais, Cervantes, perhaps Goethe, and perhaps Walter Scott) alongside thirteen poets (Homer, Virgil, Dante, Shakespeare, etc.). Moreover, Wood's subheading, "Poets — Dramatists — Novelists," acknowledges novels in a way that Ward's anthology does not. Thus, Arnold's later decision to reprint his claims for poetry clearly commits him to a narrower use of the genre term than Wood had envisioned (in addition to ascribing such power to poets beneath Wood's small number of worthies). "The Study of Poetry" might be read as a retraction of Wood's more flexible conception of poetry.

38. Volumes appearing after 1880 would include poets from Addison to Rossetti (vols. 3 and 4) and, after Arnold's death, from Browning to Rupert Brooke (vol. 5). Arnold himself appears in volume 5, as he might reasonably have hoped when writing his introduction.

39. Miller, *Disappearance of God,* 14.

40. For an overview of Coleridge and Carlyle in this context, see Ashton, *German Idea.*

41. Charles Hennell's *Inquiry concerning the Origin of Christianity* (1838) was still more neglected. George Eliot would write consolingly to Sara Hennell (Charles's sister), "And perhaps you have felt inclined, as I have, to be a little impatient at the 'fuss' made about Renan's book, as well as Colenso's doings, by an English public which supposes that these men are finding out new heresies. However, such impatience is unreasonable" (*Letters* 4: 104–5).

42. As Shaffer rightly puts it, "Colenso's book on the Mosaic question is, however affecting from the point of view of his personal history, no more than the rankest provincial amateur might have penned in a lonely vicarage a hundred years previously" (*"Kubla Khan,"* 268).

43. Another popular work in this genre is J. R. Seeley's *Ecce Homo* (1865), which has still less claim than *La vie de Jésus* to be called a higher critical work, and whose author lacked the benefits of extensive German scholarship. Still, it appeared (anonymously) to a great deal of hubbub in British literary circles, and Gladstone wrote of it with characteristic hyperbole: "I know of, or recollect, no production of equal force that recent years can boast of. . . I hail the entrance into the world of a . . . noble book" (qtd. in Soffer, "History and Religion," 137).

44. Hardy, *Complete Poetical Works,* 1: 198–99.

45. Eliot, *Middlemarch,* 70.

46. Trollope, *Barchester Towers,* 90.

47. Hallam Tennyson, *Alfred Lord Tennyson,* 2: 463.

48. For more on these, see Shaw, *Lucid Veil*, and G. B. Tennyson, *Victorian Devotional Poetry*, as well as Blair's forthcoming *Form and Faith in Victorian Poetry and Religion*.

49. Scheinberg, in *Women's Poetry and Religion*, addresses many of these questions in relation to Jewish poets, for instance.

50. Chillingworth, *Religion of Protestants*, 463.

51. It is no coincidence that all of the poems chosen by Daniel Brown for his recent essay on poetry and science in the *Cambridge Companion to Victorian Poetry* treat religious themes even when they come to specifically nonreligious conclusions: Tennyson's *In Memoriam*, Arnold's "Dover Beach," Hardy's "In a Wood," Meredith's "Lucifer in Starlight," Browning's "Christmas-Eve," Hopkins's "The Blessed Virgin Compared to the Air We Breathe."

52. "Our" here refers to literary critics such as myself, rather than to historians of science. Works such as James A. Secord's fine *Victorian Sensation* do a better job of contextualizing our literary subjects than we tend to do.

53. Even so superb a literary historian as Isobel Armstrong has wondered aloud how Tennyson could articulate geological concerns even before Lyell's *Principles*: "It seems that [Tennyson] knew of these speculations before Lyell's book appeared in 1830" (*Victorian Poetry*, 57).

54. *Norton Anthology*, 1st ed., 821.

55. *Works of John Ruskin*, 115.

56. As Roy Porter has shown in *The Making of Geology* (1977), the key difference between Georgian geological registers and Victorian ones is found in their claim to be part of a geological science, "a highly complex construct of formal and informal institutions, practices, standards, beliefs and facts, forged over time" (216).

57. *Byron*, 882.

58. The *Gentleman's Magazine* wrote of *Cain* that "it is in fact neither more nor less than a series of wanton libels upon the Supreme Being and His attributes" ("Cain," 613); the *London Review*, that its "direct attacks upon the goodness of God, are such as no arguments can justify, and no criticism can sanction" ("Sardanapalus," 69); the *London Magazine*, that "the direct attacks on the goodness of God are such as we dare not utter or transcribe" ("Sardanapalus," 70); and *Blackwood's Edinburgh Magazine*, that "it is perhaps of all the effusions of the Satanic school, the best entitled to that distinction.... The office of drugging the dainties is naturally given to the apostate arch-angel" (Matthews, 215).

59. Steffan, *Lord Byron's Cain*, 313.

60.   Tout en parlant ainsi, le satyre devint
    Démesuré; plus grand d'abord que Polyphème
    Puis plus grand que Typhon qui hurle et qui blasphème,
    Et qui heurte ses poings ainsi que des marteaux,
    Puis plus grand que Titan, puis plus grand que l'Athos;
    L'espace immense entra dans cette forme noir;
    Et, comme le marin voit croître un promontoire,
    Les dieux dressés voyaient grandir l'être effrayant;
    Sur son front blêmissait un étrange orient;
    Sa chevelure était une forêt; des ondes,
    Fleuves, lacs, ruisselaient de ses hanches profondes;
    Ses deux cornes semblaient le Caucase et l'Atlas....
    ... Sa poitrine terrible était pleine d'étoiles.
    (Hugo, 429)
For "deep time," see Gilmour, *Victorian Period*, 25.

61. See Wheeler, *Death and the Future Life*.

62. Strauss, *Life of Jesus*, 3: 92.

63. As Daniel Brown seems to suggest in "Victorian Poetry and Science."

64. Wilde, *Artist as Critic*, 301.

65. Lines 300–305. "Fra Lippo Lippi" is singled out for praise elsewhere in Wilde's *Intentions* (*Robert Browning: The Poems*, 547).

66. Todorov, *Mikhail Bakhtin*, 83.

67. Barrett Browning, *Aurora Leigh*, 190.

68. For an explicit critique of this view, see "Religion: Reform, Rejection, Reconstruction," in Gilmour, *Victorian Period*, 63–110. See also R. W. Ward, "Faith and Fallacy"; McLeod, *Religion and Society*; Melnyk, *Women's Theology*; Helmstadter and Davis, *Religion and Irreligion*; Parsons, *Religion in Victorian Britain*.

1. "MRS. BROWNING'S GOSPEL"

1. Scott and Byron dwarfed the poetry sales of their contemporaries throughout the 1830s, as William St. Clair shows in *Reading Nation*, 216–19, 413–32.

2. While Hemans's latitudinarian religious views differed markedly from Keble's High Anglicanism, both viewed poetry as a conduit for religious emotion. Of their oeuvres, only Hemans's last works approach EBB's vatic ideal. See Mason, *Women Poets*; Melnyk, "Hemans's Later Poetry"; G. B. Tennyson, *Victorian Devotional Poetry*.

3. See reviews in the *Examiner* (June 1838) and *Metropolitan Magazine* (August 1838) reproduced in Kelley and Hudson, *Brownings' Correspondence*, 2: 375, 83. Hereafter cited as *Correspondence*.

4. St. Clair, *Reading Nation*, 210.

5. Stone, "Heretic Believer."

6. EBB to Hugh Stuart Boyd, September 1827, *Correspondence*, 2: 76.

7. 3.245–248. All references to this poem are from Barrett Browning, *Aurora Leigh*.

8. Unless otherwise noted, all references to *The Seraphim and Other Poems* are from Barrett Browning, *Poetical Works*, Cambridge Edition.

9. "Sounds" represents an especially clear instance of a large-scale, transatlantic tendency among post-Enlightenment minority religions to claim an aural connection to the Deity. Leigh Eric Schmidt goes so far as to claim of this period that "with the crumbling of established authorities, God had more prophets, tongues, and oracles than ever before; thus, the modern predicament actually became as much one of God's loquacity as God's hush" (*Hearing Things*, 11).

10. Mill, "What Is Poetry?" 1216.

11. Swedenborg, *Arcana Coelestia*, 10: 413–14.

12. Barrett, *Seraphim and Other Poems*, 227. *Correspondence* 4: 73–77.

13. Mermin, *Elizabeth Barrett Browning*, 21–24. Lewis, *Barrett Browning's Spiritual Progress*, 9–13.

14. She objected strongly, by contrast, to an 1831 portrait (now lost) done by her friend Eliza Cliffe. "Eliza came. Painted at the picture, which will never be like me until I change my nose mouth & eyes" (Berridge, *Barretts at Hope End*, 125).

15. Twain, *Collected Tales*, 576.

16. Barrett's habit of considering the earth to be six thousand years old also led to problems with the title poem of the *Seraphim* volume, which alludes to "Adam, dead six thousand years" (74). Since this poem is set during Christ's crucifixion, Earth ought to have been just four thousand years old, according to Ussher's calendar. A gift copy of the *Seraphim* volume presented to

Louis Capell in 1843 (and now held in the Armstrong Browning Library at Baylor University) has "six" struck through and "four" added in EBB's hand (74).

17. Wordsworth, of course, presents only EBB's most obvious model. Others, including her cousin John Kenyon, wrote similar verses.

18. Lines 102–11, in Wordsworth, *Poetical Works*, 262.

19. Newman, "Tamworth Reading Room," 230.

20. "Isobel's Child" is singled out for excerption and special praise in the *Athenaeum* (July 7, 1838) and the *Monthly Review* (September 1838); reviews reproduced in *Correspondence* 4: 376–77, 86–87.

21. "De toutes les religions qui ont jamais existé, la religion chrétienne est la plus poétique, la plus humaine, la plus favorable à la liberté, aux arts et aux lettres; que le monde moderne lui doit tout, depuis l'agriculture jusqu'aux sciences abstraites; depuis les hospices pour les malheureux jusqu'aux temples bâtis par Michel-Ange, et décorés par Raphaël" (Chateaubriand, *"Génie du Christianisme,"* 469–70).

22. Prickett, *Origins of Narrative*, 168–79.

23. "Il est temps qu'on sache enfin à quoi se réduisent ces reproches d'*absurdité*, de *grossièreté*, de *petitesse*, qu'on fait tous les jours au christianisme; il est temps de montrer que, loin de rapetisser la pensée, il se prête merveilleusement aux élans de l'âme, et peut enchanter l'esprit aussi divinement que les dieux de Virgile et d'Homère."

24. For Hemans's deep and abiding interest in Byron, see Wolfson, "Hemans and the Romance of Byron."

25. The enduring importance of this work is addressed in two works by Elisabeth Jay, the second of which reproduces this passage at some length: *Evangelical and Oxford Movements* and *Faith and Doubt in Victorian Britain*, 2–4.

26. This is but one instance of EBB's fraught relationship to Judaism, described more completely in Scheinberg, *Women's Poetry and Religion*.

27. As Steve Dillon has pointed out in "Barrett Browning's Poetic Vocation."

28. F. Elizabeth Gray points out that Victorian women's devotional verse often refused (or failed) to distinguish between Mary the Virgin, Mary Magdalene, and Mary of Bethany (*Christian and Lyric Tradition*, 128).

29. Indeed, Mason (*Women Poets*) identifies this ambition as a general aspect of nineteenth-century poetry by women.

30. [Sawtelle], "Review of the Straussian Theory," 348.

31. Parker adds, "Eichhorn had made the reasonable demand that the Bible should be treated like other ancient books" ("Das Leben Jesu," 277–78).

32. See reviews in the *Examiner* (June 24, 1838), the *Athenaeum* (July 7, 1838), *Blackwood's Edinburgh Magazine* (August 1838), the *Monthly Chronicle* (August 1838), and the *Monthly Review* (September 1838), reproduced in *Correspondence* 4: 375, 77–78, 80, 85, 86–87.

33. Review in the *Sunbeam* (October 6, 1838), reproduced in *Correspondence* 4: 400.

34. Swedenborg insisted that proper biblical exegesis required additional revelation such as he enjoyed: "Anyone may see that the Apocalypse can be explained only by the Lord; for every word in it contains arcana which could never be known without special enlightenment, i.e., revelation" (*Apocalypse Revealed*, viii–ix). Similarly, "This is really the case that no one can possibly know [the Hebrew Bible] except from the Lord. It may therefore be stated in advance that of the Lord's Divine mercy it has been granted me now for some years to be constantly and uninterruptedly in company with spirits and angels, hearing them speak and in turn speaking with them" (*Arcana Coelestia*, 2).

35. Qtd. in Swedenborg, *Apocalypse Revealed*, iii.

36. As Inge Jonsson points out, Swedenborg's notions of correspondence and the spirit world evolve considerably over the course of his writings, but he returns often to this idea (Jonsson, *Emanuel Swedenborg*, 108).

37. Qtd. in Barrett Browning, *Aurora Leigh*.

38. Swinburne, *Aurora Leigh*, x.

39. Lodge, *Modes of Modern Writing*, 25.

40. Woolf, *Second Common Reader*, 230–31. For a good discussion of Woolf's response to EBB, see Chaney, "Poet-Prophet's Book."

41. As Dino Felluga nicely remarks of the Victorian verse novel, "What distinguishes the verse novel's approach from novelistic critiques is an ability to question domestic ideology not just at the level of content, or even of the form of the content, but at the level of, what Hayden White . . . has dubbed 'the content of the form'—the ideologies that are inextricably connected to form" ("Verse Novel," 177).

42. Bakhtin, *Dialogic Imagination*, 3–41. For a more involved discussion of Bakhtin and the Victorian verse novel, see Felluga, "Verse Novel."

43. See Davies, "Aurora," 58–59.

44. See Armstrong, *Victorian Poetry*, 345.

45. "Fausses quand elles essayent de prouver l'infini, de le déterminer, de l'incarner, si j'ose le dire, les religions sont vraies quand elles l'affirment. Les plus graves erreurs qu'elles mêlent à cette affirmation ne sont rien comparées au prix de la vérité qu'elles proclament. Le dernier des simples, pourvu qu'il pratique le culte du coeur, est plus éclairé sur la réalité des choses que le matérialiste qui croit tout expliquer par le hasard et le fini" (Renan, *La vie de Jésus*, 38).

46. Barrett Browning, *Complete Works*, 2: 157.

47. Bayne, "Strauss's New Life," 317. S. G. Bulfinch writes, "It may be doubted whether any work of modern times has produced so great and excitement as the 'Life of Jesus,' by Dr. Strauss" ("Strauss's Life of Jesus," 145). And G. E. Ellis states, "All of our readers must have at least heard of Dr. Strauss's book, and, we are bound to believe, have some idea, more or less defined, of its contents" ("Mythical Theory," 313).

48. Eliot, *Daniel Deronda*, 38.

49. [Ellis], "Mythical Theory," 314.

50. Bayne, "Strauss's New Life," 317.

51. The scandal would still be exciting enough a decade later for Swinburne to use it in the "Hymn to Proserpine": "Of the maiden thy mother men sing as a goddess with grace clad around; / Thou art throned where another was king; where another was queen she is crowned" (75–76).

52. Gibbon, *Decline and Fall*, 4: 111.

53. Some conservative publications, such as the *Dublin University Review*, conceded this despite their antipathy to Strauss: "The old coarse way of the English and French infidels, who account for everything in religion by fraud, forgery and falsification [is] badly calculated for the German meridian" (Anon., "Strauss' Leben Jesu," 270).

54. Barrett Browning, *Complete Works*, 2: 422.

55. Strauss, *Old Faith and the New*, 301.

56. Anger, *Victorian Interpretation*, 22–48.

57. Barrett Browning, *Complete Works*, 2: 421.

58. Smart, *Poetical Works*, 1: 7.

59. Shaun Irlam's *Elations* addresses the importance of this antithesis for early Romantic English poetics.

60. Qtd. in *Aurora Leigh*, Norton Critical Edition, 338–39.

246 Notes to Pages 65–68

61. A similar letter was written the following March to Julia Martin, in which she expresses gratification at having written "the Bible of the Age" (March 10, [1857]).

2. TENNYSON'S PRECIOUS METHOD

1. The *Athenaeum* review begins, "Mr. Tennyson has enriched the world with his best and most artistic work" (Anon., "Idylls," 73). Coventry Patmore in the *Edinburgh Review* concludes that "the specimens we have been enabled to give in these pages will satisfy our readers that the volume from which they are taken constitutes an accession of no small importance to the classical literature of England, and will be read with admiration wherever the language of England is spoken" (262). The *Eclectic Review* writes that "the *Idylls of the King* may be ranked as Tennyson's masterpiece" (Anon., "Tennyson's 'Idylls,'" 294), and that "no poem so perfect in its workmanship; so deep in its interest, and yet so free from all the factitious artifices which commonly appeal to public sympathy; so suffused throughout with the blending of truest nature and highest poetic revelation, has appeared in our day" (287). From the *British Quarterly:* "The literary history of the cycle of romance which has gathered round the name of Arthur vindicates its claim to be treated as a living power in Britain" (Anon., "Idylls," 482). The *Irish Quarterly:* "There is no doubt now on our minds that this is the most perfect of our Laureate's works, and that English literature is greatly the richer of these charming Idylls" (Anon., "Idylls," 836). The *Dublin University Magazine:* "Tennyson has given us the 'Idylls,' and endowed our poetical treasures with a work, as calm and strong, as fresh and deep, as the best of our Elizabethan singers could have produced" (Anon., "Victor Hugo," 221). The *New Rugbeian:* "Whether men choose to ascribe it to the beauty of the subject, or our poet's manner of treating it, he has quite cleared himself of the imputation, somewhat deservedly cast upon him, of not being able to write continuous pieces" (Lee, "Idylls," 267).

Similiar enthusiasm came from abroad. From the *Revue Britannique:* "Or, la *Revue d'Edimbourg* et l'*Athenæum* sont d'accord pour proclamer les *Idylles* l'œuvre la plus parfaite de Tennyson, celle où il a déployé le plus d'art dans l'agencement des mots; la plus parfaite, malgré la surabondance un peu monotone des mots d'origine saxonne, à l'exclusion de ces mots d'origine latine ou française" (Anon., "Nouvelles des Sciences," 329). From Browning's friend Joseph Milsand: "C'est une de ces oeuvres parfaites d'exécution et dictées par une inspiration parfaitement délicieuse que l'Angleterre a le bonheur d'avoir reçue dernièrement de M. Alfred Tennyson. Avec le pauvre Keats . . . M. Alfred Tennyson est peut-être le poëte le plus artiste que l'Angleterre ait jamais eu" ([Milsand], "Alfred Tennyson," 322). From the *Bibliothéque Universelle:* "Je ne crois pas d'avoir jamais lu quelque chose de si frais, de si suave, de si chaste. Cette poésie repose comme repose le chant des oiseaux par une matinée de printemps. . . . Ce qu'il y a de plus pur dans la poésie antique n'en saurait donner l'idée qu'en y joignant ce je ne sais quoi de tendre que nous devons à l' Evangile, et qui jette sa teinte même en dehors de la poésie religieuse" (J.-L., "Angleterre," 126).

2. Gladstone, "Tennyson's Poems," 464.

3. Gladstone subsequently republished an augmented version of this essay in his memoir *Gleanings of Past Years* (1879) after becoming prime minister. For Tennyson's relationship to changing Victorian technological culture, see Rudy, *Electric Meters*, 44–75.

4. A great many reviewers urged Tennyson to expand *The Idylls* from the 1859 edition, or at least to reprint them with the 1842 "Morte d'Arthur" in subsequent editions ("for the benefit of our children," as one earnest reviewer put it). [Hasell], "Idylls," 610.

5. The most thorough account of this phenomenon is in Tucker, *Epic*.

6. "In the *Idylls of the King* he [Tennyson] has dwelt less than in former poems on personal

feelings, and from the beginning of the volume to the end there is no trace of sympathy with morbid consciousness: but, in assuming a higher moral tone, his style never tends to become thin, didactic, or declamatory" (Anon., "Idylls," *Saturday Review,* 76).

7. Kirstie Blair and Daniel A. Harris have independently charted Arthur Hallam's reading in German criticism and traced his future brother-in-law and fellow Cambridge Apostle Edmund Lushington's acquaintance with Strauss (via Eliot), in addition to noting Tennyson's Cambridge connection to Connop Thirlwall and Julius Hare. Hare helped Thirlwall to translate Schleiermacher's 1827 study of Luke, and Thirlwall helped Hare with Niebuhr's *History of Rome* (1828–32). Certainly Tennyson's acquaintance with Broad Church scholars meant that he likely knew of the higher criticism before most. By the 1850s, Tennyson could hardly escape the controversies of contemporary biblical scholarship, when his friend F. D. Maurice (addressee of "Come when no graver cares employ") was dismissed from King's College London for his universalism, and when another friend, Benjamin Jowett, was mailing Tennyson English translations of the Baron Bunsen's most recent works. See Blair, "Alfred Tennyson," 496–511, and Harris, "Personification in 'Tithonus.'" On Niebuhr, Thirlwall, and Hare, see also Pearsall, *Tennyson's Rapture.*

8. Hughes, *Manyfacèd Glass,* 51–52.

9. "As to Macaulay's suggestion of the Sangraal I doubt whether such a subject could be handled in these days, without incurring a charge of irreverence. It would be too much like playing with sacred things. The old writers *believed* in the Sangraal" (*Letters* 2: 244).

10. When Ambrosius questions Percivale on the textual authenticity of the Grail legend, his critique functions on multiple levels: suggesting desire for proper authority ("From our old books I know / That Joseph came of old to Glastonbury . . . For so they say, these books of ours, but seem / Mute of this miracle" [59–66]), but also acknowledging a kinship between the Bible and related mythology ("These ancient books—and they would win thee—teem, / Only I find not there this Holy Grail, / With miracles and marvels like to these / Not all unlike" [541–44]).

11. See Armstrong, *Victorian Poetry,* especially 41–111.

12. Sedgwick, *Between Men,* 119.

13. From among the poem's final pieces, only the 1842 fragment "Morte d'Arthur" precedes "Nimuë" in composition date. Eventually, Tennyson would incorporate "Morte d'Arthur" into "The Passing of Arthur" (1869). "Nimuë" was published for private circulation alongside "Enid" even before the 1859 *Idylls;* the British Library copy shows extensive revisions Tennyson's hand, but only to "Enid." Tennyson did add six additional lines to "Merlin and Vivien" in the 1873 edition, and 140 lines to the 1875 text.

14. Strauss also appears twice in Mark Pattison's copious appendices.

15. [Parker], "Das Leben Jesu," 311.

16. *Oxford Dictionary of Quotations,* 534.

17. I address the Homeric Question in chapter 1. For a discussion of Sappho's name in relation to the Homeric Question, see Prins, *Victorian Sappho.* For more on the Shakespeare Question, see LaPorte, "The Bard, The Bible," and Shapiro, *Contested Will,* 17–79.

18. Pals, *Victorian "Lives" of Jesus.*

19. Malory, *Works,* xiv.

20. Eliot, "In Memoriam." Eliot's curt dismissal of Tennyson's narrative interest has made it much harder to reassess this work. The first significant scholarly study of the *Idylls,* for instance, John D. Rosenberg's *The Fall of Camelot* (1973), immediately surrenders Eliot's chief claim that "Tennyson's essential genius" had little to do with "conventionally epic portions" (21). Still, as Carol Christ first pointed out, Eliot more closely describes his own narrative deficiencies than Tennyson's (*Victorian and Modern Poetics*).

21. Qtd. in Hallam Tennyson, *Tennyson: A Memoir,* 464.

22. Alexander Geddes, for instance, helped to pioneer the higher criticism because he felt that such a new hermeneutics would make biblical literalism untenable, resolving things in favor of his own Roman Catholic tradition. Ironically, the Catholic establishment found his views too dangerous.

23. Said, *Orientalism,* 806.

24. Shea and Whitla, *Essays and Reviews,* 482.

25. As writes Anne Mozley in *Bentley's Quarterly Review:* "We cannot tell how far the pure Saxon idiom of the Idylls is the effect of intention, or whether the Latin share in our vernacular naturally kept out of his way" (172). *Scribner's Monthly* (5 [January 1879]) notes both the alliteration and the diction in a later idyll: "Alliteration also prevails in almost every line or sentence, and more than in any other modern poem. Is this . . . the effect of the Laureate's mousing among pre-Chaucerian ballads? It somewhat palls upon the ear, as does also the poet's habit of playing upon his own words and seemingly reiterating them for that purpose. We are compensated for all this by a stalwart presentation of that fine old English which Emerson has called 'a stern and dreadful language'" (qtd. in Andrew, *Annotated Bibliography,* 167).

26. Stanley, *Essays,* 188–89. I am grateful to Kirstie Blair for this reference.

27. The vowel of "aught," /ɔ/, is usually called an "open o," and that of "want," /ɒ/, a "turned script a." Naturally, the pronunciation of these vowels varies with Tennyson's readership, both geographically and chronologically. See *The Oxford Dictionary of Current Usage.*

28. The linguists G. K. Pullum and W. A. Ladusaw note of the two sounds that "American dialects generally do not show a /ɔ/-/ɒ/ phonological distinction (and even in Southern British there is a concomitant length difference)"; they add even that "the need for both symbols is not felt by many American linguists" (*Phonetic Symbol Guide,* 9).

The famous Victorian phonologist Henry Sweet agrees. He even suggests that the sounds were unfixed at this point in history, for on /ɒ/, Sweet's own publications do not agree. His 1877 *Handbook of Phoenetics* identifies it as a "narrow," and suggests it be pronounced in the manner of "Occ. Sc. bʉt" (16), but by his 1892 *Primer of Phoenetics,* he has decided that /ɒ/ is rather "wide," and suggests that it be pronounced like the Swedish "mɑt" (21).

29. [Hayward Abraham], "Byron and Tennyson," *Quarterly Review* 131 (1871): 354–92; qtd. in Andrew, *Annotated Bibliography,* 142.

30. Richard Holt Hutton, "Tennyson," *Macmillan's Magazine* 27 (1872): 143–67; qtd. in Andrew, *Annotated Bibliography,* 159.

31. [A. Mozley], "Tennyson," 162.

32. The most frequently voiced complaint about "Merlin and Vivien" in Victorian reviews was that Tennyson makes Vivien so wicked. In Malory, Merlin is a lecherous, scary brute who might well deserve his fate at Nimuë's hands: "And always Merlin lay about the lady, for to have her maidenhead; and she was ever passing weary of him, and fain would have been delivered of him; for she was afraid of him, because he was a devil's son, and she could not put him away by any means" (Tennyson, *Poems,* 393). Conversely, in the medieval French prose *Merlin,* Vivien eventually thinks better of her decision to imprison Merlin: "and often time she regretted what she had done, for she had thought that the thing which he taught her could not be true, and willingly would have let him out if she could" (395). Tennyson's version, by contrast, neither punishes Vivien's betrayal of Merlin nor makes her repent of it. Neither does his Merlin succumb to mere sexual appetite, as in Malory and the French prose *Merlin.* Rather, Tennyson's hero gives in to the false promises of love. These aspects of *Merlin and Vivien* disturbed Tennyson's contemporaries and received surprisingly harsh criticism as each successive version of *The Idylls* appeared. Tennyson nonetheless declined to alter them.

33. Part 1 (Paris, 1793), part 2 (Paris, 1795), and part 3 (New York, 1807); Paine, *Theological Works.*

34. Nash, *Paine's Age of Reason*, 82.

35. Qtd. in Norton, *History of the English Bible*, 319.

36. Burgon, *Inspiration and Interpretation*, 233.

37. As famously depicted in Anderson, *Imagined Communities.*

38. Pick, *Hopkins Reader*, 128–29.

39. Qtd. in Browne, *Charles Darwin*, 2: 152.

40. Trollope, "Henry Taylor's Poems," 129–30.

41. "And Jesus said unto them, A prophet is not without honour, save in his own country, and in his own house" (Matthew 13:57 KJV). The expression was apparently proverbial when Jesus used it.

42. In 1828, for instance, F. D. Maurice offered an extensive reading of Byron's *Cain* as a Christian apology in order to promote the installation of the Byron monument among the English poets in Westminster Abbey. See [Maurice], "Lord Byron's Monument."

43. On Tennyson's distance from Tractarian poetics, see Kirstie Blair's forthcoming work, *Form and Faith in Victorian Poetry and Religion.*

44. Quoted in G. B. Tennyson, *Sartor Called Resartus*, 291.

45. Roughly half of "Timbuctoo" comes directly from "Armageddon."

46. Tennyson, *Poems*, 73.

47. Naturally, to view the former poem as a version of the latter goes against the grain of scholarship that presents the earliest verses as "unfinished" and maintains that the "real" or "complete" Tennyson poems are those he sanctioned late in his career. However, if the editorial theory of the last thirty years (exemplified most prominently in the work of Jerome J. McGann) has shown us anything about the material life of poetry, it is that the meaning of a poem can neither be contingent upon its publication history nor upon a poet's explicit authorization of a given version. See McGann, *Critique of Modern Textual Criticism* and *Textual Condition.*

48. For more on Tennyson's Miltonic debts, see Gray, *Milton and the Victorians*, 92–129.

49. Armstrong, *Victorian Poetry*, 265.

50. As Matthew Rowlinson observes in *Tennyson's Fixations*, the more the visionary claims to see, the less capable he seems to be of describing his vision (24–34).

51. William Smith's *Dictionary of the Bible* (1895) suggests that this identification was first made by Jean François Van de Velde in his *Prodromus Danielicus* (1710), coauthored with Jean Gérard Kerkherdere, but problems of biblical geography became increasing fraught in the nineteenth century, and even conservative publications confronted these questions. The conservative "Biblical Cabinet, or Hermeneutical, Exegetical, and Philological Library of Edinburgh" that espoused Bishop Usher's chronological table (that which dates the Creation at 4004 BC) also translated Johann Frederick Röhr's *Palästina, oder, Historisch-geographische Beschreibung des jüdischen Landes zur Zeit Jesu* (1819), with its open doubts about the population figures listed in the Hebrew scriptures: "The immense population which we occasionally find spoken of in the Scripture does not, indeed, correspond with this extent [of land]. . . . Perhaps less than half this number may be nearer the truth, and even from this we might make a large deduction" (28–29).

52. Blair, "Alfred Tennyson," 497.

53. I do not go quite so far as Herbert F. Tucker, who identifies the poet of "Timbuctoo" as "standing with [Milton's] Satan in the abyss he would replenish with his own light" (*Doom of Romanticism*, 64), but I agree that it is in this direction (and not that of Alan Sinfield's demythologizing) that the poem's imagery all tends.

54. Hallam, *Letters*, 326.

55. As Coleridge wrote in ca. 1825, in response to the same Deist critique, "Are all these testimonies and lights of [Christian] experience to lose their value and efficiency, because I feel no warrant of history, or Holy Writ, or of my own heart for denying, that in the framework and outward case of this instrument a few parts may be discovered of less costly materials and of meaner workmanship? . . . Does not the universally admitted canon—that each part of Scripture must be interpreted by the spirit of the whole—lead to the same practical conclusion as that for which I am now contending:—namely, that it is the spirit of the Bible, and not the detached words and sentences, that is infallible and absolute?" (*Confessions of an Inquiring Spirit*, 72–73).

56. For a like assessment of Tennyson's growing facility with myth, see Joseph, *Tennyson and the Text*, 161–90.

57.   "And, Dr. Jenkinson, please," Mrs. Sinclair went on in a voice of plaintive innocence, "not to think me a terrible blue-stocking, because I ask you these questions; for I really hardly know any Greek myself—except perhaps a verse or two of the New Testament; and that's not very good Greek, I believe, is it? But the gentleman who translated so much to me, when he came to these little poems I speak of, was continually, though he was a very good scholar, quite unable to translate them. Now, why should that have been, I want to know? Are Greek love-poems very hard?"

"Well," said the Doctor, stammering, yet reassured by Mrs. Sinclair's manner, "they were probably—your friend perhaps—well—they were a little obscure perhaps—much Greek is—or . . ."

"Corrupt?" suggested Mrs. Sinclair naively.

(Mallock, 110–11)

58. Strauss, *Der Alte Und Der Neue Glaube*.

59. "Verstehe er? die Bibel? Wie viele Theologen verstehen sie denn? wollen sie verstehen? Ja, man meint die Bibel zu verstehen, weil man gewohnt ist, sie nicht zu verstehen" (Strauss, *Der Alte Und Der Neue Glaube*, 121; *Old Faith and the New*, 301).

60. Parker, *None Like It*.

61. By "brawling," Tennyson clearly means the *OED*'s secondary definition: "Clamour; indecent or offensive noise; scolding." Tennyson liked the word and seems to have associated it with conventional mid-century Christian morality, as when he wrote the Duchess of Argyll shortly after finishing "Nimuë" that "a blustering mouth" who had seen it "apears to have gone brawling about town, saying that such a poem would corrupt the young, that no ladies could buy it or read it etc. etc." (*Letters* 2: 179). His early poem "The Palace of Art" (1832) uses the word specifically to signify divisive religious opinion: "I care not what the sects may brawl" (1: 210).

62. Hallam Tennyson, *Tennyson: A Memoir*, 524.

63. See note 7, above.

64. Qtd. in Jump, *Tennyson: Critical Heritage*, 398.

3. CLOUGH'S DEVIL IN THE DETAILS

1. "I John, who also am your brother, and companion in tribulation, and in the kingdom and patience of Jesus Christ, was in the isle that is called Patmos, for the word of God, and for the testimony of Jesus Christ. / I was in the Spirit on the Lord's day, and I heard behind me a great voice, as of a trumpet / Saying. . ." (Revelation 1:9–11).

2. Clough, naturally, could only know the (more muted) 1850 version of this passage.

3. Riede, *Allegories of One's Own Mind*, 107.

4.   What though the music of thy rustic flute
       Kept not for long its happy, country tone;
           Lost it too soon, and learnt a stormy note
       Of men contention-tossed, of men who groan,
       Which tasked thy pipe too sore, and tired thy throat
           It failed, and thou wast mute!
       ("Thyrsis," 221–26)

5. In "Swinburne's Tragedies" (1866), Lowell writes, "I have a foreboding that Clough, imperfect as he was in many respects, and dying before he had subdued his sensitive temperament to the sterner requirements of his art, will be thought a hundred years hence to have been the truest expression in verse of the moral and intellectual tendencies, the doubt and struggle towards settled convictions, of the period in which he lived" (*Works* 2: 121). Lowell himself echoes a review in the *Boston Review* of the 1862 American Clough edition, which explains, "The man is 'representative' because he tried the pathway of religious doubt. . . . Because he did not succeed, he is worthy of notice in these pages. . . . The young men who are first in intellectual power are weakest in their belief in religious truth. Clough is the very type and leader of these" (Anon., "Arthur Hugh Clough," 133).

6. Similar sentiments are expressed by Walter Bagehot in the *National Review*, William Allingham in *Fraser's Magazine*, Henry Sidgwick in the *Westminster Review*, and R. H. Hutton in the *Spectator*, as well as in anonymously published articles.

7. Anon., "Poems and Prose Remains," 25–26.

8. Clough did have some early advocates, such as Bagehot, but he only gradually attained a broader readership. It was with some justice that an anonymous *Boston Review* writer noted in 1863, "It happened to Clough, as to many other recent English writers, to be more truly recognized in America than in England. We are in more sympathy with such earnest, searching minds, than the mass of Englishmen" ("Arthur Hugh Clough," 136).

9. John Schad, for instance, begins an engaging recent study with *"Swinburne is right, Clough is a bad poet"* (*Arthur Hugh Clough*, 1).

10. Browning, *Poems*, 3.

11. Clough, *Poems*, xxii.

12. Marjorie Perloff and Craig Dworkin ("Sound of Poetry") rightly describe the autobiographical tendency of Romantic lyric as a major impediment to our appreciating alternate views of poetry; E. Warwick Slinn (*Victorian Poetry*) provides the best counterexample to this autobiographical trend in Clough studies.

13. Except where noted, poetry citations and line numbers are taken from the Phelan edition (*Clough—Selected Poems*), as being the most accessible scholarly edition. No definitive version exists for such poems as "Epi-Strauss-ism," "Easter Day," or *Dipsychus* because Clough never published them, and his MSS often contain incompatible versions, none of which are clearly authoritative.

14. Anthony Kenny rightly points out that this unexpected clipping of the lines makes us almost physically sensible of the absence marked by the missing feet, an absence that corresponds to the disappearance of the Evangelists (*God and Two Poets*, 76–77).

15. Clough, *Correspondence*, 182.

16. This prejudice was so well established that in 1848 Clough's provost, E. Hawkins, would take for granted that his problems with conventional scriptural interpretation must concern the Hebrew scriptures. Hawkins noted to himself, "I suspect he doubted about the O[ld]

T[estament]," and he wrote to Clough, "I suspect, however, that many of your difficulties turn upon the O[ld] Test[amen]t" (Clough, *Correspondence,* 221–26).

17. For Clough, this new position forcibly also entailed contradictions. His rhetoric in this letter, for instance, derives from the scriptural training Clough received at the hands of Dr. Thomas Arnold, his Rugby mentor. As Isobel Armstrong notes, Arnold was profoundly committed to a theology of Christian conscience because it honored the individual experience of scripture, instead of deferring to such interpretative authorities as are found in High Church Anglicanism and Roman Catholicism. Yet the individual conscience is here enlisted not to interpret the Bible, but to replace it altogether in the event that "Matthew, Mark, Luke, and John, or even St. Paul, were to fall" (Armstrong, *Arthur Hugh Clough,* 9).

18. Strauss, *Life of Jesus,* 397.

19. This apologetic strain in Strauss is underrepresented in Clough criticism (and indeed elsewhere). The first and most obvious reason for this is that Strauss eventually gave up the idea of reforming Christian theology. The second reason, though, was that his mid-century critics took his apostasy for granted and identified him (albeit wrongly) with the deism of Voltaire or Thomas Paine. The *Life of Jesus* was widely condemned even in Germany, and Strauss was thereafter seen as an iconoclast, not a reformer.

20. As Houghton rightly points out, the sun's western progress also suggests that the "Eastern" genius of the Gospels must be supplemented by Western theologies (*Poetry of Clough,* 52–53). Yet it might be supposed that this Eastern genius will regain its radiance in the morning, when the sun comes around again. For an analysis of the theological difficulties presented by Clough's metaphor, see Netland, "Problem of Metaphor."

21. Clough, *Poems and Prose Remains,* 417. When Clough resigned his Oriel fellowship in the fall of 1848, Hawkins urged him to formulate a systematic examination of his religious ideas. Whether the *Notes* were the direct result of this urging, they present the closest he came to what Hawkins seems to have had in mind.

22. Victorian critics did not generally admit the success of "Easter Day" as poetry, but many were so impressed with its sentiments that they resorted to the paradox that Clough's very prosiness becomes poetic. As Henry Sidgwick put it, "The intensity of the blended feeling fuses a prosaic material into poetry very remarkably" ("Poems and Prose Remains," 278). Symonds advances something similar: "'Easter Day' is unique in the history of literature. It is a poem fully worthy of that name, in which a close and difficult reasoning is expressed in concise words—such words as might have been used by a commentator on the Gospels, yet so subtly manipulated by the poet, with such a rhythm, such compactness, such vitality of emotion, as to attain the dignity of art by mere simplicity and power" (Thorpe, *Clough: Critical Heritage,* 229).

23. As might be expected, Clough's early reviewers negatively associated him with the higher critics, and his supporters tended to apologize for his theology. *St. James's Magazine* represents the fruition of this tradition: "When we speak of Clough's scepticism, it must be understood that scepticism as to creeds, not as to religion, is meant. For Clough had preeminently what Mrs. Browning says all poets must possess: 'a religious passion in his soul'" (Mayer, "Charles Kingsley and Arthur Hugh Clough," 266). Between such apologetics and a changing late-century intellectual climate, Clough's name increasingly freed itself from association with the higher critics. Soon after, regular Christian journals such as the *Primitive Methodist Quarterly* and the *Wesleyan Methodist Magazine* would recommend his poetry and denounce the higher criticism in the same issue. A positive late-century Clough review even appeared in the *Homiletic Review,* which insisted that "Clough's poetry is too little known" to Christian preachers (Murray, "Clough and His Poetry," 293).

24. Anon., "Arthur Hugh Clough," 287.

25. On Victorian bardolatry, see LaPorte, "The Bard, the Bible."

26. Armstrong, "And Beauty? A Dialogue," in *Radical Aesthetic*, 174–94. McGann, *Swinburne.*

27. Booth, "Male Sexuality."

28. Symonds, *Letters,* 1: 670.

29. Symonds, "Arthur Hugh Clough," 592.

30. Blanche Clough's earlier editions tended to omit works that risked damaging her husband's reputation. Symonds encouraged her to publish more of them.

31. The exceptional case that Clough makes of Christian history in the "Notes"—its *particularly* entire uncertainty—represents an inversion of the exceptionalism practiced by so many of his contemporaries with reference to biblical history. The indefatigable Rev. William Smith, for instance, used different scholarly principles in his groundbreaking *Dictionary of Greek and Roman Biography and Mythology* (to which Clough contributed seventy-seven short biographies) and his subsequent *Dictionary of the Bible* (1863), a work that goes so far as to defend the Mosaic authorship of the Pentateuch. By the standards of Smith's prior reference books, this is a bit like crediting Apollo with the invention of the lyre.

32. Thorpe, *Clough: Critical Heritage,* 445.

33. Sometimes Clough did not even bother to entitle his experiments. Thus, "Alcaics" is an English variation on Alcaeus's ancient Greek hendecasyllabic couplets, and so forth.

34. For a more thorough treatment of Clough's hexameters, see Gray, "Clough and His Discontents."

35. Saintsbury, indeed, would observe of Clough that "he happened at a particular period to be steeped in Greek verse, and at the same time overflowing with 'criticism of life'. . . . It so happened that he could write elastically and spontaneously at the given time in the given manner; the manner being in itself a stimulus peculiarly fit in his case. He never seems to have written prose with any such facility" (Thorpe, *Clough: Critical Heritage,* 351).

36. Clough's contributions to Arnold's thinking are also (posthumously) acknowledged in these lectures (Arnold, *Classical Tradition,* 150–51).

37. Ovid, *Heroides and Amores,* 319.

38. See Watson, *Victorian Hymn.*

39. "Aber man soll doch ja nicht meinen, daß Lessings Nathan oder Goethes Hermann und Dorothea schwerer zu verstehen seien und weniger 'Heilswahrheiten,' weniger auch goldene Sprüche enthalten, als ein paulinischer Brief oder eine johanneische Christusrede" (Strauss, *Der Alte Und Der Neue Glaube,* 301; *The Old Faith and the New,* 121).

40. "Wenn doch jede Religion herkömmlich ihre heiligen Bücher hat, daß für die Religion der Humanität und Sittlichkeit, zu der wir uns bekennen, Lessings Nathan das heilige Grundbuch bildet" (Strauss, *Der Alte Und Der Neue Glaube,* 308; *The Old Faith and the New,* 132).

41. When *Dipsychus* appeared, William Henry Smith of *Macmillan's Magazine* predicted confidently, "Henceforth, he will be known as the author of 'Dipsychus'" (89). John Dowden of the *Contemporary Review* agreed: "Now published for the first time in its completeness [is] what we cannot but regard as the most remarkable of all the writings of Clough—the unfinished poem entitled 'Dipsychus'" (513).

42. McLeod, *Secularization in Western Europe,* 25.

43. Houghton and many others assume that Clough's idea comes from Goethe, but, as Chorley points out, Clough confessed to not having read Goethe's version well (*Clough, the Uncommitted Mind,* 251).

44. Symonds, "Arthur Hugh Clough," 607–8.

45. Some manuscripts explicitly identify Malebranche as a model.

46. Marlowe, *Tragical History of Doctor Faustus,* 3.45–54, in *Norton Anthology,* 776.

47. In other places it will of course depart from Marlowe's script, but the principle of the demon's summons remains constant both here and elsewhere:

> *D:* How shall I call him? Mephistophiles?
>
> *S:* I come, I come.

See Clough, *Poems and Prose Remains,* 2: 143.

48. Maynard, "Victorian Innocence Abroad."

49. Kierstead describes *Dipsychus* and *Amours* as "semi-autobiographical records of the poet's response to the spectacle of modern Italy and to the ever-present 'Byron'" ("Where 'Byron Used to Ride'"). On the myth of Byron, see McGann, *Fiery Dust,* and Elfenbein, *Byron and the Victorians.*

50. Wilde, *Critic as Artist,* 307.

51. Chorley, *Clough, the Uncommitted Mind,* 254.

52. Neil, "Criticism and Theological Use," 263.

53. Brooke, *Four Victorian Poets,* 35.

54. Pascal, *Shakespeare in Germany,* 15.

55. Joyce, *Ulysses,* 25.

56. Eagleton, *Literary Theory.*

57. Eagleton, *Reason, Faith, and Revolution.*

58. In my discussion of the gondola episode, I cite Norrington's Oxford edition (*The Poems of Arthur Hugh Clough*). Phelan and Norrington render the manuscript differently, but Norrington represents Blanche Clough's version—the version to which Victorian reviewers responded. The quotation here is taken from 4.3–8 in the Oxford edition.

59. *Dipsychus* was written during the early years of the Christian Socialist movement, and clearly shows its influence, despite the fact that Clough seems to have harbored reservations about the practicality of the movement. These reservations are suggested by an 1853 letter he received from J. A. Froude: "I quite agree with what you say of the Maurice affair. . . . As thinkers Maurice and still more the Mauricians, appear to me the most hopelessly imbecile that any section of the world have been driven to believe in" (Clough, *Correspondence,* 446).

60. Polonius features often in *Dipsychus,* in fact, from the beginning of the drama: "Still nesting on thyself" (1.1.6).

61.   Ma name'sh Levi Moshesh: I tink I vash born,
>   Dough I cannot exactly remember,
>   In Roshemary-Lane, about tree in de morn,
>   Shome time in de mont of November.
>   My fader cried "clothesh," trough de shtreetsh ash he vent,
>   Dough he now shleeping under de shtone ish,
>   He made by hish bargains two hundred per shent,
>   And dat vay he finger'd de monish.
>
>   Ma fader vash vise: very great vash his shenshe:
>   De monish he alwaysh vash turning:
>   And early he taught me poundsh, shillingsh, and penshe;
>   "For," shaysh he, "dat ish all dat'sh vorth learning.
>   Ash to Latin and Greek, 'tish all nonshenshe, I shay,
>   Vhich occasion to shtudy dere none ish;

But shtick closhe to Cocker, for dat ish de vay,
To teach you to finger de monish."
(1–16; Peacock, *Palmyra*, 133–34)

62. Anon., "Clough's Life and Poems," 410.

63. Butler, *Way of All Flesh*, 55.

64. Froude, *Nemesis of Faith*, 24, 42.

65. Carlyle, *Carlyle Reader*, 303.

4. ROBERT BROWNING'S SACRED AND LEGENDARY ART

1. Peterson, *Interrogating the Oracle*, 56, 96. The situation was similar in America, where Browning societies proselytized his religious importance and where the cult of Browning eventually produced a magnificent shrine in Waco, Texas: the Armstrong Browning Library.

2. For more on Browning's hermeneutics, see Shaw, *Lucid Veil*.

3. Furnivall, "Forwards," 25.

4. Thomson, "The Ring and the Book," 682–85. Furnivall privately disputed Thomson's view of the poem as a religious work, but Thomson maintained this position over Furnivall's objections in his 1882 presentation to the Browning Society entitled "Notes on the Genius of Robert Browning."

5. McGann, *Towards a Literature of Knowledge*, 7–8.

6. This is also true of *Aurora Leigh*, but *The Ring and the Book* pursues the question more doggedly and comprehensively—not least because it purports to be historically true.

7. It can be instructive to consider how gifted twenty-first-century writers make this same point, as when the late David Foster Wallace complains of a cruise ship publicity brochure that "after reading [Frank] Conroy's essay on board, whenever I'd look up at the sky it wouldn't be the sky I was seeing, it was the *vast lapis lazuli dome of the sky*" (287). For Browning, as for Wilde, Foster Wallace has no real cause for complaint, for it is never the sky we are seeing, but always another artist's lapis lazuli dome. Foster Wallace, *A Supposedly Fun Thing I'll Never Do Again*.

8. J. Hillis Miller presents perhaps the best-known case that "'The Ring and the Book,' like the frailest of Browning's lyrics, leads only to a momentary and evanescent perception. Like all his other poems, it expresses man's incapacity to understand or possess God" (*Disappearance of God*, 153).

9. As an anonymous reviewer in *Harper's* contrasts the sureness of Collins's conclusion with the ambiguous fate of Paul Emanuel in Brontë's *Villette*: "Of ten critical readers of [*Villette*], five will be sure that he was drowned, and the other five will be just as sure that he came home, married Lucy Snowe, and lived 'happily ever after.' No such difficulties will confront the readers of any novel by Wilkie Collins" (qtd. in *The Moonstone*, 556).

10. Hillis Miller, similarly, writes that "one of the effects of reading 'The Ring and the Book' is a sense of vertigo which results from seeing how plausible all these contradictory points of view can be made" (151–52). Bailey, "Somatic Wisdom," 586.

11. Subsequent scholarship on the importance of Gothic literature risks making this contemporary appreciation seem natural, but Browning's readers felt it to be extraordinary.

12. Dorothy Mermin and Herbert F. Tucker aptly characterize the episode as an "adventure in homemade Higher Criticism" (*Victorian Literature*, 75).

13. To be sure, he was prized by discriminating readers such as Elizabeth Barrett Browning (unsurprisingly), Dante Gabriel Rossetti, and Algernon Charles Swinburne, but condemned or dismissed by many more.

14. This is clear even in the opening lines of *The Ring and the Book*; the poet finds his story at the bookstall next to "The Life, Death, Miracles of Saint Somebody," and "Saint Somebody Else, his Miracles, Death, and Life,—" (1.80–81).

15. Clough, *Prose Remains*, 416.

16. Müller, *Auld Lang Syne*, 88.

17. Another example is that of the recently discovered Saint Filomela, who appears in Anna Jameson's *Sacred and Legendary Art*, 672.

18. Blackbourn, *Marpingen*, 17–57.

19. Buchanan's *Athenaeum* article insists that "from the first to the last, Pompilia haunts the poem with a look of ever-deepening light" ("The Ring and the Book," 399–400). H. B. Forman of the *London Quarterly Review* agrees, claiming, "Pompilia is so little dependent on anything but the nobility of her character and treatment for the interest she excites, the exquisite pleasures her speech yields, and the genuine help to be got therefrom in breasting the troubles of every day, that we feel confident in the efficiency of time to make this work a popular poem" (356), and "Pompilia's character is one which makes analysis a superfluity by reason of its mere simplicity and purity. . . . With Pompilia, every reader must know, before he has turned many pages of her death-bed speech, that he is reading good and beautiful poetry, which places him face to face with a good and beautiful soul" ("Epic of Psychology," 353). John Morley's *Fortnightly Review* confirms the prevalence of this view: "When the first volume of Mr. Browning's new poem came before the critical tribunals . . . it was pronounced a murky subject, sordid, unlovely, morally sterile . . . [yet] Pompilia convinced them that the subject was not, after all, so incurably unlovely" ("On 'The Ring and the Book,'" 544). Later in the century, Sir Henry Jones keeps this hermeneutic alive with his claims that "Pompilia shone with a glory that mere knowledge could not give" (*Browning*, 333). And Harriet Gaylord confirms its longevity with *Pompilia and Her Poet*, an unqualified encomium on Pompilia's "white soul" that went through three editions in the 1930s. Even John Doherty's almost entirely unsympathetic report in the *Dublin Review* nonetheless concedes, "The character of Pompilia . . . is itself an exquisite conception . . . a type of simplicity, innocence, and purity. . . . There is something of the supernatural in it" ("The Ring and the Book," 60). See also Austen, "Pompilia."

20. The historical witnesses to Pompilia's death provide warrant for Browning's idea. Her confessor Fra Celestino Angelo records, "I have discovered and marveled at an innocent and saintly conscience in that ever-blessed child," who "died with strong love for God . . . and with the admiration of all bystanders, who blessed her as a saint." Nicolo Constantio, Placido Sardi, and the Marquis Nicolo Gregorio similarly add, "We have witnessed her dying the death of a saint" (Hodell, *Old Yellow Book*, 45–48).

21. Dalberg-Acton, "German Schools of History."

22. Curle, *Robert Browning and Julia Wedgwood*, 152; Hodell, *Old Yellow Book*, 282.

23. Hodell, *Old Yellow Book*; Corrigan, *Curious Annals*. Such selectiveness need not betoken Browning's bad faith, however; the poem's structure dramatizes the inevitable selectiveness of any history.

24. The *London Quarterly Review*, for example, maintains that Pompilia's utter simplicity and purity make analysis "a superfluity," calling her monologue "good and beautiful poetry, which places [the reader] face to face with good and beautiful soul" (Forman, "Epic of Psychology," 353). The *Edinburgh Review* writes of the poem's protagonists, "In English literature the creative faculty of the poet has not produced three characters more beautiful or better for men to contemplate than these three [Caponsacchi, Pompilia, and the Pope]" ("The Ring and the Book," 91).

25. My argument complements, and in some instances qualifies, the following studies:

Auerbach, *Romantic Imprisonment*, 92–106; Brown, "Pompilia: The Woman (in) Question"; Tucker, "Representation and Repristination"; Walker, "Pompilia and *Pompilia*"; and Candace Ward, "Damning Herself Praiseworthily."

26. The original *Sacred and Legendary Art* (hereafter *SLA*) went through ten editions and was reprinted into the twentieth century. In the manner of Lootens, Judith Johnston, and Clara Thomas, I refer to this work under this title, although "Sacred and Legendary Art" as an umbrella title also applies to Jameson's subsequent works in the same series. See Johnston, *Anna Jameson*, and Thomas, *Love and Work Enough*.

27. Holcomb, "Anna Jameson."

28. That the Brownings did not know the two-volume *SLA* is only academically possible, given the friends' familiarity with one another's work. EBB translated verse for AJ's 1844 *Athenaeum* essay on the Xanthian Marbles, and Jameson, in turn, quotes "The Cry of the Children" in both *SLA*, vol. 1, and *Legends of the Madonna*. Jameson's famous 1846 "I have also here a poet and a poetess" letter from Paris mixes expressions of pleasure at the Brownings' elopement with complaints about the difficulty of rapidly finishing *SLA* (see MacPherson, *Memoirs*, 228–29). Further, Bate MacPherson, AJ's niece, records in her memoirs that the Brownings were Jameson's "closest associates" when at Pisa and Florence, "working out the result of [Jameson's] studies, arranging and classifying the additions to her stories" (233). Finally, when EBB thanked AJ for the reception of the second publication in the *SLA* series (*Legends of the Monastic Orders*), she observes that Jameson's "books" will be "a necessity for art students" (Barrett Browning, *Letters*, 2: 440–41).

29. Jameson, *SLA*, 468, 517, 61, 68, 74, 601, 8–9. All subsequent page numbers will be from this edition.

30. Melissa V. Gregory shrewdly points out that the generic logic of the dramatic monologue helps account not only for Victorian readers' visceral response to Browning's depictions of domestic violence but also for Browning's inclination to treat it in the first place ("Violent Lyric Voice").

31. See Austen, "Pompilia," and Friedman, "To Tell the Sun."

32. In this, as throughout, RB takes elements of the *Old Yellow Book* and expands upon them. There are only two references to Pompilia's beauty in the *Old Yellow Book,* and neither are particularly emphatic or convincing. Yet Sir Frederick Treves, even after admitting Browning's dearth of evidence for her appearance, can attest as though it were factual that "Pompilia, so the book affirms, was young, good and beautiful, with large dark eyes and a bounty of black hair. Her face was pale and her expression grave and grieffull [*sic*], like that of our Lady of All the Sorrows" (250).

33. Tucker asserts that *The Ring and the Book* "represents virginity not as a stable condition, but as a conviction dynamically effected and reaffirmed" ("Representation and Repristination," 78).

34. Walker has suggested that such elements deflate any claims that Pompilia has to Christian sanctity. Just the contrary is true, because of the poem's generic tradition. For a good discussion of the poetic rendering of this episode, see Campbell, *Rhythm and Will*, 99–124.

35. Both this numeric issue and the manuscript's revision are indicated in the Ohio *Complete Works*, 7: 346.

36. So as not to belabor the generic element of this argument, I have refrained from addressing the poem's hagiographical elements that are not specifically related to female virgin martyrs. William De Vane's St. George narrative is one such element. One might also trace the less-developed depiction of Caponsacchi and Pompilia as Saints Francis and Clare. Browning was very likely acquainted with Giotto's early-Renaissance illustration of Francis's Arezzo

exorcism; if not, it is a striking coincidence that Caponsacchi relates having repeated a prayer of exorcism to relieve Pompilia's nightmares of her own personal Arezzo demon—"'Oh, if the God, that only can, would help!/ Am I his priest with power to cast out fiends?/ Let God arise and all his enemies/ Be scattered!' By morn, there was peace, no sigh/ Out of the deep sleep" (6.1300–1304). Anna Jameson details the lives of Francis and Clare in her *Legends of the Monastic Orders,* 278–309. She relates the tale of St. Francis's Arezzo exorcism on 298.

37. Pompilia's monologue must strategically avoid questions of sex if it is to present its resemblance to hagiography. Still, at one point, she does imply herself to be a victim of what today would be called marital rape, and it is not by accident that the "New Woman" writer Mona Caird cites copiously from *The Ring and the Book* in her 1890 *Fortnightly Review* critique of the institution of marriage: "The Morality of Marriage."

38. [John Mozley], "The Ring and the Book," 546.

39. Strauss, *The Old Faith and the New,* xl.

40. The phrase is from Mantel, "'What Did Her Neighours Say?'"

41. Erskine, *Anna Jameson,* 28–29.

42. For further analyses of this poem, see Roberts, "Me/Not-Me"; Shaffer, *"Kubla Khan."*

43. To be sure, it is not hard to find anti-Catholic attitudes in Browning. But such poetry does not negate his positive use of Catholic themes elsewhere.

44. As notes DeLaura, her conflation of the "poetic" and "sacred" functions of art rearticulates themes of Alexis François Rio's *De la poésie chrétienne.*

45. Curle, *Robert Browning and Julia Wedgwood,* 144.

46. Kenyon, *Life and Letters,* 272.

47. Qtd. in Lootens, *Lost Saints,* 125.

48. Lootens, *Lost Saints,* 3.

49. This is clear in Victorian criticism. Alexandra Sutherland Orr thus writes in her 1891 biography that "Mrs. Browning's spiritual presence was more than a presiding memory in the heart. I am convinced that it entered largely into the conception of Pompilia." Hodell echoes Orr with reference to "the saintly glory of Pompilia" and "the nature of Elizabeth Barrett Browning" (*Old Yellow Book,* 281). And Gaylord cites Orr's and Hodell's enthusiastic conjectures as "convincingly evident to all close students of Browning's life and poetry," and continues, "Little by little there was a subtle hallowing of his conception of Pompilia into the spiritual embodiment of her at the shrine of whose memory the poet unremittingly worshipped" (*Pompilia and Her Poet,* 21, 27).

50. Nietzche, *Nietzche Reader,* 465.

51. As suggested in Murphy, "Reconceiving the Mother."

52. Jameson, *Legends of the Madonna,* xviii.

53. Browning, *Letters,* 309.

54. Hair, *Robert Browning's Language,* 269–83.

55. Jones takes from Kirkman the expression of Browning as a contemporary Isaiah ("Mr. Kirkman's Address," 176).

56. This attitude lasts well into twentieth-century scholarship. Take, for instance, Whitla's fine study of Browning's religious poetics, which concludes, "With the completion of *The Ring and the Book,* Browning had offered his most profound examination of faith and doubt, truth and fancy, time and Incarnation. . . . In the years afterwards, [he] merely looks again at some aspects of the old concerns" (*Central Truth,* 142).

57. Anecdote underpins a good deal of what today will seem the most intriguing work presented at the London Browning Society: in 1887, for instance, J. Llewellyn Davies's 1887 pronouncement that "A Death in the Desert" (1864) derived from the school of D. F. Strauss

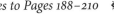

relies upon his insistence (never confirmed) that Browning wrote the whole poem before reading Ernest Renan's *Vie de Jésus* (1863).

58. Suzanne Bailey, "'Decomposing' Texts" and "Somatic Wisdom"; Roberts, "Me/Not-Me"; Johnstone, "Truth Has a Human Face."

59. Peterson, "Rereading Christmas-Eve," 363–80.

5. GEORGE ELIOT'S FITS OF POETRY

1. Briefly, Eliot felt that the first printed version of Browning's poem offered insufficient explanation of the girl's gold hoard, and Browning added three stanzas to the printed version (lines 101–15) for the second impression of *Dramatis Personae* (Browning, *Complete Works*, 6: 435).

2. Blackwood's letter is dated December 29, 1868; Eliot's response is December 31 (*Letters* 4: 497, 501).

3. James, "Legend of Jubal."

4. Eliot, *Middlemarch*, 223.

5. Lewes, *Principles of Success*.

6. Clayton, *Romantic Vision*, 39–46.

7. It is strange that this letter should become, as Martha Vogeler has it, "a text in the history of realism in the English novel"! ("Choir Invisible," 414).

8. Neither are they liberating to women in circumstances less dire than those of virgin martyrs, which is why much twentieth-century feminist criticism expresses dissatisfaction with Browning's model (as opposed, for instance, to that of Marian Erle in *Aurora Leigh*). Conversely, Browning's ethical uselessness helps account for his favor with diverse post-modernist theorists, as Adam Roberts suggests in *Robert Browning Revisited*, vii, 157–61.

9. Main, "Letters of Alexander Main to George Eliot."

10. Roberts, *Romantic and Victorian Long Poems*, 3.

11. Roberts, *Romantic and Victorian Long Poems*, 28.

12. Qtd. in Cross, *George Eliot's Life*, 3: 50.

13. The *Timoleon* project probably also derives from Harrison. When Harrison writes in May 1868 to remind Eliot of his great epic plan, she responds by telling him that she has meditated on the possibility of one: "Indeed, I not only remember your letter, but . . . have read it many times. Within these latter months, I have seemed to see in the distance a possible poem shaped on your idea" (*Letters* 4: 448). Almost certainly, the "possible poem" she mentions is *Timoleon*.

14. Anon., "Spanish Gypsy," 380.

15. Anon., "Spanish Gypsy," 188.

16. Anon., "Spanish Gypsy," 538.

17. Prickett describes the Jena group's understanding of the prose/poetry distinction in *Origins of Narrative*, 109–11.

18. Cited is the Bible's only reference to Jubal, and the fullest description of the line of Cain. The line of Seth also produced a Lamech, though, and the relation between the two Lamechs was debated by scholars.

19. Lisle, "Art and Egotism," 268.

20. Tucker, *Epic*, 424.

21. Ross, *Contours of Masculine Desire*, 217.

22. Walker, *Nightingale's Burden*, 23; Greer, *Slip-Shod Sibyls*, xv; Bennett, *Nineteenth-Century American Women Poets*, 3.

23. Bodenheimer, *Real Life.*

24. British Library AD MS 34038 makes clear that she had intended to add up to six further lines here.

25. Moers, *Literary Women,* 177.

26. British Library AD MS 34038.

27. Gray, *Christian and Lyric Tradition;* Scheinberg, *Women's Poetry and Religion.*

28. "I believe that religion too has to be modified—'developed,' according to the dominant phrase—and that a religion more perfect than any yet prevalent, must express less care for personal consolation, and a more deeply-awing sense of responsibility to man, springing from sympathy with that which of all things is certainly most known to us, the difficulty of the human lot" (*Letters* 5: 31).

29. In this, Eliot was largely right. See Neil, "Criticism and Theological Use," 260–65.

30. Strauss writes, "That little reliance can be placed on the headings of ancient manuscripts, and of sacred records more especially, is evident, and in reference to biblical books has long since been proved. In the so-called books of Moses mention is made of his death and burial: but who now supposes that this was written beforehand by Moses in the form of prophecy?" (*Life of Jesus,* 56).

31. Abrahams, "George Eliot: Her Jewish Associations."

32. Rabbinowitz, "Deuteronomy"; Ginzberg, *Legends of the Jews.*

33. Charlesworth, *Old Testament Pseudepigrapha,* 8–9.

34. Apocryphal texts' prominence in eighteenth-century illustrated family Bibles suggests interesting connections to female consumers as well, as Carpenter argues in *Imperial Bibles, Domestic Bodies,* 24–31.

35. For example, the apocryphal Sirach 44 was often read at Anglican funeral services in the nineteenth and twentieth centuries. I thank Ralph Williams for this example.

36. Blain, *Victorian Women Poets,* 174.

37. Armstrong and Bristow, *Nineteenth-Century Women Poets,* 521.

38. Though not until after Palgrave's death.

39. Jackson and Prins, "Lyrical Studies."

40. Lamartine, *Oeuvres Poétiques Complètes.* Though we have no record of her reading this poem, Eliot certainly knew Lamartine's work. When at Mâcon in June of 1876, for instance, she and Lewes made a pilgrimage to the house where Lamartine was born (*Letters* 6: 264).

41.　　Est-ce là mourir, ô prophète?
　　　Quoi! pendant une éternité
　　　Sentir le souffle qu'on lui prête
　　　Respirer dans l'humanité?

　　　. . . . .

　　　Avoir son cri sur toute bouche,
　　　Son accent dans tous les accents?

　　　Est-ce là mourir? Non! c'est vivre,
　　　Plus vivant dans le verbe écrit!
　　　Par chaque oeil qui s'ouvre au saint livre,
　　　C'est multiplier son esprit!
　　　(1144)

42. German biblical scholars, of course, presuppose multiple authorship throughout the century. In 1807, W. M. L. de Wette takes for granted his audience's understanding that "David

is as much a collective name as Moses, Solomon, Isaiah" (*Beiträge*, 1: 158). Qtd. in Cheyne, *Founders of Old Testament Criticism*, 38.

43. Cleveland, *George Eliot's Poetry*.

44. Smith, "George Eliot," 8; Bates, "George Eliot," 90.

45. Scheinberg, "Measure to Yourself," 263–64.

46. Aguilar, *Women of Israel*, 1: 204.

47. Stowe, *Women in Sacred History*, 27–28.

48. Eliot instructed her publisher to keep the poems' composition dates in the collections, in fact, as though to display her poetic development. In a letter to Blackwood on April 2, 1874, she writes, "I had better say now that I wish to restore the dates of the poems—*not* the months, but simply the years" (*Letters* 6: 38).

49. James, "Legend of Jubal," 486.

50. The autobiographical reading that James suggests is one that a poet could count upon in the Victorian period. Augusta Webster, for instance, laments this in her 1879 essay "Poets and Personal Pronouns."

51. Ruskin, *Sesame and Lilies*, 29.

52. The book of Daniel was recorded during the Maccabean War; thus, the prophesies of the book are historically accurate up to the moment of the war itself. Yet the author of Daniel, for instance, does in some sense truly prophesy the future, because the national struggle in whose service the book is written is successful—the Hebrews win the Maccabean War because they realize the faith and perseverance that the book of Daniel wishes to encourage. In this sense, Daniel's prophesies, though literary and not supernatural, nonetheless prove a valid form (perhaps, for Eliot, *the* valid form) of future telling.

53. Jackson and Prins, "Lyrical Studies," 523.

54. James, "Daniel Deronda," 486.

55. Lazarus, "Jewish Problem," 610. Emma Lazarus previously dedicated to Eliot the title poem of her 1882 volume *Songs of a Semite: The Dance of Death and Other Poems*.

56. Though, as Leah Price shows in *The Anthology and the Rise of the Novel*, such practices as Main's changed the ways that the nineteenth-century novel was understood.

57. Price expresses bafflement that Main includes so much poetry, but he plainly takes his cues from her correspondence.

58. Qtd. in Haight, *George Eliot*, 58.

CONCLUSION

1. Qtd. in Tennyson, *Sartor Called Resartus*, 291.

2. Buell, *New England Literary Culture*, 166–90. See also Dimock, *Through Other Continents*.

3. Mumford, *Ralph Waldo Emerson*, 65.

4. Stead, "Wanted, an English Bible!"

5. Carlyle's famous encomiums in *Sartor Resartus* (1833–34) and "The Poet as Hero" (1841) stand out here, but later Victorian critics demonstrated a still more zealous commitment to this ideal, as my introduction discusses in relation to Alfred Austin.

6. Other helpful recent critiques of secularization by literary scholars include Viswanathan's "Secularism in the Framework of Heterodoxy" and Vincent Pecora's *Secularization and Cultural Criticism*, which addresses secularization's ongoing reliance upon the paradigms of religious tradition.

7. LaPorte, "George Eliot" and "The Bard, the Bible."

8. Peterson, *Interrogating the Oracle*, 3.

9. As the language historian Richard W. Bailey puts it, "In the 'translation,' Smith did his nineteenth-century best to write seventeenth-century English" (*Nineteenth-Century English*, 312).

10. That said, *The Book of Mormon* has been oddly neglected in modern literary criticism.

11. Taylor, *Secular Age*, 432.

12. Hardy, *Complete Poetical Works*, 2: 36–42.

13. Leighton, *On Form*, 56.

Bibliography

Abrahams, Beth-Zion Lask. "George Eliot: Her Jewish Associations—a Centenary Tribute." *Jewish Historical Society of England Transactions* 26 (1979): 53–61.

Abrams, M. H. *Natural Supernaturalism: Tradition and Revolution in Romantic Literature.* New York: Norton, 1971.

Aguilar, Grace. *The Women of Israel.* 2 vols. Vol. 1. New York: D. Appleton, 1872.

A[llingham], W[illiam]. "Arthur Hugh Clough, 1819–1861." *Fraser's Magazine* 74 (1866): 525–35.

Allison, J. W. "Arthur Hugh Clough." *Primitive Methodist Quarterly Review and Christian Ambassador* n.s., 13 (1891): 625–36.

Anderson, Benedict. *Imagined Communities: Reflections on the Origin and Spread of Nationalism.* London: Verso, 1983.

Andrew, Aletha. *An Annotated Bibliography and Study of the Contemporary Criticism of Tennyson's "Idylls of the King," 1859–1886.* New York: P. Lang, 1993.

Anger, Suzy. *Victorian Interpretation.* Ithaca, NY: Cornell University Press, 2005.

Anonymous. "Arthur Hugh Clough." *Contemporary Review* 105 (1914): 285–88.

———. "Arthur Hugh Clough." *Boston Review* 3, no. 14 (1863): 132–38.

———. "Arthur Hugh Clough." *Once a Week* 4, no. 94 (1869): 237–40.

———. "Cain, a Mystery." *Gentleman's Magazine* (1821): 613–15.

———. "Clough's Life and Poems." *Cornhill Magazine* 14 (1866): 410.

———. "Clough's Poems." *Saturday Review* 13 (1862): 109–10.

———. "Idylls of the King." *Athenaeum* no. 1655 (1859): 73–6.

———. "Idylls of the King." *Irish Quarterly Review* 9, no. 35 (1859): 834–59.

———. "Idylls of the King." *Saturday Review* 8, no. 194 (1859): 75–76.

———. "Nouvelles des Sciences." *Revue Britannique,* 8th ser., 4 (1859): 237–40.

———. "The Poems and Prose Remains of Arthur Hugh Clough." *Saturday Review* 66 (1888): 25–26.

———. "The Religious Poetry of Arthur Hugh Clough." *Wesleyan Methodist Magazine* (1893): 513–20.

———. "The Ring and the Book." *Edinburgh Review* 130 (July 1869): 83–94.

———. "Sardanapalus, a Tragedy; the Two Foscari, a Tragedy; Cain, a Mystery." *London Review* (1822): 58–70.

———. "Sardanapalus, the Two Foscari, and Cain." *London Magazine* 5, no. 25 (1822): 66–71.

——. "The Spanish Gypsy. A Poem." *Atlantic Monthly,* September 1868, 380–84.

——. "The Spanish Gypsy. A Poem." *Edinburgh Review,* October 1868, 523–38.

——. "The Spanish Gypsy. A Poem." *London Quarterly Review,* October 1868, 160–88.

——. "Strauss' Leben Jesu." *Dublin University Magazine* 28, no. 165 (1846): 268–84.

——. "Tennyson's 'Idylls of the King.'" *Eclectic* 110 (1859): 287–74.

——. "Victor Hugo—La Légende Des Siècles." *Dublin University Magazine* 55, no. 326 (1860): 221–32.

Armstrong, Isobel. *Arthur Hugh Clough.* [London]: Longmans, 1962.

——, and Joseph Bristow. *Nineteenth-Century Women Poets.* Oxford: Oxford University Press, 1998.

——. *The Radical Aesthetic.* Oxford: Blackwell, 2000.

——. *Victorian Poetry: Poetry, Poetics, and Politics.* London: Routledge, 1993.

Arnold, Matthew. *Complete Prose Works of Matthew Arnold.* Edited by R. H. Super. Ann Arbor: University of Michigan Press, 1960–68.

Ashton, Rosemary. *The German Idea: Four English Writers and the Reception of German Thought, 1800–1860.* Cambridge: Cambridge University Press, 1980.

Auerbach, Nina. *Romantic Imprisonment: Women and Other Glorified Outcasts.* New York: Columbia University Press, 1985.

Austen, Kay. "Pompilia: 'Saint and Martyr Both.'" *Victorian Poetry* 17 (1979): 287–301.

[Austin, Alfred]. "The Poetry of the Period: Mr. Browning." *Temple Bar* 26 (1869): 316–33.

——. "The Poetry of the Period: Mr. Tennyson." *Temple Bar* 26 (1869): 179–94.

[Bagehot, Walter]. "Mr. Clough's Poems." *National Review* 15 (1862): 310–26.

Bailey, Richard W. *Nineteenth-Century English.* Ann Arbor: University of Michigan Press, 1996.

Bailey, Suzanne. "'Decomposing' Texts: Browning's Poetics and Higher-Critical Parody." In *Victorian Religious Discourse: New Directions in Criticism,* edited by Jude V. Nixon, 117–30. New York: Palgrave, 2004.

——. "Somatic Wisdom: Refiguring Bodies in *The Ring and the Book.*" *Victorian Studies* 41, no. 4 (1998): 577–91.

Bakhtin, M. M. *The Dialogic Imagination.* Translated by Caryl Emerson and Michael Holquist. Austin: University of Texas Press, 1981.

Balfour, Ian. *The Rhetoric of Romantic Prophecy.* Stanford, CA: Stanford University Press, 2002.

Bates, Katherine Lee. "George Eliot." *Literary World* 12 (January 1, 1881): 8.

Bayne, Peter. "Strauss's New Life of Christ." *Fortnightly Review* 4 (1866): 317–37.

Bennett, Paula. *Nineteenth-Century American Women Poets: An Anthology.* Malden, MA: Blackwell, 1998.

Berridge, Elizabeth, ed. *The Barretts at Hope End: The Early Diary of Elizabeth Barrett Browning.* London: John Murray, 1974.

Blackbourn, David. *Marpingen: Apparitions of the Virgin Mary in Bismarckian Germany.* Oxford: Clarendon Press, 1993.

Blain, Virginia, ed. *Victorian Women Poets.* Harlow, UK: Longman, 2001.

Blair, Kirstie. "Alfred Tennyson." In *The Blackwell Companion to the Bible in English Literature,* edited by Emma Mason Rebecca Lemon, John Roberts, and Christopher Rowlands, 496–511. Oxford: Blackwell, 2009.

——. *Form and Faith in Victorian Poetry and Religion.* Oxford: Oxford University Press, forthcoming.

Bodenheimer, Rosemarie. *The Real Life of Mary Ann Evans: George Eliot, Her Letters and Fiction*. Ithaca, NY: Cornell University Press, 1996.

Booth, Howard J. "Male Sexuality, Religion and the Problem of Action: John Addington Symonds on Arthur Hugh Clough." In *Masculinity and Spirituality in Victorian Culture*, edited by Andrew Bradstock, 116–33. New York: St. Martin's, 2000.

Brooke, Stopford Augustus. *Four Victorian Poets*. New York: G. P. Putnam's Sons, 1908.

Brown, Callum. *The Death of Christian Britain: Understanding Secularization, 1800–2000*. London: Routledge, 2001.

Brown, Daniel. "Victorian Poetry and Science." In *The Cambridge Companion to Victorian Poetry*, edited by Joseph Bristow, 137–58. Cambridge: Cambridge University Press, 2000.

Brown, Susan. "Pompilia: The Woman (in) Question." *Victorian Poetry* 34 (1996): 15–38.

Browne, Janet. *Charles Darwin: The Power of Place*. 2 vols. Vol. 2. New York: Knopf, 2002.

Browning, Elizabeth Barrett. *Aurora Leigh*. Edited by Margaret Reynolds. Athens: Ohio University Press, 1992.

———. *Aurora Leigh*. Norton Critical Edition. New York: Norton, 1996. 338–39.

———. *Complete Works of Elizabeth Barrett Browning*. Edited by Charlotte Porter and Helen A. Clarke. Vol. 2. New York: Thomas Y. Crowell, 1900.

———. *The Letters of Elizabeth Barrett Browning*. Edited by Frederic G. Kenyon. 3rd ed. 2 vols. Vol. 2. London: Smith Elder, 1897.

———. *The Poetical Works of Elizabeth Barrett Browning*. Edited by Ruth M. Adams. Cambridge Edition. Boston: Houghton Mifflin, 1974.

———. *The Seraphim*. [1838]. Gift copy presented to Louis Cappel in 1843. ABL MS D843.1. Armstrong Browning Library, Baylor University.

———. *The Seraphim and Other Poems*. London: Saunders & Otley, 1838.

Browning, Robert. *The Complete Works of Robert Browning: With Variant Readings and Annotations*. Athens: Ohio University Press, 1969.

———. *Letters of Robert Browning Collected by Thomas J. Wise*. Edited by Thurman L. Hood. New Haven, CT: Yale University Press, 1933.

———. *Robert Browning: The Poems*. Edited by John Petttigrew and Thomas J. Collins. 2 vols. Vol. 1. New Haven, CT: Yale University Press, 1981.

Bruce, Steve. *God Is Dead: Secularization in the West*. Oxford: Blackwell, 2002.

[Buchanan, R. W.]. "The Ring and the Book." *Athenaeum*, no. 2160 (1869): 399–400.

Buell, Lawrence. *New England Literary Culture*. Cambridge: Cambridge University Press, 1986.

[Bulfinch, S. G.]. "Strauss's Life of Jesus:—the Mythic Theory." *Christian Examiner and Religious Miscellany* 4, no. 39 (1845): 145–68.

Burgon, John W. *Inspiration and Interpretation: Seven Sermons by the Rev. John W. Burgon*. London: Marshall Brothers, 1905.

Butler, Samuel. *The Way of All Flesh*. Edited by James Cochrane. New York: Penguin, 1966.

Byron, George Gordon. *Byron*. Edited by Jerome J. McGann. Oxford: Oxford University Press, 1986.

Caird, Mona. "'The Morality of Marriage.'" In *Prose by Victorian Women: An Anthology*, edited by Andrea Broomfield and Sally Mitchell, 629–53. New York: Garland, 1996.

Campbell, Matthew. *Rhythm and Will in Victorian Poetry*. Cambridge: Cambridge University Press, 1999.

Carlyle, Thomas. *A Carlyle Reader*. Edited by G. B. Tennyson. Cambridge: Cambridge University Press, 1984.

Carpenter, Mary Wilson. *Imperial Bibles, Domestic Bodies: Women, Sexuality, and Religion in the Victorian Market.* Athens: Ohio University Press, 2003.

Chadwick, Owen. *The Secularization of the European Mind in the Nineteenth Century.* Cambridge: Cambridge University Press, 1975.

Chaney, Christine. "The 'Poet-Prophet's Book.'" *SEL* 48, no. 4 (2008): 791–99.

Charlesworth, James H. *The Old Testament Pseudepigrapha and the New Testament: Prolegomena for the Study of Christian Origins.* Cambridge: Cambridge University Press, 1985.

Chateaubriand, François-René. *"Essai sur les révolutions" et "Génie du Christianisme."* Paris: Gallimard, 1978.

Cheyne, T. K. *Founders of Old Testament Criticism: Biographical, Descriptive, and Critical Studies.* London: Methuen, 1893.

Chillingworth, William. *The Religion of Protestants, a Safe Way to Salvation.* Edited by Edward Knott. A new and complete edition. London: H. G. Bohn, 1854.

Chorley, Katharine Campbell Hopkinson. *Arthur Hugh Clough, the Uncommitted Mind: A Study of His Life and Poetry.* Oxford: Clarendon Press, 1962.

Christ, Carol T. *Victorian and Modern Poetics.* Chicago: University of Chicago Press, 1984.

Clayton, Jay. *Romantic Vision and the Novel.* Cambridge: Cambridge University Press, 1987.

Cleveland, Rose Elizabeth. *George Eliot's Poetry, and Other Studies.* New York: Funk & Wagnalls, 1885.

Clough, Arthur Hugh. *Clough — Selected Poems.* Edited by J. P. Phelan. London: Longman, 1995.

——— *The Correspondence of Arthur Hugh Clough.* Edited by F. Mulhauser. 2 vols. Oxford: Clarendon Press, 1957.

———. *The Poems of Arthur Hugh Clough.* Edited by A. L. P. Norrington. Oxford: Oxford University Press, 1968.

———. *Poems of Arthur Hugh Clough, Sometime Fellow of Oriel College, Oxford.* Edited by Charles Whibley. London: Macmillan, 1913.

———, and Blanche Smith Clough. *The Poems and Prose Remains of Arthur Hugh Clough, with a Selection from His Letters and a Memoir.* 2 vols. London: Macmillan, 1869.

———. *Prose Remains of Arthur Hugh Clough.* Edited by Blanche Clough. London: Macmillan, 1888.

Coleridge, Samuel Taylor. *Confessions of an Inquiring Spirit.* 1840. Menston, UK: Scolar Press, 1971.

Collins, Wilkie. *The Moonstone.* Edited by Steve Farmer. Peterborough, Ontario: Broadview, 1999.

Cox, Jeffrey. *English Churches in a Secular Society: Lambeth, 1870–1930.* Oxford: Oxford University Press, 1982.

Cross, J. W., ed. *George Eliot's Life.* 3 vols. London: Blackwood & Sons, 1885.

Culler, A. Dwight. *Imaginative Reason: The Poetry of Matthew Arnold.* New Haven, CT: Yale University Press, 1966.

Curle, Richard. *Robert Browning and Julia Wedgwood: A Broken Friendship as Revealed by Their Letters.* New York: Frederick A. Stokes Company, 1937.

Dalberg-Acton, John. "German Schools of History." *English Historical Review* 1 (1886): 7–42.

Daremberg, Charles. *Dictionnaire des antiquités Grecques et Romaines d'après les textes et les monuments.* Paris: Hachette et Cie, 1875.

Davies, Corinne. "Aurora, the Morning Star: The Female Poet, Christology and Revelation in *Aurora Leigh.*" *Studies in Browning and His Circle* 26 (2005): 54–61.

Dillon, Steve. "Barrett Browning's Poetic Vocation: Crying, Singing, Breathing." *Victorian Poetry* 39, no. 4 (2001): 509–32.

Dimock, Wai Chee. *Through Other Continents: American Literature across Deep Time.* Princeton, NJ: Princeton University Press, 2006.

[Doherty, John]. "The Ring and the Book." *Dublin Review* n.s., 8 (1869): 48–62.

Dowden, John. "Arthur Hugh Clough." *Contemporary Review* 12 (1869): 513–24.

Eagleton, Terry. *Literary Theory: An Introduction.* 2nd ed. Minneapolis: University of Minnesota Press, 1996.

———. *Reason, Faith, and Revolution: Reflections on the God Debate.* New Haven, CT: Yale University Press, 2010.

Eichhorn, Johann Gottfried. *Introduction to the Study of the Old Testament.* Translated by George Tilly Gollop. Edited by Christine J. Reeve. [London]: Printed for private circulation [by Spottiswoode], 1888.

Elfenbein, Andrew. *Byron and the Victorians.* Cambridge: Cambridge University Press, 1995.

Eliot, George. *Daniel Deronda.* Edited by Graham Handley. Oxford: Oxford University Press, 1984.

———. *Felix Holt, the Radical.* Edited by Lynda Mugglestone. New York: Penguin, 1995.

———. *George Eliot: Collected Poems.* Edited by Lucien Jenkins. London: Skoob Books, 1989.

———. *The George Eliot Letters.* Edited by Gordon Sherman Haight. 9 vols. New Haven, CT: Yale University Press, 1954.

———. *Middlemarch.* Edited by Rosemary Ashton. New York: Penguin, 1994.

Eliot, T. S. "In Memoriam." In *Selected Essays,* 286–95. New York: Harcourt Brace, 1950.

[Ellis, G. E.]. "The Mythical Theory Applied to the Life of Jesus." *Christian Examiner and Religious Miscellany* 41 (1846): 313–54.

Erskine, Beatrice. *Anna Jameson, Letters and Friendships (1812–1860).* London: T. Fisher Unwin, 1915.

Faurot, Margaret. "*Bishop Blougram's Apology:* The Making of the Poet-Shepherd." *Victorian Poetry* 31, no. 1 (1996): 1–18.

Felluga, Dino. "Verse Novel." In *A Companion to Victorian Poetry,* edited by Richard Cronin, Alison Chapman, and Antony H. Harrison, 171–86. Oxford: Blackwell, 2002.

[Forman, Harry Buxton]. "Robert Browning and the Epic of Psychology." *London Quarterly Review,* no. 32 (1869): 325–57.

Foster Wallace, David. *A Supposedly Fun Thing I'll Never Do Again.* Boston: Little, Brown, 1997.

Fraser, Hilary. *Beauty and Belief: Aesthetics and Religion in Victorian Literature.* Cambridge: Cambridge University Press, 1986.

Friedman, Barton. "To Tell the Sun from Druid Fire: Imagery of Good and Evil in *the Ring and the Book.*" *SEL* 6 (1966): 694–708.

Froude, James Anthony. *The Nemesis of Faith.* 2nd ed. London: J. Chapman, 1849.

Furnivall, Frederick James. "Forwards." *Browning Society Papers* 1, no. 1 (1881): 25–29.

Gaylord, Harriet. *Pompilia and Her Poet.* 2nd ed. New York: Modern Classics, 1931.

Gibbon, Edward. *The History of the Decline and Fall of the Roman Empire.* 5 vols. Vol. 4. Philadelphia: Porter and Coates, [188-?].

Gilfillan, George. *The Bards of the Bible.* New York: Harper & Brothers, 1853.

Gilmour, Robin. *The Victorian Period: The Intellectual and Cultural Context of English Literature 1830–1890.* London: Longman, 1993.

Ginzberg, Louis. *The Legends of the Jews.* Translated by Paul Radin. 7 vols. Vol. 3. Philadelphia: Jewish Publication Society of America, 1909.

Gladstone, W. E. "Tennyson's Poems." *Quarterly Review* 106, no. 212 (1859): 454–85.

Gray, Erik. "Clough and his Discontents: *Amours de Voyage* and the English Hexameter." *Literary Imagination* 6, no. 2 (2004): 195–210.

———. *Milton and the Victorians*. Ithaca, NY: Cornell University Press, 2009.

Gray, F. Elizabeth. *Christian and Lyric Tradition in Victorian Women's Poetry*. New York: Routledge, 2010.

Greer, Germaine. *Slip-Shod Sibyls: Recognition, Rejection and the Woman Poet*. London: Viking, 1995.

Gregory, Melissa Valiska. "Robert Browning and the Lure of the Violent Lyric Voice: Domestic Violence and the Dramatic Monologue." *Victorian Poetry* 38, no. 4 (2000): 491–510.

Hair, Donald S. *Robert Browning's Language*. Toronto: University of Toronto Press, 1999.

Hallam, Arthur Henry. *The Letters of Arthur Henry Hallam*. Edited by Jack Kolb. Columbus: Ohio State University Press, 1981.

Hardy, Thomas. *The Collected Letters of Thomas Hardy*. Edited by Richard Little Purdy and Michael Millgate. Vol. 6. Oxford: Clarendon Press, 1978.

———. *Complete Poetical Works of Thomas Hardy*. Edited by Samuel Lynn Hynes. 5 vols. Vols. 1–2. Oxford: Clarendon Press, 1982.

Harris, Daniel A. "Personification in 'Tithonus.'" In *Critical Essays on Alfred Lord Tennyson*, edited by Herbert F. Tucker, 100–24. New York: G. K. Hall, 1993.

[Hasell, Elizabeth]. "The Idylls of the King." *Blackwood's Edinburgh Magazine* 86, no. 529 (1859): 608–27.

Helmstadter, Richard J., and R. W. Davis. *Religion and Irreligion in Victorian Society : Essays in Honor of R. K. Webb*. London: Routledge, 1992.

Hemans, Felicia. *The Sceptic*. London: John Murray, 1820. Reproduced by British Women Romantic Poets Project, http://digital.lib.ucdavis.edu/projects/bwrp/Works/HemaFScept .htm.

Herder, Johann Gottfried, ed. *Theologische Schriften*. Edited by Christoph Bultmann and Thomas Zippert, Johann Gottfried Herder Werke. Frankfurt: Deutscher Klassiker Verlag, 1994.

Hodell, Charles Wesley. *Old Yellow Book: Source of Browning's "The Ring and the Book" in Complete Photo-Reproduction*. Washington, DC: Carnegie Institution of Washington, 1908.

Holcomb, Adele M. "Anna Jameson: The First Professinal English Art Historian." *Art History* 6, no. 2 (1983): 171–87.

Hopkins, Gerard Manley. *A Hopkins Reader*. Edited by John Pick. New York: Image Books, 1966.

Houghton, Walter Edwards. *The Poetry of Clough: An Essay in Revaluation*. New Haven, CT: Yale University Press, 1963.

Hughes, Linda K. *The Manyfacèd Glass: Tennyson's Dramatic Monologues*. Athens: Ohio University Press, 1987.

Hugo, Victor. *La légende des siècles*. Paris: Gallimard, 1950.

[Hutton, R. H.] "The Unpopularity of Clough." *The Spectator*, no. 2,839 (1882): 1507–09.

Irlam, Shaun. *Elations: The Poetics of Enthusiasm in Eighteenth-Century Britain*. Stanford, CA: Stanford University Press, 1999.

J.-L., M. "Angleterre: Un Poëme De Tennyson." *Bibliothèque Universelle*, n.s., 9 (1860): 118–26.

Jackson, Virginia, and Yopie Prins. "Lyrical Studies." *Victorian Literature and Culture* 27 (1999): 521–30.

James, Henry. "Daniel Deronda: A Conversation." *Atlantic Monthly* 38 (1876): 684–94.

———. "The Legend of Jubal, and Other Poems." *North American Review* 119 (October 1874): 484–89.

Jameson, Anna. *Legends of the Madonna.* 4th ed. London: Longmans, Green, 1867.

———. *Sacred and Legendary Art: Containing the Patron Saints, the Martyrs, the Early Bishops, the Hermits, and the Warrior Saints of Christendom.* 5th ed. London: Longmans, Green, 1866.

Jasper, David. *The Sacred and Secular Canon in Romanticism.* New York: St. Martin's, 1999.

Jay, Elisabeth. *The Evangelical and Oxford Movements.* Cambridge: Cambridge University Press, 1983.

———. *Faith and Doubt in Victorian Britain.* Houndmills, Basingstoke: Macmillan, 1986.

Johnston, Judith. *Anna Jameson: Victorian, Feminist, Woman of Letters.* Aldershot, Hants., UK: Scolar Press, 1997.

Johnstone, Michael. "Truth Has a Human Face." *Victorian Poetry* 38, no. 3 (2000): 365–81.

Jones, Sir Henry. *Browning as a Philosophical and Religious Teacher.* 2nd ed. Glasgow: Maclehose & Sons, 1892.

Jonsson, Inge. *Emanuel Swedenborg.* New York: Twayne Publishers, 1971.

Joseph, Gerhard. *Tennyson and the Text.* Cambridge: Cambridge University Press, 1992.

Jowett, Benjamin. *The Life and Letters of Benjamin Jowett, M.A., Master of Balliol College, Oxford.* Edited by Evelyn Abbott and Lewis Campbell. London: John Murray, 1897.

Joyce, James. *Ulysses.* Gabler Edition. New York: Random House, 1986.

Jump, John Davies, ed. *Tennyson: The Critical Heritage.* London: Routledge & Kegan Paul, 1967.

Kelley, Philip, and Ronald Hudson, eds. *The Brownings' Correspondence.* Vols. 2, 5, 4, 7, 8. Winfield, KS: Wedgestone Press, 1984–1989.

———, and Scott Lewis, eds. *The Brownings' Correspondence.* Vol. 10. Winfield, KS: Wedgestone Press, 1992.

Kenny, Anthony John Patrick. *God and Two Poets: Arthur Hugh Clough and Gerard Manley Hopkins.* London: Sidgwick & Jackson, 1988.

Kenyon, Frederic G., ed. *Life and Letters of Robert Browning.* Edited by [Alexandra] Mrs. Sutherland Orr. Boston: Houghton Mifflin, 1908.

Kierstead, Christopher M. "Where 'Byron Used to Ride': Locating the Victorian Travel Poet in Clough's *Amours De Voyage* and *Dipsychus.*" *Philological Quarterly* 77, no. 4 (1998): 377–95.

Kirkman, J. "Mr. Kirkman's Address at the Inaugural Meeting of the Society, Oct 28, 1881." *Browning Society Papers* 1, no. 2 (1881): 171–90.

Lamartine, Alphonse de. *Oeuvres Poétiques Complètes.* Edited by Marius-François Guyard. Paris: Gallimard, 1963.

LaPorte, Charles. "The Bard, the Bible, and the Victorian Shakespeare Question." *ELH* 74 (2007): 609–28.

———. "George Eliot." *Blackwell Companion to the Bible in English Literature.* Edited by Emma Mason, Rebecca Lemon, John Roberts, and Christopher Rowlands, 536–550. Oxford: Blackwell, 2009.

[Lawrance, Hannah]. "Idylls of the King." *British Quarterly* 60 (1859): 481–510.

Lazarus, Emma. "The Jewish Problem." *Century Illustrated Monthly Magazine,* February 1883, 602–11.

Lee, Warner. "The Idylls of the King." *New Rugbeian* 1, no. 9 (1859): 267–71.

Leighton, Angela. *On Form: Poetry, Aestheticism, and the Legacy of a Word.* Oxford: Oxford University Press, 2007.

Lewes, George Henry. *The Principles of Success in Literature*. Edited by Fred Newton Scott. 3rd ed. Boston: Allyn & Bacon, 1917.

Lewis, Linda M. *Elizabeth Barrett Browning's Spiritual Progress*. Columbia: University of Missouri Press, 1998.

Lichtenberger, Frédéric Auguste. *History of German Theology in the Nineteenth Century*. Translated by W[illiam] Hastie. Edinburgh: T. & T. Clark, 1889.

Lisle, Bonnie. "Art and Egotism in George Eliot's Poetry." *Victorian Poetry* 22, no. 3 (1984): 263–78.

Lodge, David. *The Modes of Modern Writing*. London: Edward Arnold, 1977.

Looper, Travis. *Byron and the Bible*. Metuchen, NJ: Scarecrow Press, 1978.

Lootens, Tricia. *Lost Saints: Silence, Gender, and Victorian Literary Canonization*. Charlottesville: University Press of Virginia, 1996.

Lowell, James Russell, and Horace Elisha Scudder. *The Works of James Russell Lowell*. Standard Library Edition. 13 vols. Vol. 2. Boston: Houghton Mifflin, 1890.

MacPherson, Gerardine Bate. *Memoirs of the Life of Anna Jameson*. Boston: Roberts Brothers, 1878.

Main, Alexander. "Letters of Alexander Main to George Eliot," 1871–76. MS 942. National Library of Scotland, Edinburgh.

Mallock, W. H. *The New Republic*. London: Chatto and Windus, 1877.

Malory, Thomas. *Malory: Works*. Edited by Eugène Vinaver. 2nd reprinted edition. Oxford: Oxford University Press, 1971.

Mantel, Hilary. "'What Did Her Neighours Say When Gabriel Had Gone?'" *London Review of Books* 31, no. 7 (2009): 3–6.

Mason, Emma. *Women Poets of the Nineteenth Century*. Tavistock, UK: Northcote House, 2006.

———, and Mark Knight. *Nineteenth-Century Religion and Literature*. Oxford: Oxford University Press, 2006.

[Matthews, John]. (Siluriensis). "Lord Byron." *Blackwood's Edinburgh Magazine* 11, no. 61 (1822): 212–17.

[Maurice, F. D.]. "Lord Byron's Monument." *Athenaeum*, nos. 48 and 49 (1828): 751–52, 67–68.

Mayer, S. R. Townshend. "Charles Kingsley and Arthur Hugh Clough." *St. James's Magazine and United Empire Review* 31, no. 7 (1877): 265–76.

Maynard, John. "Victorian Innocence Abroad: The Sexual and Religious Dialectics of an Englishman in Italy." *Annals of Scholarship* 7, no. 2 (1990): 217–34.

McGann, Jerome J. *A Critique of Modern Textual Criticism*. Chicago: University of Chicago Press, 1983.

———. *Fiery Dust: Byron's Poetic Development*. Chicago: University of Chicago Press, 1968.

———. "The Idea of an Indeterminate Text: Blake's Bible of Hell and Dr. Alexander Geddes." *Studies in Romanticism* 25, no. 3 (1986): 303–24.

———. *Swinburne: An Experiment in Criticism*. Chicago: University of Chicago Press, 1972.

———. *The Textual Condition*. Princeton Studies in Culture/Power/History. Princeton, NJ: Princeton University Press, 1991.

———. *Towards a Literature of Knowledge*. Oxford: Clarendon Press, 1989.

McKelvy, William R. *The English Cult of Literature: Devoted Readers, 1774–1880*. Charlottesville: University of Virginia Press, 2007.

McLeod, Hugh. *Religion and Society in England, 1850–1914*. Basingstoke: Macmillan, 1996.

———. *Secularization in Western Europe, 1848–1914*. New York: St. Martin's, 2000.

Melnyk, Julie. "Hemans's Later Poetry: Religion and the Vatic Poet." In *Felicia Hemans: Reimagining Poetry in the Nineteenth Century,* edited by Nanora Sweet and Julie Melnyk, 74–92. Houndmills, Basingstoke: Macmillan, 2001.

Mermin, Dorothy. *Elizabeth Barrett Browning: The Origins of a New Poetry.* Chicago: University of Chicago Press, 1989.

Mermin, Dorothy, and Herbert Tucker. *Victorian Literature: 1830–1900.* Fort Worth, TX: Harcourt, 2002.

Mill, John Stuart. "What Is Poetry?" 1835. In *Broadview Anthology of Victorian Poetry and Poetic Theory,* edited by Thomas Collins and Vivian Rundle, 1212–20. Peterborough, UK: Broadview, 2000.

Miller, J. Hillis. *The Disappearance of God: Five Nineteenth-Century Writers.* 1963. Reprint, Urbana: University of Illinois Press, 2000 [1963].

[Milnes, R. Monckton]. "Timbuctoo." *Athenaeum* 1, no. 91 (July 22, 1829): 456.

[Milsand, Joseph]. "Alfred Tennyson: Idyls of the King (Idylles Du Roi)." *Le magasin de librairie* 12, no. 47 (1860): 321–50.

Moers, Ellen. *Literary Women.* Garden City, NY: Doubleday, 1976.

Moore, Edward Caldwell. *An Outline of the History of Christian Thought since Kant.* New York: Charles Scribner's Sons, 1916.

[Morley, John]. "On 'The Ring and the Book.'" *Fortnightly Review,* n.s., 5 (1869): 331–43.

[Mozley, Anne]. "Tennyson—Idylls of the King." *Bentley's Quarterly Review,* October 1859, 159–94.

[Mozley, John Rickards]. "The Ring and the Book." *Macmillan's Magazine* 19 (1868–69): 544–52.

Müller, F. Max. *Auld Lang Syne.* New York: Charles Scribner's Sons, 1898.

Mumford, Lewis, ed. *Ralph Waldo Emerson: Essays and Journals.* New York: Doubleday, 1968.

Murphy, Patricia. "Reconceiving the Mother: Deconstructing the Madonna in *Aurora Leigh.*" *Victorian Newsletter* 91 (1997): 21–27.

Murray, J. O. "Arthur Hugh Clough and His Poetry." *Homiletic Review* 29, no. 4 (1895): 291–97.

Nash, Michael. *Paine's Age of Reason Measured by the Standard of Truth.* London: Sold by J. Mathews, 1794.

Neil, W[illiam]. "The Criticism and Theological Use of the Bible, 1700–1950." In *The Cambridge History of the Bible,* edited by Peter R. Ackroyd, Christopher Francis Evans, G. W. H. Lampe, and S. L. Greenslade, 238–94. Cambridge: Cambridge University Press, 1963–70.

Netland, John. "The Problem of Metaphor in Arthur Hugh Clough's 'Epi-Strauss-Ism.'" *Victorians Institute Journal* 23 (1995): 151–69.

Newman, John Henry. "The Tamworth Reading Room." In *Victorian Literature: 1830–1900,* edited by Dorothy Mermin and Herbert F. Tucker, 222–39. Fort Worth, TX: Harcourt, 2002.

Nietzsche, Friedrich. *The Nietzsche Reader.* Oxford: Blackwell, 2006.

Nixon, Jude V. "'Kill[ing] Our Souls with Literalism': Reading *Essays and Reviews.*" In *Victorian Religious Discourse: New Directions in Criticism,* edited by Jude V. Nixon, 51–82. New York: Palgrave, 2004.

The Norton Anthology of English Literature. Edited by M. H. Abrams. New York: W. W. Norton, 1962.

Norton, David. *A History of the English Bible as Literature.* Cambridge: Cambridge University Press, 2000.

Orr, [Alexandra] Sutherland, Mrs. *Life and Letters of Robert Browning.* Revised by Frederic G. Kenyon. Boston: Houghton Mifflin, 1908.

———. "The Religious Opinions of Robert Browning." *Contemporary Review* 60 (December 1891): 876–91.

Oxford Dictionary of Current Usage. Oxford: Oxford University Press, 1993.

Oxford Dictionary of Quotations. 3rd ed. Oxford: Oxford University Press, 1979.

Paine, Thomas. *The Theological Works of Thomas Paine . . . The Whole Preceded by a Life of Paine.* Chicago: Belfords Clarke, 1879.

Pals, Daniel L. *Victorian "Lives" of Jesus.* San Antonio, TX: Trinity University Press, 1982.

Parker, Joseph. *None Like It: A Plea for the Old Sword.* London: James Nisbet, 1894.

[Parker, Theodore]. "Das Leben Jesu." *Christian Examiner* 28 (1840): 273–3,166.

Parsons, Gerald. *Religion in Victorian Britain.* Manchester: Manchester University Press, 1988.

Pascal, R., ed. *Shakespeare in Germany: 1740–1815.* Cambridge: Cambridge University Press, 1937.

[Patmore, Coventry]. "Four Idylls of the King." *Edinburgh Review* 110, no. 223 (1859): 247–63.

Pauly, August Friedrich von, Christian Walz, and Wilhelm Sigismund Teuffel. *Real-Encyclopädie Der Classischen Alterthumswissenschaft in Alphabetischer Ordnung.* Stuttgart: J. B. Metzler, 1839.

Peacock, T. L. *Palmyra, and Other Poems.* London: W. J. and J. Richardson, 1806.

Pearsall, Cornelia. *Tennyson's Rapture: Transformation in the Victorian Dramatic Monologue.* Oxford: Oxford University Press, 2008.

Pecora, Vincent. *Secularization and Cultural Criticism: Religion, Nation, and Modernity.* Chicago: University of Chicago Press, 2006.

Perloff, Marjorie, and Craig Dworkin. "The Sound of Poetry/The Poetry of Sound." *PMLA* 123, no. 3 (2008): 749–61.

Peterson, Linda H. "Rereading 'Christmas-Eve,' Rereading Browning." *Victorian Poetry* 26, no. 4 (1988): 363–80.

Peterson, William S. *Interrogating the Oracle: A History of the London Browning Society.* Athens: Ohio University Press, 1969.

Price, Leah. *The Anthology and the Rise of the Novel.* Cambridge: Cambridge University Press, 2003.

Prickett, Stephen. *Narrative, Religion and Science: Fundamentalism versus Irony, 1700–1999.* Cambridge: Cambridge University Press, 2002.

———. *Origins of Narrative: The Romantic Appropriation of the Bible.* Cambridge: Cambridge University Press, 1996.

———. *Words and the Word: Language, Poetics, and Biblical Interpretation.* Cambridge: Cambridge University Press, 1986.

———, and Robert Barnes. *The Bible.* Landmarks of World Literature. Cambridge: Cambridge University Press, 1991.

Prins, Yopie. *Victorian Sappho.* Princeton, NJ: Princeton University Press, 1999.

Pullum, Geoffrey K., and William A. Ladusaw. *Phonetic Symbol Guide.* Chicago: University of Chicago Press, 1986.

Rabbinowitz, Joseph. "Deuteronomy." In *Midrash Rabbah,* 184–88. London: Soncino Press, 1939.

Renan, Ernest. *Vie de Jésus.* 13th ed. Paris: Calmann-Lévy, 1962.

Riede, David G. *Allegories of One's Own Mind: Melancholy in Victorian Poetry.* Columbus: Ohio State University Press, 2005.

Roberts, Adam. "Me/Not-Me: The Narrator of 'A Death in the Desert.'" In *Robert Browning in Contexts*, edited by John Woolford, 47–60. Winfield, KS: Wedgestone Press, 1998.

———. *Robert Browning Revisited*. New York: Twayne, 1996.

———. *Romantic and Victorian Long Poems: A Guide*. Brookfield, VT: Ashgate, 1999.

Robertson, John Mackinnon. *New Essays Towards a Critical Method*. London: Bodley Head, 1897.

Röhr, Johann Friedrich. *Röhr's Historico-Geographical Account of Palestine: Researches in Palestine*. Translated by David Esdaile. Edinburgh: T. Clark, 1843.

Rosenberg, John D. *The Fall of Camelot: A Study of Tennyson's "Idylls of the King."* Cambridge, MA: Harvard University Press, 1973.

Rosman, Doreen. *The Evolution of the English Churches, 1500–2000*. Cambridge: Cambridge University Press, 2003.

Ross, Marlon Bryan. *The Contours of Masculine Desire: Romanticism and the Rise of Women's Poetry*. New York: Oxford University Press, 1989.

Rowlinson, Matthew Charles. *Tennyson's Fixations: Psychoanalysis and the Topics of the Early Poetry*. Charlottesville: University Press of Virginia, 1994.

Rudy, Jason R. *Electric Meters: Victorian Physiological Poetics*. Athens: Ohio University Press, 2009.

Ruskin, John. *Sesame and Lilies. Three Lectures by John Ruskin, Ll.D.* Revised ed. New York: John Wiley & Sons, 1887.

———. *Works of John Ruskin*. Edited by E. T. Cook and Alexander Wedderburn. Vol. 36. London: Longmans, Green, 1909.

Said, Edward W. *Orientalism*. New York: Pantheon Books, 1978. [Sawtelle, H. A.]. "Review of the Straussian Theory." *Christian Review* 21, no. 85 (1856): 321–55.

Schad, John. *Arthur Hugh Clough*. Tavistock, UK: Northcote House, 2006.

Scheinberg, Cynthia. "'Measure to Yourself a Prophet's Place': Biblical Heroines, Jewish Difference and Women's Poetry." In *Women's Poetry, Late Romantic to Late Victorian*, edited by Isobel Armstrong and Virginia Blain, 263–91. New York: St. Martin's, 1999.

———. *Women's Poetry and Religion in Victorian England: Jewish Identity and Christian Culture*. Cambridge: Cambridge University Press, 2002.

Schleiermacher, Friedrich. *On Religion: Speeches to Its Cultured Despisers*. Translated by Richard Crouter. Texts in German Philosophy. Cambridge: Cambridge University Press, 1988.

———. *Über Die Religion: Reden an Die Gebildeten Unter Ihren Verächtern*. Hamburg: F. Meiner, 1958.

Schmidt, Leigh Eric. *Hearing Things: Religion, Illusion, and the American Enlightenment*. Cambridge, MA: Harvard University Press, 2000.

Secord, James A. *Victorian Sensation*. Chicago: University of Chicago Press, 2000.

Sedgwick, Eve Kosofsky. *Between Men: English Literature and Male Homosocial Desire*. New York: Columbia University Press, 1985.

Shaffer, Elinor S. *"Kubla Khan" and the Fall of Jerusalem: The Mythological School in Biblical Criticism and Secular Literature, 1770–1880*. Cambridge: Cambridge University Press, 1975.

Shannon, Edgar Finley. *Tennyson and the Reviewers: A Study of His Literary Reputation and of the Influence of the Critics upon His Poetry, 1827–1851*. Reprint ed. [Hamden, CT]: Archon Books, 1967.

Shapiro, James. *Contested Will: Who Wrote Shakespeare?* New York: Simon & Schuster, 2010.

Shaw, W. David. *The Lucid Veil: Poetic Truth in the Victorian Age*. Madison: University of Wisconsin Press, 1987.

Shea, Victor, and William Whitla, eds. *Essays and Reviews: The 1860 Text and Its Reading.* Charlottesville: University Press of Virginia, 2000.

[Sidgwick, Henry]. "The Poems and Prose Remains of Arthur Hugh Clough." *Westminster Review* 92, no. 182 (1869): 175–86.

Slinn, E. Warwick. *Victorian Poetry as Cultural Critique.* Charlottesville: University of Virginia Press, 2003.

Smart, Christopher. *The Poetical Works of Christopher Smart.* Edited by Karina Williamson. Vol. 1. Oxford: Clarendon Press, 1980.

Smith, J. Oliver [Mrs.]. "George Eliot." *Literary World* 12 (February 26, 1881): 90.

Smith, William. *A Dictionary of the Bible: Comprising Its Antiquities, Biography, Geography, and Natural History.* 1863. Reprint, Hartford, CT: S. S. Scranton, 1896.

———. *Dictionary of Greek and Roman Biography and Mythology.* Boston: C. C. Little & J. Brown, 1849.

———. *A Dictionary of Greek and Roman Antiquities.* 3rd American Edition, Carefully Revised and Containing Numerous Additional Articles Relative to the Botany, Mineralogy and Zoology of the Ancients, by Charles Anthon, LLD. New York: Harper & Brothers, 1843.

[Smith, William Henry]. "'Dipsychus' and the Letters of A. H. Clough." *Macmillan's Magazine* 15 (1866): 89–102.

Soffer, Reba N. "History and Religion: J. R. Seeley and the Burden of the Past." In *Religion and Irreligion in Victorian Society: Essays in Honor of R. K. Webb,* edited by Richard J. Helmstadter and R. W. Davis, 133–50. London: Routledge, 1992.

St. Clair, William. *The Reading Nation in the Romantic Period.* Cambridge: Cambridge University Press, 2004.

Stanley, Arthur Penrhyn. *Essays, Chiefly on Questions of Church and State.* London: John Murray, 1884.

Stead, W. T. "Wanted, an English Bible! A Suggestion for Its Compilation." *Daily Paper* (October 4, 1893): 25–26.

Steffan, Truman Guy. *Lord Byron's "Cain": Twelve Essays and a Text with Variants and Annotations.* Austin: University of Texas Press, 1968.

Stone, Marjorie. "A Heretic Believer: Victorian Religious Doubt and New Contexts for Elizabeth Barrett Browning's 'A Drama of Exile,' 'The Virgin Mary' and 'The Runaway Slave at Pilgrim's Point.'" *Studies in Browning and His Circle* 26 (2005): 7–40.

Stowe, Harriet Beecher. *Women in Sacred History.* New York: J. B. Ford, 1873.

Strauss, David Friedrich. *Der Alte Und Der Neue Glaube. Ein Bekenntniss.* 10th ed. Bonn: Emil Strauss, 1879.

———. *The Life of Jesus, Critically Examined.* Translated by George Eliot. 3 vols. Vol. 3. 1846. Reprint of 1st edition, Bristol: Thoemmes Press, 1998.

———. *The Old Faith and the New. A Confession.* Translated by Mathilde Blind. 3rd English edition. London: Asher, 1874.

Swedenborg, Emanuel. *The Apocalypse Revealed.* Translated by Alice Spiers Sechrist. New York: Swedenborg Foundation, 1968.

———. *Arcana Coelestia; The Heavenly Arcana Contained in the Holy Scripture or Word of the Lord, Unfolded.* 12 vols. Vol. 10. New York: Swedenborg Foundation, 1951.

———. *Arcana Coelestia; The Heavenly Arcana Contained in the Holy Scripture or Word of the Lord, Unfolded.* Translated by John Faulkner Potts. 12 vols. Vol. 1. New York: Swedenborg Foundation, 1949.

Sweet, Henry. *A Handbook of Phonetics, Including a Popular Exposition of the Principles of Spelling Reform.* Oxford: Clarendon Press, 1877.
——. *A Primer of Phonetics.* Oxford: Clarendon Press, 1892.
Swinburne, Algernon Charles, ed. *Aurora Leigh.* London: Smith, Elder, 1898.
Symonds, John Addington. "Arthur Hugh Clough." *Fortnightly Review* 24 (1868): 589–617.
——. *Letters.* Edited by Herbert M. Schueller and Robert L. Peters. Vol. 1. Detroit: Wayne State University Press, 1967.
Taylor, Charles. *A Secular Age.* Cambridge, MA: Harvard University Press, 2007.
——. *Sources of the Self: The Making of the Modern Identity.* Cambridge, MA: Harvard University Press, 1989.
Tennyson, Alfred Lord. *The Letters of Alfred Lord Tennyson.* Edited by Cecil Y. Lang and Edgar F. Shannon Jr. 2 vols. Cambridge, MA: Harvard University Press, 1987.
——. *The Poems of Tennyson: In Three Volumes.* Edited by Christopher B. Ricks. 2nd ed. 3 vols. Harlow: Longman, 1987.
Tennyson, G. B. *Sartor Called Resartus: The Genesis, Structure, and Style of Thomas Carlyle's First Major Work.* Princeton, NJ: Princeton University Press, 1965.
——. *Victorian Devotional Poetry: The Tractarian Mode.* Cambridge, MA: Harvard University Press, 1981.
Tennyson, Hallam. *Alfred Lord Tennyson: A Memoir.* London: Macmillan, 1905.
Thomas, Clara. *Love and Work Enough: The Life of Anna Jameson.* London: Macdonald, 1967.
Thomson, James. *Poetical Works of James Thomson.* 2 vols. Vol. 1. London: Bell & Daldy, 1866.
——. "The Ring and the Book." *Gentleman's Magazine* 251 (1881): 682–95.
Thorpe, Michael, ed. *Clough: The Critical Heritage.* London: Routledge & K. Paul, 1972.
Thorslev, Peter L. "Byron and Bayle: Biblical Skepticism and Romantic Irony." In *Byron, the Bible, and Religion,* edited by Wolf Z. Hirst, 58–76. Newark: University of Delaware Press, 1991.
Todorov, Tzvetan. *Mikhail Bakhtin: The Dialogical Principle.* Minneapolis: University of Minnesota Press, 1984.
Treves, Frederick. *The Country of "The Ring and the Book."* London: Cassell, 1913.
Trollope, Anthony. *Barchester Towers.* Edited by Robin Gilmour. New York: Penguin, 1982.
——. "Henry Taylor's Poems." *Fortnightly Review* 1 (1865): 129–46.
Tucker, Herbert F. *Epic: Britain's Heroic Muse, 1790–1910.* Oxford: Oxford University Press, 2008.
——. "Representation and Repristination: Virginity in *The Ring and the Book*." In *Virginal Sexuality and Textuality in Victorian Literature,* edited by Lloyd Davis, 67–87. Albany: SUNY Press, 1993.
——. *Tennyson and the Doom of Romanticism.* Cambridge, MA: Harvard University Press, 1988.
Twain, Mark. *Collected Tales, Sketches, Speeches, and Essays, 1891–1910.* New York: Library of America, 1992.
Viswanathan, Gauri. *Outside the Fold: Conversion, Modernity, and Belief.* Princeton, NJ: Princeton University Press, 1998.
——. "Secularism in the Framework of Heterodoxy." *PMLA* 123, no. 2 (2008): 466–76.
Vogeler, Martha S. "The Choir Invisible: The Poetics of Humanist Piety." In *George Eliot: A Centenary Tribute,* edited by Gordon S. Haight and Rosemary T. VanArsdel, 64–83. London: Macmillan, 1982.

Walker, Cheryl. *The Nightingale's Burden: Women Poets and American Culture before 1900.* Bloomington: Indiana University Press, 1982.

Walker, William. "Pompilia and *Pompilia.*" *Victorian Poetry* 22 (1984): 47–63.

Ward, Candace. "Damning Herself Praisworthily: Nullifying Women in *The Ring and the Book.*" *Victorian Poetry* 34 (1996): 1–14.

Ward, R. W. "Faith and Fallacy: English and German Perspective in the Nineteenth Century." In *Victorian Faith in Crisis: Essays on Continuity and Change in Nineteenth-Century Religious Belief,* edited by Richard J. Helmstadter and Bernard V. Lightman, 39–70. Stanford, CA: Stanford University Press, 1990.

Ward, Thomas Humphry. *The English Poets.* London: Macmillan, 1880.

Watson, J. R. *The Victorian Hymn: An Inaugural Lecture.* Kendal: Printed for the University of Durham by T. Wilson & Sons, 1981.

Webster, Augusta. "Poets and Personal Pronouns." In *A Housewife's Opinions,* 150–56. London: Macmillan, 1879.

Wheeler, Michael. *Death and the Future Life in Victorian Literature and Theology.* Cambridge: Cambridge University Press, 1990.

Whitla, William. *The Central Truth: The Incarnation in Robert Browning's Poetry.* Toronto: University of Toronto Press, 1963.

Wilde, Oscar. *The Artist as Critic: Critical Writings of Oscar Wilde.* Edited by Richard Ellmann. New York: Random House, 1968.

Wolfson, Susan J. "Hemans and the Romance of Byron." In *Felicia Hemans: Reimagining Poetry in the Nineteenth Century,* edited by Nanora Sweet and Julie Melnyk, 155–80. Houndmills, Basingstoke: Palgrave, 2001.

Woolf, Virginia. *The Second Common Reader.* New York: Harcourt, Brace, 1932.

Wordsworth, William. *The Poetical Works of William Wordsworth.* Edited by E. de Selincourt. Oxford: Oxford University Press, 1952.

———. *The Prelude.* New York: Norton, 1979.

Index

Abrahams, Beth-Zion Lask, 215, 217
Abrams, M. H., 240n12
Aeschylus, 41–42, 185, 197, 206
Aguilar, Grace, 213, 222
Anderson, Benedict, 249n37
Anger, Suzy, 63, 240n14
Anthony, Saint, 112
Aristotle, 56, 224
Armageddon, 32,
Armstrong, Isobel, 96, 121, 123, 146, 220, 242n53, 245n44, 247n11, 252n17, 253n26, 260n37
Armstrong Browning Library, 255n1
Arnold, Matthew, 2–5, 8, 12–15, 62, 77, 113, 115, 121, 123–24, 125, 128, 137, 143, 150, 194–95, 214, 232, 241nn37–38, 253n36; "Dover Beach," 3, 242n51; *The Function of Criticism at the Present Time*, 5, 15; "The Future," 8; *God and the Bible*, 121; and the higher criticism, 8, 12–15, 62, 77, 194, 214, 232; *Lectures on Translating Homer*, 124; *Literature and Dogma*, 12–14, 77, 121, 194, 214; "Obermann Once More," 5; "Stanzas from the Grand Chartreuse," 2; *The Study of Poetry*, 12–13, 62, 115; "Thyrsis," 113, 150
Arnold, Thomas, 113, 128, 252n17
Ashton, Rosemary, 241n40
Auerbach, Nina, 178, 257n25
Augustine, Saint, 109
Austin, Alfred, 11–12, 89–90, 202, 261n5

Austen, Jane, 10
Austen, Kay, 166, 177, 257n31

Bagehot, Walter, 134, 137, 251n6, 251n8
Bailey, Richard W., 262n9
Bailey, Suzanne, 158, 188
Bakhtin, M. M., 21, 52–53
Balfour, Ian, 239n8, 240n9, 240n11
Balzac, Honoré de, 10
Barnes, Robert, 241n26
Barrett Browning, Elizabeth, 2–4, 17, 21, 23–66, 89, 107, 111–12, 177–82, 190–91, 197, 206, 211, 213–14, 218, 222, 231–32, 234–35, 252n23, 255n13; *Aurora Leigh*, 3, 21, 25, 27, 48–66, 112, 178–80, 190, 198, 206, 211, 255n6; "Bertha in the Lane," 36; *Casa Guidi Windows*, 178; and conversion narrative, 38, 44–45, 53; "The Dead Pan," 45, 55; desire to revitalize Christian poetics, 38–41, 44–46; *A Drama of Exile*, 37; "Earth and Her Praisers," 30–37, 49; as evangelical, 2, 17, 23–25, 30–37, 45, 66; *The Greek Christian Poets*, 38–39; and the higher criticism, 4, 24, 28, 30–31, 37, 45, 48, 54–66; "Insufficiency," 36; "Isobel's Child," 36–37, 244n20; *The Seraphim*, 24, 37, 40–48, 53–55, 63, 197, 206; *The Seraphim and Other Poems*, 23, 25, 64; *Sonnets from the Portuguese*, 36, 206; "Sounds," 25–30, 35, 37, 47, 112; as Swedenborgian poet, 24, 27, 48–56, 65–66

Hopkins, Gerard Manley, 16, 89–90, 242n51
Horace, 218–20
Horne, R. H., 48, 146
Houghton, Walter, 3, 252n20, 253n43
Hudson, Ronald, 243n3
Hughes, Linda K., 69–70, 85
Hugo, Victor, 20; "Le Satyre," 20, 242n60
Hume, David, 5–6, 8, 61, 87, 128
Hutton, Richard Holt, 84, 248n230, 251n6
Huxley, Nettie, 89

Ibn Ezra, Abraham, 162
Ingelow, Jean, 207
Irlam, Shaun, 240n12, 245n59

Jackson, Virginia, 219, 225
James, Henry, Jr., 191, 204, 222–23, 227–28
James, Henry, Sr., 48–49
James, William, 188
Jameson, Anna, 166–81, 194, 257n28; *Sacred and Legendary Art,* 166–68, 173, 175–76, 182–83, 256n17, 257n26, 257n28
Jasper, David, 240n12
Jay, Elisabeth, 244n25
Jerome, Saint, 93
Jews. *See* Judaism
John, Saint, 26–30, 47, 63, 96, 127, 174, 180
Johnston, Judith, 257n26
Johnstone, Michael, 188
Jones, Henry, 185, 256n19, 258n55
Jonsson, Inge, 245n36
Joseph, Gerhard, 250n56
Josephus, 74
Jowett, Benjamin, 7, 9, 16, 77, 80–82, 84, 88, 98, 103, 128, 247n7
Joyce, James, 142
Judaism, 17, 146, 186, 214–18, 244n26, 261n55

Kant, Immanuel, 34
Keats, John, 135, 246n1
Keble, John, 23, 91, 243n2
Kelley, Philip, 243n3
Kenny, Anthony, 251n14
Kenyon, John, 45–46, 48, 55, 244n17
Kierkegaard, Søren, 121
Kierstead, Christopher, 254n49
Kirkman, J., 185, 258n55

Klopstock, Friedrich Gottlieb, 4, 38
Knight, Mark, 3, 239n3

Lamartine, Alphonse de, 220–22, 260nn40–41
Landon, Letitia Elizabeth (L.E.L.), 29, 47
LaPorte, Charles, 247n17, 253n25, 261n7
Layard, A. H., 105
Lazarus, Emma, 228, 230, 261n55
Leighton, Angela, 236
Lessing, G. E. (the Wolfenbüttel Fragmentist), 8, 14, 127
Lewes, George Henry, 89, 189–90, 194, 200, 203, 210, 213–14, 228, 230
Lewis, Linda M., 243n13
Lisle, Bonnie, 259n19
Lodge, David, 51–52
Longfellow, Henry Wadsworth, 123–24, 137
Lootens, Tricia, 178, 257n26
Lowell, James Russell, 114, 149, 251n5
Lowth, Robert, 8–10, 64, 87
Lyell, Charles, 1, 17–18, 88

Mabinogion, the, 79, 109
Macaulay, Thomas Babington, 158, 247n9
MacPherson, Geraldine Bate, 257n28
Main, Alexander, 198–204, 210, 228, 230
Malebranche, Nicolas de, 130–31, 254n45
Mallock, W. H., 103
Malory, Thomas, 76, 78–79, 93, 109
Mantel, Hilary, 173
Marlowe, Christopher, 131, 254n47
Martin, Julia, 246n61
Mary of Galilee (the Virgin Mother), 59–60, 163–64, 166, 173, 178–79, 181–84, 197, 237, 257n32
Mason, Emma, 3, 239n3, 243n2, 244n29
Maurice, F. D., 128, 247n7, 249n42, 254n59
Maynard, John, 131–32
McGann, Jerome, 121, 155, 240n11, 249n47, 253n26, 254n49
McKelvy, William R., 3, 143, 239n3, 239n6
McLeod, Hugh, 2, 243n68, 253n42
Melnyk, Julie, 243n68, 243n2
Menken, Adah Isaacs, 217
Meredith, George, 242n51
Mermin, Dorothy, 243n13, 255n12
Meyers, F. W. H., 109, 198, 236

Recent Books in the
Victorian Literature and Culture Series

Barbara J. Black
On Exhibit: Victorians and Their Museums

Annette R. Federico
*Idol of Suburbia: Marie Corelli and
Late-Victorian Literary Culture*

Talia Schaffer
*The Forgotten Female Aesthetes: Literary
Culture in Late-Victorian England*

Julia F. Saville
*A Queer Chivalry: The Homoerotic
Asceticism of Gerard Manley Hopkins*

Victor Shea and William Whitla, Editors
*"Essays and Reviews": The 1860
Text and Its Reading*

Marlene Tromp
*The Private Rod: Marital Violence, Sensation,
and the Law in Victorian Britain*

Dorice Williams Elliott
*The Angel out of the House: Philanthropy
and Gender in Nineteenth-Century England*

Richard Maxwell, Editor
The Victorian Illustrated Book

Vineta Colby
Vernon Lee: A Literary Biography

E. Warwick Slinn
*Victorian Poetry as Cultural Critique:
The Politics of Performative Language*

Simon Joyce
*Capital Offenses: Geographies of Class
and Crime in Victorian London*

Caroline Levine
*The Serious Pleasures of Suspense:
Victorian Realism and Narrative Doubts*

Emily Davies
Emily Davies: Collected Letters, 1861–1875
Edited by Ann B. Murphy
and Deirdre Raftery

Joseph Bizup
*Manufacturing Culture: Vindications
of Early Victorian Industry*

Lynn M. Voskuil
*Acting Naturally: Victorian
Theatricality and Authenticity*

Sally Mitchell
*Frances Power Cobbe: Victorian
Feminist, Journalist, Reformer*

Constance W. Hassett
Christina Rossetti: The Patience of Style

.